EDEXCEL
A LEVEL
HISTORY

Active Book included

Paper 3:
Protest, agitation and parliamentary reform in Britain, c1780–1928

Peter Callaghan | Edward Gillin | Adam Kidson
Series editor: Rosemary Rees

ALWAYS LEARNING

PEARSON

Published by Pearson Education Limited, 80 Strand, London, WC2R 0RL

www.pearsonschoolsandfecolleges.co.uk

Copies of official specifications for all Edexcel qualifications may be found on the website: www.edexcel.com

Text © Pearson Education Limited 2016

Designed by Elizabeth Arnoux for Pearson

Typeset and illustrated by Phoenix Photosetting, Chatham, Kent

Produced by Out of House Publishing

Original illustrations © Pearson Education Limited 2016

Cover design by Malena Wilson-Max for Pearson

Cover photo © Mary Evans Picture Library: The March of the Women Collection

The rights of Peter Callaghan, Edward Gillin and Adam Kidson to be identified as authors of this work have been asserted by them in accordance with the Copyright, Designs and Patents Act 1988.

First published 2016

19 18 17 16

10 9 8 7 6 5 4 3

British Library Cataloguing in Publication Data

A catalogue record for this book is available from the British Library

ISBN 978 1 447 985426

Copyright notice

Printed in the UK by CPI

Websites

Pearson Education Limited is not responsible for the content of any external internet sites. It is essential for tutors to preview each website before using it in class so as to ensure that the URL is still accurate, relevant and appropriate. We suggest that tutors bookmark useful websites and consider enabling students to access them through the school/college intranet.

A note from the publisher

In order to ensure that this resource offers high-quality support for the associated Pearson qualification, it has been through a review process by the awarding body. This process confirms that this resource fully covers the teaching and learning content of the specification or part of a specification at which it is aimed. It also confirms that it demonstrates an appropriate balance between the development of subject skills, knowledge and understanding, in addition to preparation for assessment.

Endorsement does not cover any guidance on assessment activities or processes (e.g. practice questions or advice on how to answer assessment questions) included in the resource, nor does it prescribe any particular approach to the teaching or delivery of a related course.

While the publishers have made every attempt to ensure that advice on the qualification and its assessment is accurate, the official specification and associated assessment guidance materials are the only authoritative source of information and should always be referred to for definitive guidance.

Pearson examiners have not contributed to any sections in this resource relevant to examination papers for which they have responsibility.

Examiners will not use endorsed resources as a source of material for any assessment set by Pearson.

Endorsement of a resource does not mean that the resource is required to achieve this Pearson qualification, nor does it mean that it is the only suitable material available to support the qualification, and any resource lists produced by the awarding body shall include this and other appropriate resources.

Contents

How to use this book

STRUCTURE

This book covers Paper 3, Option 36.1: Protest, agitation and parliamentary reform in Britain, c1780–1928 of the Edexcel A Level qualification.

You will also need to study a Paper 1 and a Paper 2 option and produce coursework in order to complete your qualification. All Paper 1/2 options are covered by other textbooks in this series.

EXAM SUPPORT

The examined assessment for Paper 3 requires you to answer questions from three sections. Throughout this book there are exam-style questions in all three section styles for you to practise your examination skills.

Section A contains a compulsory question that will assess your source analysis and evaluation skills.

A Level Exam-Style Question Section A

Study Source 12 before you answer this question.

Assess the value of the source for revealing Napier's attitude towards the Chartists, and the strength of Chartist organisation in 1839.

Explain your answer using the source, the information given about it and your own knowledge of the historical context. (20 marks)

Tip
Remember to comment briefly on the language and tone of the extract, and what they reveal about Napier's attitude.

Section B contains a choice of essay questions that will look at your understanding of the studied period in depth.

A Level Exam-Style Question Section B

'In the years 1790–1819, British radicalism failed to achieve its objectives because the power of the state was too strong.'

How far do you agree with this statement? (20 marks)

Tip
Your answer should consider two distinct points: the power of the state, and the weaknesses of British radicalism.

Section C will again give you a choice of essay questions, but these will assess your understanding of the period in breadth.

A Level Exam-Style Question Section C

To what extent was reform of the franchise in the years 1832–1928 influenced by extra-parliamentary pressure? (20 marks)

Tip
You need to know when pressure from outside parliament influenced ministers and MPs, and you should reach a judgement on the importance of the suffragettes in the making of the Acts of 1918 and 1928. You should also analyse the significance of other relevant factors, such as the collapse of the Tory Party in 1830, the intention of most politicians to secure some advantages for their party, and the importance of other factors.

The Preparing for your exams section at the end of this book contains sample answers of different standards, with comments on how they could be improved.

FEATURES
Extend your knowledge

These features contain additional information that will help you gain a deeper understanding of the topic. This could be a short biography of an important person, extra background information about an event, an alternative interpretation or even a research idea that you could follow up. Information in these boxes is not essential to your exam success, but still provides insights of value.

EXTEND YOUR KNOWLEDGE

The Parliament Act after 1911
The Liberals used the Parliament Act to pass the Irish Home Rule bill and the Welsh Church disestablishment bill in 1914. The Labour Party came to power in 1945, and further reduced the House of Lords' powers of delay to allow the passage of measures to nationalise industries. Later governments have threatened to use the Act on several occasions, but compromises between the House of Lords and the House of Commons have usually been made.

The Parliament Act 1911 expressed the hope of replacing the House of Lords with an elected chamber. Despite several changes to the composition of the Upper House, the practice of election has never been attempted.

Knowledge check activities

These activities are designed to check that you have understood the material that you have just studied. They might also ask you questions about the sources and extracts in the section to check that you have studied and analysed them thoroughly.

ACTIVITY
KNOWLEDGE CHECK

1 'The extent of the Contagious Diseases Acts was limited to regions of military and naval significance.'

   a) List the regions the legislation affected.

   b) What do you think the geographical limits of the Contagious Diseases Acts tell us about the government's priorities with regard to prostitution?

2 Why do you think the government took the measures that it did to protect its armed forces between 1864 and 1869?

Summary activities

At the end of each chapter, you will find summary activities. These are tasks designed to help you think about the key topic you have just studied as a whole. They may involve selecting and organising key information or analysing how things changed over time. You might want to keep your answers to these questions safe – they are handy for revision.

ACTIVITY
SUMMARY

The geography of discontent, 1790–1819
For this activity, you will need a map of England, some pins and a number of small pieces of card.

1 On the map, pin and label areas of radical activity, with relevant dates.

2 What can you learn about the changing geography of radical protests in the years 1790–1819?

3 How can you best explain the change?

Thinking Historically activities

These activities are found throughout the book, and are designed to develop your understanding of history, especially around the key concepts of evidence, interpretations, causation and change. Each activity is designed to challenge a conceptual barrier that might be holding you back. This is linked to a map of conceptual barriers developed by experts. You can look up the map and find out which barrier each activity challenges by downloading the progression map from this website: www.pearsonschools.co.uk/historyprogressionsapproach.

---

progression map reference

THINKING HISTORICALLY Cause and consequence (6c)

Connections

Extract 3 and Sources 5–7 show some typical aspects of the 1789 French Revolution. Work in groups or individually and answer the following:

1 Read Extract 3. How might this be seen as similar to Chartist beliefs regarding the British political system?

2 Read Source 5.

   a) What did Chartists believe about the strength of their support?

   b) How is this similar to revolutionary ideas about the French monarchy?

3 Look at Sources 6 and 7. What did the Chartists copy from the French Revolution?

4 a) Make a list of other similarities between the Chartists and the French Revolutionaries.

   b) How did their understanding of the revolution affect the attitudes and actions of the Chartists?

5 Why is it important for historians to see these links across time and be able to explain how causal factors can influence situations much later in time?

Getting the most from your online ActiveBook

This book comes with three years' access to ActiveBook* – an online, digital version of your textbook. Follow the instructions printed on the inside front cover to start using your ActiveBook.

Your ActiveBook is the perfect way to personalise your learning as you progress through your A Level History course. You can:

- access your content online, anytime, anywhere
- use the inbuilt highlighting and annotation tools to personalise the content and make it really relevant to you.

Highlight tool – use this to pick out key terms or topics so you are ready and prepared for revision.

Annotations tool – use this to add your own notes, for example links to your wider reading, such as websites or other files. Or, make a note to remind yourself about work that you need to do.

*For new purchases only. If the access code has already been revealed, it may no longer be valid. If you have bought this textbook secondhand, the code may already have been used by the first owner of the book.

Introduction
A Level History

WHY HISTORY MATTERS

History is about people, and people are complex, fascinating, frustrating and a whole lot of other things besides. This is why history is probably the most comprehensive and certainly one of the most intriguing subjects there is. History can also be inspiring and alarming, heartening and disturbing, a story of progress and civilisation and of catastrophe and inhumanity.

History's importance goes beyond the subject's intrinsic interest and appeal. Our beliefs and actions, our cultures, institutions and ways of living, our languages and means of making sense of ourselves are all shaped by the past. If we want to fully understand ourselves now, and to understand our possible futures, we have no alternative but to think about history.

History is a discipline as well as a subject matter. Making sense of the past develops qualities of mind that are valuable to anyone who wants to seek the truth and think clearly and intelligently about the most interesting and challenging intellectual problem of all: other people. Learning history is learning a powerful way of knowing.

WHAT IS HISTORY?

History is a way of constructing knowledge about the world through research, interpretation, argument and debate.

Building historical knowledge involves identifying the traces of the past that exist in the present – in people's memories, in old documents, photographs and other remains, and in objects and artefacts ranging from bullets and lipsticks, to field systems and cities. Historians interrogate these traces and *ask questions* that transform traces into *sources of evidence* for knowledge claims about the past.

Historians aim to understand what happened in the past by *explaining why* things happened as they did. Explaining why involves trying to understand past people and their beliefs, intentions and actions. It also involves explaining the causes and evaluating the effects of large-scale changes in the past and exploring relationships between what people aimed to do, the contexts that shaped what was possible and the outcomes and consequences of actions.

Historians also aim to *understand change* in the past. People, states of affairs, ideas, movements and civilisations come into being in time, grow, develop, and ultimately decline and disappear. Historians aim to identify and compare change and continuity in the past, to measure the rate at which things change and to identify the types of change that take place. Change can be slow or sudden. It can also be understood as progressive or regressive – leading to the improvement or worsening of a situation or state of affairs. How things change and whether changes are changes for the better are two key issues that historians frequently debate.

Figure 1 Fragment of a black granite statue possibly portraying the Roman politician Mark Antony.

Debate is the essence of history. Historians write arguments to support their knowledge claims, and historians argue with each other to test and evaluate interpretations of the past. Historical knowledge itself changes and develops. On the one hand, new sources of knowledge and new methods of research cause *historical interpretations* to change. On the other hand, the questions that historians ask change with time and new questions produce new answers. Although the past is dead and gone, the interpretation of the past has a past, present and future.

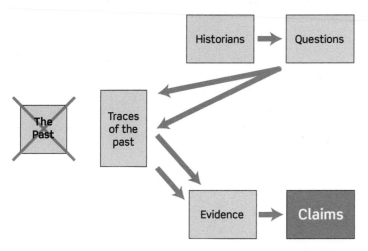

Figure 2 Constructing knowledge about the past.

THE CHALLENGES OF LEARNING HISTORY

Like all other Advanced Level subjects, A Level history is difficult – that is why it is called 'advanced'. Your Advanced Level studies will build on knowledge and understanding of history that you developed at GCSE and at Key Stage 3 – ideas like 'historical sources', 'historical evidence' and 'cause', for example. You will need to do a lot of reading and writing to progress in history. Most importantly, you will need to do a lot of thinking, and thinking about your thinking. This book aims to support you in developing both your knowledge and your understanding.

History is challenging in many ways. On the one hand, it is challenging to build up the range and depth of knowledge that you need to understand the past at an advanced level. Learning about the past involves mastering new and unfamiliar concepts arising from the past itself (such as the Inquisition, Laudianism, *Volksgemeinschaft*) and building up levels of knowledge that are both detailed and well organised. This book covers the key content of the topics that you are studying for your examination and provides a number of features to help you build and organise what you know – for example, diagrams, timelines and definitions of key terms. You will need to help yourself too, of course, adding to your knowledge through further reading, building on the foundations provided by this book.

Another challenge is to develop understandings of the discipline of history. You will have to learn to think historically about evidence, cause, change and interpretations, and also to write historically, in a way that develops clear and supported argument.

Historians think with evidence in ways that differ from how we often think in everyday life. In history, as Figure 2 shows, we cannot go and 'see for ourselves' because the past no longer exists. Neither can we normally rely on 'credible witnesses' to tell us 'the truth' about 'what happened'. People in the past did not write down 'the truth' for our benefit. They often had clear agendas when creating the traces that remain and, as often as not, did not themselves know 'the truth' about complex historical events.

A root of the word 'history' is the Latin word *historia*, one of whose meanings is 'enquiry' or 'finding out'. Learning history means learning to ask questions and interrogate traces, and then to reason about what the new knowledge you have gained means. This book draws on historical scholarship for its narrative and contents. It also draws on research on the nature of historical thinking and on the challenges that learning history can present for students. Throughout the book you will find 'Thinking Historically' activities designed to support the development of your thinking.

You will also find – as you would expect given the nature of history – that the book is full of questions. This book aims to help you build your understandings of the content, contexts and concepts that you will need to advance both your historical knowledge and your historical understanding, and to lay strong foundations for the future development of both.

Dr Arthur Chapman
Institute of Education
University College London

QUOTES ABOUT HISTORY

'Historians are dangerous people. They are capable of upsetting everything. They must be directed.'
Nikita Khrushchev

'To be ignorant of what occurred before you were born is to remain forever a child. For what is the worth of human life, unless it is woven into the life of our ancestors by the records of history.'
Marcus Tullius Cicero

Protest, agitation and parliamentary reform in Britain, c1780–1928

The 1929 General Election was an election of firsts. It was the first time that an election was held under universal suffrage in the UK, with women having equal voting rights to men, and it was the first time that the Labour Party gained a majority of seats in parliament. These two firsts aptly demonstrate how far the parliamentary system had been reformed in the preceding 150 years.

At the start of the period covered in this book, around five percent of the population of Great Britain was eligible to vote and the allocation of Members of Parliament across the country was deeply outdated. The franchise was limited to men over the age of 21 who either owned a large amount of property in a county or met one of the many complex requirements of living in a borough. Corruption and bribery were rife and safe seats could be purchased for those with the money. For the parliamentary system to have reached the position of the 1929 General Election, huge changes had to have taken place in the intervening years.

SOURCE 1

An advertisement for a fictional rotten borough published in the satirical caricature magazine *The Looking Glass*, No. 10 from October 1830. The caption reads '*To be sold, the estate of ROTTEN DOWN. Two cottages rather dilapidated a Paddock & a Pig-sty, Lowest price 25,0000£. NB returns two Members to P——t*'.

Timeline

- **1794** – Habeas corpus is suspended; leaders of London Corresponding Society put on trial
- **1832** – Representation of the People Act (known as the First Reform Act) passed
- **1842** – Second Chartist Petition presented to parliament
- **1859** – Liberal Party formed
- **1867** – Representation of the People Act (known as the Second Reform Act) passed
- **1884** – Representation of the People Act (known as the Third Reform Act) passed
- **1886** – Contagious Diseases Act repealed
- **1903** – Women's Social and Political Union (WSPU) formed
- **1915** – Glasgow Rent Strike
- **1919** – Black Friday riots in Glasgow
- **1927** – Trades Disputes Act passed

1819 – The Peterloo Massacre; the government passes the Six Acts

1839 – Chartist National Convention held; First Chartist Petition presented; Newport Rising takes place

1848 – Chartist hold rally on Kennington Common; Third Chartist Petition presented

1864 – Contagious Diseases Act passed

1872 – Ballot Act passed

1885 – Redistribution Act passed

1893 – Independent Labour Party formed

1911 – Parliament Act passed

1918 – Representation of the People Act (known as the Fourth Reform Act) passed

1926 – The General Strike

1928 – Representation of the People (Equal Franchise) Act passed

The changes to the organisation of voting and parliament throughout the 19th and early 20th centuries will be examined in the Aspects in Breadth (Chapters 1 and 2). The Reform Acts would not only change the electorate but would influence the make-up of politics itself, as the aristocracy started to lose its hold on power and the machinery of political parties became increasingly influential.

However, the change effected over the 19th century was not achieved without prolonged struggle. From the beginning of the period under study there were voices from many different sections of society calling for reform of such an unrepresentative electoral system. Even before the mass movements of the Chartists in the 1830s, there were attempts to bring pressure to bear on the ruling elite through agitation and protest. The Aspects in Depth (Chapters 3–7) will look at specific examples across the period and provide examples of both how the methods of protest changed and how successful these attempts were in challenging the established authority. The actions of key individuals and their roles in driving the change called for by these protests will be examined, as well as the splits and divisions these strong-willed characters often brought about.

From the ultimately failed attempts of the Chartists to increase the franchise, to the successes of those campaigning for the repeal of the Contagious Diseases Act and female suffrage, and the clashes with the increasingly powerful trade union movement, the response of government was nearly always one of opposition and repression. The deployment of the army at Peterloo in 1819, and again a hundred years later in Glasgow during the Battle of George Square on Black Friday, shows the lengths to which the authorities were prepared to go to restore order in the face of mass protest. The impact of legislative efforts of successive governments to prevent or curtail agitation and reform will also be considered across the period.

SOURCE

2 A struggle between police and demonstrators during the 1926 General Strike as a policeman tries to take a flag out of a protester's hands.

Reform of parliament, c1780-1928

KEY QUESTIONS

- How effective were pressures for change to the franchise in the years c1780–1928?
- How significant were changes in the distribution of seats in the years c1780–1918?

KEY TERMS

Constitution
A set of laws and agreed principles that set out rules on how a country is governed. Although Britain does not have a single written constitution, it does have a set of constitutional rules that are based largely on custom and practice.

Vested interests
In politics, individuals or groups of people who benefit from existing political arrangements, usually at the expense of others.

INTRODUCTION

In 1780, in common with all European countries, Britain did not possess a written **constitution**.

Instead, the country's system of government and its electoral system were both governed by a haphazard collection of laws and customs that had grown up since the 15th century and the early years of the reign of Henry VI. It is perhaps too generous to refer to a 'system', because neither the right to vote nor the national distribution of seats were organised in any rational way. Over the next 150 years, a number of significant reforms were carried out, which were intended to make the electoral system reflect the changing distribution of the population and the new economic forces which had grown up through the industrialisation of the country. By 1928, despite the retention of a monarchy and an unelected House of Lords, Britain had been transformed into a parliamentary democracy based on universal suffrage.

For half a century from 1780, no changes were made to the electoral system. In part, this was due to the powerful opposition mounted by **vested interests** in the House of Commons and the House of Lords: even the great reforming prime minster Pitt the Younger was unable to pass a mild reform in 1785. Far more important, however, was the impact on British politics and society of the French Revolution. What had begun as a modest programme of constitutional reforms in 1789, had, by 1793, degenerated into the execution of the king and queen, a reign of terror throughout France, and war against the leading powers of Europe. Fearing that Britain might become infected with a revolutionary spirit, Pitt and his successors turned against reform for a generation.

Ideas for parliamentary reform might have been held back for a time, but a number of long-term factors were at work which meant that sooner or later change would have to be addressed. Since the mid-18th century, the industrialisation of the Midlands and northern England had led to the rapid growth of towns and cities such as Liverpool, Manchester, Oldham and Stockport.

1789 – Outbreak of the French Revolution

1795 – Seditious Meetings Act leads to a fall in radical activity

1828-30 – Wellington's government

1830 – Earl Grey becomes prime minister

1832 – First Reform Act becomes law

| 1780 | 1790 | 1800 | 1810 | 1820 | 1830 | 1840 |

1792 – Founding of the London Corresponding Society

1812-27 – Lord Liverpool's government

1829 – Catholic Relief Act

1831 – Russell introduces the first reform bill

At the same time, new social classes were growing in number – middle-class manufacturers and traders, along with a large working class that manned the factories. By the 1820s, many leading politicians recognised that change was necessary and would have to be managed carefully.

In 1832, after two years of parliamentary debate, accompanied by extra-parliamentary protests, the First Reform Act passed into law. Contemporaries dubbed it the 'Great Reform Act', but many were disappointed by its provisions, which excluded the bulk of working-class men from the **franchise**. Nonetheless, the Act set a valuable precedent for further change. In 1867, the Conservative Party's leading minister in the House of Commons, Disraeli, managed the passing of the Second Reform Act, which to the surprise of many, enfranchised large numbers of the urban working classes. The Liberal leader, Gladstone, continued this process in 1884 with a third Act, which extended the vote to many agricultural labourers in the counties.

Despite all these changes, there were still some 40 percent of adult males who had not received the vote. At that time, the franchise was not given to men unconditionally, but only to those who had a stake in the country through the ownership or tenancy of property. The First World War would undermine this principle, while at the same time bringing about a dramatic change in the status of women.

By 1916, all political parties agreed that it was indefensible that young men could be sent to fight and to die in the war, but did not have the right to vote. This injustice was remedied with the Reform Act 1918, which finally ended the system of property qualifications and established universal male suffrage. The Act also took the first tentative steps in the direction of female suffrage by enfranchising women over the age of 30. General elections over the next decade showed that there had been no dramatic changes to the voting system, and the 1928 Act finally conceded universal suffrage for all men and women aged 21 or over.

While the change over time from a small number of male voters in 1780 to universal suffrage by 1928 was an important development in parliamentary reform, the simultaneous changes in the distribution of parliamentary seats have sometimes been overlooked. A major alteration to the distribution of seats, which is still in operation today, came with the Redistribution Act 1885. Two-member constituencies had been established as early as 1430, but in 1885 most of these were swept away with the creation of single-member seats, which remain recognisable today. This change proved to be very beneficial to the Conservative Party through the creation of suburban seats around the large cities, which insulated these areas from both the Liberal and, later, the Labour parties in the cities.

KEY TERM

Franchise
The right to vote, also known as the suffrage.

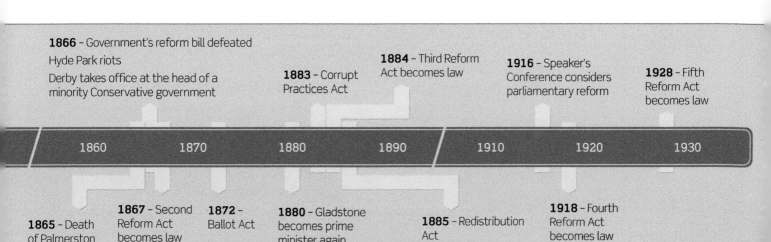

1866 – Government's reform bill defeated
Hyde Park riots
Derby takes office at the head of a minority Conservative government

1883 – Corrupt Practices Act

1884 – Third Reform Act becomes law

1916 – Speaker's Conference considers parliamentary reform

1928 – Fifth Reform Act becomes law

1860   1870   1880   1890   1910   1920   1930

1865 – Death of Palmerston

1867 – Second Reform Act becomes law

1872 – Ballot Act

1880 – Gladstone becomes prime minister again

1885 – Redistribution Act

1918 – Fourth Reform Act becomes law

HOW EFFECTIVE WERE PRESSURES FOR CHANGE TO THE FRANCHISE IN THE YEARS c1780–1928?

The franchise c1780 and its significance for representation of the people

The right to vote in elections held in Britain today belongs to all men and women aged 18 and over whose names are included on the electoral register, which is drawn up each year. An exception to this rule was made in 2014, when young people in Scotland aged 16 and 17 were allowed to vote in the referendum on independence. In 1780, however, only adult males could vote. The county franchise was uniform across the country, but in the boroughs the right to vote varied from one constituency to another.

The county franchise

In the English and Welsh counties, the right to vote had been established during the reign of Henry VI in 1430, giving the vote to all **freeholders** of property worth 40 shillings (£2) a year. This simple qualification had established a uniform county franchise that remained unchanged for 400 years. Over time, however, inflation and the rising price of land had increased the number of men qualified for the franchise.

The borough franchise

Historian Eric Evans described pre-reform elections as a 'haphazard business', and this description certainly applied to voting rights in the **boroughs**. Unlike the county franchise, the right to vote in the English boroughs was not uniform, with very wide variations from one seat to another.

At one extreme were open boroughs, where the vote was exercised by many men who met various qualifications, such as the direct payment of the local poor rates. Preston, in Lancashire, was one of the most open boroughs in the country. Here, the vote was given to all men, whether resident or not, who were in the **constituency** at the time of the election. The electorate in open boroughs ran into thousands. Around 20 boroughs had large electorates of over 1,000 men, notably Westminster, with its 11,000 voters. These boroughs were noted for their sturdy independence, and were not very susceptible to influence.

Scot and lot boroughs gave the vote to males who paid their local tax, or scot; while in potwalloper boroughs the vote could be exercised by those who possessed a hearth where they could boil, or wallop, their pots. These boroughs also had electorates of at least several hundred men.

Seats with large numbers of voters were the exception rather than the rule. Many boroughs had very small electorates, rarely exceeding 100 voters.

In burgage boroughs, the right to vote belonged to men who owned various properties, and ownership of these votes was carefully protected. Sometimes the inhabitants of a town would challenge the burgage owners, but to no avail.

Corporation boroughs were towns where the only voters were members of the town council. These councils were **self-perpetuating cliques** who filled vacant seats on the council by nomination rather than election. Most corporation boroughs were, by modern-day standards, extremely corrupt, and the electors of several towns were quite content to sell their votes to the highest bidder. The Suffolk town of Sudbury was notoriously corrupt in this respect: in the 1761 election, the town advertised its two seats for sale to the highest bidder. Sudbury was so corrupt that it was disfranchised in 1844.

Treasury boroughs were parliamentary seats that came under the control of government departments, which were the chief employers in a town. Many ports along the south coast of England, such as Portsmouth and Plymouth, were under the influence of the Admiralty, and returned MPs who would give unswerving support to the government of the day.

Finally, many constituencies were described as pocket or rotten boroughs. Most of the property in a pocket borough was owned by one person, who therefore was able to nominate his chosen candidates for election to parliament. Rotten boroughs had once been areas of economic activity, but over time had become depopulated, but still retained their parliamentary representation. In the late Middle Ages, Dunwich in Suffolk had been a well-known international port with substantial trade to and from Europe.

KEY TERMS

Freeholder
A male who owned land or property outright.

Borough
A town or small city that had once been given special privileges by royal charter.

Constituency
One of the areas into which the country was divided for election purposes. These varied considerably in geographical size and population.

Self-perpetuating clique
A small group of individuals who had the power to maintain their position indefinitely.

Frequent heavy storms and coastal erosion meant that the port had long ago been claimed by the sea, but the tiny village which remained still retained two MPs. Old Sarum in Hampshire had been a thriving community in the Middle Ages, but its inhabitants moved to what is now Salisbury. By 1780, Old Sarum was little more than a heap of mossy stones frequently visited by people curious to see one of the most corrupted boroughs in the country, and perhaps to glimpse one of its seven electors.

The size of the electorate

It is impossible to assess with any accuracy the size of the electorate in 1780 because the registration of electors was not established until the Reform Act 1832. However, a survey carried out in 1780 estimated that in England and Wales there were 214,000 electors out of a population of eight million. As late as 1831 in Scotland, where the right to vote was much more restricted, just 4,500 men in a population of 2.6 million qualified for the vote.

Elections and 'interests'

To a modern observer, the old representative system appears hopelessly corrupt and in need of long-overdue and radical reform, but this was not how it appeared to contemporaries. Indeed, until the 1790s, there was no significant pressure for parliamentary reform from any section of society. Eighteenth-century opinion was broadly content with an electoral system that was not concerned with a system based on population, but rather was able to represent various national 'interests', such as agriculture, trade and banking.

General elections today witness contests in virtually every parliamentary seat between a number of political parties with different ideologies and programmes. This was not the case in the 18th century. In the election of 1784, for example, there were only 72 contests, and in several constituencies there were no contested elections at all throughout the 18th century. Elections could be very expensive affairs, as rival candidates sought to persuade electors to vote in their favour, often accompanied by substantial bribes. 'Treating', which included the provision of large quantities of food and beer to voters and non-voters alike, was an accepted practice.

SOURCE

The Election, Chairing the Member, 1755. This painting, by the famous painter and engraver William Hogarth, illustrates the boisterous involvement of many different classes in elections in the middle of the 18th century. The painting shows a victorious candidate for the Oxfordshire constituency being carried through the streets in a traditional, though chaotic, celebration of his election.

Although the electorate was small in 1780, elections were often very colourful affairs, with thousands of people turning up to watch the progress of the poll. The county of Hertfordshire experienced many contested elections in the 18th century, and the extent of popular involvement in the election is shown in Source 2.

SOURCE 2

Ipswich Journal, 1 May 1784, describing local involvement and campaigning in a Hertfordshire election.

Thursday the election for Hertfordshire came on at the county town. Mr Plumer rode in from Ware, at the head of a most numerous cavalcade of freeholders, attended with a band of music. Lord Grimston's party then appeared, and made a respectable show, though their numbers were nothing like equal to Mr. Plumer's. His Lordship had his band of music likewise. Mr. Plumer's flags were simply decorated with the words 'Plumer and independence', while those of Lord Grimston held out 'Grimston, and the rights of the King and of the people'. After the two parties had occupied the ground for a full hour, Mr Halsey rode in at the head of his friends, and a very creditable figure they made. His flags bore the words 'Halsey and Plumer, independence and no aristocracy'. At length all the three parties adjourned to the town-hall, and the poll began. At the close the numbers stood as follows: For Mr. Plumer, 1900. Lord Grimston, 1297, Mr. Halsey, 1073.

Some historians, notably Frank O'Gorman, have analysed the unreformed electoral system, and have concluded that in many ways it actually worked quite well. O'Gorman argued that an important feature of the system was that it was concerned, not with numerical, but with virtual representation. MPs sat at Westminster, not as representatives of the voters who had put them there, but in order to champion those interests that made up the economic and political life of the nation. This explains why there were so many seats in the south of England, representing the great agricultural interests of the day, along with the government's control of the royal dockyard towns such as Plymouth and Portsmouth on the south coast. Men purchased boroughs, not to represent themselves, but rather to champion a powerful interest such as trade, shipping, banks or brewing. In 1820, the Alexander brothers purchased Old Sarum in order to further their interests in the East India Company and in merchant banking in Calcutta. Even the slaves of the West Indies sugar plantations had an indirect voice through the election of anti-slavery MPs such as William Wilberforce.

As long as the electoral system represented the overall interests of the nation, it continued to enjoy broad support. However, from the second half of the 18th century new forces were coming to bear on industry and the economy. The industrialisation of parts of the Midlands, Lancashire and the north-east of the country led to a gradual change in the balance of the economy, away from the agricultural south and east and towards the growing and densely populated towns further north. Industrialisation also changed the social structure of the country, with the emergence of a new middle class of factory owners, managers and bankers, and of an even larger urban working class. Industrial interests were not strongly represented in the parliaments of the late 18th century, and pressure began to grow for these new forces to be represented within parliament.

ACTIVITY
KNOWLEDGE CHECK

Old Corruption

Many contemporaries referred to the electoral system in the late 18th century as 'old corruption'. They, and several later historians, condemned the representative system as hopelessly out of date and in need of drastic reform.

1 Write down four points that agree with this viewpoint, and four points that challenge it.

2 What overall conclusion can you draw?

Pressures for change and reasons for resistance

The impact of the French Revolution

Before 1830, parties and governments were not deeply concerned with trying to change the electoral system. In 1785, the prime minister, William Pitt, introduced a modest proposal to buy out 36 small boroughs and transfer their seats to the counties and to London, but he was defeated on the issue and did not return to reform thereafter.

It was the outbreak of the French Revolution in 1789, and its impact on British politics and society, that sparked a serious interest in reform and widespread demands for change. The various movements for reform, however, were divided on aims and methods. At one extreme were several radical movements demanding extensive reform. The Society for Constitutional Information, which championed full universal suffrage, had been founded in 1780 by Major Cartwright, but made little headway in its early years. The London Corresponding Society, founded in 1792, promoted the rights of the skilled working class, and gained wide support among northern towns and cities.

Other groups supported ideas that were much less radical. Alarmed by the spread of radical and democratic ideas, a number of leading Whig politicians formed the Friends of the People in 1792. They hoped to control the pace of change by promoting modest amendments to the electoral system: their stated objective was simply to obtain 'a more equal representation of the people in Westminster'. Their support of reform in the House of Commons in 1793 came at an unfortunate time for the Whigs. The French king, Louis XVI, had been executed, Britain was now at war with France, and Pitt's government was more concerned with the successful prosecution of the war than with considering domestic reform. Whig motions for reform were heavily defeated, and the Friends of the People disbanded. Thereafter, the government moved rapidly to suppress reform activity. **Habeas corpus** was suspended in 1794, and the Seditious Meetings Act 1795 led to a significant decline in the influence and activities of reform groups. Leading members of the London Corresponding

KEY TERM

Habeas corpus
A writ that can be issued by any court, requiring prison officials to provide legal proof that they have the power to detain a prisoner. If this proof is not provided, the prisoner will be released.

Society were charged with **sedition**, and the society, along with its provincial groups, was outlawed under the Corresponding Societies Act 1799.

> **KEY TERM**
>
> Sedition
> Open activities, whether through speeches, demonstrations or organisations, which are deliberately intended to provoke violence or rebellion against the established government of a country.

Post-war unrest, 1815–30

The work and influence of the radical reformers in the 1790s, and in the years 1815–20, are covered in detail in Chapter 3 (pages 64–83). The French wars ended in 1815, but Britain did not enjoy a post-war period of domestic peace. Growing unemployment, economic distress and the impact of industrialisation produced a toxic mixture of grievances. Matters were made worse by the Corn Law 1815. The law was aimed at protecting the economic interests of the landed class through the imposition of a duty on imported corn. Working people feared that the price of bread would rise as a result, while manufacturers feared that their workers would demand higher wages to protect themselves and their families. There was widespread opposition to the Corn Law, which was intensified thanks to a bad harvest in 1816. A number of extra-parliamentary protests were organised throughout the country under the general watchword of 'reform'. In the short term, popular protests failed in the face of determined opposition by the government and local authorities, who were not afraid to use military force against radical agitation. A reform meeting, held at Spa Fields in London in 1816, developed into a riot which was suppressed by the city authorities with military support; and in 1819, volunteer yeomanry were responsible for the deaths of 11 people in the famous 'Peterloo Massacre' (see Chapter 3, pages 68–70). In the long term, however, the events of the post-war years led to a revival of interest in parliamentary reform, which became more organised and effective in the late 1820s.

> **EXTEND YOUR KNOWLEDGE**
>
> The Corn Laws
> The Corn Laws were introduced at the end of the Napoleonic Wars to counter the threat of cheap foreign imports flooding the British market. The laws, introduced by Liverpool's government, imposed duties on imports in order to protect farmers' profits. The Corn Laws were modified in 1828 and abolished altogether in 1846. They were regarded by middle-class industrialists and by the working class as an example of parliament protecting the interests of the large landowners.

By 1820, the government had neutralised most radical activity and the pressure for political reform had subsided. In part, this was due to a general revival in the economy and the decline of distress, which seemed to confirm the belief of the radical journalist William Cobbett: 'I defy you to agitate any fellow with a full stomach'. Another reason for the political calm in the years after Peterloo was the expert leadership of the prime minister, Lord Liverpool, who held together a government of reformers and conservatives. This period of relative tranquillity was shattered following Liverpool's death in 1827, when, after the brief administrations of Canning and Goderich, the Duke of Wellington became prime minister in 1828. Over the next few years, the unity of the Tory Party would be shattered, and its long political supremacy, dating back to Pitt's administration formed in 1783, would come to an end. The end of Tory dominance came, not so much through the growing confidence of their political opponents, but through internal divisions, especially over religious issues.

> **EXTEND YOUR KNOWLEDGE**
>
> Lord Liverpool (1770–1828)
> Liverpool was prime minister during the period 1812-27, and was the longest-serving prime minister of the 19th century. He steered the country through many domestic and foreign crises, but was associated in the public mind with the repressive policies of 1815-20. During the 1820s, Liverpool was able to support a number of liberal measures. He was a talented politician, and managed to hold his government together despite extra-parliamentary pressure for change. He was also able to keep a number of talented ministers in the government, even though a number of them, such as Peel, Home Secretary between 1822 and 1827, and Canning, foreign secretary during the same time, held widely different political views.

Many Tory backbenchers were strong supporters of the Anglican Church and of its dominant role in national life, and were opposed to measures which might weaken its supremacy. In 1828, the Whig leader, Lord John Russell, challenged the Anglican Church with his proposal to repeal the Test and Corporation Acts. These Acts dated back to the reign of Charles II and prevented Protestant dissenters such as Baptists and Congregationalists from holding government offices. By the 1820s, the Acts were not rigorously enforced, and were largely symbolic. At first, Wellington opposed repeal, but then gave his reluctant support, despite some opposition from his own backbenchers.

A further measure of religious reform, the Catholic Relief Act 1829, had far more serious implications for the unity of the Tory Party. In 1828, Vesey Fitzgerald was appointed to the Board of Trade, and had to seek re-election in his Irish constituency of County Clare. It was assumed that his election would be a formality. However, the leader of the **Catholic Association** in Ireland, Daniel O'Connell, decided to challenge existing anti-Catholic laws by standing against Fitzgerald. O'Connell defeated Fitzgerald easily, but was unable to take his seat because he would not swear the oath of allegiance to the Crown. Wellington was a long-standing opponent of Catholic relief, but he recognised that to deny O'Connell his seat could lead to widespread and destabilising unrest throughout Ireland. His views were confirmed by his colleague Sir Robert Peel (Source 3).

> **KEY TERM**
>
> Catholic Association
> Founded in 1823 by the Irish politician Daniel O'Connell, with the single aim of ending all political and religious disabilities for Catholics, in Ireland and throughout Britain. The association charged a membership fee of just one penny a month. It therefore attracted a huge membership throughout Ireland, and was the first political organisation which mobilised mass support for its cause.

SOURCE 3
Sir Robert Peel, in a memorandum to the Duke of Wellington in 1829 on the large military presence in Ireland.

In the course of the last six months, England, being at peace with the whole world, has had five-sixths of the infantry force of the United Kingdom occupied in maintaining the peace and in police duties in Ireland. I consider the state of things which requires such an application of military force much worse than open rebellion.

The state of society in Ireland will soon become perfectly incompatible with trial by jury in any political cases. The Roman Catholics have discovered their strength in respect to the elective franchise. Let us beware that we do not teach them how easy it will be to paralyse the Government and the law, unless we are prepared to substitute some other system of criminal jurisprudence for the present system.

Wellington, therefore, reluctantly supported the Catholic Relief Act 1829, which repealed most anti-Catholic legislation. The electoral power of Irish Catholics was limited by a further Act which raised the Irish franchise qualification from 40 shillings to £10. After a further by-election, O'Connell took his seat in the House of Commons in 1830.

EXTEND YOUR KNOWLEDGE

Duke of Wellington (1769–1852)
Wellington's successful campaigns against Napoleon had established his position as a national hero by 1815. Yet his political career was much less successful. He was prime minister during the period 1828–30, when his profound conservatism led him to oppose any measures of parliamentary reform, and led to the fall of his government in 1830. He was succeeded as Tory leader in 1833 by Peel, and did not serve in government again. His prestige and national popularity only recovered after he retired from political life in 1846.

While many Tory MPs were prepared grudgingly to accept the repeal of the Test and Corporation Acts, they bitterly criticised Wellington for passing Catholic relief. Some of the more extreme Tories, known as the ultras, now began to give their support to parliamentary reform. They believed that MPs in a reformed parliament would have to take account of widespread anti-Catholic feeling in the country, and would not have supported Catholic relief.

ACTIVITY
KNOWLEDGE CHECK

Forces making for parliamentary reform
1 Examine the importance of each of the following factors in promoting the cause of parliamentary reform:

  a) The French Revolution and its impact on British domestic politics.

  b) Post-war economic and social distress.

  c) The government's response to religious issues, 1828–30.

2 In your opinion, which of these factors was the most significant in driving the cause of reform?

Representation of the People Act 1832
The fall of Wellington's government, 1830
In June 1830, George IV died. The **general election** that followed saw Wellington returned to office, but his standing within the Tory Party was damaged by the return of several MPs who supported parliamentary reform. Wellington, who had tried to resist the religious changes of 1828–29, was not prepared to support any reform measure, and made this clear in an unwise speech in the House of Lords in November (Source 4).

SOURCE 4

Wellington speaking in the House of Lords, 2 November 1831. His speech was recorded in the Lords' official record, using the formal 'third-party' language of the day.

He had never read or heard of any measure up to the present moment which could in any degree satisfy his mind that the state of the representation could be improved, or be rendered more satisfactory to the country at large than at the present moment. He was fully convinced that the country possessed at the present moment a Legislature which answered all the good purposes of legislation, and this to a greater degree than any Legislature ever had answered in any country whatever. He would go further and say, that the Legislature and the system of representation possessed the full and entire confidence of the country.

Soon afterwards, the government was defeated on a vote in the House of Commons and Wellington resigned. The Whig leader, Earl Grey, formed a government of Whigs and other reforming groups – the first Whig government since the Ministry of All the Talents in 1806–7. The new ministry would change the course of British politics dramatically.

Pressure for franchise reform in 1830
The fall of Wellington's government in November 1830 removed the most important barrier to political reform. When Grey took office at the end of 1830, most people, inside and outside parliament, expected that he would address the issue of franchise reform. **Extra-parliamentary pressure** had become so intense that some sort of reform was almost inevitable.

KEY TERMS

General election
The election of representatives to the House of Commons from constituencies throughout the UK.

Extra-parliamentary pressure
Agitation for change or reform that originated from outside parliament.

There were several conditional (long-term) and contingent (short-term) factors that promoted the cause of reform.

Conditional factors
• The French revolution had a profound influence on British political life. Reformist ideals, especially those promoting liberty and equality, had become widespread and were strongly supported by many sections of society, particularly those who were excluded from the franchise.

- Many working people, especially those in industrial towns, were becoming increasingly politicised. A large number of pamphlets and newspapers spread radical political ideas to a wide and receptive audience. The most influential journal of all was William Cobbett's *Weekly Political Register.*

- The early 19th century saw the growth of large political meetings in many parts of the country. Some of these focused on a single issue, such as opposition to the Corn Laws, but many others, including the Peterloo meeting of 1819, demanded a comprehensive reform of parliament.

Contingent factors

- The Tory Party had been in power since 1812. During the late 1820s, party unity began to fragment, mostly because of religious issues, but also because of Wellington's unbending opposition to change.

- The country faced severe economic crises in the late 1820s. The harvests of 1828–30 were poor, resulting in higher food prices in the towns.

- Agricultural distress was widespread in the southern and eastern counties of England. The hardship experienced by farm workers was so severe that in 1830 it sparked the Swing Riots.

- Extra-parliamentary protests became increasingly organised, notably with the creation in 1830 of the Birmingham Political Union by the banker Thomas Attwood. Attwood intended to bring together into one single organisation the new industrial middle classes and the skilled working class, united by the single aim of parliamentary reform.

- Events in France once again influenced reform activity in Britain in the early 1830s. The 1830 July revolution in Paris swept the Bourbon king, Charles X, from the throne and replaced him with Louis Philippe, who was more acceptable to the French middle classes.

- In 1830, working people were prepared to take up the issue of franchise reform. They saw reform, not as an end in itself, but as a means of ensuring a better life for themselves and their families. Cobbett sums up their hopes and ambitions in 1831 in Source 5.

SOURCE 5

From Cobbett's *Weekly Political Register*, 1 April 1831. Cobbett was a radical journalist whose *Weekly Political Register* reached a national audience. He was a vigorous champion of the poor, especially agricultural labourers. *Rural Rides*, recounting his tours of southern and eastern England in the mid-1820s, remains in print today.

Will a reform of Parliament give the labouring man a cow or a pig; will it put bread and cheese into his satchel instead of infernal cold potatoes; will it give him a bottle of beer to carry to the field instead of making him lie down to drink out of the brook; will it put upon his back a Sunday coat and send him to church, instead of leaving him shivering with an unshaven face and a carcass half covered with a ragged smock-frock? Will parliamentary reform put an end to the harnessing of men and women by a hired overseer to draw carts like beasts of burden; will it put an end to the system which caused the honest labourer to be fed worse than the felons in the jails?... The enemies of reform jeeringly ask us, whether reform would do these things for us; and I answer distinctly that IT WOULD DO THEM ALL!

The Swing Riots (1830)

Since the late 18th century, major changes had taken place in the countryside. The growth in the rural population created a surplus of agricultural labourers, which led to a decline in wages. Matters were made worse by the introduction of agricultural machinery, especially the threshing machine. A succession of poor harvests from 1828 sparked the Swing Riots in 1830 (so-called because many farmers were sent threatening letters signed by the fictitious Captain Swing). The riots, centred on southern England and East Anglia, were characterised by arson on a large scale and the destruction of threshing machines. They were suppressed in 1831: 19 men were executed, 500 were transported and a further 600 were imprisoned. The scale of the riots was a factor in persuading the government to introduce parliamentary reform.

Agricultural unrest continued on a small scale after 1831. There were several attempts to form trade unions for farm workers, but these were ended with the Tolpuddle Martyrs case (see Chapter 4, page 86).

The reform bills of 1831–32

TIMELINE: THE CRISIS OF REFORM, 1830–32

1830
Revolution in France

Outbreak of the Swing Riots

Fall of Wellington's government

Earl Grey appointed prime minister at the head of a Whig-dominated government

1831
March: Russell introduces the first reform bill

April: Government defeated in the House of Lords; general election called

June: Whigs return with a substantial majority; second reform bill introduced

October: House of Lords rejects the second reform bill; rioting breaks out throughout the country

1832
March: Third reform bill passed in the House of Commons

May: Lords attempt to wreck the bill; government resigns; the Days of May; Whigs return to power

June: Third reform bill becomes law

December: First election under the Reform Act; Whigs take 441 seats, the Tories 175

Grey decided on a comprehensive reform which he hoped would settle the issue once and for all. In his instructions to the committee, formed to draw up a reform measure, he wrote that he wanted it to be substantial enough to satisfy public opinion and to remove the possibility of further innovations.

In March 1831, Lord John Russell presented the first reform bill (the third version of which later passed as the **Representation of the People Act 1832**) to the House of Commons. MPs on all sides were stunned by the radicalism of the measure. Russell proposed to retain the historic county franchise, the 40-shilling freeholder, but his proposals for the borough franchises appeared to be almost revolutionary in their scope. Under the terms of his bill, Russell intended to sweep away all existing voting qualifications in the boroughs and replace them with a uniform franchise of £10 householders, i.e. those who occupied property with an annual value of £10.

KEY TERM

Representation of the People Act
Between 1832 and 1928, there were five parliamentary reform Acts. They were officially entitled Representation of the People Acts, but almost all contemporaries and later historians have referred to the first three measures as the Reform Act 1832, the Second Reform Act 1867, and the Third Reform Act 1884.

EXTEND YOUR KNOWLEDGE

Lord John Russell (1792-1878)
Russell's strong support for individual liberties led him to support the repeal of the Test and Corporation Acts in 1828. His role was vital in steering reform through parliament in 1831-32. During the 1830s, Russell expressed the view that the Reform Act was a final settlement, but a further reform bill which he supported as prime minister in 1866 was unsuccessful.

Sir Robert Inglis was one of the leading opponents of reform. A leading Tory backbencher, Inglis came to prominence through his bitter opposition to measures which he believed would weaken the position of the Church of England within national life.

SOURCE 6

Sir Robert Inglis speaking in the House of Commons, 1 March 1831.

This House is not a collection of Deputies... We are not sent here day by day to represent the opinions of our constituents. We are sent here to legislate, not for the wishes of any set of men, but for the wants and the rights of all...

Our constitution is not the work of a code-maker; it is the growth of time and events beyond the design or the calculation of man... There is no evidence that our house was ever elected upon any principle of a representation of population... [the House of Commons] is the most complete representation of the interests of the people, which was ever assembled in any age or country. It is the only constituent body that ever existed, which includes within itself, those who can urge the wants and defend the claims of the landed, the commercial, the professional classes of the country; those who are bound to uphold the prerogatives of the Crown, the privileges of nobility, the interests of the lower classes, the rights and liberties of all people. How far, under any other than the present circumstances, the rights of the distant dependencies, of the East Indies, of the West Indies, of the colonies, of the great corporations, of the commercial interests generally... could find their just support in this house, I know not.

ACTIVITY
KNOWLEDGE CHECK

Differing views on the reform bill
1 Read Source 6. In your own words, outline the argument that Inglis makes against the reform bill.
2 To what extent is Inglis' argument more persuasive than Wellington's in Source 4?

Debates on the proposals revealed great divisions between the supporters and opponents of reform, and on 22 March the bill passed its second reading by just one vote (302-301). The narrowness of the government's victory meant that the bill was unlikely to pass into law. When Grey was defeated on an amendment, the government resigned and William IV dissolved parliament, calling a general election.

The last general election to the unreformed parliament returned the Whigs and their allies with a majority of more than 130 seats over the Tories. A second reform bill was introduced that passed easily through the House of Commons. A significant amendment to the county franchise came with the Chandos Clause. Proposed by the Marquis of Chandos, the amendment would extend the electorate in the counties beyond the 40-shilling freeholders by enfranchising tenant farmers who paid a rent of £50 a year for their land. The proposal would lead to a significant increase in the county electorate, and would grant the vote to a number of tenant farmers.

The bill was sent to the House of Lords in October 1831, where the peers, who were not influenced by popular pressure throughout the country, rejected the measure by 41 votes. The peers' action led to violent rioting in many towns and cities. The disturbances in Bristol were especially serious. Several hundred young men assembled in Queen Square and rioted for three days, during which they burned down the Bishop of Bristol's palace and attacked several homes and businesses.

Grey and his colleagues spent the winter of 1831–32 trying to win over sufficient peers to allow the bill to pass. A third reform bill passed through the House of Commons in March 1832, and the House of Lords passed the second reading by just nine votes. However, on 7 May, the House of Lords tried to wreck the bill by voting to postpone discussions on the redistribution of seats. Grey believed that the only way to secure the third reform bill's passage through the House of Lords was if William IV would create a large number of pro-reform peers. When the king refused Grey's request, the government resigned.

The action of the peers led to the Days of May, when national protests were organised in favour of the bill and against the Lords. Attwood and the Birmingham Political Union played a prominent role in the protests, which were aimed at preventing the return of Wellington as prime minister. In the end, Wellington was unable to form a government, largely because Peel would not support him, Grey returned to office, and William IV agreed to the creation of sufficient peers to allow the bill to pass. Faced with this unprecedented threat, the Lords gave way and passed the third reform bill in June 1832.

EXTEND YOUR KNOWLEDGE

The Days of May (1832)
The Days of May was a period of large-scale extra-parliamentary protest aimed at preventing Wellington becoming prime minister. Trade came to a standstill in some cities, large public demonstrations were held, and many petitions were presented to parliament protesting the action of the House of Lords. The Birmingham Political Union and other organisations urged people to take their money out of the banks, and London was placarded with the slogan 'to stop the duke, go for gold'. Many contemporary observers believed that a revolutionary situation was developing, and it was only halted with Grey's return to office.

The impact of the Reform Act on the franchise

In the counties, the old 40-shilling franchise was retained, and the Chandos amendment gave the vote to tenant farmers who rented property worth £50 a year.

The Reform Act swept away the confusing number of borough qualifications. For the first time, a standard borough franchise was established, enfranchising male householders with a house worth £10 a year.

In the English counties the electorate was increased by 55 percent, from 240,000 voters to 370,000. The borough electorate rose from c200,000 to 280,000 men, an increase of 40 percent. The most dramatic changes came in Scotland, where the pre-reform electorate of 4,500 soared to over 64,000 voters.

The uniform borough franchise appeared to be a radical measure, but it was hedged round with qualifications. Electors had to have been resident in their home for at least one year, and had to pay the **poor rates**. Many men in industrial towns moved house very often in search of work, and thus did not qualify for the vote. Equally, a uniform national franchise of £10 enfranchised many men in towns where rents were high, such as London, but its impact was much less in the northern towns such as Manchester and Leeds, where rents were much lower.

Several boroughs actually saw a reduction over time in the size of the pre-reform electorate. Those men who already had the vote in 1832 were allowed to retain their right to vote, but over time their numbers inevitably dwindled, and some boroughs saw a significant fall in the size of their electorate in the years to 1867.

Many people were bitterly disappointed with the Reform Act. The skilled working classes had high hopes of being admitted to the franchise, but the borough franchise of £10 was too high a hurdle for most of them. One way in which they expressed their grievances was to support the Chartist movement (see Chapter 4, pages 84–105), which flourished in the late 1830s and 1840s.

KEY TERM

Poor rate
An annual charge made on every property in a parish. The money raised was used exclusively to relieve the poor.

ACTIVITY
KNOWLEDGE CHECK

The extent of reform in 1832

1 The Representation of the People Act 1832 is popularly referred to as 'The Great Reform Act'. Study the factors that led to reform, and the changes that the 1832 Act made to the franchise.

2 In your opinion, does the Act deserve to be known as 'The Great Reform Act'?

EXTEND YOUR KNOWLEDGE

Historians and the Reform Act 1832

Historians have interpreted the Reform Act in different ways. J.R.M. Butler, in *The Passing of the Great Reform Bill* (1914), suggested that the Act moved the UK towards a fully democratic system, and Stephen Farrell's article in *History Today* (July 2010) is entitled *Reform Act: A First Step Towards Democracy*. Other historians have been less complimentary. Norman Gash, writing in *Aristocracy and People* (1979), asserted that the Act was 'no more than a clumsy but vigorous hacking at the old structure to make it roughly more acceptable'. On the other hand, Eric Evans, in *The Forging of the Modern State* (1983), suggests that, while the Reform Act can be seen as an aristocratic measure, designed to preserve as much of the old system as possible, it nonetheless paved the way for further change, and 'opened the door on a new political world'.

Politicians realised that, if parliament could be subject to a fundamental reform, the whole philosophy of reform could be extended to other areas of national life. The 1830s and 1840s would witness a flurry of reforms, to the Poor Law and to local government, as well as the growing regulation of mines, factories and banks. Moreover, the Act of 1832 marked the beginning, not the end, of parliamentary reform. The history of parliament during the succeeding century was punctuated by further electoral reform.

Representation of the People Act 1867

The revival of interest in parliamentary reform

In 1834, the Tory leader and future prime minister, Sir Robert Peel, declared his belief that the Reform Act was 'a final and irrevocable settlement of a great constitutional question', and most politicians agreed that further changes to the constitution were not necessary. Even Russell, the champion of reform in 1831–32, spoke in 1837 against further electoral changes, thus earning for himself the nickname of 'Finality Jack'. The Chartist movement of the 1830s and 1840s revived interest in the issue for a while (see Chapter 4, pages 84–105), but thereafter it appeared that the public became indifferent to further political change. Reform bills were introduced by the Liberals in 1859 and 1860, but evoked very little interest or enthusiasm.

One major obstacle to reform was removed in October 1865, with the death of the prime minister, Viscount Palmerston. Palmerston had agreed with Peel that parliamentary reform was a settled issue and he vigorously opposed those members of his government who were prepared to take up the issue. The most prominent Liberal minister who came out in favour of reform was William Gladstone, who declared in 1864 that 'every man who is not presumably incapacitated by some consideration of personal fitness or of political danger is morally entitled to come within the pale of the constitution'. On Palmerston's death in 1865, Russell, who had steered the 1832 Act through parliament, became prime minister, and reform was once again placed on the political agenda.

EXTEND YOUR KNOWLEDGE

William Gladstone (1809–98)

Gladstone was elected to parliament in 1832 and soon made his mark as a 'stern, unbending Tory'. He held minor offices in the 1830s and 1840s, but left the Tory Party when it split in 1846 (see Chapter 2, page 50). In 1859, Gladstone was one of a number of leading politicians who came together to form the Liberal Party. Between 1868 and 1894, he held office as prime minister on four occasions, more than any other politician before or since. His later years in office were dominated by his unsuccessful attempts to grant Home Rule to Ireland.

Gladstone's Liberalism encompassed gradual political reforms, financial orthodoxy and a strong sense of moral duty, which stemmed from his deeply held religious beliefs. He stamped his political views on the Liberal Party for a generation.

Unlike 1831–32, there was no substantial pressure from outside parliament for reform before 1865. The economic distress of the late 1840s had gradually declined, and was followed by sustained growth as the Industrial Revolution drove Britain to a position of economic pre-eminence in the world. With no real grievances to drive demands for reform, the 1850s and early 1860s were largely free from political agitation.

By 1865, however, developments at home and abroad had reawakened interest in parliamentary reform, and pressure for franchise reform grew. The growth of mass-circulation newspapers allowed people to follow the unification struggle in Italy of 1859–60, and the Polish revolt of 1863, with great interest. The American Civil War (1861–65) had a major impact on public opinion. The war, and the naval blockade of the south, meant that the southern states were unable to export raw cotton to the textile mills of Lancashire. The subsequent cotton famine was accompanied by widespread unemployment and distress in northern towns and cities. Nonetheless, the mill workers were unwavering in their support for Lincoln and the northern states, and against the southern institution of slavery. Their attitude persuaded many, especially leading Liberals and radicals, that a limited extension of the franchise to 'the respectable working classes' would not pose a serious threat to the existing political order.

The demand for reform was driven by a number of organised groups, similar to Attwood's Birmingham Political Union of the early 1830s. The Reform Union, formed in 1864, gained support among the prosperous middle classes, who saw reform as a means of furthering their own commercial interests, as well as challenging what they regarded as the inefficiency and waste of national government. Newspaper reports on the Crimean War (1854–56) had demonstrated the incompetence of the military and civilian leadership, which had caused a large number of deaths in the armed forces. The National Reform Union believed that franchise reform would lead to a more efficient and effective government. At home, the Northcote–Trevelyan report of 1854 condemned the inefficiency of the civil service and recommended that entry to the service should be based on merit rather than class. The Reform Union supported institutional as well as parliamentary reform: it promoted a moderate extension of the franchise and the introduction of a secret ballot.

The Reform League, formed in 1865, was a much larger and more formidable body. It differed from the Reform Union because of its commitment to universal manhood suffrage rather than the more modest household suffrage favoured by the Reform Union. The league had a strong following among trade unionists and the skilled working class, who hoped that parliamentary reform would lead to improved trade union rights as well as more extensive labour laws. Although the league was far more radical than the Reform Union, both organisations agreed to work together to promote parliamentary reform.

By the end of 1865, the Reform Union and the Reform League had developed strong national organisations that could call on widespread backing to pressure MPs into supporting franchise reform.

The Tories and the Second Reform Act

Russell had become prime minister in October 1865, with Gladstone as his Chancellor of the Exchequer. In March 1866, Gladstone introduced a reform bill in the House of Commons. This was a modest affair, which would reduce the borough franchise from £10 to £7, and extend the county franchise to tenants paying an annual rent of £14 or more. Gladstone's proposals would add around 200,000 voters in the boroughs and 170,000 voters in the counties. Vigorous opposition from Disraeli and the Conservatives, and from many uncompromising Whigs, led by Robert Lowe and the **Adullamites**, caused the bill to fail and led to the government's resignation in June. A minority Conservative government took office, with Lord Derby as prime minister and Benjamin Disraeli as Chancellor of the Exchequer.

KEY TERM

Adullamite
An anti-reform faction within the Liberal Party whose members were opposed to any change to the electoral system. Robert Lowe was the leading Adullamite: his speeches could not conceal his hatred of the working classes, describing them as 'unreflective and violent people'.

EXTEND YOUR KNOWLEDGE

Benjamin Disraeli (1804–81)
The son of a Jewish Italian father, Disraeli was elected as a Tory MP in 1837. He became a bitter opponent of Peel in the 1840s because the latter did not promote him to high office. Disraeli played a pivotal role in bringing down Peel's government in 1846 over the repeal of the Corn Laws. He served briefly as Chancellor of the Exchequer in 1852 and 1858–59, and it was as chancellor for a third time that he steered the Second Reform Act through parliament in 1866–67.

Unlike Gladstone, Disraeli was keen to attack social injustice, and passed several important social reforms during his ministry of 1874–80, which appealed to the new mass electorate. He promoted ideas of 'one-nation Conservatism', which influenced the development of the Conservative Party long after his death. His importance is described in Chapter 2 on page 51.

Few people expected the Conservatives to take up the issue of franchise reform, but Derby and Disraeli had several reasons for doing so. The Conservative Party had been in the political wilderness for 20 years, ever since they split over the issue of the Corn Laws in 1846. Derby and Disraeli had held office briefly in 1852, and in 1858–59. On both occasions their governments were little more than holding operations, which ended once the Liberals had regrouped and were ready to return to office. Derby and Disraeli were no longer prepared to govern simply at the pleasure of their political opponents. Instead, they were keen to restore the image of the Tory Party to operate as a major political force. Now that reform was on the political agenda, they decided to seize the initiative and put forward their own proposals. Disraeli was even prepared to outflank the Liberals with a substantial and radical measure.

The Tories' decision to reform was also influenced by events outside parliament. The Reform League organised meetings in Trafalgar Square in support of Gladstone's reform bill and, following the defeat of the bill, the league organised a number of mass protests and disturbances. A meeting of 200,000 people at Hyde Park in July became a riot, as railings were torn down and the police had to call for support from the Life Guards. Despite these setbacks, the league continued to pressure parliament over the winter of 1866–67.

The economic situation declined dramatically in 1866. In May, the financial house of Overend and Gurney collapsed, leading to a run on the banks and the collapse of many companies. The rest of 1866 saw little improvement in the economic situation. Heavy rains had wiped out many crops, and meat prices shot up as the virulent rinderpest disease wiped out many herds of cattle.

Thus, there were a number of factors pressuring for reform in 1865–67, as well as significant attempts to resist change.

Factors promoting reform
- Since 1860, there had been a dramatic rise in the circulation of the popular press, a reflection of growing interest in politics and reform.

- The Reform Union and the Reform League organised mass demonstrations, including the Hyde Park riots, to put pressure on MPs to support parliamentary reform.

- Economic distress was widespread, especially in the cotton towns of northern England as a result of the cotton famine.

- The Conservative Party was ready to take up the cause of reform.

Factors promoting resistance
- The more conservative Liberals, known as the Adullamites, offered strong resistance in parliament to any reform measure.

- Not all Conservatives were prepared to support reform. Their resistance was led by Cranborne, later Lord Salisbury.

- There was little genuine enthusiasm within parliament for reform.

- The landed gentry, who had sided with the South in the American Civil War, feared a dilution of their power and influence.

It was against a background of economic and social distress, as well as extra-parliamentary pressure, that Disraeli introduced his reform proposals in February 1867. The very idea of reform led to splits within the Tory Party, as three ministers, Cranborne, Carnarvon and General Peel, immediately resigned. Disraeli withdrew his original proposals and decided on a far-reaching and radical measure, which was introduced in March.

The Reform Act 1832 had resembled very closely Russell's original proposals of 1831. However, the Second Reform Act 1867 bore very little resemblance to Disraeli's original proposals. What began as a proposal to enlarge the borough electorate by 227,000 was changed dramatically as it passed through the House of Commons, and ended up doubling the national electorate.

SOURCE
7

The Hyde Park riots of 1866. Supporters of the Reform League are tearing down railings in the park, while the police attempt to maintain order. From an engraving printed in the *Illustrated London News*, 4 August 1866.

THE RIOT IN HYDE PARK.

THE MOB PULLING DOWN THE RAILINGS IN PARK-LANE.

Disraeli's bill of 18 March 1867 proposed to give the county franchise to those who rented land worth £15 a year, a substantial reduction on the £50 rent level set in 1832. Disraeli also proposed to extend the borough suffrage to all householders of two years' residence who paid rates directly to their local authority. However, this apparently radical measure was hedged around with qualifications. Lodgers in towns would not qualify, nor would the large number of **compounder** tenants. To offset the new borough electorate, a number of 'fancy franchises' were proposed, granting the vote to university graduates, members of 'learned professions' and those with £50 in the bank.

The leaders of the National Reform Union and the Reform League felt that the Tory proposals were too modest, and decided to put further pressure on parliament with demonstrations in London and throughout the country. Despite the government's attempts to ban it, a meeting in Hyde Park was arranged for 6 May. A crowd of 200,000 people turned up to listen to speeches demanding reform, with 15,000 special constables, police and the armed forces held in reserve in case rioting broke out. Contemporaries suggested that the era of mass political activity had returned, for such a huge demonstration of popular feeling had not been seen since the Chartist demonstrations of the 1830s and 1840s. However, it is not clear whether the meeting influenced either the government or the House of Commons.

Disraeli's strategy on the reform bill had been decided long before the Hyde Park meeting. He was ready to accept substantial amendments to the bill as long as they were not proposed by the Liberal front bench. He wanted to ensure that the final Act could not be claimed by the Liberals as reflecting their own proposals, but that it was a Tory measure through and through. While he rejected some measures, such as the proposal by John Stuart Mill to concede votes for women, he accepted some very radical amendments that changed the bill almost beyond recognition.

KEY TERM

Compounder
A tenant who paid a combination of rent and rates to the landlord of the property, who then paid the rates separately to the local authority.

Disraeli's intention to accept a number of amendments in order to save his bill led to dramatic changes in the proposed borough franchise. The residency qualification of two years was reduced to one year, and the vote was extended to lodgers, also of one year's residency, who paid rent of £10 a year. A third amendment was the most important of all. Proposed by a Newark MP, Hodgkinson's amendment would abolish the distinction between compounders and those who paid their rates in person. This measure alone would enfranchise 500,000 men. To universal astonishment, not least to Hodgkinson himself, Disraeli accepted an amendment whose effect was to create household suffrage as the basis of the borough franchise. Disraeli quietly dropped the 'fancy franchises' and the bill passed into law in August 1867.

The impact of the Representation of the People Act 1867 on the franchise

Gladstone's franchise proposals of 1866 would have extended the national franchise by around 370,000 men. Disraeli's Act, in comparison, virtually doubled the electorate, to two million voters.

In the counties, the historic 40-shilling franchise was retained. The electorate was increased by giving the vote to owners or leaseholders of land worth £5 a year, and landowners whose property had a rateable value of £12 a year. The reform expanded the county electorate from 540,000 to 800,000.

The borough franchise was given to all householders who had lived in a property for 12 months, and to lodgers, also of 12 months' standing, who occupied lodgings worth £10 in rent. The extension of the borough franchise was impressive. The borough electorate in 1866 numbered around 510,000 voters: the Second Reform Act created an urban electorate of 1,200,000. The number of working-class voters rose significantly, and in many constituencies, such as Sheffield and several London boroughs, the majority of the electorate was now drawn from the working class.

Despite the apparent radicalism of the Act, universal male suffrage had not been conceded. It is true that one in three adult males could now vote, instead of one in five before 1867, and that, for the first time, the majority of electors were working class. However, the franchise remained, as it had always been, based on property and a stake in the country. While householders were granted the vote, other male members of their family were not so fortunate. Moreover, the one-year residency qualification effectively disqualified the large number of people who moved house or lodgings, even within the same town, in search of employment.

There was little common ground between the bills introduced by Liberal and Conservative governments in 1866–67, but they shared one characteristic: neither party was prepared to concede the vote to what was known as the 'residuum'. These were the very poorest urban classes, unskilled, largely uneducated labourers, whose families lived in appalling conditions in slum properties. For the residuum, life was a constant struggle simply to survive. Not only were they ignored by the political parties, but the skilled working classes, who viewed themselves as the 'aristocracy of labour', regarded the residuum with undisguised contempt.

ACTIVITY
KNOWLEDGE CHECK

Similarities and differences

The following list of factors influenced the passing of both the Reform Act 1832 and the Second Reform Act 1867:

- Influences from overseas
- Party advantage
- The state of the economy
- The press
- Extra-parliamentary pressure
- The extension of the franchise.

1 List these factors in a table, with two further columns headed 'Similarities' and 'Differences'. Complete the table with one or two sentences highlighting similar and different ways in which each factor influenced the two Acts. For example, although both Acts extended the franchise, you might decide that the 1867 changes were more radical simply because the vote was given to far more people than in 1832.

2 When you have completed your table, write a short paragraph on which of the two Acts was, in your opinion, more far-reaching. Give reasons for your choice.

As the reform bill made its final passage through the House of Lords, Derby commented that 'we are making a great experiment' and 'taking a leap in the dark'. In 1832, the existing electorate had increased by 50 percent to 650,000, but the Second Reform Act saw a doubling of those entitled to vote to almost two million. The Reform Act 1867 marked the beginning of a clear shift of political influence, away from the traditional agricultural interests in the south of England and towards the manufacturing towns of the Midlands and the north.

The parties had to adjust to the new electoral landscape in many ways. Working-class voters expected reforms that tackled their grievances. The 1830s and 1840s had seen a number of reforms following the 1832 Act, and there was a similar burst of reform after 1867. Throughout the 1870s, both Liberal and Conservative governments responded to the new political environment with a wide range of reforms that tackled issues such as education, urban housing, public health and the rights of trade unions. The parties also recognised that they had to win the support of the electorate, and thus national party organisations were established to take the party's messages to the new voters (see Chapter 2, pages 56–57).

Representation of the People Act 1884

The election of 1880, which returned Gladstone to office for a second time, was the third to be fought under the terms of the Reform Act 1867. Despite the gloomy predictions of many politicians, such as Derby, who saw the Act as a 'leap in the dark', the elections of 1868, 1874 and 1880 saw no fundamental shift away from the traditional contests between Tories and Liberals (though the rise of the Irish Home Rule Party, which took 63 seats in 1880, marks the beginning of a new and difficult phase in Anglo-Irish relations).

Extra-parliamentary pressure played a significant part in the reform crises of 1831–32 and 1866–67, but there was no significant pressure from inside or outside parliament for further changes to the electoral system. However, Gladstone found it difficult to justify the maintenance of separate borough and county franchises, with household suffrage in the boroughs, but a more restrictive £12 suffrage in the counties. The experience of living with the Second Reform Act suggested to Gladstone that it would be safe to enfranchise agricultural labourers in the countryside. He may have been influenced by partisan advantage, since many assumed that any new county voters, such as small tenant farmers and agricultural labourers, would be likely to vote for the Liberals, and thus weaken the hold of the Tories and the aristocratic landowners in the counties.

Although there was no pressure for a further extension to the franchise, Gladstone introduced a reform bill in 1884. The measure proposed to replace the separate and unequal franchises for counties and boroughs with a single national qualification granted to male householders and £10 lodgers. It passed easily through the House of Commons, but was blocked in the House of Lords, thanks to the intervention of the Conservative leader Lord Salisbury. Salisbury was aware of the simple electoral fact that the Liberals' strength came from the boroughs, while the Tories dominated the county seats. Salisbury feared that the widening of the franchise would weaken the Conservative Party dramatically and establish Liberal dominance over towns and countryside alike. The rejection of the bill thus reflected the concerns of both Salisbury and his party.

In October 1884, Queen Victoria urged the parties to negotiate to end the deadlock. Party leaders met at Salisbury's London home and agreed the Arlington Street compact: the Tories would allow the reform bill to pass as long as it was followed by a major redistribution of seats. Following the Arlington Street compact, the Third Reform Act passed into law with little debate. For the first time in British parliamentary history, there was a uniform national electoral qualification based on household suffrage in towns and counties. Once again there was a dramatic increase in the size of the electorate, which rose by 84 percent to 5.5 million: some 2.5 million new voters were admitted to the franchise, a far greater numerical increase than in 1832 or 1867.

Contemporary observers, and many historians, believed that the Third Reform Act had established a democratic electoral system in Britain, but this was far from the case. Household suffrage excluded many adult males. The sons of householders, servants, members of the armed forces, as well as most of the 'residuum', the many unskilled and casual labourers who did not meet the residency qualification, and, of course, women – all these remained disfranchised. Recent research has suggested that the Act excluded 40 percent of adult males from the franchise, an issue that was not addressed until the First World War.

Representation of the People Act 1918

Many Victorian politicians expressed alarm at successive increases in the size of the electorate brought about by the Reform Acts of 1832–84. The increase in numbers of a few hundred thousand men in 1832, 700,000 in 1867, and even the 2.5 million enfranchised in 1884, pale into insignificance beside the Fourth Reform Act 1918, which tripled the electorate from 7,000,000 to 21,000,000 and, for the first time, gave the vote to over eight million women.

In 1916, Britain had been at war for two years. An election had been due in 1915, but was postponed until after the war. An election would have been impractical because, despite the work of the boundary commissioners, equal electoral districts had been impossible to maintain, and the electoral registers were hopelessly out of date. Moreover, an election fought under the 1884 franchise would have meant that hardly any soldiers fighting on the Western Front would have qualified to vote.

The government addressed the issue of reform with the appointment of the Speaker's Conference of 1916, at which representatives of the main political parties drew up a number of proposals for electoral reform.

The conference proposed two significant changes. Firstly, all adult males aged 21 and over were to be given the vote. The war service of younger men was also recognised with a proposal that men aged 19–20 who had fought in the war would be entitled to vote in the post-war election. Universal male suffrage, the central demand by radical reformers for a century, was finally conceded in the Fourth Reform Act 1918, and Britain had taken one of the last steps towards becoming a fully fledged democracy.

The triumph of adult male suffrage, and the enfranchising of over five million adult males, however, has been overshadowed in the popular imagination by the proposals made to the Speaker's Conference on women's suffrage.

The Speaker's Conference decided that the issue of female suffrage could no longer be ignored. However, leading politicians were reluctant to give the vote to women on the same terms as men. The huge loss of life on the Western Front would have made female voters the majority in the post-war electorate.

SOURCE 8

The Labour Leader Keir Hardie addressing a large suffragette meeting in Trafalgar Square, 1908.

As a result, the Speaker's Conference moved towards female suffrage in a very cautious fashion. The 1918 Act enfranchised women aged 30 and over, as long as they were householders or the wives of householders, university graduates or rented property valued at £5 per annum. These restrictive terms meant that over 20 percent of women over 30 did not qualify for the vote because they were unable to meet the stringent qualifications.

Women were now able to stand for election to parliament, and several did so in the 1918 election. The first woman to be elected was Countess Marckievicz, a member of the Irish party Sinn Fein, but she never took her seat, since Sinn Fein's 73 members had agreed to boycott parliament. The first woman to sit in the House of Commons, Nancy Astor, took her seat in 1919.

A commonly held view on the granting of votes for women in 1918 is that it rewarded women for their war work, whether in munitions, on farms or as nurses on the Western Front. However, most women involved in these activities were under 30, and so failed to qualify for the vote in 1918. The opponents of equal suffrage for men and women were perhaps influenced by the memory of the violent suffragette agitation which had clouded politics in the years before 1914, and feared its revival in the difficult post-war era.

Representation of the People Act 1928

The general elections in the years 1918–24 saw little change in voting habits, and this persuaded political leaders that it would not be dangerous to introduce universal suffrage for both men and women. However, providing equal voting rights to women after 1918 was not without controversy. There has been historical debate over how equal franchise rights were achieved in 1928. Feminist societies, notably the National Union of Societies for Equal Citizenship (NUSEC), which had formed from the National Union of Women's Suffrage Societies (NUWSS) in 1918, continued to point out the inequalities between female and male voters. Just 1 in 15 of employed women could vote as the majority of professional women rented their accommodation and therefore failed to meet the property qualifications to vote.

The reform of 1918 kept working women disenfranchised. The Labour Party's failed 1919 women's emancipation bill, which would provide equal suffrage rights to women from the age of 21, was followed by equal franchise bills almost every year in the early 1920s. The Labour government of 1924 fell before it had a chance to introduce any suffrage reform. Between 1918 and 1927, the NUSEC kept the question of equal franchise open in parliament. More important than public pressure or Labour's efforts was the Conservative Party's determination, under Prime Minister Stanley Baldwin's leadership, to attract women voters. Until 1927, the majority of the party's backbench MPs opposed equal franchise for women on reaching 21, but the party's leadership believed that women were the key to the party's future. The women's organisation in the party was the fastest growing element within it, with more than a million female Conservative Party members by 1928. Women were more likely than men in the 1920s to vote Conservative. The Conservative Party tended to do much better in constituencies with higher proportions of female voters, while

Labour struggled in areas where more women voted. Baldwin supported equal franchise from 1924, and in 1927 his cabinet agreed to extend the franchise to women at the age of 21. They wanted to secure new women voters as Conservative supporters.

Despite this Conservative support for equal suffrage, in 1927 opponents of equal suffrage mounted one last attempt to prevent the reform. The *Daily Mail* published several articles claiming that reform meant giving the vote to 'flappers'. The newspaper portrayed these women as young, single, sexually active and politically ignorant women. This stereotype was aimed at stirring up Conservative opposition to Baldwin's extension of the franchise. Those opposed also claimed that the extension would create a majority of women voters who would vote as a single unified bloc, which would bring about the feminisation of political culture. Nevertheless, the 1928 equal franchise bill passed comfortably in the Commons by 387 to 10 votes, becoming in law the Representation of the People Act. This Act gave women the vote on the same terms as men, adding a further 5.2 million women to the electorate. Within just ten years, women had gone from being completely unenfranchised to a majority position in the electorate, with 14.5 million women voters, compared with 12.25 million men. Millicent Fawcett, a leading campaigner for the suffrage and for women's rights, was present in parliament when the bill completed its passage into law. She wrote: 'It is almost exactly 61 years ago since I heard John Stuart Mill introduce his suffrage amendment to the reform bill on 20 May 1867. So I have had extraordinary good luck in having seen the struggle from the beginning'.

A Level Exam-Style Question Section C

To what extent was reform of the franchise in the years 1780–1928 influenced by extra-parliamentary pressure? (20 marks)

Tip
You need to know when pressure from outside parliament influenced ministers and MPs, and you should reach a judgement on the importance of the suffragettes in the making of the Acts of 1918 and 1928. You should also analyse the significance of other relevant factors, such as the collapse of the Tory Party in 1830, the intention of most politicians to secure some advantages for their party, and the importance of other factors.

ACTIVITY
KNOWLEDGE CHECK

Why did it take so long to achieve universal adult suffrage?

1 The transition from an aristocratic electoral system to one based on universal adult suffrage took almost a century. Explain briefly how each of the following points helped or hindered the process of change in the years 1832–1928:
- The prevailing state of the economy
- The attitude of the working class to franchise reform
- The campaign for women's suffrage.

2 Which other factors, in your opinion, were of major importance either in promoting or hindering the process of change?

HOW SIGNIFICANT WERE CHANGES IN THE DISTRIBUTION OF SEATS IN THE YEARS c1780–1918?

Each of the Reform Acts passed in the years 1832–1918 included provisions for the redistribution of parliamentary seats to take account of changes in the franchise. The national distribution of seats in 1780 became increasingly indefensible with the growth of new areas of population in the Midlands and the north. Although the Whig government's reforms in 1832 did not attempt to make constituencies of fairly equal size in terms of population and the number of electors, MPs did try to create an electoral map that was broadly acceptable to the new electorate.

The problems of representation, c1780

- There were 558 parliamentary seats in England, Scotland and Wales. This number rose to 658 after the Act of Union of 1800 abolished the Irish parliament and provided 100 Irish seats for the Westminster parliament.

- There were 122 county seats, with each county, regardless of size, represented by two MPs.

- The boroughs and the universities of Oxford and Cambridge comprised a total of 436 seats. The number of electors in each borough varied dramatically. Smaller boroughs consisting of 500–1,000 voters were sometimes under the direct control of the government, notably naval bases along the south coast of England.

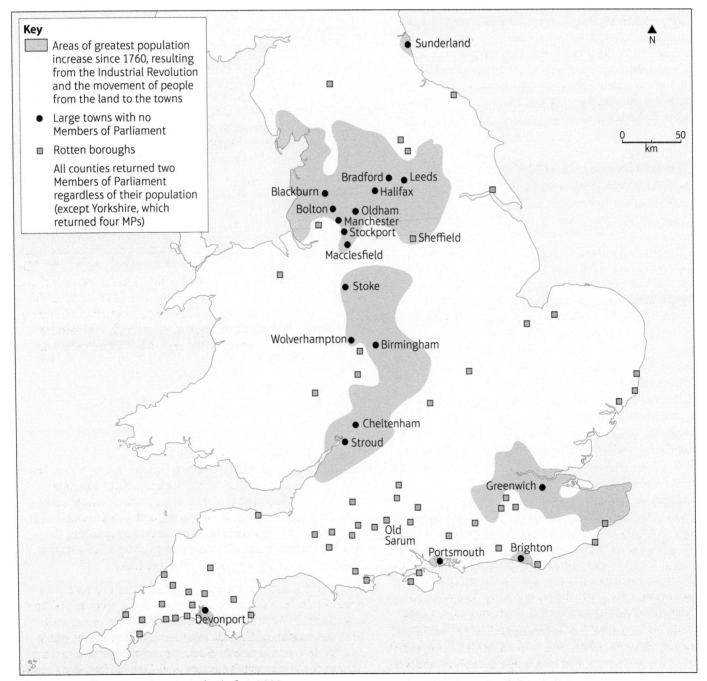

Key

Areas of greatest population increase since 1760, resulting from the Industrial Revolution and the movement of people from the land to the towns

● Large towns with no Members of Parliament

▢ Rotten boroughs

All counties returned two Members of Parliament regardless of their population (except Yorkshire, which returned four MPs)

Figure 1.1 Parliamentary representation before 1832.

- In many smaller boroughs, the electors were quite content to sell their votes to the highest bidder. The Suffolk town of Sudbury was notoriously corrupt in this respect, and in 1844 it lost both of its MPs.

- The practice of sending two MPs to parliament to represent each county in the UK had been a consistent feature of the electoral system since the reign of Henry VI. The granting of MPs to boroughs was a more haphazard affair. In many cases, seats were allocated to towns that possessed some economic or religious significance. Although depopulation or economic decline reduced the population and the electorate in many boroughs, they retained the right to send one or two MPs to parliament.

Figure 1.1 shows that the distribution of seats at the end of the 18th century was heavily weighted towards the south and south-west of England. To the south of a line drawn between Bristol and London were seats that returned 40 percent of all MPs to Westminster. Cornwall returned 44 MPs in all, just one seat fewer than the 45 MPs elected for the whole of Scotland. Moreover, the representative system did not take into account the changes in the distribution of population that had been taking place throughout the 18th century. The growing populations of industrial areas, especially in the Midlands, Lancashire and Yorkshire, were not reflected in the electoral system. By 1780, Lancashire's population was four times that of Cornwall (1,300,000 compared with 300,000), but Lancashire returned just 14 MPs to Cornwall's 44.

The failure of Pitt's proposals

Pitt had displayed his commitment to parliamentary reform before becoming prime minister in December 1783. He was following in the footsteps of his father, Pitt the Elder, who had proposed some measures of reform in the 1750s and 1760s, but without success. Pitt entered parliament in 1781 as member for the pocket borough of Appleby in Westmorland, and soon made his mark as a champion of parliamentary reform. He was influenced by Christopher Wyvill, whose Yorkshire Association was founded in 1780 with the aim of eliminating corruption in parliament. Early in 1782, Pitt proposed the creation of a committee to address several issues concerning parliamentary representation, but was easily defeated. In May 1783, he made a more specific proposal, to disfranchise a number of corrupt boroughs and transfer their seats to the counties. Once again, his measure was defeated, though by a smaller margin than before.

Pitt made a third attempt at reform in 1785. In April, he introduced a detailed measure that would abolish 36 corrupt boroughs and transfer their seats to London and to the counties. Borough owners would be given financial compensation for the loss of what was regarded as their personal property. Pitt hoped that his personal standing as prime minister might gain him support, especially from the independent MPs, though opposition to the measure remained strong. George III was openly hostile to the measure, and there was no groundswell of opinion in the country as a whole for reform. Fox, who was Pitt's chief opponent in the House of Commons, had long supported reform, and was ready to support Pitt on the issue. However, he refused to accept

Pitt's suggestion that £1 million should be made available to compensate the owners of seats. Fox and his supporters therefore opposed the bill presented to parliament in April 1785.

In his speech proposing the reform bill, Pitt referred to the opponents of the measure, and the reasons why they could not support reform (Source 9).

SOURCE 9 From the speech that Pitt made in the House of Commons on 18 April 1785 in support of his reform proposals. Here, Pitt identified the principal opponents of the bill, and the reasons for their opposition.

Those who, with a sort of superstitious awe, reverence the constitution so much as to be fearful of touching even its defects, had always reprobated every attempt to purify the representation. They acknowledged its inequality and corruption, but in their enthusiasm for the grand fabric, they would not suffer a reformer, with unhallowed hands, to repair the injuries which it suffered from time. Others who, perceiving the deficiencies that had arisen from the circumstances, were solicitous of their amendment, yet resisted the attempt, under the argument, that when once we had presumed to touch the constitution in one point, the awe which had heretofore kept us back from the daring enterprize of innovation might abate, and there was no foreseeing to what alarming lengths we might progressively go, under the mask of reformation. Others there were, but for these he confessed he had not the same respect, who considered the present state of representation as pure and adequate to all its purposes, and perfectly consistent with the first principles of representation.

Pitt's bill was defeated in the House of Commons by 248 votes to 174. He remained a supporter of parliamentary reform, but in the years after 1785 he had more pressing issues to contend with. The French Revolution, and the explosive growth in radical activity and ideas, meant that Pitt never took up the issue again. In 1792, the Whig Charles Grey introduced a reform proposal that was almost identical to that championed by Pitt. Pitt strongly opposed the measure, which he claimed would lead to the overthrow of the British constitution.

Reasons for resistance to and key changes brought about by reform

Representation of the People Act 1832

Most extra-parliamentary pressure for reform in the years c1780–1830 focused on demands for the extension of the franchise, with redistribution being only a secondary issue. Concern over widespread corruption in the boroughs, and the ease with which their members could be dragooned into supporting the government of the day, were brought into sharp relief with the controversy over Catholic relief in the late 1820s.

The decision made by Wellington's government to pass a Relief Act in 1829 was opposed in many areas, especially in the universities. Peel had served as MP for Oxford University since 1817. His support of Catholic relief led him to resign his seat in January 1829 and force a by-election in an attempt to regain the support of the university's electors. Anti-Catholic feeling in Oxford was so strong that Peel was defeated in February, just a few days before he was due to introduce the relief bill in the House of Commons.

A solution to Peel's predicament came from the town of Westbury in Wiltshire. Sir Manasseh Lopes, one of the town's MPs, and owner of the borough, resigned his seat. Within a week, a by-election was held and the town's three electors awarded the seat to Peel. Manoeuvres such as these influenced many people to support demands for a more equitable distribution of seats.

In 1830, the prime minister, Earl Grey, ordered a comprehensive review of the whole electoral system that would inform the government's proposals in the reform bill. The review's findings revealed the impact of industrialisation and population change, and highlighted the widespread variations in the distribution of seats:

- Thirty-three English towns had a population of over 10,000 people, but returned no MPs. They included Manchester and Salford (133,788), Birmingham (85,416) and Leeds (83,796).

- Twenty-seven English boroughs had had no contested elections in the previous 30 years.

The Reform Act 1832 introduced important changes to the franchise, which added the propertied middle classes to the electorate, but changes to the distribution of seats were in many ways more radical:

- Fifty-six boroughs with a population below 2,000 lost both of their parliamentary seats.

- Thirty boroughs of between 2,000 and 4,000 people lost one MP.

- Forty-four new borough seats were created, with many of them going to the new industrial towns and cities in the Midlands and the north.

- The influence of the new borough seats was partially offset by the granting of 65 extra seats to the counties.

The Whigs had been determined to remove the worst excesses of the old representative system, but did not intend to introduce any mathematical uniformity in the distribution of seats. The new seats, especially in the boroughs, were created to reflect economic interests rather than the populations of the towns. Salford in Lancashire had an electorate of 1,497, while Reigate in Surrey had just 153; both towns returned one MP. In the Scottish counties, Perthshire's 3,180 electors returned one MP, as did Sutherland's electorate of just 84.

Figure 1.2 shows the extent to which redistribution gave large towns separate representation in parliament after 1832. Anomalies remained, however: Tamworth in Staffordshire, for example, remained under the control of Peel's family. Peel's father had represented the seat since 1790, and on his death in 1830 Peel left Westbury to take control of the family seat. There were also many larger towns, especially in Yorkshire and Warwickshire, which did not have separate representation. Although London and the counties gained several seats, they remained under-represented in terms of population.

ACTIVITY
KNOWLEDGE CHECK

Pitt and Grey
Some historians have argued that it was the level of support in parliament that explains the failure of Pitt's proposals in the 1780s and Grey's success in 1832. Suggest two other reasons to explain the different outcomes of both men's measures.

Representation of the People Act 1867

By the mid-1860s, organisations such as the Reform League began to campaign not only for universal suffrage, but also for measures to remedy the imbalance in the distribution of seats. For instance, 334 borough MPs represented a total of 9.5 million people, while the 11.5 million people in the counties had just 162 members. To many contemporaries, the most important feature of the Reform Act 1867 was the substantial increase in the size of the electorate brought about by the introduction of household suffrage in the boroughs. A measure of redistribution was undertaken, though it appeared to be less substantial or significant than the changes made in 1832.

Disraeli, however, believed that redistribution was 'the very soul of the question of reform'. He realised that extending the vote to many of the working classes might, in the short term at least, work to the disadvantage of the Conservatives, and tried to limit its significance through changes to the electoral map.

The Act made changes to the number of seats in both boroughs and counties:

- Boroughs with a population below 10,000 lost one or both of their MPs.

- Eleven new constituencies were created, and the number of MPs for Liverpool, Manchester, Leeds and Birmingham was increased from two to three.

- The English and Welsh counties were allocated an extra 25 MPs.

- Scotland was given five more seats, and three new university seats were created.

The most important feature of the 1867 redistribution was its impact, not in the new boroughs, but in the counties. Firstly, a further 25 seats for the counties led to a strengthening of the landed interest, whose members tended to favour the Conservatives rather than the Liberals. Secondly, the creation of new borough seats meant that their electorates would not be voting in the counties, where they might challenge the entrenched power of the nobility and the large landowners.

The 1868 election result suggests that Disraeli had miscalculated the effects on the Conservatives of redistribution. Rather than increasing its representation, the party lost eight seats as Gladstone's Liberals stormed to power with a substantial majority. In the longer term, however, the Conservatives established themselves as a major force in British politics, partly as a result of the changes brought about by Lord Salisbury in 1885.

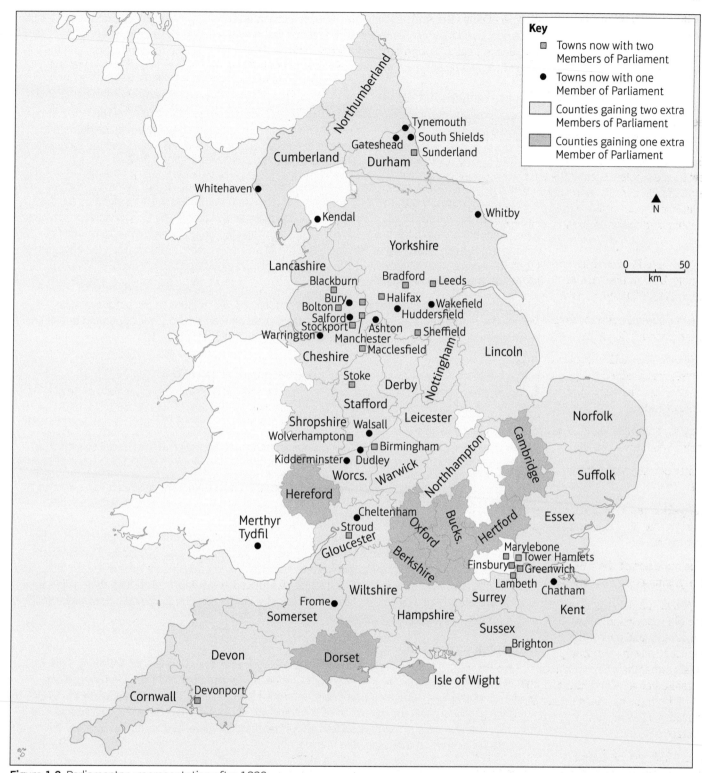

Figure 1.2 Parliamentary representation after 1832.

Ballot Act 1872

The year 1868 saw the first general election fought under the Reform Act 1867, and Gladstone's Liberal Party secured a strong parliamentary majority. Gladstone was concerned by the publicity given to the widespread corruption and intimidation that took place before and during the poll, and therefore he proposed measures to tackle corruption and protect electoral secrecy with the introduction of the secret ballot. The corrupt practice measures were dropped, but the government pressed on with the secret ballot, which had been one of the points demanded by the Chartist movement in the 1830s and 1840s.

Some MPs believed that the bill would reduce corrupt practices and save many voters from their baser instincts. These members believed many of the new electorates were open to bribery or intimidation, which would be reduced by the secret ballot.

The bill was not controversial, and passed easily into law in 1872. While it may have ended some of the worst forms of malpractice, its initial effects were not clear, and the influence of landlords in the counties and factory owners in towns continued to affect some electors. Perhaps the most important short-term effect of the ballot was seen in Ireland. Supporters of Irish Home Rule were now less open to intimidation, and the Home Rule movement grew dramatically over the next 20 years.

Corrupt Practices Act 1883

Issues of parliamentary reform loomed large during Gladstone's second ministry (1880–85). Many MPs were scandalised by the widespread bribery and corruption that had taken place during the 1880 election, one of the most corrupt and expensive elections for many years, and the Liberals prepared to tackle an issue of growing importance.

An unforeseen consequence of the redistribution of seats carried out in 1867 was that, once borough seats were freed from the aristocratic influence that controlled the surrounding counties, they became open to electoral competition. Many candidates, Liberal and Conservative, spent large sums of money trying to secure the votes of the growing electorate. Their methods included simple bribery, treating (the provision of free food and drink) and 'colourable employment' (the engaging of voters in nominal jobs). Historian H.J. Hanham's research suggested that, between 1865 and 1884, 64 English boroughs 'possessed a corrupt element', of which 21 were 'extremely corrupt'.

Sudbury had been disfranchised for corruption on a large scale in 1844, but dubious practices remained a prominent feature in electoral contests. A Royal Commission was appointed in 1880 to investigate the 1880 election that took place in Sandwich in Kent (Source 10).

SOURCE

10 Report of the Royal Commission on the election in Sandwich, 1881.

Observing the nature and manner of the bribery committed at the contest between Mr. Crompton Roberts and Sir Julian Goldsmid, the general expectation that money would be distributed in bribery, the almost universal willingness and even avidity to accept bribes, the great proportion of the population implicated, the ease with which the most extensive bribery was carried out, the organisation for the purpose of bribery, which was far too facile and complete to be inexperienced, the readiness on the part of many to accept bribes from both sides, and the total absence of a voice to warn, condemn, or denounce, we cannot doubt that electoral corruption had long and extensively prevailed in the borough of Sandwich.

The Corrupt Practices Act 1883 set stringent limits on campaign expenses. In England and Wales, candidates could spend no more than £710 for the first 2,000 voters and £40 for each additional 1,000 voters. Candidates and their agents were required to keep detailed records of expenditure, and stiff penalties could be imposed if malpractice was proved in the courts. Although there was some evidence of illegal practices after 1883, the Act finally brought an end to the culture of electoral corruption that had existed for centuries.

Redistribution Act 1885

The Redistribution Act 1885 was the work of the Tory leader, the Marquess of Salisbury. This is perhaps a little surprising, since, as Viscount Cranborne, he had resigned from Derby's cabinet in 1867 in opposition to Disraeli's proposed reforms. However, the Conservative victory in 1874 convinced Salisbury that the extension of the franchise had not damaged the Tory Party, and that franchise changes were in many ways less important than the national distribution of seats. In 1884–85, he worked on this issue with unusual energy.

EXTEND YOUR KNOWLEDGE

Marquess of Salisbury (1830–1903)

Lord Salisbury was MP for Stamford in Lincolnshire from 1853 until 1868, when he was elevated to the House of Lords on the death of his father. As an MP, he had opposed the Reform Act 1867, and resigned from the government in protest. He was a member of Disraeli's cabinet between 1874 and 1880, and as foreign secretary played a leading role in European affairs. On Disraeli's death in 1881, Salisbury became Tory leader in the House of Lords, and was responsible for the terms of the Redistribution Act 1885. Salisbury was prime minister on three occasions: 1885–86, 1886–92 and 1895–1902. He was largely responsible for the development of 'Villa Toryism', which was widely supported by the suburban electorate, but he was very reluctant to carry out large-scale social reforms promoted by radical members of his cabinet. He embodied the traditional qualities of aristocratic conservatism.

One of the effects of the rising population in towns and cities was the development of the suburb. These were areas outside the city centres where middle-class factory owners and managers settled, free from the overcrowding and pollution of the centres of towns, but within easy reach by train or tram. In electoral terms, the suburbs, whose residents were largely Conservative voters, possessed only limited value to the Conservatives. If they voted within their county, they simply increased an existing Conservative majority; if their homes were within the borough's boundaries, their votes were often insufficient to dent a healthy Liberal majority.

The Arlington Street compact favoured the creation of equal electoral districts (like the ballot, a demand made by the Chartists). Salisbury went even further with his proposal to establish single-member constituencies. This was a radical departure from the existing practice that dated back to the 15th century: in 1885, 70 percent of all MPs sat in multi-member constituencies. Salisbury believed that equal electoral districts that would choose just one MP would provide significant electoral benefits for the Tories. Many suburbs would become constituencies separate from the towns, providing a possible inbuilt advantage for the Conservative Party.

In 1884, boundary commissioners were appointed to determine the new electoral geography. They drew up proposals based on one parliamentary seat for a population of around 50,000. The Redistribution Act 1885 saw 28 boroughs with populations of over 50,000 remain as two-member constituencies, but in all other cases single-member seats were established. The number of seats for each large city would now reflect population size. Liverpool, for example, had nine seats; Leeds had five. There were substantial changes made in the counties, again dependent on population size. Smaller counties such as Cumberland and Norfolk gained no extra MPs; the number of county seats in Lancashire rose from eight to 23, and in Yorkshire from ten to 26.

Taken together, the changes brought by the reforms of 1883–85 transformed the electoral landscape. Hanham believed that 'the years 1880–86 marked a significant break in electoral politics'. The main reason for this dramatic change is arguably down to redistribution rather than to the wider franchise established in 1884. Henceforth, political life was dominated by class rather than by interests. As Lang pointed out, 'redistribution in effect, grouped constituencies by class: middle-class suburbs, working-class inner-city areas, landed class counties and so on'. The general election of 1885 confirms this view: for the first time MPs drawn from industry and commerce outnumbered those related to the aristocracy.

Salisbury proved justified in his view that the single-member suburban constituencies would become Conservative strongholds and essential to the party's success for many years. Indeed, Evans noted that 1885 'provided what was probably the biggest single boost his party ever received. The electoral hegemony of the Conservative Party in the years 1886–1997 owed more to the shrewd cynicism of the Marquess of Salisbury than it did to the meretricious chicanery of the Earl of Beaconsfield'.

Representation of the People Act 1918

The year 1918 saw no major redistribution of seats in England. Some major towns and cities gained seats, a process which, like 1867, limited the growth of urban influence in the counties. The Easter Rising in Ireland, in 1916, prompted a general rearrangement of Irish seats designed to increase the influence of the Unionist Party, the Irish equivalent of the Conservatives.

Between 1832 and 1918, patterns of redistribution were designed to provide some advantage to the party in power. The process was taken out of the hands of politicians in 1944, when independent boundary commissions were established to monitor the size of each constituency's electorate and recommend boundary sizes where appropriate. Parliament may not amend the boundary commission's decisions; they must be accepted or rejected as a whole.

A Level Exam-Style Question Section C

'Redistribution of seats was carried out mainly to reflect changes in Britain's economic landscape.' How far do you agree with this opinion on parliamentary redistribution in the years 1780–1918?
(20 marks)

Tip

You should analyse redistribution in the years 1780–1918, focusing on the extent of change and the increasing representation given to towns and cities. Then consider other relevant factors making for redistribution, such as attempts to eliminate corruption, and the aim of making the representative system overall acceptable to the growing electorate.

THINKING HISTORICALLY — Cause and consequence (7a & b)

Questions and answers

Questions that historians ask vary depending on what they think is important. It is the questions that interest us that define the history that is written. These questions change with time and place. Different historians will also come up with different answers to the same questions, depending on their perspectives and methods of interpretation, as well as the evidence they use.

Below are three historians who had different areas of interest.

G.M. Trevelyan	E.P. Thompson	Michel Foucault
A political historian who lived in the late 19th and early 20th centuries.	An economic and political historian who lived in the 20th century.	A French philosopher and historian of ideas who lived in the 20th century.
Was interested in the idea that humanity is constantly advancing through history towards democracy.	Was interested in the role of radical political movements and how they contributed to historical change in the 19th century.	Was interested in how governments control society and the techniques they adopted to maintain order.
Believed that Britain's political system was a triumphant product of progressive historical change.	Was politically left-wing, and worked to emphasise the part played by the working classes in English history.	Believed that the extension of liberties to individuals was actually a way for governments to continue governing. Argued that extensions of political representation to the middle and working classes were ways of avoiding revolution and maintaining the peace.

These are some key events in the reform of parliament between 1780 and 1928:

Reform Act 1832	Ballot Act 1872	Chartist movement of the 1830s and 1840s
French Revolution	Second Reform Act 1867	Lack of political representation for women in the 19th century
Women's suffrage in 1918	Failure of reform bills in 1831 and 1832	Third Reform Act 1884

Work in groups of between three and six to answer these questions:

1   Which of these events would have been of most interest to each historian? Explain your answer.

2   Each take the role of one historian and devise a question that would interest them about each of the events.

3   Discuss each event in turn. Present the questions that have been devised for each historian and offer some ideas about how they would have answered them.

4   For each event, decide as a group which question is the most interesting and worthwhile of the three.

Answer the following questions in pairs:

5   Identify the different ways that each historian would approach writing an account of the passing of the Reform Act 1832.

6   In what ways would Trevelyan and Thompson differ in their explanations of the significance of the Chartist movement of the 1830s and 1840s? What would be the focus of their arguments?

Answer the following questions individually:

7   All three historians may produce very different accounts and explanations of the same piece of history. Of the three historians, whose account would you prefer to read first? Explain your answer.

8   Do the differences in these accounts mean that one is more valid than the others?

9   Explain why different historical explanations are written by different historians.

10 Explain why different explanations of the same event can be equally valid.

ACTIVITY
KNOWLEDGE CHECK

The Redistribution Act 1885

1 How far do you agree that the Redistribution Act was the most important change to the electoral system in the years 1867–85?

2 Write three paragraphs in which you agree with the statement in question 1, focusing on the Redistribution Act.

3 Write a further three or four paragraphs on the reforms passed in the years 1867–83, highlighting one change that you think could be considered as more important than the Act of 1885. Explain your reasons.

ACTIVITY
SUMMARY

Key turning points

1 The table below shows the changing size of the British electorate in the years 1780–1928.

1780	214,000
First Reform Act 1832	800,000
Second Reform Act 1867	2,000,000
Third Reform Act 1884	5,400,000
Fourth Reform Act 1918	21,400,000
Fifth Reform Act 1928	26,700,000

The figures suggest that the Fourth Reform Act 1918 was the most significant of the Reform Acts because of the substantial increase in the size of the electorate.

a) Give reasons to support the view that the 1918 Act was the most important of the Reform Acts.

b) Choose one of the other Acts that might be considered the key turning point in the changes to the franchise in these years. Explain your choice.

2 The Acts of 1832 and 1867, and the Redistribution Act 1885, saw major changes in the distribution of seats across Britain. Which development do you think was more important in the creation of a more representative electoral system in these years: the extension of the franchise or the redistribution of seats? Explain your choice.

  WIDER READING

Briggs, A. *The Age of Improvement, 1783–1867*, Longman (1986)

Brown, R. *Revolution, Radicalism and Reform, 1780–1846*, Cambridge (2000)

Evans, E.J. *Parliamentary Reform, c1770–1918*, Pearson (2000)

Evans, E.J. *The Forging of the Modern State, 1783–1870*, Longman (1996)

Gash, N. *Aristocracy and People, 1815–65*, Arnold (1979)

Lang, S. *Parliamentary Reform, 1785–1928*, Routledge (2005)

O'Gorman, F. *Voters, Patrons and Parties: The Unreformed Electoral System of Hanoverian England, 1734–1832*, Oxford (1989)

Partridge, M. 'Gladstone and parliamentary reform, 1832–94', *History Review* (September 2003)

Pearse, R. 'The Great Reform Act, 1832', *History Review* (March 2007)

Whitfield, B. *The Extension of the Franchise, 1832–1931*, Heinemann (2001)

Woodall, R. 'The Ballot Act of 1872', *History Today* (July 1974)

3.2 Changing influences in parliament: the impact of parliamentary reform, c1780–1928

KEY QUESTIONS

- How far did the influence of the Crown and the aristocracy over elections and parliament change in the years c1780–1928?

- To what extent did political parties change in the years c1780–1928?

INTRODUCTION

KEY TERMS

Executive
Executes, or carries out, the law and is responsible for the everyday administration of the state.

Legislature
In Britain, this consists of the House of Commons and the House of Lords. The legislature is responsible for passing and amending laws (legislation), and ensures that the executive power is exercised lawfully.

The various reform Acts passed in the years 1832–1928 changed, sometimes dramatically, the British electoral system. They were also responsible for long-term changes in the power and influence of both the **executive** and the **legislature**.

In 1780, the Crown exercised significant executive powers within the political system. Parliamentary reforms gradually weakened that power. William IV (r1830–37) and Queen Victoria (r1837–1901) found that the traditional royal prerogatives of appointing and dismissing ministers, and whole governments, could not be maintained within an increasingly representative parliament. From 1841, it was the outcome of general elections that decided which party would take office.

The traditional aristocracy dominated political life in both the House of Lords and the House of Commons in 1780. During the 19th century, this influence over the House of Commons waned, as more middle-class and working-class men (and women from 1918) were elected to parliament. The power of the House of Lords in the legislative process was challenged in the early 20th century, and the Parliament Act 1911 removed their veto powers over legislation.

The most significant changes of all can be seen in the development of the political parties. Aristocratic in both composition and outlook in the late 18th century, they were compelled to reform and adapt to the new electoral system. The Tory Party, after some early setbacks, managed change with considerable success, and since 1874 the Conservative Party has been the most successful electoral machine in the country. The Whigs controlled government and parliamentary life for most of the 18th and early 19th centuries. However, they found it difficult to adapt to the new electoral landscape, and in 1859 united with Liberals and Peelites to form the Liberal Party.

1780 - Dunning's motion on the power of the Crown: the drive for economic reform

1834 – William IV's dismissal of Melbourne's government

Peel's Tamworth Manifesto

1841 – The election victory of Peel and the Conservative Party

1852 – Conservative minority government led by Derby

1858-59 – Derby's second minority government

| 1780 | 1830 | 1840 | 1850 | 1860 |

1832 – Tories suffer their worst election defeat of the 19th century, winning fewer than 30 percent of votes

1839 - Victoria and the Bedchamber Crisis

1846 – The split in the Conservative Party over the repeal of the Corn Laws

1858 – Abolition of the property qualification for MPs

EXTEND YOUR KNOWLEDGE

The Whigs

The Whigs emerged as a political group in the 1680s when they opposed the succession of the Catholic James Stuart to the throne. They dominated politics in the years 1715–60, but lost influence during the years of Pitt's supremacy in the 1780s and 1790s. They returned to power in 1830 as the champions of parliamentary reform. The Whigs were always a close-knit group of aristocratic families, and found it impossible to survive alone in an age of popular involvement in politics. They were founding members of the Liberal Party in 1859, but broke with Gladstone in 1886 over Irish Home Rule. The last remnants of the Whig faction merged into Salisbury's Conservative Party in the 1890s.

Under Gladstone and his successors, the Liberals passed a number of important social and political reforms, and in the years before 1914 were responsible for the creation of a basic welfare state. The Liberals split during the First World War between supporters of Asquith and Lloyd George. Lloyd George resigned as prime minister in 1922, and Liberalism as a political creed was unable to cope with the ideology of the rising Labour Party. Some Liberal ministers served briefly in the national governments of the 1930s, but it was not until the formation of the coalition government in 2010 that the party as a whole returned to office.

Many working-class men were enfranchised by the Third Reform Act in 1884. Most of them supported the Liberal Party, and they were more interested in trade union activity than in forming a political movement that would promote specifically working-class interests. In the election of 1892, three working-class candidates, including Keir Hardie, were elected as independent Labour MPs. In 1893, the Independent Labour Party was founded, and it went on to form the nucleus of the Labour Party, created in 1906. By 1922, Labour had become the second largest party in parliament, replacing the Liberals as the main challenger to the Conservative Party. In 1924, Labour took office for the first time, as a minority government.

HOW FAR DID THE INFLUENCE OF THE CROWN AND THE ARISTOCRACY OVER ELECTIONS AND PARLIAMENT CHANGE IN THE YEARS c1780–1928?

The extent of Crown and aristocratic influence on elections and in parliament c1780

The Crown and politics

George III came to the throne in 1760. His Hanoverian predecessors, George I (r1714–27) and George II (r1727–60) spoke very little English, and had been content to leave government in the hands of their Whig ministers.

1872 – Disraeli's speeches at Crystal Palace and the Free Trade Hall

1886 – The split in the Liberal Party over Irish Home Rule, and the secession of the Whigs

1893 – Independent Labour Party founded

1911 – Payment of MPs introduced

1924 – First Labour government formed

1870 — 1880 — 1890 — 1900 — 1910 — 1920

1866 – Derby's third minority government and the Second Reform Act

1874 – The election victory of Disraeli and the Conservative Party

1892 – Keir Hardie elected as Independent Labour candidate for West Ham South

1900 – Creation of the Labour Representation Committee

George III, however, upset established conventions because he was keen to play an active role in government. As a result of the king's involvement in political affairs, the 1760s was a decade of political instability, as the king ignored the views of parliament by appointing ministers who could not claim the support of the House of Commons. This experiment in royal government proved impossible to sustain, and in 1770, the king appointed Lord North as prime minister, a politician who could count on the support of the House of Commons.

However, the Crown's influence in government and parliament was not confined to direct royal involvement in government. Since 1714, a large network of **patronage** had developed, which was used by monarchs and their ministers to ensure the loyalty of individual MPs. Financial incentives, especially **sinecures** and generous pensions, were lavished on individuals in order to secure their support for the government of the day. These practices were increased significantly by George III and North, and whole new avenues of patronage were opened up during Britain's war against the American colonies from 1775.

Aristocratic involvement in elections and in parliament

In the late 18th century, aristocratic influence over elections, and over the House of Commons, was substantial. The House of Lords and the House of Commons were the two branches of the legislature, but the social composition of both was very similar. The head of an aristocratic family sat in the House of Lords, while his male siblings and sons often sat in the House of Commons, an arrangement that survived well into the 19th century.

Most of the aristocracy were very large landowners, with substantial estates scattered throughout the country. With land came wealth and influence, and many peers deployed both in order to give them control over elections to the House of Commons. Their influence was felt most strongly in the counties, whose electors often cast their votes for the local aristocrat's preferred candidate, either through a habit of deference or because they feared repercussions if they voted for another candidate. In the smaller boroughs, the aristocracy could deploy substantial sums of money among a small number of voters to ensure the election of their chosen candidate.

The strength of the aristocracy in the late 18th and early 19th centuries is reflected in the composition of the cabinets of the time. In Pitt's first period of government from 1783–94, his cabinet included just three members of the House of Commons against nine members of the House of Lords. When Grey formed his ministry in 1830, which was to pass the Reform Act, once again, there were only three MPs. For most politicians, the dominance of the aristocracy in both the House of Lords and the House of Commons was regarded as a normal state of affairs.

Economic reform in the 1780s

George III

By the late 1770s, opposition to the use of patronage by the Crown and the government was growing outside parliament. The American war had broken out in 1775, and was to have a profound effect on British politics. A whole swathe of government contracts were issued for ships, uniforms, arms and provisions, and these were usually granted to favoured suppliers, at a substantial cost to the government's finances. Inevitably, taxes were increased to pay for the war. Property and business taxes rose, and there was widespread opposition from the landed gentry in the counties to the rising tax on land. The land tax, based on the value of individual landholdings, was set at 2 shillings in the pound for most of the 18th century. The cost of war, and the requirement to pay the interest on the burgeoning national debt, led to a tax of 4 shillings in 1779.

It was the combination of rising taxation and widespread royal and government patronage that stimulated extra-parliamentary opposition to North's government. In 1779, Rev. Christopher Wyvill inspired the formation of the Yorkshire Association, which was supported by the county's gentry and landowners, and was soon imitated in several other counties. The associations campaigned for major reductions in both taxation and government spending. They believed that both these objectives could be achieved, in part, by a substantial reduction in the network of Crown and government patronage. More ominously for the government, several associations believed that patronage could only be reduced by parliamentary reform, and promoted universal suffrage as a remedy against corruption. In 1779–80, a **petitioning movement** grew out of the association counties, with petitions presented to parliament demanding a reduction in the number of posts that were at the Crown's disposal.

Burke and economic reform in the 1780s

The Yorkshire Association established close links with the Rockingham Whigs, who were the most influential opposition group in the House of Commons. One of Rockingham's leading supporters was Edmund Burke, who would become one of the primary opponents of the French Revolution in the 1790s. In 1780, Burke presented a reform plan to the House of Commons that reflected the demands of the associations in Yorkshire and other counties. Burke attacked the high expenditure that went on maintaining the royal court, especially the number of royal sinecures. Offices such as the Groom of the Stole and the Groom of the Wardrobe were simply honorary titles, though profitable, and Burke reserved particular contempt for the office of the royal turnspit. This post, supposedly involving the roasting of joints of meat for the royal dining table, was held by an MP.

Burke's reform project, he claimed, would lead to a substantial reduction in expenditure, and would enable the government to reduce taxes accordingly. He also believed that economic reform would weaken growing demands for parliamentary reform. Burke was a long-standing champion of the existing electoral system and favoured reform rather than widespread innovations. He felt that the abolition of Crown and government patronage would lead to the revival of the independence of individual MPs, and thus make parliamentary reform unnecessary. This explains why his scheme of economic reform was entitled 'A bill for the better security of the independence of parliament'.

Burke presented a wide-ranging bill for economic reform in March 1780, but was unable to secure its passage through the House of Commons. Nonetheless, reform had become an important feature of the Rockingham Whigs' programme. In April, the Whig MP Dunning secured the passage of two motions in the House of Commons, calling for the reduction of royal influence over the House of Commons. The Whigs were unable to capitalise on their success, but Dunning's motions showed the growing unease felt by many MPs about the influence of the Crown in the country's political life.

Burke carried out some reforms when he was appointed paymaster in Rockingham's short-lived government of March to July 1782. The paymaster of the armed forces held substantial sums of money for long periods, and could use their profits for his own benefit. Burke could have enriched himself, but he ended the practice by placing all the paymaster's funds into the Bank of England, and setting the paymaster's salary at £4,000 a year. He followed this measure with the Civil Service Act, which abolished over 130 royal and government sinecures, saving in the process over £70,000 a year.

Burke's campaigns against institutional corruption had some achievements to their credit, and established his own reputation as a cautious reformer. Rockingham's death in July 1782 ended his short time in office, but he had established the possibility of reform and paved the way for future changes carried out by Pitt.

Pitt and reform

When Pitt became prime minister in December 1783, he had to tackle a number of issues that he inherited from North's time in office. The fall of North's government in 1782, and the end of the American war in 1783, contributed to the collapse of the Yorkshire Association and similar bodies, but the Whigs and many independent MPs continued their attacks on corruption and government extravagance. Like Burke, Pitt was prepared to take some action to reduce patronage and sinecures, but he did so more out of a desire for administrative efficiency than for ideological reasons.

Pitt's main aim as prime minister was to bring the national finances under control. The American war had led to a major increase in the size of the national debt, so Pitt was forced to reform government administration in order to reduce costs. He moved cautiously in reducing sinecures because he realised that it would be difficult to tackle a wide range of vested interests head-on. Instead of abolishing sinecure posts outright, he waited until the office holder died and then allowed the position to lapse. This approach was painfully slow for many of his supporters, but by the time of his death in 1806 a large number of offices had vanished.

Pitt's actions were important. In the 1770s, George III had been able to maintain North in office by the widespread use of sinecures and pensions. By 1800, this was no longer possible. Henceforth, ministers would have to rely increasingly on the support of parliament if they were to remain in office.

The process of economic reform had been fairly successful in eliminating the worst feature of corruption in government, but many sinecures and pensions remained in existence long after 1800.

In 1819, for example, Cobbett, with his usual journalistic flair, attacked both the economic reformers and Burke in a single article. Cobbett notes that pensions often outlived their recipients (Source 1).

SOURCE

The radical reformer and journalist William Cobbett, from an article published in his *Weekly Political Register* on 1 May 1819. Cobbett founded the *Register* in 1802, but its circulation was restricted by its high cover price of one shilling. From 1816, he published a cheaper version as a two-penny pamphlet that reached a circulation of over 40,000. Pensions and sinecures were two of Cobbett's chief targets.

The economical reformers are the cunningest crew, but they deceive nobody. Amongst economical reformers is Lord Milton the lofty, who makes speeches of three hours long, about a part of Mr. Croaker's salary [Croaker was an office holder], but who says not a word about the two thousand five hundred pound a year, that have been paid to the Executors of Burke for the last twenty-four years, and is still to be paid to them for three lives yet unexpired! Here are sixty thousand pounds already, actually paid, to the executors of this reptile alarmist, this worst of all mankind, this most base and mischievous of men. He and his wife both had pensions for their lives; but this that I have now mentioned is paid to this fellow's executors. There will be no good in England till those who procured this grant be compelled to pay back the sums which it has taken from the people.

The reasons for declining royal influence over the House of Commons

Economic reform since 1782 had contributed to the declining influence of the Crown over the House of Commons, a process that was accelerated after 1810 by the fading mental powers of George III. The Reform Act 1832 was especially important in reducing the influence of successive monarchs over parliament as a whole. Before 1832, governments relied on the favour of the monarch, and the huge amount of Crown patronage that they could use to secure the support of MPs. With economic reform reducing Crown patronage, and parliamentary reform fostering the development of clearly defined parties, the scope for royal involvement in government was considerably reduced.

William IV and Melbourne's government, 1834–35

The Whigs and their allies won the general election of 1832 with a substantial majority, and it was widely expected that they would provide stable government for several years. In 1834, however, William IV, who was worried about the Whigs' proposals for reforms to the Irish Church, dismissed the prime minister, Lord Melbourne, and invited Peel to form a government. Since Peel's Conservatives held only 175 seats, he asked for an immediate dissolution of parliament. In the election of January 1835, the Conservatives added 100 seats to their number, but this was not sufficient to allow for the formation of a stable government. Peel resigned and Melbourne returned to office.

The events of 1834–35 were a convincing demonstration of the effects of the Reform Act on the political world. In 1783, George III had taken the initiative in dismissing the Fox–North coalition, had granted Pitt a dissolution in 1784, and had supported his young minister with all the patronage funds at his disposal. Economic reform had reduced the Crown's influence over the House of Commons, placing William IV in a less fortunate position. Elections after the Reform Act presented the electorate with a clear choice in most constituencies between Whigs and Conservatives, making it easier to discern which party had gained a majority of seats. William IV and his successors could no longer choose a prime minister if he could not rely on a parliamentary majority in the House of Commons.

Victoria and the Bedchamber Crisis, 1839

Victoria came to the throne in 1837 at the age of 18. She was unprepared for her new role, and relied heavily on the advice of her Whig prime minister, Lord Melbourne. Melbourne resigned in 1839 following a defeat in the House of Commons, and Victoria invited Peel to form a government. Although the Conservatives did not have a parliamentary majority, Peel believed that he could count on the support of some Whig MPs in order to pass important legislation. It was customary for an incoming prime minister to appoint his allies to posts within the royal household, including the ladies of the bedchamber. Acting on Melbourne's advice, Victoria refused to change her ladies. Peel refused to become prime minister under such restrictions, and Melbourne returned to office.

EXTEND YOUR KNOWLEDGE

Queen Victoria (1837–1901)
Victoria was fifth in line to the throne on her birth. The deaths without children of three of George III's sons made her heiress to the throne in 1830, and she succeeded William IV in 1837. She lost her initial popularity with the Bedchamber Crisis of 1839, but her marriage to Prince Albert restored some of her prestige. Victoria had strong political views, as well as personal opinions about her prime ministers, but these were not made public during her reign. She detested Gladstone, who she felt 'addresses me as if I were a public meeting', but displayed a strong affection for Disraeli. Her reign of 63 years was surpassed by Elizabeth II in 2015.

For the rest of her long reign, Victoria did not act against the wishes of her prime ministers, and indeed was unable to do so. Elections usually produced majorities for one party or the other, and Victoria had no choice but to appoint the leader of the majority party as prime minister. Although she had strong personal views about the abilities of her ministers, she never expressed them openly.

George V (r1910–36)

George V succeeded to the throne on the death of his father Edward VII, and was immediately involved in a major constitutional crisis over the House of Lords (see pages 143–4). Throughout the crisis of 1910–11, the king, despite his personal reservations, followed the advice given to him by his ministers.

One of the theoretical powers that a monarch possesses is the right to reject a bill passed by both Houses of Parliament. This power has been used only rarely, the last time being in 1707, when Anne rejected a bill to reform the Scottish militia. In 1914, after bitter parliamentary debates, a bill to grant Home Rule to Ireland passed through the House of Commons and the House of Lords. George V privately opposed the measure because he believed that Home Rule would lead to civil war in Ireland, between the Unionists, who wanted to retain the union with Ireland, and the Irish Nationalists. George seriously considered applying a royal veto to the measure, but finally gave his royal assent in September 1914, because the outbreak of the First World War meant that Home Rule was suspended until the war's end.

For the rest of his reign, George V observed both the spirit and the letter of the conventions of government, remaining aloof from the political infighting that followed the fall of Lloyd George's government in 1922. However, the election of December 1923 threatened to drag the king into the political arena. The Conservatives held 258 seats, Labour 191 and the reunited Liberals 158. The Conservatives had lost 86 seats, and thus their parliamentary majority, and the prime minister, Baldwin, believed that he had no real mandate to continue in office. It was the accepted convention that the leader of the next-largest party should be invited to form a government. George V appointed Ramsay MacDonald in January 1924, and was widely praised for his tactful and helpful attitude towards the new Labour cabinet members.

Parliamentary reform, especially the First Reform Act, severely restricted the ability of the monarchy to become involved in elections and the processes of government. Victoria and her successors reigned as constitutional monarchs. They possessed wide powers in theory, but all of these powers were exercised by the government of the day. Writing after the Second Reform Act 1867, the writer W. Bagehot suggested that 'the sovereign has, under a constitutional monarchy such as ours, three rights – the right to be consulted, the right to encourage, the right to warn.' These principles have been followed to the present day.

ACTIVITY
KNOWLEDGE CHECK

The declining influence of the Crown

1 Compile a list of the different factors that were at work in the years c1780–1928 in reducing the influence of the Crown in politics.

2 Write a short paragraph outlining the significance of each factor.

3 Choose the factor that you think is the most important, and write a short paragraph explaining your choice.

The reasons for declining aristocratic influence over the House of Commons, c1780–1928

The impact of reform on aristocratic influence, 1832-65

Those who had campaigned so vigorously for reform in the hope that British political life might change dramatically were to be bitterly disappointed, especially with regard to aristocratic influence in politics and government.

SOURCE
2

A painting by Sir George Hayter of the first session of the reformed House of Commons held in February 1833.

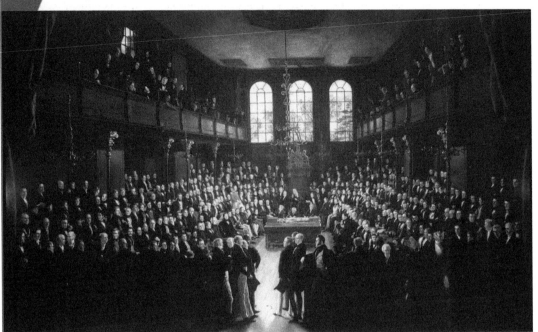

Aristocratic influence over parliament remained after 1832, and there is evidence that it was strengthened in several respects. In the counties, the increased number of seats worked to the benefit of the aristocracy, with a strengthening of control over elections and the choice of MPs. Moreover, the tenants of agricultural land, who were enfranchised by the Chandos Clause (see Chapter 1, page 18), depended on the goodwill of the landowners and voted in accordance with their wishes. The Reform Act had abolished many small boroughs, but the historian Gash calculated that around 60 seats remained under direct aristocratic control in the reformed parliament.

The historian Aydelotte carried out a number of investigations into the parliament of 1841–47. He confirmed Greville's observation that the composition of the House of Commons was changed very little by the Reform Act. A fifth of MPs elected in 1841 came from the middle classes, almost the same proportion as before 1832, with over 70 percent of MPs related to peers or to the country gentry. These numbers barely changed in the years to 1867. Thus, aristocratic influence was maintained, and indeed strengthened, almost in spite of the reform and redistribution measures of 1832.

The decline of aristocratic influence over elections and the House of Commons, 1865–1928

In the 20 years after 1865, the electoral system changed considerably. The Second and Third Reform Acts, the Ballot Act, the Corrupt Practices Act and the Redistribution Act 1885 all combined to change the electoral geography of the country, along with the influence of the aristocracy and other interests within parliament.

Aristocratic influence had managed the small post-1832 electorate with some ease. This influence was hard to maintain with the establishment of household suffrage, in the boroughs in 1867 and the counties in 1884. The large new electorate was influenced by increasingly well-organised political parties, rather than by aristocratic or middle-class interests. The Ballot Act 1872 went some way towards ending the intimidation of tenants in the countryside and artisans in the towns, while the Corrupt Practices Act 1883 wiped out electoral corruption at a stroke.

The creation of the single-member constituency in 1885 was a significant factor in reducing aristocratic influence in the House of Commons. Local Conservative and Liberal associations were often reluctant to nominate candidates linked to the nobility and gentry, preferring to support men whose attitude to politics was more professional.

Until 1880, members of the nobility were able to deploy their substantial wealth at elections in support of their chosen candidates. The general election of that year was one of the most expensive on record. From 1880, there was a gradual decline in the wealth of nobility and gentry alike. The last 20 years of the 19th century saw a fall in agricultural prices, as farmers struggled to compete with imports of cheap American corn. The landed interest was also hit by the introduction of death duties in 1894. Partly as a result of these electoral and economic developments, only 10 percent of MPs elected in 1906 came from aristocratic or gentry families.

The changing nature of government also led to the decline of the aristocratic amateur in politics.

From the 1860s, government intervention in the economic and social life of the country increased substantially, as parliament dealt with issues such as living and working conditions in towns and changing attitudes towards education and trade unionism. The status of an MP, in the House of Commons and in his constituency, became functional rather than decorative, a change that many MPs found uncongenial.

By 1928, aristocratic influence over elections, and over the House of Commons, had all but disappeared. Universal male suffrage in 1918, and full female suffrage by 1928, had led to the emergence of new and more powerful electoral organisations, notably the Labour Party. At the same time, changing economic circumstances were reducing the aristocracy's landed power. A comprehensive system of death duties was introduced in 1894, which, over time, contributed to the break-up of a number of landed estates.

Although the traditional aristocratic interest in the House of Commons was unable to survive the growing democratisation of politics, the nobility retained substantial influence within government. Lord Salisbury's cabinet of 1895–1900 consisted of ten peers and nine MPs, and, as late as 1924, Baldwin's Conservative cabinet consisted of 14 MPs and seven peers.

Parliament Act 1911

Chapter 1 outlined the process whereby the House of Commons went from being an aristocratic stronghold in the 1780s to a fully democratic chamber by 1928. Radical and reforming groups had called for reform of the House of Commons throughout the 19th century, to make it more representative of the population as a whole. There were fewer demands for reform from the House of Lords, though some leading politicians, such as Gladstone, did consider the possibility of moderate reform, partly to redress the substantial influence of landowners.

Membership of the House of Lords grew from around 350 c1780 to 623 in 1910. The House of Lords consisted of hereditary peers and 26 bishops, including the Archbishops of Canterbury and York. A number of lords who were qualified in the law were empowered to hear appeals against legal decisions in the courts. The peers' main function was to act as a revising chamber, examining and amending bills sent from the House of Commons. On a few occasions, the Lords put up strong resistance to the will of the House of Commons. Their stand against Grey's reform bill in 1831–32 weakened their political standing, but for the next 30 years they reverted to their traditional revising functions.

A long-standing convention ensured that the House of Commons had full control over financial matters. In 1860, Gladstone introduced the Paper Duties bill, which would repeal the duty on paper and reduce the cost of all printed materials, including newspapers. The government and the House of Commons gave the measure only lukewarm support, and the House of Lords threw out the bill. Gladstone then consolidated all money bills into a single Finance bill, thus establishing the annual Budget. The House of Lords would not challenge the House of Commons' supremacy over financial affairs until 1909.

The House of Lords was bitterly opposed to Gladstone's long campaign to grant Home Rule to Ireland. His first attempt at Home Rule failed to pass the House of Commons in 1886, but a further attempt in 1892 did gain the House of Commons' support. The lords, many of whom had substantial landholdings in Ireland, rejected the bill outright, showing that they were prepared to reject measures when their own personal or political interests were threatened. The Liberals promised reform of the Upper House, but failed to make concrete proposals before their defeat in the 1895 election ushered in a decade of Conservative rule.

The election of 1906

The Conservatives fought the general election of 1906 as a divided party, and suffered the worst electoral defeat in their history. In the election that followed the Reform Act 1832, they were reduced to 185 MPs, but in 1906 they sank even lower, to 156 MPs. It was clear that they would have very little impact in the House of Commons when faced with the serried ranks of 397 Liberals, 82 Irish and 29 Labour MPs. The Liberals had a majority of 125 over all parties, and of 241 over the Conservatives.

Balfour and other Conservative leaders were not prepared to give up power so easily, and were prepared to use the House of Lords, not simply as a revising chamber, but as a body ready to oppose the Liberals' legislative programme. Historian Robert Blake suggests some reasons why they were unable to come to terms with their overwhelming defeat in his book *The Conservative Party from Peel to Thatcher*, published in 1985. He notes that Balfour commented after his personal defeat in Manchester in January 1906, 'It is a duty of everyone to ensure that the great Unionist party should still control, whether in power or whether in opposition, the destinies of this great Empire.' Blake suggests that if this is taken literally this is a denial of parliamentary democracy. Many Conservatives did seem to behave as though the result of 1906 was a freak result and that the public – with the guidance of the House of Lords – would come to its senses.

Parliament after 1906

The House of Lords mounted a campaign in 1906–8, aimed at wrecking social reform legislation, including the education bill of 1906, and a measure to abolish plural voting. The House of Lords was careful not to attack measures that might bring it into conflict with organised labour. It agreed the Workmen's Compensation Act 1906, which looked after the interests of those injured at work, and the law of 1908, which imposed an eight-hour working day in the mining industry. The government's response to the House of Lords' behaviour was limited to passing resolutions condemning the actions of the Upper House, but doing no more. It was left to Lloyd George and the 1909 Budget to bring the conflict between the House of Lords and the House of Commons to a head.

In 1908, the Liberal government was remodelled following the resignation of Campbell-Bannerman. Asquith became prime minister, with Lloyd George as Chancellor of the Exchequer. In 1909, Lloyd George drew up a Budget aimed at increasing government revenue. This move was essential, since the introduction of old-age pensions in 1908, and the Admiralty's demands for naval expansion, could not be funded out of existing taxation. Many measures were uncontroversial, such as an increased income tax and duties on petrol and spirits. However, three proposals were explosive. Lloyd George proposed a tax on the unearned increase in land values; a further tax on undeveloped land; and a super tax on incomes above £8,000 a year. The House of Lords regarded these three measures not as simple tax increases, but as a class-based assault on the landed aristocracy. In September 1909, it rejected the whole Budget by 350 votes to 75.

Two days later, the House of Commons resolved that the House of Lords' action breached the constitution. Parliament was dissolved and an election was called for January 1910. The Liberals campaigned on the simple slogan of 'Peers vs People', but the electorate appeared uninterested in grave constitutional issues. The Liberals had achieved their huge majority of 1906 more from Tory divisions than popular enthusiasm for the Liberals' manifesto, and their years in government had only a few substantial achievements to their credit. The election result was a virtual stalemate. The Liberals secured 274 seats; the Conservatives 272. The Liberals remained in office, but depended on the support of 71 Irish MPs and the 41 seats won by the Labour Party.

Though slightly chastened by the election result, the government pressed on with its policy of restricting the power of the House of Lords. In April 1910, it introduced the parliament bill into the House of Commons. This was an attempt to establish the primacy of the House of Commons over the House of Lords once and for all.

Before the bill could be considered by the peers, King Edward VII died suddenly on 6 May. His successor, George V, had not been briefed by his father on the crisis, and was uncertain how to act. In an attempt to avoid a major crisis at the beginning of the king's reign, an inter-party constitutional conference was convened in June. No agreement was reached, and the conference fell apart in November. George V was now faced with the same situation that William IV had to resolve in 1832. Asquith requested a second general election, but also asked the king to agree to the creation of sufficient liberal peers (the prime minister had drawn up a list of 250 candidates) to ensure the passage of the parliament bill through the House of Lords. The king reluctantly agreed, as long as his promise was kept secret.

The second election of 1910, held in December, produced an outcome almost identical to the January results. Liberals and Conservatives both won 272 seats, the Irish Party 74 and the Labour Party 42.

In May, the parliament bill was sent back to the House of Lords, and it was expected that the peers would finally give way. Instead, they mutilated the measure out of all recognition. A large number of Conservative peers, known as the 'Ditchers' because they vowed to 'die in the last ditch', refused to let the bill pass. Asquith now informed the Conservative leadership of the king's undertaking to create peers. This promise had only a limited effect on the Ditchers, but in August the parliament bill passed through the House of Lords by 131 votes to 114. Under the Parliament Act, the House of Lords could not reject or amend any money bill. Other bills passed by the House of Commons in three successive sessions but rejected by the House of Lords would simply bypass the Upper House and become law. Finally, the life of a parliament, fixed at seven years in 1715, was reduced to five years.

EXTEND YOUR KNOWLEDGE

The Parliament Act after 1911
The Liberals used the Parliament Act to pass the Irish Home Rule bill and the Welsh Church disestablishment bill in 1914. The Labour Party came to power in 1945, and further reduced the House of Lords' powers of delay to allow the passage of measures to nationalise industries. Later governments have threatened to use the Act on several occasions, but compromises between the House of Lords and the House of Commons have usually been made.

The Parliament Act 1911 expressed the hope of replacing the House of Lords with an elected chamber. Despite several changes to the composition of the Upper House, the practice of election has never been attempted.

ACTIVITY
KNOWLEDGE CHECK

The changing power of the aristocracy over the House of Commons, c1780–1914

1 Draw up a list of the various ways in which the aristocracy influenced the membership and the power of the House of Commons c1780 and in 1914.

2 How had these powers changed, and how do you explain these changes?

A Level Exam-Style Question Section C

How far do you agree that changes to the franchise in the years c1780–1928 were the most important reason for the declining influence of the aristocracy over the House of Commons? (20 marks)

Tip

Outline the power of the aristocracy at the start of the period, c1780. Then consider the stated factor of changes to the franchise, along with other relevant points you wish to discuss. These might include the redistribution of seats, the changing nature of political leadership, and the declining economic power of the aristocracy through, for example, the repeal of the Corn Laws.

TO WHAT EXTENT DID POLITICAL PARTIES CHANGE IN THE YEARS c1780–1928?

The change in political parties' role in parliament and in elections

Parliamentary parties, c1780–1830

KEY TERM

Whigs and Tories
Originally terms of abuse. A 'Whig', or whiggamor, was a Scottish cattle-driver of the early 17th century, while 'Tory' was originally a description of an Irish rebel.

Although the terms 'Tory' and 'Conservative' were originally quite different in meaning, they have become interchangeable over time.

In the early 1780s, although **Whigs and Tories** were terms in common use, they did not refer to clearly defined political parties. The distinguished historian Namier devoted much of his career to studying 18th-century British politics, and claimed that it was not possible to refer to different political parties in parliament during the first 20 years of George III's reign. However, events in the years 1783–1830 led to the gradual development of a two-party system in the House of Commons.

After the Fox–North coalition fell from power in December 1783, Pitt took office as prime minister and remained in post until 1801. During the 1780s, parties in parliament became more identifiable, with the Whigs coming together under Fox, while their opponents gathered together in support of Pitt. The Whigs split in the early 1790s over the French Revolution, and many Whig MPs changed their allegiance and supported the government.

Between c1780 and 1830, the different political beliefs of Whigs and Tories became more distinctive. The years 1783–1830 were a period of almost unbroken Tory rule, which clarified their political ideas. Some of the hallmarks of their political philosophy included the maintenance of law and order and defence of property, strong armed forces and moderate economic policies. This helps to explain their repressive response to demands for political and constitutional reform during their time in office, especially in the years 1790–1820. Tory government became more moderate in the 1820s. There was some relaxation of restrictions on trade union activities, which Pitt had introduced during the wars with revolutionary France. At the Home Office, Peel carried out far-reaching legal reforms, including reducing the number of crimes that could carry the death penalty, and reforming the appalling conditions that could be found in most prisons.

Their long period in opposition meant that the Whigs were also able to develop their ideology. In 1792, some young Whig MPs formed the Friends of the People, an organisation committed to parliamentary reform, especially widening the franchise. Although the organisation folded within two years, many Whigs maintained their support for reform, which gained wider acceptance in the 1820s.

Fox died in 1806, leaving his supporters leaderless and divided. He had championed some fundamental Whig beliefs that guided the party throughout the 19th century. He fought against any increases in the executive power, whether by the king or the government, and he supported parliamentary reform in order to increase the effectiveness of the House of Commons. Fox was a strong supporter, despite its unpopularity, of religious toleration for both Catholics and nonconformists. His greatest achievements came in 1806, when parliament passed his resolution calling for the abolition of the slave trade, a measure that passed into law in 1807.

In the 1820s, the Whigs were concerned with broad moral and religious issues, including slavery within the British Empire and the political disabilities of both nonconformists and Catholics; and these matters were to underpin Whig beliefs for the next 40 years.

By the late 1820s, the various Whig factions began to unite as an effective political force under the leadership of Earl Grey. They took advantage of Tory divisions over religious issues by supporting both the repeal of the Test and Corporation Acts in 1828, and the passing of Catholic emancipation in 1829. By 1830, the Whigs were at last able to return to power and tackle the issue of parliamentary reform.

The historian Frank O'Gorman has identified a number of major issues that divided politicians in the years 1760–1832, which accelerated the trend towards the creation of a two-party system in parliament and the country. Between 1760 and 1800, the role of the monarchy in politics, the American War of Independence and the impact of the French Revolution had the cumulative effect of reducing the number of independent MPs, while increasing the number of those who adopted one or other of the party labels. From 1800 to 1832, political life was increasingly divided, especially by issues of religious toleration and the growing demands for parliamentary reform. The Reform Act 1832 established a clear political divide between Whigs and their allies on the one hand, and an identifiable Conservative Party on the other.

The changing nature of the parliamentary Whig and Tory parties, 1830–46

The years 1830–32 marked a key stage in the parliamentary roles of both the Whig and Tory parties. The religious legislation of the years 1828–29 had split the Tories: O'Gorman wrote that Catholic emancipation was 'one of the greatest shocks to the Tory Party in its entire history'. The opposition led by Peel and Wellington threatened to weaken its position in political life altogether. Peel was attacked by many within his party for abandoning his long-standing opposition to Catholic relief. He knew that he could not betray the party still further by giving any support to parliamentary reform in 1831–32. Demoralised and bitterly divided, the Tory party was soundly defeated in the general election of December 1832.

In the years 1833–34, the Whig government passed a number of reforms designed to please the new middle-class electorate.

Wilberforce and many humanitarians had campaigned for years for the abolition of slavery within the British Empire, and the Abolition Act was passed in 1833. In the same year, a Factory Act acted on the report of a select committee and limited the hours of work for factory children. The Poor Law Amendment Act 1834 attempted to rationalise the provision of poor relief. Outdoor relief was to be abolished, and the poor were to be cared for only in workhouses.

By 1834, the Whigs' reforming impetus had died down, and they encountered many difficulties in their attempts to settle Irish grievances. They were also opposed by a Tory party that had begun to reorganise and reform itself after the disaster of 1832.

Peel, who succeeded Wellington as Tory leader, realised that the parliamentary party had to be able to accommodate the changes brought about since 1828. Failure to do so might well consign the party to increasing irrelevance and to permanent opposition in the House of Commons.

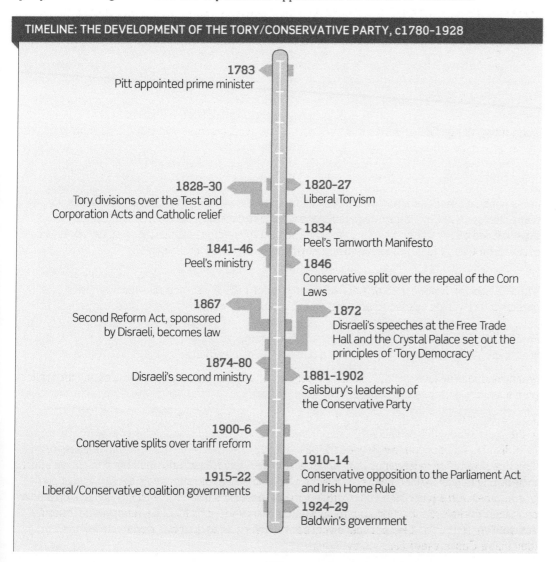

TIMELINE: THE DEVELOPMENT OF THE TORY/CONSERVATIVE PARTY, c1780–1928

1783
Pitt appointed prime minister

1820–27
Liberal Toryism

1828–30
Tory divisions over the Test and Corporation Acts and Catholic relief

1834
Peel's Tamworth Manifesto

1841–46
Peel's ministry

1846
Conservative split over the repeal of the Corn Laws

1867
Second Reform Act, sponsored by Disraeli, becomes law

1872
Disraeli's speeches at the Free Trade Hall and the Crystal Palace set out the principles of 'Tory Democracy'

1874–80
Disraeli's second ministry

1881–1902
Salisbury's leadership of the Conservative Party

1900–6
Conservative splits over tariff reform

1910–14
Conservative opposition to the Parliament Act and Irish Home Rule

1915–22
Liberal/Conservative coalition governments

1924–29
Baldwin's government

Between 1832 and 1841, Peel worked to reform his party's beliefs so that he could present a set of political ideas that would be accepted and, indeed, welcomed by the new electorate. While some in his party were ready to maintain their opposition to the Reform Act and to continue their support for the established Church of England, Peel knew that these policies did not provide a sufficiently popular programme suitable for a party seeking to return to power.

During the election campaign of 1834–35, when he headed a minority government, Peel took the unusual step of issuing a statement of his party's beliefs to the electorate. Before 1832, candidates for election had confined themselves to issuing broad general statements to their own constituents. Peel's Tamworth Manifesto, though ostensibly addressed to his 570 Staffordshire constituents, received wide publicity and discussion in national and local newspapers. Unlike modern party manifestos, Peel's *Letter to the Electors of Tamworth* was not a programme for government, but an attempt to show the post-reform Conservative Party in a favourable light.

SOURCE

3 From Peel's Tamworth Manifesto, December 1834. Peel was MP for Tamworth between 1830 and his death in 1850. The borough was under the control of the Peel family: Peel's father, brother and son represented the constituency at different periods.

The Reform Bill, it is said, constitutes a new era, and it is the duty of a Minister to declare explicitly – first, whether he will maintain the Bill itself, and, secondly, whether he will act upon the spirit in which it was conceived.

With respect to the Reform Bill itself, I consider it a final and irrevocable settlement of a great Constitutional question – a settlement which no friend to the peace and welfare of this country would attempt to disturb, either by direct or by insidious means.

Then, as to the spirit of the Reform Bill, and the willingness to adopt and enforce it as a rule of government: if, by adopting the spirit of the Reform Bill, it be meant that we are to live in a perpetual vortex of agitation; if this be the spirit of the Reform Bill, I will not undertake to adopt it. But if the spirit of the Reform Bill implies merely a careful review of institutions, civil and ecclesiastical, undertaken in a friendly temper, combining, with the firm maintenance of established rights, the correction of proved abuses and the redress of real grievances, – in that case, I can for myself and colleagues undertake to act in such a spirit, and with such intentions.

The Tamworth Manifesto showed that Peel intended to return to the policies of mild reform that had characterised the Liberal Toryism of the 1820s, not the unyielding opposition to change which the Tory Party had displayed in the years 1828–32. His moderate position gained favour with many voters in the 1835 election, when the Tories increased their representation at Westminster to 279 seats.

Peel's political beliefs were reflected in the adoption of the name of the Conservative Party. For many electors, the 'Tory' Party was associated with the repressive policies that maintained public order carried out by Pitt and his successors from the 1790s to the early 1820s. 'Conservative' was a more subtle term, which was not associated with repression. Rather, it suggested the maintenance of established institutions in Church and state, but did not suggest an unthinking hostility to reform.

The Whigs were disconcerted to see Peel back in office in 1834–35, and realised that the parliamentary Whigs needed to broaden their support by forming alliances with other parties. In February 1835, the Whigs reached an agreement with radical and Irish MPs known as the Lichfield House compact. The three groups agreed to work together to bring down Peel's government, and in return, the Whigs would work to remedy a number of Irish problems.

Some historians believe that the Lichfield House compact marks the birth of the Liberal Party, but others are less convinced. While the term 'Liberal Party' came into general use from 1835, and Lord John Russell adopted the Liberal label in 1839, the Lichfield House agreement was a temporary solution to an immediate problem. Liberalism as a clear set of political beliefs did not emerge for another 20 years.

The Whigs returned to power in 1835 under Melbourne, but the radicalism that had characterised their policies since 1830 had waned considerably. Their last great reform was the Municipal Corporations Act 1835, which ended the monopoly in local politics enjoyed by often unelected and highly corrupt groups, replacing them with councils elected by all male ratepayers. This single measure conferred substantial local power to the middle classes, and was eagerly taken up by nonconformists and radicals.

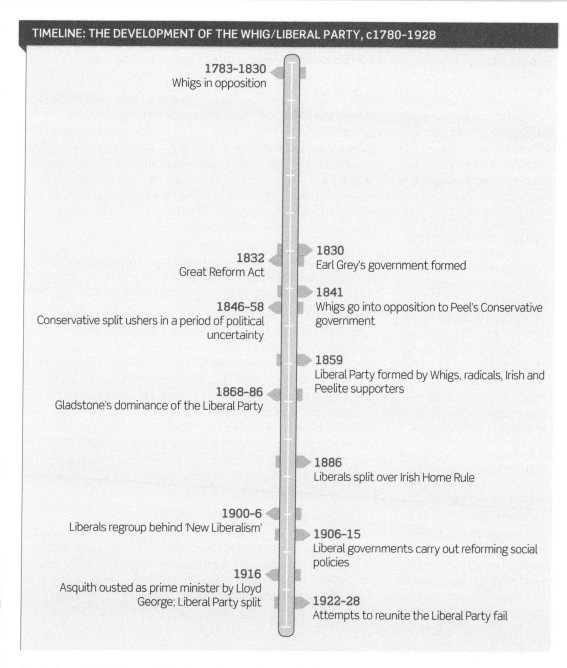

TIMELINE: THE DEVELOPMENT OF THE WHIG/LIBERAL PARTY, c1780–1928

1783–1830
Whigs in opposition

1832
Great Reform Act

1830
Earl Grey's government formed

1841
Whigs go into opposition to Peel's Conservative government

1846–58
Conservative split ushers in a period of political uncertainty

1859
Liberal Party formed by Whigs, radicals, Irish and Peelite supporters

1868–86
Gladstone's dominance of the Liberal Party

1886
Liberals split over Irish Home Rule

1900–6
Liberals regroup behind 'New Liberalism'

1906–15
Liberal governments carry out reforming social policies

1916
Asquith ousted as prime minister by Lloyd George; Liberal Party split

1922–28
Attempts to reunite the Liberal Party fail

By the late 1830s, the coalition formed at Lichfield House began to fall apart. Many Whig MPs were uneasy at the rate of reform, with some even transferring their support to the Tories, and there were growing divisions between the aristocratic Whig leadership and the forces of middle-class radicalism.

Several of the radical MPs represented seats that had been allocated to the industrial towns and cities of the Midlands and the north, and they championed the interests of the manufacturing classes. On some political issues they agreed with the Whigs, with both groups favouring a reduction in the powers of the Crown and the Church of England. Many leading radicals, such as Richard Cobden, the MP for Stockport, wanted to go further than the Whigs, in promoting social reform to tackle urban problems, such as housing and public health. Many manufacturers who supported the radicals opposed any policy that would interfere with their business interests. Thus, they opposed military action abroad and, above all, they championed free trade. Therefore, it was a disunited Whig coalition that faced the electors in the general election of 1841.

The political changes carried out by the Conservative Party in the 1830s paid dividends in 1841, when the party returned to power with a majority of 76 seats overall. Conservative success was impressive in the English county seats, with 124 of the 144 seats returning to the party fold in 1841; in 1832, they had managed just 42 seats. However, they also made inroads into their opponents' territory in the towns and smaller boroughs. The new post-1832 electorate was attracted by the

Conservatives' willingness to adopt broad and moderate reforms, and the election marked the beginning of urban Toryism, which was to become more significant later in the century.

Conservative dominance in the House of Commons was to last for just five years as, once again, the party split over issues connected with Ireland and with the Protestant ascendancy. In 1845, Peel proposed to increase the state grant to the Catholic seminary at Maynooth, where young Irishmen were trained to become priests, from £9,000 to £26,000pa. The measure passed only with Whig support and demonstrated the fragility of Conservative unity.

In the end, Peel's parliamentary party collapsed over the issue of agricultural protection. Since 1815, the Corn Laws had limited the importation of foreign corn in order to protect domestic farmers from competition. The issue of protection came to a head in 1845 when the Irish potato crop, the staple food for most of the population, was attacked by the potato blight. There was widespread famine and starvation throughout Ireland, and Peel decided that the only way to relieve distress was to repeal the Corn Laws completely and allow unrestricted imports of foreign corn. Like the Maynooth grant, repeal was passed only with Whig support, but its effect on the Conservative Party was devastating. Prominent Conservatives, led by Bentinck, Stanley and Disraeli, determined to bring Peel down. The government was defeated on the Irish coercion bill and resigned in 1846.

Peel had substantial achievements to his credit in the recovery of Conservatism after the debacle of 1832. However, many of his opponents within the party could not forgive his abandonment of traditional Tory values, whether in 1828–29 or 1845–46. The party had recovered from its difficulties over reform in the early 1830s, but the divisions of 1846 proved impossible to heal. Peel and his supporters remained a separate parliamentary grouping, but during the 1850s they merged into what would become the Liberal Party. The remaining Conservatives had to regroup once again. Although they retained the party name, the historian Blake believes that it was a brand-new party that developed after 1846, and he dates the modern Conservative Party from that year. The party was to remain in the political wilderness for 28 years, until Disraeli formed a majority Conservative government in 1874.

ACTIVITY
KNOWLEDGE CHECK

The changing nature of political parties, c1780–1846

1 Draw up two lists of factors that outline the various ways in which
   a) the Conservative Party and b) the Whig Party and its allies changed in the years c1780–1846.

2 Which party saw the greater changes?

Conservatives and Liberals, 1846–86

The fall of Peel's government in 1846 and the split within the Tory Party ushered in a period of instability and political regrouping that lasted for 20 years. Many Peelites, though maintaining a separate political identity, tended to support the Liberal

governments led by Russell and Palmerston. The Peelite leader Aberdeen even formed a Whig–Peelite government, supported by radicals and Irish members, which lasted from 1852 to 1855.

In 1858, Lord Derby formed his second minority Conservative government. Repeating the action they had taken in 1835, the Whigs and their allies united once more to bring down the government. This time, however, the agreement held together once its purpose had been achieved. A broad coalition of reform-minded MPs, Whigs, radicals, Irish and, crucially, Peelites formed a single and recognisable Liberal Party. This explains why most historians prefer 1859 to 1835 as the date of the founding of the Liberal Party. In particular, John Vincent, in his book *The Formation of the British Liberal Party, 1857–68*, published in 1972, challenged the idea that the Liberal Party was formed by the Lichfield House compact in 1835 and suggests 1959 as more probable date. However, he claimed that Liberalism had few clearly defined policies at that time.

During the 1860s, the development of the Liberal Party was encouraged by the financial reforms carried out by Gladstone as Chancellor of the Exchequer. Regarded in his youth as 'the rising hope of the stern, unbending Tories', Gladstone's political conversion took him from Toryism and support of Peel, to the Liberalism of the 1860s and beyond. His financial reforms reflected the spirit of the age, with the promotion of lower taxation (he even considered abolishing the income tax) and far-reaching free trade measures. As the old aristocratic Whig leadership faded away (Palmerston died in 1865 and Russell retired in 1868), Gladstone became leader of the Liberals and formed his first government in 1868.

In the 20 years after the split of 1846, the Conservative Party held office only briefly on two occasions, both times as a minority government. Although they were the largest single party in the House of Commons, they were easily outnumbered by a coalition of Whigs, Liberals, radicals, Peelites and Irish members. The Peelites were the most talented MPs within the Conservative Party, and their departure left the party in the hands of Bentinck (who died in 1848), Stanley (later Lord Derby) and Disraeli.

The Conservatives maintained their opposition to **free trade** in agriculture for only a few years. Many supported a rebranding as the Protection Party, but Disraeli realised that there could be no return to **protection**, a policy with only limited electoral appeal.

KEY TERMS

Free trade
An economic system that allows the free importation of goods without the imposition of duties.

Protection
An economic policy that imposes restrictions on goods coming into a country. Protection is often carried out by imposing duties on imported goods in order to protect domestic industries from foreign competition. The Corn Laws were a notable example of protecting British agriculture from cheap imports of corn.

Derby and Disraeli both hoped to sponsor a major piece of legislation in order to show that the Conservatives could be taken seriously as a governing party. This explains why Disraeli went to great lengths to secure the passage of the Second Reform Act 1867 (Chapter 1). The new electorate, however, did not appear very grateful. The 1868 election brought Gladstone's Liberal Party to power with a healthy majority of 116 seats over the Conservatives.

Like Peel before him, Disraeli had to ensure that Conservative ideology was in tune with the ideas of the new electorate. By 1872, many Liberals were becoming disillusioned with Gladstone's government. It was more concerned with institutional and political issues rather than social reforms, and Gladstone's insistence on tackling Irish problems did not appeal to voters in other parts of the UK. In 1872, Disraeli made a determined bid to broaden Tory appeal and win over the post-1867 electorate. Traditional supporters such as the landed and wealthier middle class formed the base of the party, but as successive elections since 1846 had shown, this support was not enough to convert into a majority of seats. In his speeches of 1872, Disraeli decided to appeal to working-class voters and thus create a truly national party.

Disraeli's speech to the National Union of Conservative and Constitutional Association (NUCCA) members in 1872 attacked the constant innovations introduced by Gladstone since 1868, and set against these the continuity of traditional Conservative beliefs.

SOURCE

Disraeli speaking in the Free Trade Hall, Manchester, April 1872. He was addressing the NUCCA, founded by him in 1867 to co-ordinate the work of local party associations.

> Our opponents assure us that the Conservative party has no political programme... If by a programme is meant a plan to despoil churches and plunder landlords, I admit we have no programme. If by a programme is meant a policy which assails or menaces every institution and every interest, every class and every calling in the country, I admit we have no programme. But if to have a policy with distinct ends, and these such as most deeply interest the great body of the nation, be a becoming programme or a political party, then, I contend, we have an adequate programme, and one which, here or elsewhere, I shall always be prepared to assert and to vindicate.
>
> Gentlemen, the programme of the Conservative party is to maintain the Constitution of the country.

The Free Trade Hall speech contained no specific proposals, but Disraeli went on to develop these in his speech to the NUCCA a few months later. The three objectives that Disraeli set out were to form the foundations of 'Tory Democracy', and were to prove an effective programme for Tories for the rest of the 19th century. The Conservatives went on to win the election of 1874, giving them their first majority for nearly 30 years. In the years 1874–76, Tory Democracy was put into action as towns and cities were

empowered to tackle issues such as slum clearance and public health. Most of these reforms were permissive, enabling rather than compelling local authorities to take action. Many cities, notably Birmingham, took on their new powers with enthusiasm, but others failed to do so, which weakened the impact of the reforms.

SOURCE

Disraeli speech to the NUCCA, Crystal Palace, June 1872. Here, Disraeli suggests that the continuity of Conservative beliefs in the importance of national institutions could be combined with a programme of social reform to improve conditions in towns and cities. The Crystal Palace speech was the second time Disraeli had addressed the NUCCA in three months, a sign of the importance he ascribed to the organisation.

> I have always been of the opinion that the Tory party has three great objects. The first is to maintain the institutions of the country...
>
> There is another and second great object of the Tory party. It is to uphold the Empire of England...
>
> Another great object of the Tory party is the elevation of the condition of the people. It is a large subject. It involves the state of the dwellings of the people, the moral consequences of which are not less considerable than the physical. It involves their enjoyment of some of the chief elements of nature – air, light, and water. It involves the regulation of their industry, the inspection of their toil. It involves the purity of their provisions, and it touches upon all the means by which you may wean them from habits of excess and of brutality.

Disraeli lost the election of 1880 and died the following year. In purely electoral terms, he must be judged to be a failure, losing five of the six general elections that he fought as a party leader between 1852 and 1880. However, he had ensured that Conservatism survived the potentially disastrous split of 1846. The inward-looking protectionists of the 1840s had been transformed into a national party that was able to draw its support from many sections of the community. Between 1881 and 1928, despite further damaging divisions, once again over free trade and protection, Conservatism remained an electoral force to be reckoned with. Indeed, the years 1885–1906 were a period of almost unbroken Conservative rule.

Although Vincent wrote that the Liberal Party was 'not the instrument of a creed', there were many clearly defined characteristics of Gladstonian Liberalism that were reflected in the legislation passed during his four ministries (1868–74, 1880–85, 1886 and 1892–94).

One feature of Gladstone's Liberalism was the investigation and rationalisation of the institutions of the country. During his first ministry, the Education Act 1870 allowed for schools to be established where provision by the Church of England and voluntary associations was insufficient. This led to the creation of board schools across the country, providing non-denominational education for children aged 5–13. The Act, and later amendments, had a massive effect on the development of almost universal literacy by the end of the century. Changes were made to the civil service and the armed forces, traditionally the preserves of the aristocratic amateur. The civil service was thrown open to public competition, the purchase of commissions in the armed forces was abolished, and the army became more humane with the abolition of flogging in peacetime.

SOURCE

6

An 1880s illustration from the magazine *Vanity Fair* showing Gladstone (centre) and leading MPs in parliament. Joseph Chamberlain is second left from Gladstone.

Gladstone was a firm believer in the old Foxite principle of **retrenchment**. Thanks largely to his work as Chancellor of the Exchequer in the years 1859–66, the principles of free trade had been accepted, and his preference for a peaceful foreign policy, which did not involve expensive overseas commitments, kept direct and indirect taxes at a low level.

A third feature of Liberalism in this period was Gladstone's long-held belief that government intervention to improve 'the condition of the people' was harmful and often counterproductive. He accepted the principles of self-help promoted by the writer Samuel Smiles, and believed that individuals had to take action by themselves to improve their lives and those of their families. This political belief reflected his strong Christian principles, which regarded the family as the focal point of religious and moral development.

Gladstone's political beliefs thus embodied the classic Liberalism of the 19th century: low taxes and expenditure, individual freedom and self-help, and a **laissez-faire** attitude towards social questions. These policies might have been sufficient in the 1850s and 1860s, in what was still a largely agricultural society, but they failed to take account of the rapid changes in economic life caused by the speedy industrialisation of the country. The new electorate created by the Second Reform Act in 1867 hoped for more direct improvements, especially in the towns, which helps to explain Disraeli's success in the 1874 election.

Above all, Gladstone's ministries are identified by his powerful, almost obsessive, interest in Ireland. On learning that he was to become prime minister in 1868, he said simply, 'My mission is to pacify Ireland'. He provided some temporary solutions to Irish problems in his first ministry, with the disestablishment of the Irish Church in 1869 and a Land Act in 1870. His second ministry of 1880–85 was dominated by the Irish question. A further Land Act in 1881 helped to pacify the country by reducing evictions of peasants from their tenancies, but Gladstone had to deal with a powerful and increasingly confident Irish Parliamentary Party of 63 MPs. Under their leader Parnell, they obstructed parliamentary business on many occasions, thus weakening the government's legislative achievements. The Third Reform Act 1884 gave the vote to the Irish peasantry, and they voted in large numbers for the Irish Party in 1885, helping it to secure 86 seats and giving it the balance of power in the House of Commons.

In 1886, the Liberals and Irish combined to force out Salisbury's government, and Gladstone took office, committed to granting Home Rule to Ireland. The Home Rule bill failed in the House of Commons, and Salisbury returned to power. An important effect of Gladstone's concern with Home Rule was that he split his party in 1886. Chamberlain and his supporters, along with the last of the Whigs, left the party and transferred their allegiance to the Conservatives as the Liberal Unionists. In his last ministry of 1892–94, Gladstone introduced a second Home Rule bill that passed the House of Commons but was massively rejected by the House of Lords.

Gladstone's Liberalism had achieved much. It rationalised many institutions of the state and encouraged the growth of a strong capitalist economy. The party's reluctance to carry out reforms that would directly improve social conditions was not popular with a growing electorate, and contributed to its rejection by the electorate in the years 1895–1905. Gladstone had made Ireland a central feature of Liberal action, and the failure to provide a comprehensive solution to the Irish question was to have a marked influence on British politics, especially in the years 1912–22.

ACTIVITY
KNOWLEDGE CHECK

Conservatism and Liberalism

1 By 1886, the political beliefs of the Conservative and Liberal parties had become clearly defined. Create a spider diagram showing their different attitudes towards economic policies, political reforms, social policies, reform of institutions, and Ireland.

2 Which party's policies would appeal more to:

   a) the working classes in towns and cities

   b) trade unionists

   c) businessmen and merchants?

Conservatives and Liberals in a democratic age, 1886–1928

In the 20 years after Disraeli's death, the Conservative Party was led by Lord Salisbury. Salisbury was to win three general elections, and was prime minister for over 13 years. His success was partly due to the divisions among his Liberal opponents, but also because Salisbury was able to preserve his party's unity.

Salisbury was largely responsible for the adoption of single-member constituencies in the Redistribution Act 1885. This single measure did more than anything else to ensure Tory electoral dominance for the rest of the century. Henceforth the growing number of 'villa Tories', who lived in the suburbs of large towns and cities, would no longer be outvoted by Liberal and radical voters in multi-member constituencies. In 1885, Tory candidates won in 114 of the 226 borough seats; by 1900, that number had risen to 177.

Conservative fortunes were given an unexpected boost in 1885–86. Many supporters of Gladstone's government, especially the remnants of the once great Whig Party, felt increasingly uneasy at the radical direction of Gladstone's leadership. When, in 1886, Gladstone proposed Home Rule for Ireland, the coalition of interests that was the Liberal Party broke up. The Whigs, led by Hartington, and the radicals under Joseph Chamberlain, withdrew from the party. Over the next few years, they gave their support to Salisbury's Conservatives. The split of 1886 had important consequences. In the election of July 1886, 319 Conservatives, supported by 78 former Liberals (now known as Liberal Unionists), faced a rump of 191 Liberals and 86 Irish members. The election result ushered in a period of Conservative ascendancy that was to last almost unbroken for 20 years.

During his premierships of 1886–92 and 1895–1902, Salisbury worked to preserve party unity at all costs. He refused to support Chamberlain's radical programme, preferring instead to establish a consensus in the cabinet rather than persuading ministers to a particular point of view. Salisbury had learned from both Peel and Gladstone that radical changes in policy could split a party, however well argued they might be.

Salisbury's ability to maintain party unity was not inherited by his successor, his nephew Arthur Balfour. In 1903, Chamberlain proposed the introduction of protective tariffs, arguing that tariffs would protect British industry from unfair foreign competition. At the same time, preferential tariffs would be established with the territories of the British Empire, in order to stimulate imperial trade and strengthen ties between Britain and its overseas possessions. His tariff reform programme was welcomed by many Conservatives, but it opened up deep divisions within the party. Liberals had long championed free trade with almost religious fervour, and tariff reform was an important factor in reuniting the party in strong opposition against the proposals. Tariff reform was not a popular electoral issue, and Liberal propaganda that contrasted the size of free trade and tariff loaves of bread struck a chord with the electorate. Tariff reform, combined with Balfour's failure to address a number of pressing social issues, contributed to the devastating Tory defeat in the 1906 election. They were reduced to 157 seats, their lowest total ever.

The years 1906–28 were a period in their history of which the Conservatives could not be very proud. They had been in power almost continuously since 1886, and many Tories had come to regard themselves as the natural party of government. They used the House of Lords to block several of the Liberals' social reforms, and provoked a major constitutional crisis in 1909–11 over the Parliament Act. They went on to force a second, much more dangerous confrontation in 1912–14. Now that the Parliament Act had removed the House of Lords' absolute veto over legislation, Irish Home Rule would inevitably pass into law by 1914. In 1912–13, two armed militia groups were formed in Ireland. The Ulster Volunteers were determined to use any means necessary to resist Home Rule in the north of Ireland, while the Irish Volunteers' objective was to safeguard Home Rule. Bonar Law, who succeeded Balfour in 1911, promised the Ulster Volunteers almost unqualified support. Thus, the Conservative Party came perilously close to supporting an armed rebellion against Britain's lawful government, and it was only the outbreak of war in Europe that defused the situation – for the time being, at least.

Gladstone had resigned as party leader in 1894, leaving the Liberals in a weakened and demoralised state. The split over Ireland in 1886 showed no prospect of healing, and the second Boer War of 1899–1902 threatened to tear the party apart yet again. Many Liberals, including prominent MPs such as Asquith and Grey, supported the Conservative government's conduct of the war.

SOURCE
7   Conservative election poster, 1906. Tariff reform was a key issue in the election, and the poster shows the tariff reform tug pulling the British constitution off the rocks of socialism and towards the safe harbour in the background.

More radical members attacked the war as representing the worst features of British **imperialism**, especially the concentration camps built to house Boer women and children. The divisions began to heal with the end of the war in 1902, and the party reunited in vigorous opposition to Chamberlain's tariff reform programme. The unpopularity of protective tariffs was a major contributing factor to the Liberals' landslide victory in 1906, with a majority of 125 seats over all opposition parties combined.

KEY TERM

Imperialism
The extension of national influence and power over other countries through colonisation. This can be done via military, naval, diplomatic or economic force.

The government's political beliefs were characterised as 'New Liberalism' and were promoted by radicals such as Lloyd George. The Gladstonian ideas of laissez-faire and individual self-help were challenged by the Boer War, and by investigations into poverty in Britain in the early 1900s. Almost one-third of potential recruits for the South African war were rejected because of their poor physical condition, caused by poverty, poor diet and insufficient health provisions. The investigations of Charles Booth in London, and Seebohm Rowntree in York revealed that nearly 30 percent of people in these two cities were living below the poverty line and were unable to provide for their basic everyday needs. Armed with this information, and aware of the growing electoral strength of the Labour Party, the Liberals carried out a far-reaching programme of social reforms.

EXTEND YOUR KNOWLEDGE

David Lloyd George (1863–1945)
Many historians regard Lloyd George as one of the greatest political figures of the 20th century. He was one of the driving forces behind the Liberals' social reforms in the years 1906-14, and gained immense popularity for the introduction of the old-age pension in 1908. Lloyd George's vigorous leadership during the First World War, as minister of munitions and then as prime minister, was a major factor in Britain's victory in 1918. He was responsible, along with US President Wilson and France's prime minister Clemenceau, for shaping the post-war maps of Europe and the Middle East. He played a crucial role in the partition of Ireland into Northern Ireland and the Irish Free State in 1921-22.

Several reforms targeted children and old people. Councils were given powers to introduce free school meals, medical inspections were introduced, and free scholarships enabled poor children to take up places in secondary schools. Old-age pensions were introduced in 1908, though the payment of five shillings (25p) did not cover basic needs, and applied only to those over the age of 70.

The government also aimed at improving the lives of workers. Labour exchanges were established in 1909, and were very successful in helping men and women to find jobs. Perhaps the Liberals' most far-reaching reform was the National Insurance Act 1911. Although it was applied to only a minority of workers, it provided health and unemployment insurance to assist people through difficult times.

In the years 1910–14, the government was preoccupied with the crisis over the House of Lords and the re-emerging Irish question. The two elections of 1910 destroyed the majority gained in 1906, leaving the government dependent on the votes of the Irish Nationalist Party. A third Home Rule bill was introduced in 1912, and became law in 1914, only to be suspended with the outbreak of war.

In his 1935 work, *The Strange Death of Liberal England*, George Dangerfield suggested that the Liberal Party was terminally weakened by the crises of 1910–14: the fight for the Parliament Act; the threat of civil war in Ireland, which was actively encouraged by the Conservatives; suffragette violence led by the Pankhursts; and the growing militancy of the trade unions. Other historians believe that it was the First World War and its aftermath that destroyed Liberalism as a major political force.

The war had a devastating effect on classic Liberal principles of peace, reform and retrenchment. Peace and reform were not on the political agenda during the war, and retrenchment was naturally impossible, since the costs of the war required substantial increases in taxation. In 1916, for the second time in 30 years, the Liberal Party split. Asquith had formed a wartime coalition government with the Conservatives in 1915. His ineffective leadership led the Conservatives to bring him down in 1916, when Lloyd George was installed as prime minister. Asquith and his followers went into opposition, while the majority of Liberal MPs gave their support to Lloyd George.

The party split was intensified in the post-war election of December 1918. The coalition parties won a crushing victory: 127 coalition Liberals were elected, while Asquith's supporters were reduced to 37 MPs. A worrying development for the Liberals was the rise of the Labour Party. The 1918 election was the first to be fought under the Fourth Reform Act: 57 Labour members were elected, 15 more than in December 1910.

Lloyd George's coalition broke up in 1922, and there was a gradual reconciliation between the two party factions. However, the elections of 1923 and 1924 confirmed that the Liberals had been overtaken by Labour as the main opposition to the Conservatives in the House of Commons. No member of the Liberal Party was to hold government office between 1922 and 2010.

In the years c1780–1928, the two main parties in British politics reinvented themselves on several occasions. The Conservatives managed this with extraordinary success, dominating the parliamentary scene under Disraeli and his successors. The Liberals were less fortunate. They transformed themselves from the aristocratic Whigs of the late 18th century into a mass party supported by middle- and working-class voters under Gladstone; and New Liberalism had taken the party into a more socially aware direction. However, the growing electorate, especially the mass electorate of men and women created in 1918, seemed prepared to trust the Labour Party rather than the Liberals to deliver much-needed social reforms.

ACTIVITY
KNOWLEDGE CHECK

Individuals and the process of change 1886-1928

1 In the years 1886-1928, the Conservative and Liberal parties both had leaders who influenced the pace of change in politics and national life.

   a) Outline briefly the contribution to the Liberal Party of Gladstone, Asquith and Lloyd George.

   b) Outline the significance of Salisbury and Chamberlain to the Conservative Party.

2 Choose two other factors that explain the changing nature of the Conservative and Liberal parties in these years.

3 How far do you agree that the role of individuals was the most important factor driving changes to British political parties in these years? Explain your answer.

Party organisation and membership

The impact of the Reform Act 1832 on party organisation and membership

With the passing of the Reform Act and the Whig victory in the election of December 1832, prospects for the Conservative Party looked gloomy. The party held only 150 seats in the election, and had few policies to offer to the new electorate. Party organisation was poor, both nationally and locally. Although the Carlton Club was formed in London in 1832, it functioned as a social club for Tory MPs rather than as a central hub for organising the party in parliament and the country. During the 1830s, however, Peel, who emerged as the Tory successor to Wellington, promoted a number of significant reforms designed to revive Toryism as a political creed, and develop party organisation with the single aim of winning elections.

Peel expanded the Carlton Club's role to forge links between the national party and constituencies in the country, and appointed F.R. Bonham to reorganise the party nationally. Working from the Carlton Club, Bonham encouraged the creation of Conservative associations in the constituencies, which provided a social and political focal point for local supporters. Bonham also worked to ensure a high turnout for the party in general elections. Under the Reform Act, constituencies were required to create an electoral register that contained the names of all those who possessed the property qualifications needed to vote. The party established registration societies, which ensured that their supporters were registered for elections. These societies also challenged the right to vote claimed by their political opponents.

For their part, the Whigs and their allies showed little interest at first in matching the Tories' organisation. The Reform Club was founded in London in 1836, and became the unofficial headquarters of the Liberals, but did not form the same links with the constituencies that the Tories were developing. Instead, it was interested in developing the radical political ideas that were put forward by many of its members, which included most Liberal MPs and party grandees in the House of Lords.

By the late 1830s, the importance of party organisation had become clear. In the nine years between 1832 and 1841 there were no fewer than four general elections, which coincided with the creation of a new electorate and a growing political consciousness among voters. Party organisation was often the key decider in determining the outcome of an election. Membership of the two main parties grew steadily. While many of the new electors were committed to the growing Liberal Party, the Conservatives also saw a rise in membership in towns and cities. Middle-class voters, especially those who had campaigned for the Reform Act, became disillusioned with the Whig government, particularly as its reforming impetus faded in the late 1830s. They were also attracted to Peel's version of Conservatism, which had been stamped on his party by the Tamworth Manifesto.

The election of 1841 was the first fought by two clearly defined political parties. The well-organised Conservative Party swept to power with an overall majority of 76, a tribute to Bonham's organisational skills and the work carried out by local party associations. The year 1841 was the first time that the role of the monarch in a general election was insignificant. Victoria strongly favoured Melbourne and his government, but the electors had taken the choice of appointing a government out of her hands. Peel's victory was the first time a sitting government was forced from office by the decision of the electorate.

Changing party organisations, 1867-1914

The Reform Acts of 1867 and 1884 were a key factor in the further development of party organisations and membership. One of the most significant developments in the organisation of political parties came in Birmingham.

Joseph Chamberlain was mayor of Birmingham in the years 1873 to 1876. He was one of the city's leading businessmen, and a strong supporter of the Liberal Party. Chamberlain was one of the chief organisers of the Birmingham Caucus, which took party organisation to a new level. The Reform Act 1867 had created a number of multi-member constituencies, allowing the election of three MPs and giving local electors two votes in the process. It was expected that two MPs would be elected from one party, and the third from another. Chamberlain devised a strategy whereby the local Liberal Party would canvass the entire city and draw up a list of supporters. They would then guide electors in how to cast their votes so that they were spread evenly among all three Liberal candidates, and thus ensure their success in the election. The caucus system proved highly successful, and for many years Birmingham was represented in parliament by three Liberal MPs.

The caucus was adopted with varying degrees of success by other multi-member constituencies. It was instrumental in the creation of the National Liberal Federation (NLF) in 1877, which intended to spread the caucus system throughout the country, and thus emulate the success of the Conservative Party's organisation. Although the NLF could not formulate Liberal policies, it did encourage the promotion of radical political ideas. In 1883, the NLF conference adopted proposals for extending the suffrage to women, though Gladstone failed to adopt the scheme in the Reform Act 1884. In 1914, however, the proposal was aired once more, and helped persuade Asquith to consider female suffrage at the Speaker's Conference in 1916.

Disraeli lost the 1868 election, and in the following years encouraged reforms in party organisation. The NUCCA had been founded in

1867, and under the guidance of J.E. Gorst, whom Disraeli entrusted with party reorganisation, brought together local associations into a central organisation. Gorst also established the Central Office, which oversaw the selection of candidates for election. He recognised the importance of the new urban electorate, and supported the creation of Conservative clubs as social and recreational centres, especially for working men. Party organisation was reinvigorated thanks to Gorst, and made an important contribution to the Conservatives' election success in 1874.

The Conservatives were the first party to win over women to the party's cause. Disraeli died in 1881, and the Primrose League was formed in 1884 in his memory (it was widely believed that the primrose was Disraeli's favourite flower). The league was open to men and women who were prepared to uphold the Conservative cause, expressed in its motto of 'Empire and Liberty'. In the year of its foundation it could claim just 957 members, but membership rose to over one million in 1891, and reached two million in 1910; around half of its members were women. The league was never involved in the development of policies, but rather maintained a programme of social events and fundraising efforts for the national party. It flourished until the outbreak of war in 1914, but declined rapidly thereafter. In 1918, the granting of female suffrage and the opening of the Conservative Party's membership to men and women decreased the importance and usefulness of the Primrose League.

In the years 1867–1914, both political parties acknowledged the new electoral dispensation created by the Second and Third Reform Acts of 1867 and 1884. A number of Conservative and Liberal working men's associations were established in industrial towns and cities. These were intended to attract factory workers and others to their parties, and succeeded in their aim, especially in the factory towns in Lancashire and Yorkshire. The Conservative clubs, in particular, attracted large working-class numbers. They had low membership fees and became a popular focus for social gatherings.

Political organisation in a democratic age, 1918–28

The parliamentary reforms of 1918 and 1928 completed Britain's transition to a fully democratic political system by extending the vote to all men and women over the age of 21. Political parties quickly realised that they would have to create a mass party membership to respond to a mass electorate. The Conservative Party was well placed in terms of organisation and existing membership to achieve this. Since 1867, they had attracted members from both the middle and working classes, while the Primrose League ensured the active involvement of women in the party. Many middle-class Liberals had switched to the Conservatives during Gladstone's long tenure of the premiership, alarmed by the growing radicalism of the party and by Gladstone's attempts to tackle the Irish question. By the mid-1920s, the Conservatives had a large base of support, which proved invaluable in providing effective canvassing of the electorate and in getting Conservative supporters to the polls on election day.

The Liberal Party fared much less well in these years. They had operated a very successful party machine after 1900, and had forged links with the Labour Representation Committee (LRC), which helped ensure their landslide victory in 1906. However,

the growing divisions within the governing party from 1910 took their toll on party organisation. The Liberal Party's split in 1916 between the supporters of Asquith and Lloyd George weakened the party as an electoral machine; and many of its members switched their allegiance to the growing Labour Party after 1918.

Since 1832, political parties had been compelled to adapt their organisation in the country and to extend membership to the new and growing electorate. Peel and Disraeli had managed this with considerable success, partly because their policies appealed to the voters, but also because they could draw on considerable funds to create and develop new political organisations. The Liberals followed the Conservatives' example, and by the 1880s had a substantial national network of associations that attracted many middle-class and working-class members. They were less successful in attracting women to the party's cause, which was to prove a factor in their decline from 1914.

The growth of the Labour Party

Throughout the 19th century, various organisations were formed, dedicated to improving the lot of the poorest and the dispossessed in British society. In the years after the end of the Napoleonic Wars, working-class grievances had been expressed

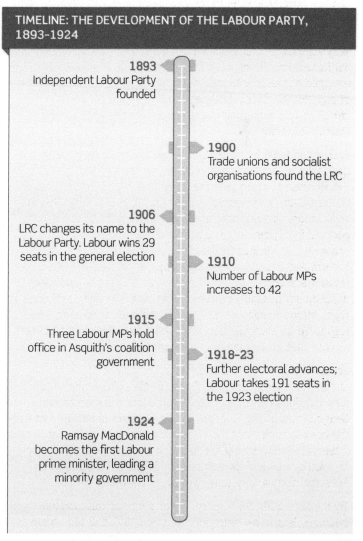

TIMELINE: THE DEVELOPMENT OF THE LABOUR PARTY, 1893–1924

1893 Independent Labour Party founded

1900 Trade unions and socialist organisations found the LRC

1906 LRC changes its name to the Labour Party. Labour wins 29 seats in the general election

1910 Number of Labour MPs increases to 42

1915 Three Labour MPs hold office in Asquith's coalition government

1918–23 Further electoral advances; Labour takes 191 seats in the 1923 election

1924 Ramsay MacDonald becomes the first Labour prime minister, leading a minority government

through rioting and unrest, such as the Spa Fields riots of 1816, and what became known as the Peterloo Massacre in 1819 (see Chapter 3, pages 68–70). Many working-class men allied briefly with middle-class organisations during the reform crisis of 1830–32, but were bitterly disappointed by the Reform Act itself. During the late 1830s and 1840s, working-class activity became more organised through the Chartist movement (see Chapter 4, pages 84–105), but real progress in promoting working-class interests came only after the parliamentary reforms of 1867–85.

The Second and Third Reform Acts extended the franchise to many working-class males, most of whom were content to support the Liberal and Conservative parties. Even though the Redistribution Act 1885 led to the creation of identifiably working-class constituencies, this change did not lead to the election of large numbers of working-class MPs.

During the 1880s, the socialist ideas that were influencing European politics, especially in France, Germany and Russia, began to take hold in Britain. In 1884, three socialist organisations were formed. Two of these, the Social Democratic Federation (SDF) and its offshoot the Socialist League, embraced Marxist political ideals, promoting class struggle as a prelude to a socialist revolution. A third body, the Fabian Society, took a more gradualist line, hoping to influence the policies of existing parties. While these organisations had no electoral success, they were influential in shifting the political climate slightly, away from laissez-faire individualism and towards a more collectivist attitude towards society.

A trend that would have greater significance for working-class organisation was the growth of the trade union movement. For many years, trade unions had been organised to promote the interests of skilled workers such as engineers and miners, regarded as the 'aristocracy of labour'. By 1874, these trade unions could boast a combined membership of one million men.

The economic downturn of the 1870s and 1880s led to the growth of 'New Unionism', which organised large numbers of unskilled workers such as dockers and railwaymen. Trade societies for women were formed, and the strike by women workers at the Bryant and May match factory in London in 1888 highlighted the changing nature of trade union activity. By the early 1890s, the leaders of New Unionism were ready to combine to form a political organisation that would fight for better social and working conditions.

In 1893, a number of trade union delegates and representatives from the Fabians and the SDF met in Bradford and founded the Independent Labour Party. The party adopted a programme that rejected the Marxist agenda of the SDF and its supporters. They proposed a number of progressive social reforms, including free education at school and university, a legal minimum wage, free access to medical treatment and comprehensive welfare provision.

The hopes invested in the new party were difficult to sustain. A total of 28 Independent Labour Party candidates stood in the 1895 election, but none was elected, and the party secured a mere 44,000 votes. Moreover, the party's open hostility to the Boer War in 1899 made it easy for its opponents to denounce the Independent Labour Party as unpatriotic. The Trades Union Congress (TUC) decided that further action was required to sponsor parliamentary candidates. In February 1900, the LRC was formed, supported by many trade unions and socialist organisations, and by the Independent Labour Party itself.

In 1901, the House of Lords ruled in the *Taff Vale* case that unions were liable for loss of profits caused by strike action, and the Amalgamated Society of Railway Servants was forced to pay the Taff Vale Railway Company the sum of £23,000 in damages. The judgment dismayed the unions, and they affiliated in large numbers to the LRC, turning it into a mass political movement. The link between Labour and the unions benefited both parties: the unions promoted their own interests through the party, while Labour gained widespread electoral support from trade union members.

In 1903, the Liberals agreed an electoral pact with the LRC. Liberals would not put forward candidates in an agreed number of seats, thus giving LRC candidates a free run against the Conservatives.

Taken together, *Taff Vale* and the electoral pact contributed to a major advance for the LRC in 1906, when they won 29 seats and 254,000 votes. Shortly after the election, the LRC changed its name to the Labour Party. This was an inspired choice. Conservatives and Liberals had always been identified in terms of their philosophy and political outlook. The use of the term 'Labour Party' suggested that it was aimed at promoting the interests of a class rather than of a set of political beliefs.

From 1906 to 1918, the Labour Party made only slow progress, partly because its broad support for New Liberalism's agenda, including the Trades Disputes Act 1906, which reversed the *Taff Vale* judgment, meant that the party did not develop a clear political identity of its own. In the Taunton by-election of 1909, Frank Smith suggested to the electors that Labour had a strong influence on Liberal policies.

It was in the years 1918–24 when Labour established itself as a major political force. During the war, the party had gained some experience in government, when Labour members were given three minor positions in Asquith's coalition government of 1915. The Fourth Reform Act 1918 established a mass electorate of 21 million, and increased the number of seats in areas where Labour support was concentrated. Taken together, these developments contributed to Labour taking 57 seats in the 1918 election, with the support of two million voters. The party advanced further still in the 1922 election. It won 142 seats and was the largest single party in opposition to the Conservatives in the House of Commons.

After 1918, the Liberal Party was quickly replaced by the Labour Party as the dominant left-wing political party in the House of Commons. However, after the 1923 General Election, fought on the issues of free trade and protection, the Labour Party was unable to come to power on its own. The Conservatives were still the largest party, with 258 seats, but it was not enough to have a majority. Therefore, in January 1924, the Liberals were needed to form the first Labour government. Labour had 191 seats, combined with 158 Liberals. The government's dependence on Liberal support meant that it was unable to carry out a wide-ranging reform programme. However, its legislation did make clear some of the reforms it would champion in later years. Its main achievement was the Housing Act, which promoted the construction of 500,000 houses to be rented out at controlled rents. Other measures included improved pensions and unemployment benefits, extended secondary education and expanded health provision. However, the Labour minority government only lasted until 1924, when Conservative opposition led to a motion of no confidence in the House of Commons and the resignation of Ramsay MacDonald's administration.

In the 1924 election, the Conservatives triumphed with 412 seats to Labour's 151. The real drama of this election though was the collapse of the Liberals, who lost 118 seats, leaving them with only 40. Much of this Liberal calamity has been attributed to their part in the formation of the first Labour government in 1923. Many Liberal voters feared socialism and a future Labour government and so switched to the Conservatives. The 1924 election effectively polarised British politics into a two-party system in which the Liberals were doomed to a marginal position.

The Liberal element continued to decline throughout the 1920s but was still of importance for Labour. In the 1929 General Election, Labour secured the greatest number of seats, 287, but this was still not enough for a majority. The Labour government of 1929 could only form on the agreement that the Liberals would not join the Conservatives in opposing them. By this stage, the Liberals had just 59 seats and could only hope to exert influence through an alliance with Labour.

Neither the rise of Labour in the early 20th century nor the decline of Liberalism as a political force were inevitable developments. Liberalism, especially under Gladstone, had been a popular and broadly based party that achieved much in the late 19th century. New Liberalism after 1906 seemed to be taking the party away from the classic Liberalism of the 19th century into more collectivist areas, and there was a growing acceptance that the state rather than the individual could be responsible for radical improvements to society. The Conservative experience after 1846 showed that a divided party could not be electorally successful. The Liberal split of 1916 was devastating for the party's fortunes, and was largely responsible for the party's growing weakness and decline to 1928 and beyond.

On the other hand, the Labour Party was boosted by a number of fortunate events between 1900 and 1928. The electoral pacts agreed in 1903, and the effects of the Fourth Reform Act 1918, were both instrumental in the substantial growth of the party and its support, which had, by 1923, made Labour a serious contender for government. It is perhaps ironic that it was the Liberal leader Asquith who supported the formation of the first Labour government in 1924 and sustained it in office.

ACTIVITY
KNOWLEDGE CHECK

The Labour Party

1 Examine the development of the Labour Party as a political force in the years to 1924.

2 Explain how the following helped or hindered the party's growth:

a) the Lib–Lab pact

b) trade union support

c) the party's political beliefs

d) the decline of the Liberal Party.

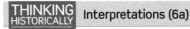
THINKING HISTORICALLY   Interpretations (6a)

Ever-changing history

Our interpretations of the past change as we change. This may be because our social attitudes have changed over time, or perhaps because historians have constructed a different theory, or perhaps technology has allowed archaeologists to discover something new.

Work in pairs.

1 Make a timeline that starts with the Labour Party's success in the 1906 election and ends 50 years in the future. Construct reactions that illustrate the point that time changes history. In the future box, you can speculate on how people might react to the event in 50 years' time. Below is an example.

1906	1914	1945	2010	2066
The Labour Party wins 29 seats in the general election.	Industrial worker: 'The moment a party representing the working classes gained some political influence.' Liberal politician: 'A moment that encouraged our party to bring in new political reforms.'	Labour politician: 'The start of our rise to political power.' Liberal politician: 'A disaster. The end of our party's chances of winning an election.'	Industrial worker: 'The moment our working-class party joined the political system that prevents us working classes from having any influence.' Labour politician: 'Beginning of the two-party system, dominated by the Labour and Conservative Parties.' A gender historian: 'An insignificant moment. Women had to fight for their rights without any help from Labour's growing political influence.'	?

Answer the following questions.

2 Identify three factors that have affected how Labour's success in the 1906 general election has been interpreted over time, or might affect it in the future.

3 If a historian was to write a book proposing a radically new interpretation of Labour in the 1906 general election, how might other historians react? What would affect their reaction?

4 How will the future change the past?

The extent of change in the social make-up of the House of Commons by 1928

Parliament in 1780 was dominated by the landed interest, and around one-fifth of all MPs were the sons or brothers of peers. Aristocratic influence was sustained and even extended through Pitt's widespread creation of new peers in the 1780s and 1790s. Other forms of property were represented in the House of Commons, such as brewing and flour milling, with around 110 MPs gaining their fortunes as merchants, bankers and industrialists. A handful of MPs could boast a rags-to-riches career, such as Joseph Pitt, the son of a West Country carpenter who became, in turn, a banker, brewer and the owner of several parliamentary boroughs.

The extension of the franchise and the redistribution of seats throughout the 19th century did not necessarily lead to a change in the social composition of the House of Commons. The increasing number of county seats simply entrenched the power of the county gentry, while redistribution actually worked against the interests of those merchants and bankers who had purchased and controlled seats before 1832. Between 1832 and 1867, the social make-up of the House of Commons barely changed at all: there was certainly no influx of middle-class men to represent the new electorate, and the working class remained unrepresented. The historian Vincent analysed the occupational background of 456 Liberal MPs who sat in parliament between 1859 and 1874. Of these, 198 were large landowners, 151 were businessmen, and only 20 were identified as radicals.

There was some change brought about after the Reform Acts of 1867 and 1884–85, but it was glacially slow. Two miners, supported by the Liberals and trade unions, were elected in 1874, but they were exceptions in a House of Commons where lawyers, businessmen and the landed gentry predominated. Real change came only after 1900, with the growth of the Labour Party. In 1900, there were 11 'Lib–Lab' MPs, supported by the Liberals, but the 1918 election returned 63 Labour members, 56 of whom came from working-class backgrounds.

Women had begun to play a significant role in local politics following the passage of the Local Government Act 1894, which allowed women to be elected onto local bodies such as parish and district councils. The Representation of the People Act 1918 enfranchised women over 30, but did not address the issue of women standing for parliament. This was remedied by the Parliament (Qualification of Women) Act, which was rushed through parliament in November 1918, in time for the general election in December. At 27 words, it is the shortest Act in the history of parliament: 'A woman shall not be disqualified by sex or marriage for being elected to or sitting or voting as a member of the Commons House of Parliament.'

Seventeen of the 1,623 candidates for the election were women, including some leading suffragette campaigners. The only successful candidate was Countess Markievicz, who won a seat in Dublin for Sinn Fein, the Irish nationalist party. Along with her fellow Sinn Fein MPs, the countess refused to take her seat.

The first woman to sit in the House of Commons was Viscountess Nancy Astor. In 1919, her husband succeeded to a peerage, which meant his seat for Plymouth fell vacant, and his wife took the seat in a by-election. However, progress for women overall was slow, as they faced two major obstacles: they had to be selected by one of the major parties; and they had to stand in seats where they had a chance of success.

Year	Conservative	Labour	Liberal	Other	Total
1918	0	0	0	1	1
1922	1	0	1	0	2
1923	3	3	2	0	8
1924	3	1	0	0	4

Figure 2.1 Women MPs, 1918-24.

EXTEND YOUR KNOWLEDGE

Women in parliament
Between 1918 and 2015, only 450 women were elected as MPs, with their numbers rising from one MP in 1918 (Countess Markievicz) to 191 in 2015. A handful of women have reached high political office, often as members of the Labour Party. Margaret Bondfield became the first woman to hold government office in 1924, when she was appointed under-secretary at the ministry of labour. Bondfield went on to become the first woman cabinet minister, as minister of labour in 1929–31. For the Conservatives, Margaret Thatcher became the first woman prime minister in 1979. In 2016, Teresa May became the UK's second woman prime minister.

Abolition of the property qualification for MPs, 1858

The property qualification had been introduced in England in 1711 as a means of excluding radical opponents of the governments of the day. County MPs were required to hold land that produced an annual income of £600, and borough MPs had to prove an income of £300 a year. Men, therefore, had to have substantial private means before they could even consider standing for parliament.

By 1832, the property qualification had become an absurd fiction. Shady dealings with bankers and landowners could provide any MP with fictitious qualifications drawn up before or after their election, and thus circumvent the property requirements. When the matter was debated in the House of Commons in 1838, its opponents claimed that over half of all MPs had obtained their property qualifications by fraudulent means.

The abolition of the qualification was one of the demands made by the Chartists in the late 1830s as one of their Six Points (see Chapter 4, page 85). In 1842, Chartist representatives met in Birmingham to discuss their aims and strategy. One of the delegates, Bronterre O'Brien, spoke on the injustice of the property qualification (Source 8).

SOURCE

8

Bronterre O'Brien speaking to Chartist delegates at their conference in Birmingham, April 1842. O'Brien was a leading Irish Chartist.

The only qualification that ought to be required in a member of parliament was the free choice of his constituents. To give a constituency the right of choosing a representative, and at the same time to circumscribe this choice to a particular class, was to give the right with one hand, and to take it away with the other. To establish a property qualification was like giving sparrows the right to choose their protectors, but circumscribing this choice to hawks.

The property qualification was a major concern for the Chartists. Many of its members believed that there was little point in universal male suffrage if voters could only choose rich men as their representatives. In 1852, a leading Chartist, Samuel Carter, was elected as MP for Tavistock. Carter was a leading businessman in his town, owning a large house and a tannery. However, a select committee of the House of Commons decided that he did not meet the precise terms of the property qualification, and he lost his seat.

The issue was brought to a head in 1858 with the case of Edward Glover. Glover was elected to parliament in the 1857 election, but did not possess the necessary property required for election. In the first and only case of its kind, Glover was barred from the House of Commons, tried at the Old Bailey for making a false declaration to the House of Commons and imprisoned for three months. The government decided to address the issue in 1858. It supported abolition on the grounds that existing law required no property qualification for Scottish MPs, and that the system had become universally recognised as a sham. Abolition became law in 1858, though some peers opposed repeal on the grounds that it appeared to be a concession to the Chartists, since it met one of their Six Points.

The impact of abolition was only gradual. While election was now open to all men, the absence of payments for MPs deterred working-class men from standing for election. The problem was partially solved from the 1870s onwards, when trade unions began to subsidise a handful of MPs, but this had little effect on the social composition of the House of Commons.

The payment of MPs, 1911

The payment of MPs, introduced in 1911, was in some ways a revival of an ancient practice. Ever since medieval times, when towns first sent representatives to the parliament in London, it had become established practice for local bodies to pay money to their MPs to help cover their expenses and to compensate them for their absence from their home and their work. In return, MPs were expected to report to their constituents on events in parliament and to confirm their regular attendance at Westminster. The practice gradually died out over time until, by 1700, it had become a very rare practice as the composition of the House of Commons changed. Many constituencies chose wealthy men to represent them who were able to defray their costs from their own funds.

During the 19th century, the issue of paying MPs was raised several times, inside and outside parliament. As the franchise widened, a number of politicians wanted to broaden the composition of the House of Commons to include men who could not meet the cost of travelling and living expenses. Payment of MPs was one of the demands made by the Chartist movement in the 1830s. Chartists supported proposals for paying MPs £500 a year, with their attendance records published annually.

The issue took on a wider significance after the franchise reform of 1867. It was argued that, since many working men now had the vote, they ought to be represented in parliament by men drawn from the poorer classes. Gladstone was converted to the idea of payment of MPs in the 1880s, and it was formally adopted by the Liberal Party in the Newcastle programme of 1891.

One solution to the issue was provided by trade unions, who sponsored individuals at elections and provided financial support to their MPs. Keir Hardie, who was elected as MP for West Ham South in 1892, was sponsored in this way by the Miners Federation. From 1904, the emerging Labour Party provided up to £200 a year to support its MPs.

The Labour Party and the unions both suffered a major setback with the *Osborne* judgment of 1909. Osborne was a Liberal supporter who objected to the political levy collected by his union, the Amalgamated Society of Railway Servants. The case went to the House of Lords, which ruled that it was illegal for unions to collect a levy from their members to be used for political purposes. The judgment was received with outrage in parliament and in the country, and campaigns were organised to reverse the ruling.

The matter was resolved thanks to a number of events in 1910 and 1911. The two elections of 1910 had destroyed the Liberals' substantial parliamentary majority, and they needed the support of minority parties to get their measures through parliament. They thus decided to support the payment of MPs in order to repair some of the damage caused by the *Osborne* judgment, and to secure the broad support of Labour's 42 MPs.

In August 1911, the House of Commons approved a resolution from the Chancellor of the Exchequer, Lloyd George, for paying ordinary MPs (but not government ministers) a sum of £400 a year. This was a substantial amount of money in 1911, and the payment of MPs was to have far-reaching effects in future years. It was a contributory factor in the subsequent growth of the Labour Party, which had 191 MPs by 1924, and it brought into public life men who might otherwise never have had a political career. Ernest Bevin worked as a labourer and lorry driver in the West Country. Elected as MP for Wandsworth Central in 1940, he is widely regarded as one of the most outstanding foreign secretaries of the century.

ACTIVITY
KNOWLEDGE CHECK

Changes to Britain's political representation

1 a) How different do you think the House of Commons was in 1928 from how it had been in 1832?

  b) How had such changes taken place?

2 To what extent do you think parliament was more representative of British society in 1928 than it had been in 1780?

ACTIVITY
SUMMARY

The House of Commons

1 Investigate the principal features of the House of Commons c1780, and how far these changed over time in the years to 1928. You may wish to use the following table:

	c1780	1833	1875	1928
Membership				
Powers				
Government support				
Opposition to the government				
Significance of elections				

2 a) In your judgement, which of these features changed the most in the given period?

  b) Which feature changed least of all?

3 What does your investigation suggest about the impact of parliamentary reform on parliament?

WIDER READING

Behagg, C. *Working-Class Movements, 1815–1914*, Hodder and Stoughton (1991)

Blake, R. *The Conservative Party from Peel to Thatcher*, Fontana (1985)

Hurd, D. 'Sir Robert Peel: The making of a party', *History Today* (July 2007)

Pearce, E. 'Resisting reform in the Lords, 1911', *History Today* (June 1998)

Pearce, R. and Stearne, R. *Government and Reform, 1815–1914*, Hodder and Stoughton (1994)

Powell, D. 'The decline of the Liberal Party', *History Review* (September 2009)

Rathbone, M. 'Benjamin Disraeli: Conservative leader and prime minister', *History Review* (December 2006)

Watts, D. *Tories, Conservatives and Unionists*, Hodder and Stoughton (1994)

A Level Exam-Style Question
Section C

How far do you agree that change to the electoral system in the years 1780–1928 was the most important factor driving changes in the organisation and membership of the Liberal and Conservative parties in the years 1832–1928? (20 marks)

Tip
You may find it best to assess organisation and membership together rather than separately. A chronological approach is fine, but your argument may be made sharper by considering each party separately.

3.3 Radical reformers, c1790–1819

KEY QUESTIONS

- How significant was extra-parliamentary protest, 1790–1819?
- How effective was the government's response to protest in the years to 1819?
- What was the impact of the radical reformers themselves?

INTRODUCTION

In 1789, the French Revolution broke out in Paris. Over the next three years, a wide-ranging series of reforms reduced the power of the monarchy, abolished feudal privileges and many of the rights enjoyed by the Catholic Church and the aristocracy, and proclaimed the principles of *liberté, égalité* and *fraternité*. These revolutionary ideas, which challenged the very nature of existing governments and regimes, spread rapidly throughout Europe. In Britain, while there was no serious threat to the existence of the Hanoverian monarchy itself, many liberal and radical thinkers took heart from events in France. Political debates and discussions in London and throughout the provinces were encouraged by new political organisations and by radical national and local newspapers. The standard bearer for conservative forces in Britain was Edmund Burke, whose *Reflections on the Revolution in France* was a comprehensive assault on the revolution, and a gloomy prediction that France would ultimately degenerate into chaos. Radicals, on the other hand, were more optimistic. Some hoped that events in France would encourage demands for reform in Britain, especially parliamentary reform. A few, notably Tom Paine and Thomas Spence, hoped that Britain would follow the French example with the establishment of a republic and universal male suffrage.

Most politicians, Tory and Whig alike, gave a cautious welcome to the French Revolution. They expected that it would develop along the lines of the **Revolution of 1688–89**, which had established a constitutional monarchy in Britain under William and Mary. Their hopes were dashed as events in France became more violent, especially after the September Massacres of 1792 and the execution of Louis XVI in 1793. Pitt's government feared that the calls for reform in Britain might lead to outbreaks of rebellion on the French lines, and throughout the 1790s his government took strong action, supported by king and parliament, against radicals and their activities. The maintenance of domestic stability became even more important from 1793, when war broke out between Britain and France. War encouraged the development of a strong current of nationalist sentiment in Britain, and widespread patriotic feelings supported the suppression of radical activities. By 1799, the government had imposed domestic harmony by means such as the suspension of habeas corpus (see Chapter 1, page 14), attacks on the freedom of the press, and the banning of large-scale meetings and demonstrations.

(see Chapter 1, page 14)

KEY TERM

Revolution of 1688–89
In 1688, the Stuart king, James II, abandoned his throne and fled the country. Parliament offered the crown jointly to William, Stadtholder of the Netherlands, and his wife Mary, a daughter of James II. In the years 1689–1701, a number of laws clarified the powers of the monarchy and parliament, and established a constitutional monarchy in Britain.

1789 – Outbreak of the French Revolution

1792 – Royal proclamation issued against seditious writings
Founding of the London Corresponding Society (LCS) by Thomas Hardy

1794 – Trial of the leaders of the LCS

| 1789 | 1791 | 1792 | 1793 | 1794 | 1795 |

1791 – Tom Paine's *The Rights of Man Part 1* is published

1793 – France declares war on Britain

1795 – Treason Act and Seditious Meetings Act

The return of peace in 1815, and the difficulties of adjusting to a peacetime economy, saw the re-emergence of a radical movement that suggested a real threat of revolution. The radicalism of the 1790s had been centred in London, but post-war unrest was a national, and thus more threatening, phenomenon. Economic and social distress was widespread, and was a fertile ground for radical agitation. Between 1815 and 1819, Liverpool's Tory government introduced a number of measures aimed at maintaining law and order that many contemporaries and later historians condemned as unnecessarily oppressive.

EXTEND YOUR KNOWLEDGE

Lord Liverpool (1770–1828)

Liverpool's government lasted from 1812 to 1827, making him the longest-serving prime minister of the 19th century. He was responsible for the successful ending of the wars with France, dealing with post-war unrest and encouraging growing prosperity during the 1820s. His leadership skills may be inferred by the fact that, within three years of his resignation, his party was bitterly split over religious and reform issues, which allowed the Whigs to take office in 1830.

The most notorious event in these years was the breaking up of a huge meeting at St Peter's Fields in Manchester in August 1819, which left 11 dead and 400 wounded. This action, which has entered popular folklore as the Peterloo Massacre, marked the end of the years of unrest, as the economy gradually revived in the 1820s and demands for reform declined.

HOW SIGNIFICANT WAS EXTRA-PARLIAMENTARY PROTEST, 1790–1819?

The London Corresponding Society, 1792–93

The success of the American Revolution and the early events of the French Revolution contributed to a growing interest in political affairs among working people, especially the skilled working class. The circulation of radical newspapers grew, and several organisations were formed that promoted the ideas of republicanism and parliamentary reform.

In 1780, Major John Cartwright formed the Society for Constitutional Information (SCI), an organisation that promoted social and political reform. Its members were mostly middle-class industrialists, who were interested in discussing political affairs, but were not prepared to go beyond this into radical activity. From 1783, its support fell as its members joined other organisations, and it ceased to exist after 1795.

In the early 1790s, a number of corresponding societies were established in London and in provincial towns, drawing their membership from the growing ranks of the skilled working classes. These societies spread their political ideas through printed pamphlets, and many individuals communicated directly with their counterparts in Paris.

1812 – First Hampden Club founded in London by John Cartwright

1816 – Spa Fields riot

1819 – Mass meeting at St Peter's Fields, Manchester (Peterloo Massacre)

The Six Acts

| 1812 | 1815 | 1816 | 1817 | 1818 | 1819 |

1815 – End of the Napoleonic War

1817 – Pentridge (Pentrich) Rising

The 'Gagging Acts'

The most important of these new organisations was the London Corresponding Society (LCS), founded in 1792 by a shoemaker, Thomas Hardy, and supported by skilled craftsmen in London. Hardy was strongly influenced by the SCI, and thus the LCS promoted the twin causes of universal suffrage and annual parliaments. Some members were keen on adopting issues of social and political reform, but Hardy and other leaders were reluctant to champion these causes, arguing that these reforms would come about as a natural consequence of parliamentary reform.

SOURCE

A savage commentary by James Gillray on a meeting of the LCS, published in 1798. The sketches on the wall are of Tom Paine and Horne Tooke, who worked with Cartwright to establish the SCI. Gillray was a noted portrait painter and caricaturist, and was one of the first to produce cartoons with a political message.

The LCS worked to promote the political education of its members by publishing pamphlets promoting their views. Their aims were set out in a key pamphlet issued in November 1792, the *Address of the London Corresponding Society to the other Societies of Great Britain*. They explained their basic aims, and made clear that their methods would be peaceful: they intended to petition parliament rather than organise mass, and potentially violent, demonstrations.

The organisation of the LCS marked a new departure for radical groups. The society never tried to limit its membership to any particular class. It adopted the slogan 'that our membership be unlimited', and charged a very low subscription fee. It kept the size of local associations deliberately small to enable all of its members to take part in discussions and debates. Pitt was worried by the structure of the LCS. He believed that the society was not so much a political organisation, but had the potential to become a military body. Government spies infiltrated the society, but reported that the LCS operated strictly within the law.

Inevitably, there was a backlash from conservative groups against the LCS and other radical organisations, especially as events in France moved from the moderate position of 1789 into more extreme activity in 1791–93. A number of loyalist societies were established, whose members viewed the radicals as being disloyal to both king and country. The Association for Preserving Liberty and Property against Republicans and Levellers was formed in 1792, and a network of these organisations grew up nationally. While the corresponding societies were largely supported by skilled workers, association membership was drawn almost exclusively from the middle classes. The government welcomed the **Association movement** and played its part by using the loyalist Press to promote patriotic propaganda, by giving secret help to the associations, and by taking action against the reformers.

KEY TERM

Association movement
By the early 1790s, the landed and propertied classes, influenced by Burke and other conservative writers, and by the growth of radical movements, came to believe that a general national conspiracy was being organised that intended social and political revolution. Following promptings from the press, many local landowners and others began to form associations, with the sole intention of providing support for the government whenever it was needed.

The Association movement was the first part of a process of creating a united loyalist front against radicalism. In the years to 1815, many of its members also served as armed volunteers, ready to take action against internal or external enemies.

The Spa Fields meeting, 1816

The government's determination to destroy reforming activity, and the growth of national feeling during the Napoleonic War, had effectively silenced British radicalism in the early years of the 19th century. However, peace abroad was not accompanied by tranquillity at home, and from 1815 Lord Liverpool's government faced a number of challenges to its authority.

Compared with other parts of the country, London had remained relatively quiet after 1815. The more extreme radical groups were divided on their aims and methods, while support was growing for the moderate reforming programme of middle-class leaders such as Sir Francis Burdett.

EXTEND YOUR KNOWLEDGE

Sir Francis Burdett (1770–1844)
Burdett was a radical MP who was a long-time supporter of reforms. During his parliamentary career he supported many measures, such as parliamentary reform, an end to Catholic disabilities, and the abolition of corporal punishment in the armed forces. Though widely respected for his radicalism for many years, he became far more conservative in his views in the 1830s and 1840s.

Reform meetings in London during the early months of 1816 proved uncontroversial, and were concerned as much with the relief of the poor as with political reform. The followers of Thomas Spence were unhappy with such a moderate stance, and planned a mass meeting in east London, which they hoped would lead to violent rioting and disorder.

EXTEND YOUR KNOWLEDGE

Thomas Spence (1750–1814)
Spence was a self-taught radical who developed his own political ideas, which were revolutionary in their implications. He called for the abolition of both monarchy and aristocracy, and, uniquely for the time, universal suffrage for men and women. His message was an influential one, and he favoured active revolution on the French model to overthrow the entire social and political order.

Spence died in 1814, but his influence outlived him. The Spencean Philanthropist Society was formed in 1815. Its members were to play a major role in revolutionary activity in London until 1820, especially during the Spa Fields riot of 1816.

The radical leader and speaker, Henry 'Orator' Hunt, was invited to address a meeting called to take place at Spa Fields in east London in November. The crowd of 10,000 people was the largest gathering seen in London since the anti-Catholic **Gordon riots** of 1780. The meeting's aim was not contentious: Hunt was asked to present a petition to the Prince Regent, urging him to reform parliament. In his speech, Hunt championed the moral force behind the petition, but came dangerously close to suggesting the use of physical force if the petitioners' demands were not met.

KEY TERM

Gordon riots
Riots organised by Protestant groups against measures to reduce official discrimination against Catholics. Around 50,000 people took part, and inflicted widespread destruction in London. The riots damaged Britain's reputation abroad and made it difficult for the government to secure European allies in the American War of Independence.

Almost inevitably, Hunt was not received by the Prince Regent, and a second protest meeting was called for 2 December. Once again Hunt was due to speak, but he was pre-empted by Spenceans who stirred up sections of the crowd and urged them to take a course of direct action. A number of people left the meeting, looted a number of gunsmiths, and set off to seize the Tower of London and the Royal Exchange. Had they been successful, they might have attempted a coup against the government, but the quick action of the Lord Mayor of London and his force of constables dispersed the rioters and arrested their leader.

The trial of the ringleaders in 1817 exposed the role of government informers and spies in the Spa Fields affair. The defence was able to prove that a government informer named Castle had encouraged the riot, and that he had duped the ringleaders into taking extreme action. In the light of this revelation, the jury acquitted all the defendants.

Spa Fields exposed many of the difficulties faced by radical reformers in the post-war years. The use of government **spies and agents provocateurs** made it almost impossible to outwit the forces of order, who were usually well informed about intended courses of action.

KEY TERM

Spy and agent provocateur
In the absence of a national police force, the government relied on a large and effective spy network that provided the Home Office with information about radical activity. Agents provocateurs were government agents who infiltrated radical groups in order to persuade their members to break the law.

The division between those who supported peaceful protest and others who tended towards violence made unified action impossible. The *Leeds Mercury*, a strong supporter of the radicals, condemned the Spa Fields riot without reservation (Source 2).

From an editorial by the editor of the *Leeds Mercury*, Edward Baines, 7 December 1816. The *Mercury* had a wide circulation in Yorkshire and Lancashire, and represented moderate Whig opinions.

The two meetings which have already been held under the auspices of Mr Hunt have been more injurious to the cause of Parliamentary Reform than the united efforts of all its enemies. We trust, however, that the guarded, temperate, and exemplary conduct of the friends of Reform In other parts of the kingdom will redeem the cause from that odium which the violent proceedings of Mr Hunt and his associates have thrown upon it; and we hope that the advocates of Reform will be eager to disavow and condemn the proceedings to which we have adverted and that they will adhere to the good old Constitutional mode of peaceably petitioning the Legislature, without adding to it measures, which have the appearance, at least, of being resorted to for the purpose of intimidation: than which nothing can be conceived more absurd and hopeless. In fact, a reform obtained by the intimidation of physical force would differ in nothing but in name from a Revolution, and would probably lead through the horrors of a civil war to the establishment of a military despotism, or to the misrule of a few despicable anarchists.

EXTEND YOUR KNOWLEDGE

Leeds Mercury

The *Leeds Mercury* was one of the most influential provincial newspapers of its day. Its editor and proprietor, Edward Baines, was one of the first newspapermen to include political editorials as well as news in his paper. He campaigned for several radical causes, such as the provision of parliamentary seats for industrial towns. However, he was a staunch opponent of universal suffrage and of factory legislation aimed at improving working conditions for adults and children.

The Pentridge Rising, 1817

Bamford was correct in his belief that government agents had infiltrated radical movements and were feeding information about their intentions back to London. Liverpool's government had established a Committee of Secrecy, which operated a substantial network of spies. The information that they gathered enabled them to be prepared for outbreaks of violence or rebellious activity. The significance of the spies was highlighted by the Pentridge (Pentrich) rising of 1817.

In the early months of 1817, a number of revolutionary activists held meetings in Pentridge, a village in Derbyshire, where they discussed plans for an insurrection. In May, they were joined by a Londoner who called himself Oliver. Oliver persuaded the meeting that radicals in London were preparing an uprising in the capital for 9 June, which would be supported by similar actions throughout the country. None of this was true. Oliver was in fact a former convict called Richards, and was in the pay of Lord Sidmouth, the Home Secretary. Not only did he spy on radical groups, but in this instance he acted as an agent provocateur, intending to lead the Pentridge activists into illegal and treasonable activities. The activists were convinced by Oliver's reports, and on 9 June their leader, Jeremiah Brandreth, led 300 men towards Nottingham, intending to seize the city. Once again,

the system of spies proved effective. The rebels were intercepted by a regiment of soldiers before they could reach the city: many men fled, but 80 were arrested.

A week after the attempted rising, the *Leeds Mercury* published a detailed investigation that exposed Oliver's role in the rising. Its editor, Edward Baines, blamed the government rather than the activists for the whole affair. Those who believed that Castle's involvement in the Spa Fields riot was an isolated incident, now realised that ministers had been using such tactics for some years. Public revulsion had no effect on the trial of the ringleaders. Fourteen men were transported, and Brandreth, along with two others, was hanged and beheaded in public.

ACTIVITY
KNOWLEDGE CHECK

The development of extra-parliamentary protest

Study the aims and methods of the LCS, the Spa Fields meeting and the Pentridge Rising. Outline three ways in which the radical movement after 1815 differed from that of the 1790s.

Peterloo, 1819

The actions taken by the government in 1816 and 1817, coupled with some improvements in the economy, meant that radical activities were damped down for a brief period. In 1818, Henry Hunt stood for election to parliament, but his advocacy of parliamentary reform was unpopular with the electorate, and he was soundly defeated. Radical clubs and societies remained in existence, and although the *Political Register* ceased publication in 1817 after Cobbett fled to the USA, a flourishing radical press continued to argue the case for reform.

The last significant protest of these years took place, not in London, but in Manchester. The city and its surrounding mill towns provided fertile ground for working-class radicalism to flourish. There was a long tradition of trade unionism in the region, and large textile mills, employing hundreds of people, had given rise to a working-class identity that was separate from their middle-class employers.

Working-class activity in Manchester was exemplified by the march of the Blanketeers in 1817. The Blanketeers were textile workers who intended to march to London to petition the Regent to take steps to improve the cotton trade. A crowd of around 10,000 saw off some 300 marchers from Manchester, but they did not get very far. At Stockport, six miles south of Manchester, the local **yeomanry** arrested many of the marchers and dispersed most of the rest, and the remaining Blanketeers failed to get beyond Macclesfield in Cheshire.

KEY TERM

Yeomanry

Young volunteers recruited from the ranks of middle-class traders and businesses, with no sympathy for radical causes. They lacked effective training, and were unprepared to deal with large gatherings of people.

Radical activity in Manchester continued to fluctuate in line with economic conditions, and the downturn in the textile industry in 1818 gave rise to a sustained campaign of mass meetings and demands for parliamentary reform. Radical activists decided to stage a meeting in Manchester in 1819, and invited Henry Hunt to address the gathering.

The meeting was held on 16 August at Saint Peter's Fields. It attracted some 80,000 men, women and children, perhaps the largest crowd that had ever gathered in Britain. Most came from Manchester itself, but their numbers were swelled by contingents from surrounding towns, including Oldham, Stockport and Ashton-under-Lyne. The careful organisation of the different groups was explained by the radical leader Samuel Bamford in his description of the preparations made in Middleton, a cotton town outside Manchester (Source 3).

SOURCE

3 Samuel Bamford, *Passages from the Life of a Radical*, 1842. Bamford was a prominent leader of local reformers in the town of Middleton, a few miles north of Manchester. His autobiography provides invaluable eyewitness accounts of life in northern towns in the years to 1820.

By eight o'clock on the morning of Monday, the 16th of August, 1819, the whole town of Middleton might be said to be on the alert: some to go to the meeting, and others to see the procession.

First were selected twelve of the most decent-looking youths, who were placed in two rows of six each, with each a branch of laurel held in his hand, as a token of amity and peace; then followed the men of several districts in fives; then the band of music, an excellent one; then the colours of blue... and green... Next were placed the remainder of the men of the districts in fives... Every hundred men had a leader, who was distinguished by a sprig of laurel in his hat... and the whole were to obey the directions of a principal conductor, who took his place at the head of the column, with a bugleman to sound his orders.

Several groups carried banners calling for universal suffrage and annual parliaments. Hunt arrived at the meeting at 1pm, and began to address the crowd. The magistrates, who were watching from a nearby house, issued a warrant for the speaker's arrest, and ordered the Manchester and Salford Yeomanry to ride through the crowd and arrest Hunt.

As they moved towards the hustings where Hunt was speaking, the sheer density of the crowd held up their progress, and this caused the men, and their horses, to panic. Some stones were thrown at the troops, who defended themselves by hacking at the crowd with their sabres. Other forces moved in to disperse the crowd, which rapidly scattered, leaving 11 dead and over 500 injured.

SOURCE

4 This source describes the events that took place at St Peter's Fields in Manchester on 16 August 1819. It is taken from the *Annual Register*, a publication that was first produced in 1758 under the editorship of the Whig politician Edmund Burke. The *Annual Register* was soon established as one of the most authoritative and respected journals in print.

A little before noon on the 16th August, the first body of reformers began to arrive at St. Peter's Field. These persons bore banners, surmounted with caps of liberty, and bearing the inscriptions, 'no corn laws', 'annual parliaments', 'universal suffrage', 'vote by ballot'. Large bodies of reformers continued to arrive from the towns in the neighbourhood of Manchester, all proceeded by flags and many of them in regular marching order. Two clubs of female reformers advanced, one of them numbering more than 150 members. The congregated multitude now amounted to a number roundly computed at 80,000.

At length Mr. Hunt made his appearance, and after a rapturous greeting, mounted a scaffolding and began to harangue his admirers. He had not proceeded far, when the appearance of the yeomanry cavalry excited a panic in the outskirts of the meeting. They entered the enclosure and, after pausing a moment, drew their swords and brandished them fiercely in the air. The multitude gave three cheers to show that they were undaunted by this intrusion, and the orator had just resumed his speech to assure the people that this was only a trick to disturb the meeting, when the cavalry dashed into the crowd, making for the cart on which the speakers were placed. The multitude offered no resistance; they fell back on all sides. The commanding officer then approaching Mr. Hunt, and brandishing his sword, told him that he was his prisoner. Mr. Hunt said he would readily surrender to any civil officer on showing his warrant, and the principal police officer received him in charge.

A cry now arose among the military of, 'have at their flags' and they dashed down not only those in the cart, but the other dispersed in the field; cutting to right and left to get at them. From this moment the yeomanry lost all command of temper; numbers were trampled under the feet of men and horses; many were cut down by sabres; several were slain on the spot. The number of persons injured amounted to between three and four hundred. The populace threw a few stones and brickbats in their retreat, but in less than ten minutes the ground was entirely cleared of its former occupants, and filled by various bodies of military, both horse and foot.

A Level Exam-Style Question Section A

Study Source 4 before you answer this question.

Assess the value of the source for revealing the behaviour of the crowd and the actions taken by the yeomanry.

Explain your answer, using the source, the information given about its origin and your own knowledge about the historical context. (20 marks)

Tip

Check the source for evidence of bias, for example in the choice of words and phrases. Make sure that you use appropriate own knowledge in assessing the overall value of this source.

The events at St Peter's Fields provoked widespread national revulsion, leading to several outbreaks of sporadic rioting and the further growth of political unions. Peterloo, so-called in mocking irony of the Battle of Waterloo in 1815, soon entered national folklore as the symbol of savage repression of working-class people by an authoritarian government. The historian Gash has taken a different view of the events of 16 August, and of the government's policies as a whole. Gash asserted that 'Peterloo was a blunder: it was hardly a massacre', and that 'It was because Peterloo was uncharacteristic that it achieved notoriety'. The responsibility for Peterloo lay not with the government, but with the Manchester magistrates. They had become alarmed at the growing popularity of training and marching by reform groups, and the use of flags and banners gave an increasingly military flavour to protest meetings. The sheer size of the meeting at St Peter's Fields worried them. Had they arrested Hunt before or after the meeting, then deaths and injuries might well have been prevented. As it was, they, and the amateur yeomanry, had all been gripped by a sense of panic.

SOURCE

5 A contemporary cartoon showing the Manchester Yeomanry attacking the crowd at St Peter's Fields, 16 August 1819.

A Level Exam-Style Question Section B

How far do you agree that, in the years 1790–1819, radical protests posed no serious threat to the government? (20 marks)

Tip

Consider those protests that were very serious and those that had little effect. Conclude your answer by reaching an overall judgement on the question.

The extent of the success of extra-parliamentary protest by 1819

After Peterloo, the government moved swiftly to pass a raft of laws aimed at preventing further unrest and disorder. In this respect, they were remarkably successful. There were isolated outbreaks of violence in 1820–21, but for the most part, the 1820s was a period of domestic peace.

The government's response to the radicals

An important reason for the failure of extra-parliamentary pressure to achieve any concrete successes was the determination of successive governments to suppress unrest by any means in their power. Pitt in the 1790s, and Liverpool in the post-war years, relied on local magistrates to maintain order in towns and cities. They used the limited forces at their command, such as the volunteer yeomanry who were deployed with disastrous consequences at Peterloo. They could also call on local regiments where necessary, though in a pre-railway age it was difficult to move large numbers of troops with any speed to potential trouble spots. The vital role played by the magistrates explains the government's actions after Peterloo, when they congratulated the Manchester justices for their prompt action in dispersing the crowd at St Peter's Fields. To have done otherwise would have lost the government much support from the magistrates in the country as a whole.

The government also used a large network of spies, who infiltrated radical organisations and reported back to the Home Office on their activities. Their information enabled the government to take pre-emptive action to deal with unrest. The value of the spy network was shown clearly in the Pentridge Rising of 1817, when the spy, Oliver, played an important role as an agent provocateur, which caused the attempted rising to fail.

Moreover, in the years 1793–1815, Britain was at war with revolutionary and Napoleonic France. It was therefore essential for the government to promote a sense of national unity, and to suppress any internal dissent. Reform was often equated with revolution, which made the task of the radical movement all the more difficult. While radicalism was a powerful force at the time, a number of patriotic and national movements, such as the associations and the volunteers, attracted far more volunteers. Add to this the patriotic and nationalist propaganda that poured out from the press (supported by lavish government funding), and it is clear that the aims of radical protest were almost impossible to achieve.

Thirty years of radical activity and protest, therefore, appeared to have achieved nothing concrete, and in this sense extra-parliamentary protest appeared unsuccessful. None of the specific aims that united radicals, especially their support of some measures of parliamentary reform, had been achieved. This does not mean, however, that radical protest was a complete failure. Much had been achieved in terms of organisation, and in the political education of the working class as a whole. These developments were to have long-term effects, especially in the 1830s and 1840s.

The extent of radical success

In the 1790s, the forces of British radicalism were responsible for the creation of a great national debate, carried on through pamphlets, books and the press, on the meaning of the French Revolution and its significance for British government and politics. Many pamphleteers, from the conservative Burke to the brilliant radical Paine, all used forceful arguments to try to sway public opinion to their way of thinking. The influence exerted by many of them was profound and lasting.

By 1800, popular radicalism had been virtually stamped out. That it did not disappear completely was due to a number of long-term developments.

Educational provisions in the late 18th century were very limited and haphazard: a national system of state education was not established until 1870, and it was left to individuals and local bodies to make educational provisions if they wished. In 1780, Robert Raikes founded a Sunday school in Gloucester. Many parents sent their children to the school, where they were educated to read and write. Raikes' innovation was taken up by many nonconformist groups, especially the Methodists. Recent research estimates that in 1820 some 675,000 children were being educated in day schools, with a further 500,000 attending Sunday schools.

Growing literacy meant that many families were able to access newspapers and pamphlets, and this was reflected in changes in the newspaper industry. The 18th century saw major growth in the number of papers printed annually, rising from one million in 1690 to over 14 million by 1785. Pitt feared that large numbers of literate working-class men would gain access to radical printed propaganda, and thus between 1789 and 1815 the duty on newspapers rose from 1½d to 4d. This did not halt the growth of national and local newspapers, some of which were subsidised by the government. The Tory-supporting *Manchester Herald* had a healthy circulation in Manchester and nearby towns, and the independent but radical *Leeds Mercury* had a circulation of 3,000 by 1800.

The post-war reform movement differed significantly from that which had been active in the 1790s. The early reformers operated through the corresponding societies and political clubs, and spread their message through pamphlets and discussions. Despite the government's concerns, radicals as a whole were interested only in issues such as equal rights and parliamentary reform: they were not prepared to back up their demands by mass action or the use of force. This helps to explain the membership of the early reform movements. The SCI drew much of its support from the middle classes, especially the industrialists and factory owners, and the LCS was backed by the skilled artisans in London and the provinces. Their programmes held little attraction for the mass of the working and agricultural classes.

The reform programmes that developed from 1812 differed from those of the 1790s in both the nature and the extent of their support. Middle-class support remained strong, especially from those whose business activities had suffered during the war; and the skilled and literate working classes maintained their interest in reform. However, the dynamics of radicalism had changed over time. In the 1790s, the unskilled working classes in industrial towns and cities had begun to organise themselves into trade unions until they were suppressed by the Combination Acts of 1799 and 1800. As the French wars drew to a close, interest in reform revived, but workers were to become more interested in political reform. Many Hampden Clubs were established, especially in the northern textile towns, and soon had large and committed memberships. Radicalism of the 1790s had been dominated by people and organisations based in London. This situation was reversed in the post-war years, as northern radicalism, especially in Manchester, took the lead in organising protests.

 THINKING HISTORICALLY Change (8a, b & c) (I)

Imposing realities

The shape of history is imposed by people looking back. People who lived through the 'history' did not always perceive the patterns that later historians identify. For example, some people living through the Industrial Revolution may have understood that great change was taking place, but they would not have been able to understand the massive economic, social and political consequences of industrialisation.

Answer the following:

1 Explain why the conversation in the cartoon above would not have happened.

2 Consider the beginning of the French Revolution and its impact on British politics:

  a) Who would have made the decision as to when the French Revolution would start to influence British politics?

  b) Could anybody have challenged this decision?

  c) Explain why someone living in the 18th century would have been unable to make a judgement about the beginning of a new era.

3 Who living at the present time might regard the French Revolution as an important event?

4 What does this cartoon tell us about the structure of history as we understand it?

Hampden Clubs

Hampden Clubs took their name from a 17th-century MP. John Hampden challenged many of Charles I's actions, which he felt breached constitutional practices. He was one of the five MPs whose attempted arrest by the king in 1642 contributed to the outbreak of the English Civil War.

The failures of British radicalism

Despite its growing importance, post-war radicalism faced two serious problems. Firstly, there were no national figures able or prepared to take up positions of leadership. Cobbett's role was that of a journalist and propagandist, not an active agitator, and the powerful oratory of men such as Henry Hunt was not transformed into political action.

Secondly, post-war reformers faced the classic dilemma of those seeking change in society, one that was to cause problems for the Chartist movement in the 1840s (see Chapter 4, pages 84–105). Reformers were split between those, like Cobbett, who wanted to achieve change through moral force and persuasion, and those who believed that it was only through violence, or physical force, that radicals could achieve their aims. Their difficulties were compounded by the government's determination, as shown in the 1790s, to stand firm against the forces of reform and maintain law and order.

For 30 years, from 1789 onwards, politics and society in Britain were strongly affected by the French Revolution and its aftermath. War with France broke out in 1793 and lasted almost without a break for the next 22 years. French armies undertook to export the principles of freedom and equality to other countries in Europe, and Britain was not immune to the attractions of *liberté*, *égalité* and *fraternité*. In the years 1790–99, radicalism was largely the preserve of the middle classes. Even some Whigs jumped on the reform bandwagon with the formation of the Friends of the People, an aristocratic, exclusive and short-lived organisation that called for parliamentary reform.

From 1810, the reform climate changed in both nature and extent. Radicals were better organised than before, and the ideas of reform were supported by people drawn from all social classes. Most organisations still aimed for parliamentary reform, but some, notably the Spenceans, aimed at the revolutionary seizure of the state.

The economic difficulties of the post-war years were overcome, and gave way to stability and growth in the years to 1830. Although political agitation had calmed down after Peterloo, radicalism remained as a powerful influence, especially among the working classes; it was to reappear with dramatic effect through the activities of the Chartist movement of the 1830s and 1840s.

ACTIVITY
KNOWLEDGE CHECK

Changes in British radicalism, 1790–1819

1 On a sheet of A3 paper, write down a list of all the main radical protests in the years 1790–1819.

2 Highlight the ways in which the nature of these protests changed over time. Consider matters such as organisation, aims and leadership.

3 Write down ways in which British radicalism changed overall in these years. Here, you should consider matters such as the influence of printed materials, the geographical reach of radicalism, for example the gradual change from London-based organisations to regional ones, and the strength of radical leadership.

4 Work out the differences between extra-parliamentary radicalism in 1790 and that in 1819. What conclusions can you draw?

HOW EFFECTIVE WAS THE GOVERNMENT'S RESPONSE TO PROTEST IN THE YEARS TO 1819?

Late 18th-century governments had very few weapons at their disposal to counter the growth of radicalism in Britain. There was no organised police force to maintain order in the towns and, in a pre-railway age, it was difficult to move numbers of troops with any speed to potential trouble spots. The government resorted to the use of spies, who infiltrated the corresponding societies and reported back to ministers on their activities. They also relied on local magistrates to control the towns and to enforce a number of laws passed by Pitt's government in the 1790s. Their role increased in importance from 1793, when Britain went to war against revolutionary France. Thereafter, it was even more essential to suppress radical activities and to promote a spirit of national loyalty and patriotism.

The trial of the leaders of the LCS and the suspension of habeas corpus, 1794

A royal proclamation of 1792 against **seditious writings** was followed by more direct actions against reformers. In 1793, the LCS and the revived SCI sent delegates to a meeting in Edinburgh to agree on the calling of a national reform convention with the sole intention of pressing for parliamentary reform. The government saw the meeting as potentially subversive, sent in troops and arrested several of the delegates.

> **KEY TERM**
>
> Seditious writing
> Writing or speeches designed to promote rebellions against the government or the monarchy. The term 'sedition' was first used in Elizabeth I's reign.

Despite this setback, the reform societies regrouped, and early in 1794 announced the calling of a national reform convention. Their timing was unfortunate. Britain had been at war with France since 1793, and there was very little sympathy for reformers who appeared to be dividing the nation at a critical time. Armed with information provided by their network of spies, the government arrested several leaders of the LCS and SCI, and charged them with high **treason**. At the same time, parliament, prompted by Pitt, suspended habeas corpus. This action allowed the government time to interview the accused and prepare a case against them.

> **KEY TERM**
>
> Treason
> The Treason Act had been passed in 1351 during the reign of Edward III. It defined high treason in very narrow terms: aiming to kill the king; waging civil war; and supporting the king's enemies at home or abroad.

The government had become deeply concerned at the growth of the LCS. Although at its height it had no more than 5,000 members, its reform message was reaching a large and sympathetic audience. Pitt overestimated the size and the power of the LCS. The society kept its meetings deliberately small to encourage the involvement of every member, so more groups were formed as its membership grew. The government was convinced that the organisation was expanding rapidly, especially as Hardy had declared that its membership would be unlimited. It is no wonder that Pitt believed that the LCS posed a threat to the very existence of the state.

The trials of the accused took place towards the end of 1794. Despite the lengthy pre-trial examination of the defendants, the government was unable to present a convincing case to the courts. In order to support the charge of high treason, the prosecution claimed that the LCS was planning the assassination of George III. Evidence produced to support this claim was flimsy and largely invented. The jury refused to accept the evidence and, after lengthy trials, acquitted all the defendants.

The events of 1794 showed just how seriously the government, and Pitt in particular, took the threat of domestic unrest and opposition. In 1785, Pitt had proposed some limited measures of parliamentary reform, but revolution and the French war convinced him of the necessity to maintain stability at home, even if it meant imposing substantial limits on personal freedom. Although the LCS trials did not lead to any convictions, they had served their purpose for the government. Most of the LCS leadership, including Hardy, withdrew from radical politics. For the rest of the 1790s, Pitt's government continued to harass radical movements, and was prepared to change existing laws to achieve its purpose.

Treason Act 1795 and the Seditious Meetings Act 1795

The year 1795 was a time of war, distress and growing unrest. The French war had dislocated Britain's overseas trade, leading to rapidly rising unemployment in industrial towns. These difficulties were compounded by poor harvests and the inevitable rise in food prices. When stones were thrown at George III's coach, the government used the event as a pretext to take strong action.

The failure of the 1794 treason trials had persuaded ministers to amend the treason law in order to strengthen their powers against radicalism.

The existing laws against treason made it impossible to convict the LCS leaders, and the government decided to extend the definition of treason to go beyond simply treasonable actions. The Treason Act 1795 made it an offence to kill, or even to harm, the king. More ominously for reformers, treason was also defined as any intention 'to intimidate or overawe either Houses or either House of Parliament'. This meant that anybody outside parliament who called for parliamentary reform could be charged with treason.

The Treason Act was accompanied by the Seditious Meetings Act, passed in the same year. The Act restricted the size of public meetings to 50 people, unless they were approved in advance by the magistrates. Large outdoor meetings of thousands of people had been taking place in the early 1790s, but these were now effectively banned.

SOURCE

6

A contemporary anonymous cartoon illustrating the effects of the Treason and Sedition Acts of 1795. The effects of the Acts are shown by the padlock on the mouth labelled 'No Grumbling'. The man's hands are tied and he is holding a paper inscribed 'Freedom of the Press: Transportation'. The tumbledown house and the debtors' prison are comments on the prevailing state of the economy.

Some historians have seen the 1790s as a decade of repression imposed by Pitt's government, in alliance with the magistrates. It is difficult to see what other course was open to him. At a time of heightened national crisis, the government had no choice but to maintain order in Britain and to suppress those revolutionary principles that were being spread by the armies they were fighting. Although the government did employ spies and informers against the reform movement, it used parliament and the law at all times rather than resorting to openly unconstitutional activity.

Pitt's policies served their purpose. Radical activity rapidly diminished, and was supplanted for many years by the development of patriotic feeling as a result of the long years of war against France. In such an environment, there was little support for reforming ideas, which carried with them more than a whiff of treachery. Leading radicals were silenced or had escaped

abroad. Between 1792 and 1802, Tom Paine lived in France, where he continued to produce reformist pamphlets. His *Age of Reason*, published between 1794 and 1797, attacked the errors and corruption of the Christian churches, and promoted the ideas and values of natural religion, or deism. His ideas found little favour with his target audiences in Britain and France, or in the USA, where he spent the last years of his life.

ACTIVITY
KNOWLEDGE CHECK

Cartoons and satire
Choose one of the three cartoons in this chapter (Source 1, page 66, Source 5, page 70 or Source 6, opposite).

1 What message is the cartoonist trying to convey to the viewer of each cartoon?

2 How effective are the techniques of persuasion that are adopted?

3 Does the evidence of these cartoons suggest that contemporary cartoons are a useful source for historians?

The Gagging Acts, 1817

In 1815, after 22 years of almost constant conflict, the wars with France came to an end. British forces had achieved a great victory, and Britain had emerged as the leading power in Europe. However, peace abroad was not accompanied by peace at home, and in the years to 1819, Lord Liverpool's government faced a number of serious challenges to its authority.

The return of peace did not lead to an immediate improvement in the country's economy. Harvests were poor and, after a brief post-war boom, the economy fell into depression. Rising unemployment was made worse by the speedy demobilisation of 300,000 troops. The government did little to alleviate distress, clinging to the laissez-faire belief that the economy would revive in time, without the need for government intervention.

Radical activities in the years 1815–17 led ministers to believe in the existence of a broad national revolutionary conspiracy. The work of the Hampden Clubs, the Spenceans' hare-brained attempt at revolution at Spa Fields, the attack on the Prince Regent, and the Blanketeers all seemed to be a linked series of events that would lead to a general insurrection. Their view was reinforced by the information fed to the Home Secretary by the government's own spy network. In the aftermath of Spa Fields, therefore, the government decided to take firm action.

During 1817, Liverpool's government passed three measures designed to combat radical activity. The Treason Act 1795 was due to lapse on the death of George III, but the attacks on the Regent persuaded parliament to make the Act a permanent measure. Habeas corpus was suspended for all those suspected of treasonable activities. This measure gave ministers time to prepare a case against radicals, but it also took leading radicals such as Samuel Bamford out of circulation for several months before they were released without charge.

The Seditious Meetings Act 1817 built on the terms of the 1795 measure. Justices of the Peace were given the power to attend any public meeting, and could disperse it if they considered it to be an unlawful assembly. Societies and organisations whose members were required to swear a secret oath were banned outright. The government demonstrated its fear of the Spenceans by suppressing all Spencean clubs by name.

Like the 1795 Acts, the 1817 measures quickly became known as the 'Gagging Acts'. They succeeded in their aim of quelling unrest in the short term, especially in London. When most of their terms lapsed in 1818, radical activities simply sprang up once more.

The Six Acts, 1819

The most important post-war meeting was that held at St Peter's Fields in Manchester in August 1819. Peterloo appeared to the government to be a well-organised and threatening action, especially because of the discipline of the crowds, who had marched to the meeting with almost military efficiency. The government was determined to restore and maintain order. Parliament met at the end of 1819 to consider proposals from Lord Sidmouth, the Home Secretary, aimed at preventing similar disturbances in the future. By the end of the year, the so-called 'Six Acts' had all passed into law.

One of the most important of the Acts was the Unlawful Drilling Act. Many of those who attended at Peterloo were known to have been practising marching and drilling on the moors outside Manchester for many months. In his memoirs, Samuel Bamford suggested that there was nothing sinister in these activities, but that the organisers of the meeting wanted to disarm their critics by a show of 'cleanliness, sobriety and decorum'. The government took a different view, believing that the frequent practising of marches could be seen as training for a future insurrection. The Act banned unlawful military-style drilling, with the harsh penalty of transportation imposed on any lawbreakers. The Act was accompanied by the Seizure of Arms Act, which empowered magistrates to enter any property where they suspected arms were being stored; and the Misdemeanours Act reduced the ability of any arrested person from being granted bail.

Liverpool's government wanted to prevent any further huge radical demonstrations on the scale of Peterloo. The Seditious Meetings Prevention Act revived the terms of the 1795 and 1817 Acts, many of which had been allowed to lapse. Public meetings were once again limited to 50 people, and could be conducted at the level of the parish only. This measure was a significant attempt to curtail individual freedom, and was strongly opposed by the Whig opposition. It was eventually repealed in 1824.

The government knew that radicalism was strongly underpinned and influenced by its own press. The Criminal Libel Act 1819, which proved to be ineffective in operation, introduced the penalty of transportation for libellous writings. More important was the Newspapers and Stamp Duties Act 1819. The number of publications that had to pay the stamp duty was extended, and the amount to be paid was increased substantially. The effect of this measure was to reduce the number of newspapers and pamphlets that could be published profitably.

The government acknowledged how seriously they viewed the radical threat to national stability: the preamble to the Acts declared that 'every meeting for radical reform is an overt act of treasonable conspiracy against the king and his government'. The Six Acts had the desired effect. Calm was soon restored, there would not be another Peterloo, and the crisis years of 1812–19 would not be repeated. The Acts were vigorously condemned by many contemporaries, but the verdict of historians has been divided. While some historians have criticised the Tory governments of the time for their apparently repressive policies, others have noted that ministers had few weapons at their command to keep order in the country. Historian R.J. White wrote extensively on the years 1815–19. He pointed out that the government was attempting to maintain law and order with only a few weapons at its disposal. He described how little had changed in the way of peacekeeping forces since 1588. There was a small official police force in London but outside London any peacekeeping force was voluntary and amateur, and depended on the interest and public spirit of the landed gentry. In Regency England there was a great deal of disorder, but with this ad hoc 'policing' it is surprising the disorder was a not a lot worse.

A Level Exam-Style Question Section B

'In the years 1790–1819, British radicalism failed to achieve its objectives because the power of the state was too strong.'

How far do you agree with this statement? (20 marks)

Tip
Your answer should consider two distinct points: the power of the state and the weaknesses of British radicalism.

ACTIVITY
KNOWLEDGE CHECK

Government responses to protest
Study the Gagging Acts of 1817 and the Six Acts of 1819.

1 Draw up a balance sheet that includes all the Acts by name, and list ways in which the Acts dealt with radical activities.

2 Does your balance sheet suggest that the government was only acting to maintain law and order?

3 What measures might the government have taken to deal with distress?

WHAT WAS THE IMPACT OF THE RADICAL REFORMERS THEMSELVES?

The influence of Thomas Paine (1737–1809) and the *Rights of Man*

Paine was one of the most influential and colourful radicals of the 18th century. He welcomed the French Revolution of 1789, hoping that it would lead to a democratic system of government for France. He strongly opposed the conservative ideas put forward by Edmund Burke in *Reflections on the Revolution in France*, published in 1790, and issued a reply in the form of the *Rights of Man* (1791–92).

EXTEND YOUR KNOWLEDGE

Edmund Burke (1729–97)

Burke's *Reflections* were a powerful denunciation, not only of the French revolutionaries, but also of radical ideas that had been developing in Britain for many years. He attacked the speed of change in France, where reformers were attempting to sweep away the absolute monarchy of the Bourbons and introduce a constitutional monarchy within just a few months. Burke believed that radical and rapid change would only lead to disaster.

Burke's most important contribution to the debate on the French Revolution came with his thoughts on human rights and democracy. Reformers believed that individuals acquired human rights at the time of their birth, and that they were not granted as a gift from the government. Burke challenged this idea, insisting that civil and political rights could only be enshrined by law. Burke also feared democracy, referring to 'the swinish multitude' who could not be trusted to have any rational involvement in politics.

Burke's open opposition to the French Revolution sparked a period of vigorous debate between his supporters and opponents. The most significant response, and one that caught the public imagination, was made by Paine. Unlike other pamphleteers, Paine wrote in a style that was accessible to most people, not simply the educated elite. His *Rights of Man* (published in two parts in 1791–92) was the most successful attempt to counter Burke's arguments, and reached a large audience in both Britain and France. The historian Evans acknowledges the importance of Paine's work, writing that 'the publication of his *Rights of Man* is perhaps the single most important event in the history of British radicalism'.

EXTEND YOUR KNOWLEDGE

Thomas Paine (1737–1809)

Born in Norfolk in 1737, Paine emigrated to North America in 1774. In 1776, he published *Common Sense*, a hugely influential pamphlet that made a convincing case for American independence from Britain, and for the establishment of a republican and democratic system of government for the 13 colonies. He returned to England in 1787, and in 1791-92 published several versions of the *Rights of Man*, which became an immediate bestseller. He fled to France to escape prosecution in 1792, and returned to the USA in 1802, where he died in poverty in 1809. In 1964, American supporters presented a gilded statue of Paine to his home town of Thetford in Norfolk.

In Part 1 of the *Rights of Man*, Paine rejected Burke's claim that civil and political rights were created by governments. He argued that rights bestowed by governments could also be removed, making a mockery of the idea of fundamental and inalienable rights. Instead, he declared that, since all men were born equal in the sight of God, they must therefore be endowed with the same human and political rights. Any system of government that was based on hereditary rule, such as the monarchy and the House of Lords, was thus unnatural and contrary to the rights of man. For Paine, government depended not on divine or hereditary right, but on the consent of all men equally.

SOURCE

7

From the conclusion to the *Rights of Man*, Part 1, by Thomas Paine, published in 1791. Here, Paine is arguing against the principle of hereditary government, and makes a case for complete political equality based on the rule of law.

When men are spoken of as kings and subjects, or when Government is mentioned under the heads of monarchy, aristocracy, and democracy, what is it that man is to understand by the terms? As there is but one species of man, there can be but one element of human power; and that element is man himself. Monarchy, aristocracy, and democracy, are but creatures of imagination.

From the Revolutions of America and France... it is evident that the opinion of the world is changing with respect to systems of Government... All the old governments have received a shock from the revolutions that have already appeared.

When we survey the wretched condition of man, under the monarchical and hereditary systems of Government, dragged from his home by one power, and impoverished by taxes more than by enemies, it becomes evident that those systems are bad, and that a general revolution in the principle and construction of Governments is necessary.

What is government more than the management of the affairs of a Nation? It is not, and cannot be, the property of any man or family, but of the whole community, at whose expense it is supported. Sovereignty, as a matter of right, appertains to the Nation only, and not to any individual; and a Nation has at all times an inherent right to abolish any form of Government it finds inconvenient, and to establish such as accords with its interest and happiness. Every citizen is a member of the Sovereignty, and, as such, can acknowledge no personal subjection; and his obedience can be only to the laws.

As it is not difficult to perceive, from the enlightened state of mankind, that hereditary Governments are verging to their decline, and that Revolutions are making their way in Europe, it would be an act of wisdom to anticipate their approach. From what we now see, nothing of reform in the political world ought to be held improbable. It is an age of Revolutions, in which everything may be looked for.

A Level Exam-Style Question Section A

Study Source 7 before you answer this question.

Assess the value of the source for revealing radical arguments against hereditary systems of government and in favour of popular revolutions.

Explain your answer, using the source, the information given about its origin and your own knowledge about the historical context. (20 marks)

Tip
Comment on the use of language and the techniques of persuasion that Paine uses.

Arguments such as these were easy to understand, and explain the success of Paine's writings. Equally straightforward was his proposal for a wholesale reform of the British system of government, with the establishment of a republic in which all adult males would have the vote. Government would thus be carried out in the interests of all, not just of a privileged elite.

In Part 2 of the *Rights of Man*, Paine outlined a comprehensive plan for the practical application of his theories to British government and society. Among his proposals were: the creation of a national democratic assembly; the abolition of the aristocracy and its titles; the establishment of a national system of education; a reduction in taxes on the poor; and a progressive tax to be levied on all land. In many ways, these ideas were more revolutionary than those being promoted across the English Channel.

The government did not take action against Paine over the publication of Part 1 of the *Rights of Man*, even though it reached a wide audience: in the three years after its publication it sold some 200,000 copies. Ministers were concerned, however, that the price of Part 2 was within the reach of most people, and decided to suppress its incendiary message. In 1792, a royal proclamation was issued against 'divers [*sic*] wicked and seditious writings which have been printed, published and industriously dispersed'. Many saw the proclamation as aimed directly at Paine, who wisely decided to leave Britain for France.

SOURCE
8 A 1792 print of Thomas Paine displaying his 'Rights of Man', surrounded by injustices and standing on labels representing morals and justices, defending measures taken in revolutionary France and appealing to the English to overthrow their monarchy and organise a republic.

Wha WANTS ME

I am Ready & Willing to offer my Services to any Nation or People under heaven who are Desirous of Liberty & Equality

Vide Paines Letter to the Convention

Mary Wollstonecraft (1759–97)

Wollstonecraft was the author of *A Vindication of the Rights of Men*, written in 1790 as the first counterblast to Burke's *Reflections*. She argued that Burke's support of tradition could be used to justify the continued subjection of women and children. She promoted individual rights and the importance of the family as the foundation of society.

Wollstonecraft's writings reached a wide audience, and her *Vindication of the Rights of Women* became a founding tract for the later development of groups supporting female suffrage and of women's rights as a whole.

John Cartwright and the Hampden Clubs

With the suppression of the LCS and similar organisations, British radicalism had lost its sole national organisation. It proved difficult to fill the gap in the early 1800s. Enthusiasm for parliamentary reform had abated, and parliament was never likely even to consider issues of reform as long as the French war continued. Leaderless, and without direction, British radicalism was virtually extinguished for the early years of the 19th century.

From 1812, new life was breathed into the reform movement from an unlikely source. Major John Cartwright, who was in his early seventies, possessed radical credentials stretching back to the 1770s, when he published his first pamphlet calling for universal suffrage. In 1812, he formed the Hampden Club in London, named after John Hampden, one of the leading opponents of Charles I in the English Civil War. The club was an exclusive affair: its high annual subscription of two guineas (£2.10) limited its membership to a very small number of middle-class and aristocratic men.

After 1812, Cartwright toured the industrial districts in the north and the Midlands, where he saw first hand the widespread poverty and poor living conditions that existed in the cotton towns. He became convinced that the only remedy for social ills was parliamentary reform, and from 1816 encouraged the creation of regional Hampden Clubs. These were different from the London club. Membership was open to all who could pay a weekly subscription of one penny, and frequent meetings took place to discuss national news and to debate political issues. In many ways, the Hampden Clubs filled the gap left by the demise of the LCS, which had been disbanded in 1794 and formally outlawed by the government in 1799.

SOURCE

9

From *Passages in the Life of a Radical*, by Samuel Bamford, 1842. The activities of the Hampden Clubs were described by Samuel Bamford in glowing terms in his memoirs published in 1842. He suggests that the clubs gave an outlet to young men who might otherwise be inclined to riots and disorder, and promoted political education for all.

Instead of riots and destruction of property, Hampden clubs were now established in many of our large towns, and the villages and districts around them; Cobbett's books were printed in a cheap form; the labourers read them, and thenceforward became deliberate and systematic in their proceedings. Nor were there wanting men of their own class, to encourage and direct the new converts; the Sunday Schools of the preceding thirty years, had produced many working men of sufficient talent to become readers, writers, and speakers in the village meetings for parliamentary reform; some also were found to possess a rude poetic talent, which rendered their effusions popular, and bestowed an additional charm on their assemblages: and by such various means, anxious listeners at first, and then zealous proselytes, were drawn from the cottages of quiet nooks and dingles, to the weekly readings and discussions of the Hampden clubs.

One of these clubs was established in 1816, at the small town of Middleton, near Manchester; and I, having been instrumental in its formation; a tolerable reader also, and a rather expert writer, was chosen secretary. The club prospered; the number of members increased; the funds raised by contributions of a penny a week became more than sufficient for all outgoings; and taking a bold step, we soon rented a chapel which had been given up by a society of Methodists.

The rapid growth in the popularity of the regional Hampden Clubs persuaded Cartwright and others to invite local delegates to a plenary meeting in London in 1817 to settle matters of policy. They agreed on universal suffrage and annual parliaments, and approved a broad strategy of petitioning parliament to introduce reforms.

Although the Hampden Clubs worked strictly within the law, following Cartwright's maxim to 'hold fast by the laws', local authorities were not convinced of the clubs' peaceful intentions. Many local authorities used any excuse, or none, to arrest political reformers. Magistrates in Manchester and the surrounding towns employed spies who attended club meetings and filed reports, which usually exaggerated the threat posed by the radicals. Acting on these reports, magistrates arrested club members, charging them with attending seditious meetings. Bamford and other local leaders were arrested in 1817, sent to prison in London, only to be released without charge some months later. Actions such as these, by local and national officials, meant that the Hampden Clubs were unable to act effectively after 1817.

William Cobbett and the *Political Register*

Cobbett was born at Farnham in Surrey in 1763. He moved to the USA in 1792, where he soon gained a reputation as a skilled journalist. He wrote many pamphlets against the French wars that were widely circulated in the USA and Britain. In 1800, Cobbett returned to England, where the government offered him some lucrative opportunities as a journalist, but he turned these down because he preferred to maintain his independence. He established *Cobbett's Political Register*, which soon became one of the leading independent sources of impartial news: by 1805, the *Register* had a circulation of 4,000.

From 1806, Cobbett became increasingly radical in outlook. In that year he stood for parliament in Honiton, but was not elected. The experience brought home to him just how corrupt the British electoral system was, and thereafter he began to promote the cause of parliamentary reform.

In 1809, some soldiers stationed at Ely in Cambridgeshire mutinied because they had not been paid. They were court-martialled and five ringleaders were sentenced to 500 lashes each. Cobbett published a number of articles in successive editions of the *Register*, which vigorously denounced this cruel and inhuman punishment. The government used Cobbett's articles against him. In 1810, he was tried for seditious libel against the armed forces and was sentenced to two years' imprisonment. He took up journalism once again on his release in 1812, and the *Political Register* continued to flourish.

In 1816, Cobbett decided to reach a much wider audience. The *Political Register* was a very popular journal, but its cost of one shilling, which included the newspaper tax, placed it beyond the means of working-class readers, who had to club together to purchase a copy. Cobbett decided to issue a single sheet of the *Register* for just two pence, which meant that the paper would not have to pay the high newspaper duty set by the government. The first edition of the new publication, *To the Journeymen and Labourers of England, Wales, Scotland and Ireland*, was a huge success, and by the end of 1817, 200,000 copies had been printed and circulated. Cobbett's opponents labelled the new venture the '*two-penny trash*', a description that Cobbett was happy to employ.

SOURCE 10

From the first edition of the two-pence edition of the *Political Register*, entitled *To the Journeymen and Labourers of England, Wales, Scotland and Ireland*, November 1816. Here, Cobbett suggests that the working people of Britain alone were responsible for its great wealth and power. After making a powerful attack on high taxation, Cobbett urged his readers to support the causes of parliamentary reform and universal male suffrage.

FRIENDS AND FELLOW COUNTRYMEN.

Whatever the pride of rank, of riches, or of scholarship may have induced some men to believe, the real strength and all the resources of a country ever have sprung from the labour of its people; and hence it is, that this nation, which is so small in numbers and so poor in climate and soil has, for many ages, been the most powerful nation in the world. Elegant dresses, superb furniture, fine roads and canals, warehouses teeming with goods; all these are so many marks of national wealth and resources. But all these spring from labour. Without the journeymen and the labourer none of them could exist. [Cobbett went on to suggest that the impact of war was the main reason for high taxation and the cost of goods and food.]

We have seen that the cause of our miseries is the burden of taxes, occasioned by wars, by standing armies, etc. The remedy is what we have now to look to, and that remedy consists wholly and solely of such a reform in the Commons House of Parliament, as shall give to every payer of direct taxes a vote at elections, and as shall cause the Members to be elected annually.

You should neglect no opportunity of doing all that is within your power to give support to the cause of Reform. Petition is the channel for your sentiments, and there is no village so small that its petition would not have some weight. You ought to attend at every public meeting within your reach. You ought to read to, and to assist each other in coming at a competent knowledge of all public matters. Above all things, you ought to be unanimous in your object, and not to suffer yourselves to be divided.

SOURCE 11

Cobbett's influence was summed up by Samuel Bamford in his memoirs, *Passages in the Life of a Radical*, published in 1842. After noting the unrest and distress of the years 1815–16, Bamford wrote the following.

At this time the writings of William Cobbett suddenly became of great authority; they were read on nearly every cottage hearth in the manufacturing districts of South Lancashire, in those of Leicester, Derby, and Nottingham; also in many of the Scottish manufacturing towns. Their influence was speedily visible. He directed his readers to the true cause of their sufferings – misgovernment; and to its proper corrective – parliamentary reform.

ACTIVITY
KNOWLEDGE CHECK

Bamford's view

1 Samuel Bamford's memoirs are an important source for historians of this period, especially his eyewitness description of events. Study Sources 3, 9 and 11. What can you learn from these three sources about the:

   a) St Peter's Fields meeting

   b) importance of the Hampden Clubs

   c) role of William Cobbett?

The role of Henry Hunt (1773–1835) as a radical orator

In the years 1800–20, William Cobbett was the most influential radical journalist in Britain. His writings reached a very wide national audience, and he did much to spread radical ideas among the British working class. When Cobbett first produced his two-penny register in 1816, Henry Hunt was coming to the forefront of radical politics, using his remarkable powers of oratory in addressing meetings throughout the country.

Hunt was a gentleman farmer from Wiltshire. In the years to 1800, he supported the political and social outlook of men of his class, giving unqualified support to Pitt's domestic and foreign policies. His attitudes changed dramatically in 1799–1800, when he was imprisoned for a time for defying the orders of the commander of his local militia. While in prison he came into contact with some radicals who had been imprisoned for political activities. These men and their ideas had a profound influence on Hunt; he later wrote in his memoirs that his prison term was responsible for converting him wholeheartedly to the radical cause.

By 1810, Hunt had begun to gain a reputation as a brilliant orator, making powerful speeches at election meetings throughout the West Country. He failed in his bid to be elected for Bristol in 1812, and moved to London the following year. By 1815, he had established himself as one of the most important leaders of British radicalism, thanks in part to his many speeches opposing property taxes and the Corn Law of 1815.

Hunt's influence was seen most clearly at the Spa Fields meeting in November 1816. Hitherto prominent radicals, including Cartwright and Cobbett, had given their support to household suffrage as one of their main aims. At Spa Fields, Hunt proposed universal suffrage for the first time at a mass meeting. He noted in his memoirs that the effect of his speech was electrifying (Source 12).

SOURCE 12

From the memoirs of Henry Hunt, 1820–22. Hunt was imprisoned in 1820 for his part in Peterloo. While in jail he wrote three volumes of autobiography, which were published in monthly instalments.

When the day arrived [of the first Spa Fields meeting] I proposed the resolutions and the petition to his Royal Highness the Prince. The resolutions proposed by me, and unanimously passed by the most numerous meeting ever held in this country, avowed the principle of UNIVERSAL SUFFRAGE. This was the first time that universal suffrage was petitioned for at a public meeting, and I shall ever feel a pride in the reflection of being the first man who publicly proposed this measure.

The reformers of the north, south, east, and west, became instantly alive to the appeal that was made to them in the resolutions passed at Spa Fields, public meetings were held, and petitions to the House of Commons were signed, all praying for universal suffrage.

In 1819, Hunt accepted an invitation to address the mass meeting planned for 16 August at St Peter's Fields in Manchester. He insisted that the meeting would be peaceful and tightly organised. Hunt intended to urge the meeting to refuse to pay taxes, and to secure parliamentary reform by the use of 'numerical force' (a deliberately vague expression). The magistrates feared that Hunt's ability to influence public meetings would lead to violence, and sent in the Manchester Yeomanry to arrest him. He was charged with promoting a seditious conspiracy, and in 1820 he was jailed for two and a half years.

Much of the credit for the growth of British radicalism in the early 19th century must go to both Cobbett and Hunt. Cobbett was able to articulate very effectively working-class grievances and aspirations through the medium of print, but from 1815 it was Hunt who was seen as the champion of the people and of their interests. His trademark white top hat made him instantly recognisable at public meetings, and his powerful championing of radical causes brought him national popularity. Hunt's advocacy of universal suffrage inspired working people throughout the country, and was a vital factor in sustaining British radicalism in the first half of the 19th century.

ACTIVITY
KNOWLEDGE CHECK

Radical reformers' contributions

Each of the reformers mentioned in this section made different contributions to British radicalism in the years 1790–1819.

1 Draw up a table as shown below.

Radical reformer	Contribution	Significance
Thomas Paine		
John Cartwright		
William Cobbett		
Henry Hunt		

2 Describe the contribution each made to the radical movement, and then evaluate their significance.

3 In your opinion, which of the four reformers made the most important contribution to British radicalism in this period? Explain your answer briefly.

ACTIVITY
SUMMARY

The geography of discontent, 1790–1819

For this activity, you will need a map of England, some pins and a number of small pieces of card.

1 On the map, pin and label areas of radical activity, with relevant dates.

2 What can you learn about the changing geography of radical protests in the years 1790–1819?

3 How can you best explain the change?

WIDER READING

Behagg, C. *Labour and Reform: Working-Class Movements, 1815-1914*, Hodder (1991)

Brown, R. *Revolution, Radicalism and Reform, 1780-1846*, Cambridge (2000)

Gash, N. *Aristocracy and People, 1815-65*, Arnold (1979)

Ingram, R. *The Life and Adventures of William Cobbett*, Harper (2006)

Lawson, P. 'Reassessing Peterloo', *History Today* (1988)

Plowright, J. 'Lord Liverpool and alternatives to "repression" in Regency England', *History Review* (1997)

White, R.J. *Waterloo to Peterloo*, Penguin (1968)

3.4 Chartism, c1838–c1850

KEY QUESTIONS

- How far had the Chartists achieved their aims by 1850?
- To what extent did Chartist support change in the years c1838–50?
- How effective was the government's response to the Chartist challenge?

INTRODUCTION

The struggle for reform in the years after 1815 had collapsed in the aftermath of the bloodshed of Peterloo. Working-class radicalism did not disappear completely in the 1820s, but it lacked direction without the leadership of men such as Hunt and the Spenceans. There was a brief revival during the reform struggle of 1830–32, but working people were disillusioned by its outcome. They became even more radicalised by the legislation passed by the Whig government in the 1830s, especially the despised Poor Law Amendment Act 1834.

By the mid-1830s, a number of organisations had come into being, seeking further and more far-reaching parliamentary reform. Three groups, the London Working Men's Association (LWMA), the Birmingham Political Union (BPU), and the Great Northern Union, came together in 1838 with the aim of creating a national petition in support of the Six Points of the People's Charter, which had been drawn up by William Lovett of the LWMA. Over the next ten years, Chartists arranged mass demonstrations and organised three petitions, signed by millions of men and women, which were presented to parliament. Each petition was overwhelmingly rejected by the House of Commons.

Support for the Chartist movement fluctuated considerably in the years 1838–48. It was very popular in times of economic hardship and high unemployment, when its numbers swelled dramatically. Although it was hard to sustain such enthusiasm, Chartism continued to enjoy broad support among working-class radicals, though it never succeeded in attracting to its ranks the most highly skilled workers or farm workers in rural counties. Many women supported Chartism, even though it would not embrace female suffrage. They were very active in the early years, especially in activities such as supporting imprisoned Chartists and their families. However, the numbers of supporting women declined from the early 1840s, as they transferred their support to other activities, notably teetotalism and educational activities. Although a number of middle-class people joined Chartism in its early years, many were soon alienated by the violent and threatening language of a number of its speakers. As a result, a large number of middle-class supporters had left the movement by 1839.

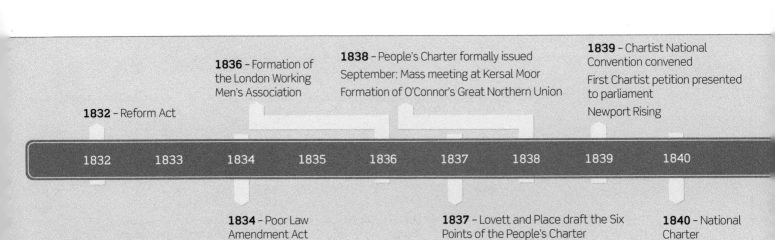

1836 – Formation of the London Working Men's Association

1838 – People's Charter formally issued
September: Mass meeting at Kersal Moor
Formation of O'Connor's Great Northern Union

1839 – Chartist National Convention convened
First Chartist petition presented to parliament
Newport Rising

1832 – Reform Act

| 1832 | 1833 | 1834 | 1835 | 1836 | 1837 | 1838 | 1839 | 1840 |

1834 – Poor Law Amendment Act

1837 – Lovett and Place draft the Six Points of the People's Charter
Revival of the Birmingham Political Union

1840 – National Charter Association established

An important reason for the failure of Chartism was the determination of Whig and Tory governments to resist radical demands and oppose Chartist violence by any means at their disposal. After the founding of the Metropolitan Police in London in 1829, similar police forces were created in other parts of the country from 1839, and these were supported by armed forces wherever they were required. Major General Napier was a key figure in countering the Chartists: his leadership of the Northern District in 1839–40 was both measured and non-confrontational, although he worked to suppress Chartist riots. Moreover, the economy began to revive from 1842, with a consequent reduction in both unemployment and distress.

HOW FAR HAD THE CHARTISTS ACHIEVED THEIR AIMS BY 1850?

What factors led to the emergence of the Chartist movement in the 1830s?

In August 1838, the Six Points of the People's Charter were approved at a meeting of leading radicals in Birmingham. The Charter was concerned only with political reform, which was to be achieved by:

- universal male suffrage
- the secret ballot
- constituencies of equal size
- the abolition of property qualifications for MPs
- annual parliaments
- payment of MPs.

These proposals were not new: most of the points had been championed in one way or another for many years. Indeed, schemes promoting universal suffrage and short parliaments can be traced back to the 'Head of the Proposals' of 1647, when army leaders met to discuss how the country should be governed after the Civil War of the 1640s. The French Revolution and post-war distress had revived interest in constitutional and political reform, though the debate was silenced by Peterloo, the Six Acts, and the economic revival of the 1820s.

Working-class interest in reform was revived in the late 1820s. Middle-class organisations such as the BPU gained widespread working-class support, and were instrumental in securing the passage of the Reform Act 1832. Working-class radicals and trade unionists had high hopes for reform, but their expectations were to be unfulfilled. Not only were they excluded from the franchise, but they were deeply opposed to what they regarded as a sustained assault by the Whig government on their rights and privileges. For many, the Whigs seemed even more repressive than Liverpool's government of the post-war years. Disillusion with the Reform Act, and with the Whig government after 1832, pushed many working people towards radical politics.

1845 – O'Connor establishes the Chartist Land Plan

1847–48 – Economic depression

1858 – Final Chartist Convention meets

| 1841 | 1842 | 1845 | 1846 | 1847 | 1848 | 1858 |

1842 – Formation of Complete Suffrage Union

Second Chartist petition presented to parliament

Plug Plot riots

1846 – Estates purchased for Chartist settlement

Repeal of the Corn Laws leads to a reduction in food prices

1848 – Third Chartist petition presented to parliament

Government investigation of the Chartist Land Plan leads to the winding up of the organisation

In explaining the origins of the Chartist movement, some historians have focused on the importance of economic factors, especially the cyclical trade depressions that punctuated the years 1838–50 and underpinned the agitation for the People's Charter in 1839, 1842 and 1848. While economic factors were significant, Chartists were opposed to many of the policies carried out by the Whigs since 1832. Not only were they disillusioned by the outcome of the Reform Act, but they vigorously opposed what they saw as Whig attacks on issues such as the rights of trade unions and their failure to provide effective reform of factory conditions. In this sense, Chartism was a response to political as well as economic circumstances.

EXTRACT

1 From the article 'Chartism revisited' by Eric Evans, published in *History Review* in March 1999.

If Chartism was merely a reaction to bad times for working people, it might be asked, why were all of the six points political? The Chartist petitions to parliament did not call for a minimum wage, for additional rights for trade unionists or for the abolition of the hated new poor law. Chartists wanted a say in how Britain was governed.

Irish Coercion Act 1833

The Catholic Relief Act 1829 had freed Catholics from most of their civil disabilities, allowing Irish Catholics to turn their attention to attacking the payment of **tithes** to the Anglican Church of Ireland. There were many violent clashes between farmers and police forces, and the breakdown of law and order compelled the government to act.

KEY TERM

Tithe
Usually around 10 percent of agricultural produce that was paid annually to fund the Anglican Church in Ireland. Opposition to these payments by Catholics resulted in the bitterly contested Tithe War of 1831–36. Tithes were abolished in 1869 when the Irish Church was disestablished from the state.

The Irish Coercion Act 1833 was one of the most repressive pieces of Irish legislation of the 19th century. The Lord Lieutenant of Ireland was given wide powers to suppress any public meetings; arbitrary arrest became commonplace; and offenders were to be tried by court martial rather than in the civil courts.

The severity of the Act shocked radicals throughout Britain. They feared that if the Whigs were prepared to act so harshly in Ireland, they might be ready to impose similar restrictions on British radicalism. There were demonstrations against the Act throughout England and Scotland. Mass meetings in Birmingham, Nottingham and Manchester marked the first stage in the revival of radical political activity, which had been dormant for many years and was a significant factor in the emergence of Chartism in the mid-1830s.

The Whigs and the trade unions

The repeal of the **Combination Acts** in 1824 led to the re-establishment of many trade unions.

KEY TERM

Combination Acts
These were passed in 1799 and 1800, prohibiting trade unions and attempts at collective bargaining. They were repealed in 1824, thanks largely to a lobbying campaign led by Francis Place. An Act of 1825 limited the scope of union activity.

Most of these were very small, often covering just one trade in one locality. In 1834, Robert Owen, a leading socialist and Scottish mill owner, established the Grand National Consolidated Trades Union (GNCTU). Owen intended to bring together workers from across the country to create a single national union, whose power would be enhanced by a substantial membership.

The Whigs took a firm stand against the GNCTU, and destroyed it within six months. Six farm labourers in the Dorset village of Tolpuddle agreed to form a trade union and swore an oath to keep their activities secret. The government considered secret oaths to be a crime; the men were duly convicted and sentenced to seven years' transportation. There was a national outcry, with widespread protests in London and the chief manufacturing towns, and an 800,000-strong national petition was presented to parliament. The sentences were cancelled within three years, and the men returned home, but the damage had been done. The GNCTU was no more, and the small localised unions continued as before.

The government's determination to limit the power of trade unions was confirmed by the Glasgow weavers' strike of 1837, which led to 18 leaders of the Spinners' Union being tried on various charges and sentenced to seven years' transportation. These attacks on trade union activity intensified the hatred felt by working people towards the Whig government, and were a significant factor in the growth of Chartism.

War of the unstamped, 1831–36

Newspapers had been taxed since 1712, not to raise money, but rather to restrict the circulation of all newspapers and keep them out of the hands of ordinary people. In 1765, Britain had imposed stamp duties on the American colonies, which were fiercely resisted by the colonists and contributed to the outbreak of the American Revolution in 1775. In the 1830s, every copy of a British newspaper paid a tax of 4 pence, which made the press far too expensive for ordinary people. In 1831, Henry Hetherington founded *The Poor Man's Guardian*, which was unstamped and sold for one penny; and within two years the *Guardian* had a weekly circulation of 220,000 copies.

The government tried to stop Hetherington from publishing the newspaper, but fines, imprisonment and the destruction of his printing presses did not deter him. It was thanks to sustained pressure from Hetherington and other radicals that the government reduced the stamp tax on newspapers to one penny in 1836, and abolished the tax on pamphlets altogether.

The success of this movement revealed that a co-ordinated campaign of extra-parliamentary pressure could force a change in government policies. It emboldened those hoping for some form of political reform, especially leading radicals such as William Lovett. Hetherington joined Lovett and others in 1836, and helped to draw up the People's Charter.

Factory Act 1833

During the late 18th century, many reformers campaigned for government regulation of the factory system, focusing their attention on the long hours worked by adults and children alike. Sir Robert Peel, father of the future prime minister, sponsored measures in the early 1820s to limit the hours that children under 16 could work in cotton factories, but without a system of regular inspections they were largely ignored.

The case for reform was taken up in 1830 by Richard Oastler, a Bradford humanitarian. At this time, there was considerable public interest in the various campaigns to abolish slavery within the British Empire (the slave trade itself had been abolished in 1807). Oastler began his reform campaign in a letter to the *Leeds Mercury* in October 1830. He made a powerful argument, comparing conditions for slaves on plantations overseas with what he called 'Yorkshire Slavery'. He organised a number of Short Time Committees in Yorkshire and Lancashire that campaigned for a ten-hour day for all factory workers. The strength of the Ten Hour movement led the Whigs to try to neutralise the committees by proposing changes of their own. Under the Act of 1833, factory owners could not employ children under the age of nine, and those aged nine to 18 could work for a maximum of 12 hours. Child workers were to be given some education, and four inspectors were appointed to enforce the Act.

The Short Time Committees had hoped that legislation would be introduced to regulate adult employment, but that had never been the Whigs' intention. They hoped that a limited reform aimed at improving the lot of young people would weaken the appeal of the Ten Hours movement overall. Many committee members later joined the Chartist movement, believing that political reforms, especially the widening of the franchise, would make it possible to take action to legislate for improved factory conditions.

Poor Law Amendment Act 1834

Of all the measures passed by the Whigs in the 1830s, it was changes to the Poor Law that produced the most sustained opposition and resistance, especially in northern towns. Until 1834, provision for poor relief was governed by the Elizabethan Poor Law of 1601, which allowed the poor to remain in their own homes and claim assistance in the form of outdoor relief. By the 1830s, this system of relief was coming under increasing strain. The population had more than doubled since 1601 and several areas of the country had been transformed by industrialisation, which had created densely populated towns in the Midlands and the north. The old Poor Law had become very expensive to maintain, and there were frequent calls for reform from middle-class ratepayers.

The Act of 1834 reflected the recommendations of a Royal Commission set up in 1832. It introduced a new principle for poor relief, that of 'less eligibility'. This meant that those who sought relief from their parish would receive less than the lowest-paid worker. The commission recommended that outdoor relief should be abolished. The poor should only be supported if they left their homes and entered the local workhouse, where conditions were deliberately made as unpleasant as possible. Although many parishes combined together to build workhouses, the instructions on outdoor relief were widely ignored. It remained the most common form of relief throughout the 19th century.

The Act was applied in the agricultural south from 1836, and met with little serious opposition. However, its operation was not suited to the economic conditions that applied in industrial towns. Trade cycles meant that textile towns often enjoyed periods of almost full employment, but economic downturns led to a period of sustained high unemployment because few jobs outside the textile industry were available. The extension of the Act to the northern towns in 1837 coincided with the start of a period of prolonged depression that lasted from 1838 to 1842. Town workers had gained valuable organisational experience with the Short Time Committees. They were able to transfer these skills into the Anti-Poor Law committees that flourished from 1837. Opposition to the 'Poor Law Bastilles', as workhouses were known, sparked rioting in several northern towns. In 1842, a food riot in Stockport led to an attack on the town's workhouse.

> **ACTIVITY**
> **KNOWLEDGE CHECK**
> **Challenges to the Whig government, 1833–36**
> 1 Draw up a list of the Whig government's actions that were challenged by working people.
> 2 Do you agree that the Poor Law Amendment Act was the single most unpopular measure passed in the years 1833–36? Support your answer with evidence drawn from the text.

The creation of the Chartist movement, 1836–38

Despite their opposition to Whig legislation in the years 1832–36, the government's opponents had been unable to secure many changes in Whig policies. However, between 1836 and 1838, various strands of radicalism came together to form the Chartist movement, the first truly national organisation of the British working class.

The London Working Men's Association (LWMA)

The LWMA was formed in 1836 by a group of men, led by William Lovett, who had campaigned against the stamp duty in the early 1830s. The LWMA was never intended to be a mass organisation of the London working classes. It had a small membership of a few hundred politically aware artisans, such as tailors and other craftsmen, and charged a fairly high monthly membership fee of one shilling. The LWMA's conservative outlook was reflected in its moderate ambitions, which included the promotion of political and social rights and, especially, the development of educational opportunities for all. Lovett and his associates believed that their aims could be achieved by organising peaceful protests, or moral force, which would persuade parliament to embrace social and political change. A more radical organisation, the East London Democratic Organisation, was formed in 1837. It appealed to the poorer members of the working class, such as dockworkers and silk weavers, and, unlike the LWMA, was prepared to consider physical force to meet its ends. It would continue to oppose the LWMA until the National Charter Association was founded in 1840, at which time it became part of this new body.

William Lovett (1800–77)
A former cabinet maker, Lovett had been involved in the National Union of the Working Classes, formed in 1831 to campaign for the Reform Act. He worked alongside Henry Hetherington in the war of the unstamped, and joined Robert Owen's GNCTU in 1834. He was secretary of the LWMA from 1836, but withdrew from Chartism in 1840, largely because of his bitter personal opposition to Feargus O'Connor. Lovett was thereafter deeply involved in promoting the education of the working class.

In May 1837, Lovett and his radical colleagues drafted a series of proposals that became the People's Charter in 1838. Their Six Points brought together the main aims of British radicalism, which had been proposed since the 1790s, and the LWMA believed that their enactment would inevitably lead to social and economic improvements. However, although some local organisations were established outside London, the LWMA would only be effective if it gained widespread national support.

The Birmingham Political Union (BPU)

Thomas Attwood's BPU had been a strong organisation of middle- and working-class people that campaigned in support of the reform bill in 1831–32. It had played a vital role in the agitation in favour of the bill, but had declined in importance once the Reform Act had passed into law.

Attwood reorganised the BPU in 1837 in response to the depression that hit several Midland towns that year. At first, the BPU failed to secure widespread support because its modest demands focused on household rather than universal suffrage. In November 1837, Attwood relaunched the movement on a more radical programme. He intended that a new set of proposals, which included universal suffrage, would be presented to parliament, backed by a huge national petition. There was a dramatic turnaround in the fortunes of the BPU, as it rapidly won thousands of supporters with a programme that closely resembled that of the LWMA.

The Great Northern Union (GNU)

The GNU was the brainchild of the Irish politician Feargus O'Connor. Elected for County Cork in 1832, O'Connor was disqualified as an MP in 1835 because he did not possess the necessary property qualifications. With a future in Irish politics closed to him, O'Connor turned his interest to radical English politics. Late in 1835, he toured northern England, where he established several local radical associations pledged to support parliamentary reform. O'Connell was a brilliant and persuasive orator and gained widespread support in the northern towns, not only from unskilled English workers, but also from the growing number of Irish immigrants working in the industrial north. In 1837, O'Connor combined his different organisations into the GNU and founded the *Northern Star* as its mouthpiece. His newspaper had an initial circulation of 10,000, rising to over 50,000 in 1839, when it gave its full support to the Chartist movement. This was a reflection of O'Connor's popularity nationally, and of the fact that the *Northern Star* reported on all Chartist activities.

By 1838, there were three distinct regional organisations that pursued similar objectives. By the end of the year, they had united in the common cause of parliamentary reform. In May 1838, the LWMA and the BPU attended a mass meeting in Glasgow of 200,000 people, where they agreed to join forces and adopt a common programme. O'Connor had not hitherto taken up the cause of the People's Charter, partly because he did not wish to lose control of the GNU, but most of all because of his deep personal disagreements with Lovett. Lovett disapproved of O'Connor's deliberate courting of unskilled workers, and of the fiery and intemperate language that characterised his speeches. He was convinced that O'Connor could not work alongside others, and that his egotism could only damage the movement. For his part, O'Connor realised that Chartism was gaining widespread national support that could easily diminish the GNU. He therefore decided to swing the GNU behind the other two organisations and attended a meeting in Birmingham in August 1838, where the People's Charter and the national petition were both adopted.

The 'People's Charter'
Lovett had employed the term 'Charter' to acknowledge the significance of the Magna Carta, or Great Charter, of 1215, when English barons forced King John to acknowledge a wide range of basic liberties. It was also a reference to the French Constitutional Charter of 1814, which preserved the liberties won by the French people during the Revolution, and restored the Bourbon kings to the French throne, but as constitutional monarchs.

The importance of the National Convention, 1839

Once the People's Charter and the national petition were adopted in August 1838, Chartists began to organise meetings throughout the country to elect delegates to the Chartist Convention, which was to meet in London in February 1839. These meetings were attended by thousands of men, women and children, a tribute both to the movement's organisational skills and the wide enthusiasm it generated. One of the largest meetings was held on Kersal Moor outside Manchester in September 1838. Estimates of the numbers attending varied widely, from O'Connor's exaggerated figure of one million to a more realistic 50,000.

From a speech given at Kersal Moor by J.R. Stephens, a leading northern Chartist and campaigner against the Poor Law. His definition of Chartism reflected the opinions of many northern Chartists.

This question of universal suffrage is a knife and fork question, a bread and cheese question. If any man ask what I mean by universal suffrage, I mean to say that every working man in the land has a right to a good coat on his back, a good hat on his head, a good roof for the shelter of his household, a good dinner upon his table, no more work on land will keep him in health at it, and as much wages as will keep him in the enjoyment of plenty, and all the blessings of life that reasonable men could desire.

Some historians have taken Stephens' interpretation as reflecting the opinions of the whole movement, which has often been seen as a straightforward response to the economic depression of the time, and was thus largely driven by social and economic conditions. However, Chartism was viewed differently in other parts of the country. For Lovett and the LWMA, the People's Charter was primarily a political document, a reaction to the limitations of the Reform Act and to the Whig government's policies. Many supporters in the Midlands, the heirs of the BPU traditions of the early 1830s, were motivated by economic rather than political factors, and were more interested in issues such as wage levels than the achievement of universal suffrage. Stephens' speech revealed that from the very outset there were differing views on what could be expected from the People's Charter.

These divisions were thrown into sharp relief when the National Convention met in London in February 1839. It was by no means a body of working-class men. Contemporary accounts noted that most of the delegates were shopkeepers and tradesmen, and several participants were doctors and newspaper editors.

Delegates were agreed that parliament was unlikely to accept the national petition; what divided them was what sort of action Chartists should take after the petition was rejected. Several delegates supported peaceful protests, such as 'exclusive dealing' (the boycotting of shops and trades whose owners opposed Chartism). An important suggestion, which split the Convention, was the notion of a **'sacred month'**, or general strike, a proposal that carried with it the possibility that violence and force might be used.

KEY TERM

Sacred month
A call for a national general strike, as well as abstaining from taxable items such as tobacco and alcohol. The aim was to disrupt the economy so seriously that the government would be forced to negotiate with the Chartists. The Convention did not take into account the fact that most workers would be unable to survive for a month without pay.

The Convention was also confronted with a dilemma that faced many radical movements before 1838, and is still faced by protest movements today. Some Convention members followed the example set by Lovett, of using peaceful pressure, or moral force, in an attempt to persuade parliament to consider the Charter.

Others followed O'Connor and his supporters by pressing for 'ulterior measures', which suggested physical force, involving violent action, even extending to armed rioting.

These different viewpoints divided the Chartists into moral and physical force groups, and their differences were stressed by Gammage in his history of the movement. However, this distinction can be overplayed. O'Connor, seen by most people as the leading advocate of physical force, referred to the issue in a speech delivered in September 1838 (Source 2).

From a report in the Northern Star, 22 September 1838, of a speech delivered by Feargus O'Connor to the Chartist Convention. Delegates were discussing possible Chartist campaigning methods.

He had never counselled the people to physical force, because he felt that those who did so were fools to their own cause; but those who decried it preserved their authority by it, and it alone. The people were determined to obtain Universal Suffrage, honestly if they could, but they were determined to have it. He counselled them against all rioting, all civil war; but still, he would say that rather than see the people oppressed – rather than see the Constitution violated while the people were in daily want, if no other man would do so – if the constitution were violated, he would himself lead the people to death or glory. (Cheers) Let the moral force men take that, and let it set them a good moral example.

The language and tone of this extract suggests that O'Connor was using the threat of physical force as a means of stirring up his audience, while at the same time intimidating the forces of law and order. At no time during his Chartist career did O'Connor plan any violent disturbances. Be that as it may, by May 1839, when the Convention moved to Birmingham, a large number of middle-class delegates had resigned in protest at speeches made by O'Connell and other Chartists that hinted at the use of physical force in support of the Charter.

In July 1839, Chartists held a meeting in Birmingham's Bull Ring, challenging a ban on such meetings imposed by local magistrates. The government was reluctant to use local troops in case there was a repetition of the Peterloo Massacre of 1819. Instead, they sent a police force from London on the recently opened London and Birmingham railway. The meeting was duly dispersed, but only after fighting between protesters and the police. At Lovett's prompting, the Convention denounced the police action, which led to his own arrest and subsequent imprisonment.

The Newport Rising, November 1839

Chartism had secured very strong support in the industrial areas of South Wales, and drilling and arming of men had been under way for many months. In August 1839, Henry Vincent, a prominent Welsh Chartist, was sentenced to 12 months' imprisonment in Monmouth jail on charges of unlawful assembly. Local organisers decided on a massive show of force in the town of Newport, in an attempt to persuade the authorities to release Vincent and other Chartist leaders.

John Frost, a member of the Convention, led one of three separate marches that totalled over 10,000 men and converged on Newport on 3 November. They surrounded the Westgate Hotel, where troops were holding several Chartists under arrest.

SOURCE

A contemporary representation of the Newport Rising, 1839, drawn by David Fiston and published in *Cassell's History*. Fiston was a British illustrator, who worked for a number of periodicals and books throughout the 19th century.

It is not clear which side fired the first shots, but troops responded immediately, firing into the crowd and quickly dispersing the mob. Order was restored in the town, but 22 men were dead and over 50 injured. In the aftermath of the riot, Frost and two associates were found guilty of high treason and sentenced to death. However, fearing further rioting, possibly on a national scale, the government ensured that the men were not executed, but were sentenced to transportation for life. The rising only strengthened the government's view that Chartism was an organisation committed to the violent overthrow of the state.

The Chartist petition, 1839

By June 1839, a massive **national petition** had been prepared, and the MP Thomas Attwood was persuaded to present it to parliament. The document was three miles long and contained 1,283,000 signatures. One-quarter of the signatories were women. As the House of Commons prepared to consider the petition, large public demonstrations were held throughout the country, in an attempt to persuade MPs to accept the document. The Home Office, anticipating widespread riots and disorder, recruited large numbers of special armed constables. A month later, on 14 July, the House of Commons voted on the petition. It was treated with undisguised contempt: fewer than half of all MPs turned up to vote, and the petition was rejected by 235 votes to 46.

By August 1839, the National Convention was in disarray. Its numbers had dwindled dramatically. The BPU, worried by the violence at the Bull Ring, withdrew its support. The Convention considered a proposal to carry out the sacred month and the strikes associated with it. Overwhelming opposition from trade unions meant that the proposal was rejected. In September, with many of its leaders, including Lovett, in prison, the Convention was dissolved. Over the next few months, the government moved decisively against Chartism, arresting several hundred of its leaders throughout the country. The whole Chartist movement was in danger of complete disintegration. Throughout the agitation for the first petition, Chartists had acted in a lawful fashion, apart from the Welsh Chartists' use of physical force at Newport.

The Chartist petition, 1842

The circumstances surrounding the second petition were different from those of 1839. The Whig government that had dominated politics in the 1830s was heavily defeated in the 1841 election at the hands of Peel's Conservative Party. Peel's entry into office coincided with a period of severe economic depression. By 1842, unemployment was widespread, with several towns experiencing mass unemployment. Evans noted that in Dundee, for example, half of all mechanics and shipbuilders were unemployed. The new Poor Law had not been designed to cope with such extreme conditions. In many towns it simply broke down under the strain, leading to severe hardship for many families.

KEY TERM

National petition
Submitting petitions to parliament was an established tradition by the 19th century. In a pre-democratic age, it was an important way of raising national or local concerns.

SOURCE

4 Surrounded by flags reading 'vote by ballot', 'universal suffrage' and 'reform', the 1842 petition is carried in procession to the House of Commons, in this anonymous print published in the same year.

The petition contained 3.3 million signatures, one-third of the adult population, and is the largest single petition that has ever been laid before parliament. Despite this impressive achievement, the second petition fared no better than the first: on its presentation to the House of Commons it was denied a hearing by 287 votes to 49.

The Plug Plot riots, 1842

The Chartists' response to their second defeat was influenced by prevailing economic conditions. Wage reductions in the Lancashire and Yorkshire cotton trades sparked a wave of strikes known as the Plug Plot, which involved strikers removing plugs from boilers and bringing a factory to a standstill. While the Plug Plot did involve individual Chartists, it was not promoted by the movement as a whole, and O'Connor denounced the strikers in the *Northern Star*. Violent activity in the north as a whole was widespread, but short-lived: the 1842 harvest was a good one, and towards the end of the year unemployment began to fall, as trading conditions improved.

EXTRACT

From A. Briggs, *Chartist Studies*, published in 1959. Here, Briggs argues that Chartism was driven by economic rather than political considerations.

Though Chartism in one sense was only a continuation under another name of the old radical reform movement and was to last in some shape or other into the 1850s, what gave it contemporary importance was the great industrial depression from 1837 to 1843. The force and intensity of Chartism at its peak came from men who knew that they were painfully worse off than other classes in society and were not prepared to reconcile themselves to that condition. Hungry bellies filled the ranks of the Chartists: the return of economic prosperity after 1843 thinned them. The chronology of effective Chartism is also that of the worst industrial depression which the country endured during the nineteenth century.

The Chartist petition, 1848

Events in the years 1847–48 gave new life to the Chartist movement. A downturn in trade led to a general depression in 1847. Many Chartists were worried by the Whig victory in the 1847 election, though they drew some comfort from O'Connor's election as MP for Nottingham.

Early in 1848, a wave of revolutionary activity swept Europe, and the fall of the French monarchy in February inspired Chartists to present a third petition to parliament.

A mass meeting was planned for 10 April 1848, to be held on Kennington Common (on the site of the present Oval cricket ground). O'Connor hoped that a massive crowd would support the petition, but driving rain and a display of force by the government deterred many: only 25,000 turned up, rather than the hoped-for 200,000. Nevertheless, the Home Office had prepared for the meeting by stationing 8,000 soldiers around London, and enlisting up to 150,000 special constables (including Gladstone, Peel and Louis Napoleon Bonaparte, the future French Emperor Napoleon III).

Surviving photographs of the meeting show a peaceful gathering of respectable people dressed in their Sunday best. Unlike the mass meetings of 1838–39, there were very few women on the common. Police forces prevented the demonstrators from crossing the Thames bridges and marching to parliament. O'Connor persuaded the meeting to disperse while he and a handful of supporters took the petition to parliament in a cab. His claimed 5.5 million signatures turned out to be fewer than two million genuine signatures. The claimed signatures of the queen and Wellington, as well as invented names such as 'Pugnose' and 'No Cheese', only made Chartism a laughing stock. Once again, the House of Commons refused to consider the petition.

SOURCE

5

Thomas Paine reviewing the outbreak of the French Revolution in his 1791 *Rights of Man*.

What are the present governments of Europe, but a scene of iniquity and oppression? What is that of England? Do not its own inhabitants say, it is a market where every man has his price, and where corruption is common traffic, at the expense of a deluded people? No wonder, then, that the French Revolution is traduced.

SOURCE

6 A popular print by the French engraver Faucher-Gudin of the execution of King Louis XVI in Paris on 21 January 1793.

SOURCE

7 An engraving of the storming of the Bastille on 14 July 1789, by Jean-Louis Prieur. Prieur was a sculptor, illustrator and engraver associated with the French Revolutionary movement.

THINKING HISTORICALLY   Cause and consequence (6c)

Connections

Sources 5–7 show some typical aspects of the 1789 French Revolution. Work in groups or individually and answer the following:

1 Read Source 5.

    a) What did Chartists believe about the strength of their support?

    b) How is this similar to revolutionary ideas about the French monarchy?

2 Look at Sources 6 and 7. What did the Chartists copy from the French Revolution?

3 a) Make a list of other similarities between the Chartists and the French Revolutionaries.

    b) How did their understanding of the revolution affect the attitudes and actions of the Chartists?

4 Why is it important for historians to see these links across time and be able to explain how causal factors can influence situations much later in time?

SOURCE 8

A depiction of the Chartist meeting on Kennington Common, 10 April 1848, which appeared in the *Illustrated London News* on 15 April. The artist who produced this for the newspaper is unrecorded.

ACTIVITY
KNOWLEDGE CHECK

Investigating a visual source

Look at Source 8. What can you learn from this illustration about the Kennington Common meeting and about the supporters of the Chartist movement?

The events of 10 April were widely ridiculed as a complete fiasco. It is easily forgotten that two million signatures on the petition was a remarkable achievement. But Chartism did not collapse on 10 April. A meeting in London in May attracted a crowd of 60,000, and in other parts of the country there were indications of significant Chartist activity. Men in Lancashire and Yorkshire held armed drills, and there were rumours of a possible rising if, as seemed possible, there was a revolutionary outbreak of violence in Ireland. Police and troops were deployed in large numbers throughout the north-west, and London saw a substantial police presence for the rest of the year. By early 1849, it was clear that Chartism no longer attracted a strong allegiance among working people, and it faded into insignificance. The 1848 petition ruined O'Connor. He was unable to regain his popularity with the people, and shortly afterwards his mental health began to fail.

In 1858, a final Chartist Convention was convened. Thereafter, pressure for reform became largely the preserve of middle-class radicals such as John Bright.

The roles of Lovett and O'Connor

William Lovett and Feargus O'Connor were two of the most prominent Chartist leaders. While they agreed on the People's Charter, they differed in many serious ways on Chartist organisations and methods. In the years 1839–42, their divisions were thrown into sharp relief, and were a major reason for Lovett's withdrawal from mainstream Chartism, as he focused his attention on educational provisions for the poor.

The National Charter Association, 1840

With the collapse of the National Convention, Chartism had lost the one organisation that had given it leadership, direction and legitimacy, and a fundamental reorganisation was necessary. At first, the initiative passed to local and well-supported organisations, but demands soon grew for a revived central organisation. Although he had been imprisoned in 1840, O'Connor was ideally placed to assume the leadership of Chartism. He was very popular in the north of England, had sustained the Chartist message through the *Northern Star*, and his popular journalism meant that he was regarded by many as the natural successor to William Cobbett. He used the *Star*'s columns to support the creation of a national body supported by a membership that paid a quarterly subscription. The National Charter Association (NCA) was formed on these lines in 1840 and gave central direction to the movement for the rest of the decade. Within two years, it had established 400 associations, required a subscription from its members, and could boast a membership of 70,000. Several historians have suggested that the NCA was the first national political party of the working class.

The NCA soon came under O'Connor's firm leadership. While other Chartist groups began to develop as single-issue associations, focusing on issues such as education, religion and temperance, O'Connor remained wedded to the guiding principle of promoting the Charter in its entirety. His attitude, along with his uncompromising manner, provoked widespread opposition from other Chartist leaders.

O'Connor was released from prison in August 1841 and celebrated his release with a triumphant national tour. With the NCA growing in influence and confidence, O'Connor proposed a second national petition. He called for a new Convention to meet in 1842, where it would arrange for the petition's presentation to parliament.

Lovett and Chartist education

Lovett had been imprisoned for sedition in 1839 after the Bull Ring riots in Birmingham. During his time in jail he focused his attention not on the People's Charter, but on educational initiatives. He became convinced that education was the key to individual advancement, and would help the very poorest in society. After his release in 1840, Lovett formed the National Association Promoting the Political and Social Improvement of the People, which was dubbed 'Knowledge Chartism' by his opponents. Lovett's initiative was not supported by many local organisations or by most of the Chartist leadership. O'Connor denounced the National Association because he felt it would distract Chartism from its central focus of the People's Charter. Lovett persevered with the movement, but it was poorly funded and failed to gain very much support. By the late 1850s, the National Association had faded into insignificance.

O'Connor and the Chartist Land Plan

Chartism made very little progress after 1842 because a combination of factors removed many of the Chartists' sources of discontent. A general economic revival and a series of good harvests relieved much economic pressure on working people. Moreover, unlike their Whig predecessors, Peel's government of 1841–46 did not pass any legislation that aroused Chartist anger. On the contrary, several of his policies were broadly welcomed. Reduced duties on imported corn and other goods proved to be very beneficial to consumers. Peel also showed a strong humanitarian instinct. He supported the Mines Act, which banned the employment of young children and women in coal mines; and the Factory Act 1844 placed further limitations on the hours worked by these two groups in factories. However, despite the Tory government's readiness to tackle some social issues, Peel remained as implacably opposed to Chartism as his predecessors.

After 1842, Chartist activity began to fragment, as leading Chartists took up single issues such as religion, temperance and involvement in local government. O'Connell opposed single-issue associations because he viewed them as a distraction from the central aims of the People's Charter. However, he realised that Chartism needed to promote one concern that would reunite Chartism and rekindle its radical enthusiasm. His solution was the Chartist Land Plan.

O'Connor's experience in Ireland in the 1820s and early 1830s had persuaded him of the importance of agricultural smallholdings, and even simple allotments, as a means of improving conditions for agricultural labourers. For some years, including the time he spent in prison, O'Connor had been working on plans that would remove workers from towns and resettle them on small farms in the countryside. At the Convention of 1845 he unveiled his Chartist Land Plan.

SOURCE

In 1846, the Chartist Land Company bought an estate in Hertfordshire and renamed it O'Connorville. This illustration shows O'Connor's ambitious plans for the estate, proposing to make the working class self-sufficient and to improve their quality of life by converting workers into farmers. The project failed, however, causing investors to lose money. The working class that O'Connor targeted had little experience of farming, and there was not enough land allocated to house the number of people and families in O'Connor's plan.

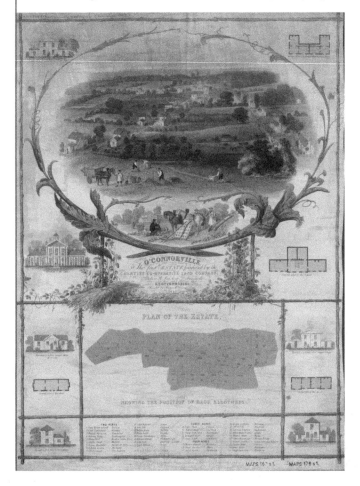

The financing of the plan was remarkably complex: Chartists could buy shares in the scheme, and ballots were to be drawn to allot smallholdings to a fortunate few. Initially, four estates were purchased, with a fifth at Dodford acquired in 1848. Only 250 families were settled under the scheme, which was wound up following a government investigation of 1848. By 1851, only 46 families remained on their smallholdings. One cottage remains today at Dodford, owned by the National Trust.

ACTIVITY
KNOWLEDGE CHECK

The Chartist Movement

1 To what extent was violence an inherent part of the Chartist movement?

2 'The goals of Chartism were too broad to be effectively campaigned for.' What evidence can you find to support this statement?

Why had Chartism failed to achieve its aims by 1850?

A divided working class

Although its petitions were supported by millions of signatures, Chartism never became a single and cohesive organisation of the entire working class. It failed to attract the support of the so-called 'aristocracy of labour', the highly paid and highly skilled craftsmen and the growing number of engineers and other skilled men working on the spreading railway network. It was never able to secure the allegiance of the large number of agricultural labourers in the country. In Suffolk, for example, Chartism was active in the large town of Ipswich, but had little support in outlying villages or in the fishing ports. Most villages were small and isolated from one another, making co-ordinated action virtually impossible. Working-class divisions became more acute in the 1840s as Chartists were diverted into other matters. The Rochdale Pioneers established the first shop of what would become a national **co-operative movement** in 1844, and the teetotal movement gained widespread support, especially among women. These developments dismayed O'Connor, whose guiding principle was to focus on the Charter to the exclusion of all other issues.

Chartism and the trade unions

Chartism was unable to gain widespread and lasting support among the trade unions. Trade union activity had been severely curtailed since 1834, when the GNCTU had collapsed and the Tolpuddle martyrs were transported to Australia. Those small unions that survived were allowed to exist, but could be prosecuted for strike actions, which were regarded under **common law** as restraint of trade.

In its early days, Chartism was supported by individual unions, who sent representatives to its meetings. The meeting at Kersal Moor in 1838 was attended by several Manchester trade unions, who marched in procession along with their union banners. However, unionists saw that the proposal for the sacred month in 1839, if carried out, would almost certainly lead to government reprisals, against individuals and the trade union movement as a whole. Their refusal to support the proposal was the deciding reason for its abandonment.

During the early 1840s, the National Charter Association tried to forge more lasting links with the unions, but were rebuffed once more. Unionists were far more concerned with economic rather than political matters, and focused their attention on wages, hours and conditions of work. The revival of unionism was demonstrated with the growing membership of individual trade unions, and with the launch of the National Association of United Trades in 1845. These changes were made possible thanks to the significant revival of trade and economic activity from 1842, and the growing confidence of individual unions. O'Connor tried to form an alliance with the burgeoning union movement, even changing the name of his newspaper to the *Northern Star and National Trades Journal*. O'Connor had no real interest in the trade unions beyond recruiting their numbers to the Chartist cause, and his attempts to win their support ended in failure.

A changing economy

In 1838, Stephens claimed that Chartism was 'a knife and fork question', and many historians have pointed out the connection between the spikes in Chartist activity in 1838–39, 1841–43 and 1847–48 and the simultaneous economic depressions. The historian Halévy claimed that 'Chartism was not a creed. It was the blind revolt of hunger'. Chartism, however, was more than simply a reaction to

KEY TERMS

Co-operative movement
This centred around consumer co-operatives. Shops were established selling goods to members and others at market prices, and any surplus was returned to members in the form of cash dividends. Chartists in England and Scotland experimented with co-operative stores in the late 1830s, before the Rochdale Pioneers founded what was to become the national co-operative movement.

Common law
This is not based on legislation passed by governments, but on decisions and precedents established by judges in the courts.

A Level Exam-Style Question Section B

How far do economic conditions explain the origins of the Chartist movement in the years 1832–38? (20 marks)

Tip

Address the stated factor of economic conditions first, then consider other relevant points before reaching a judgement on the question.

prevailing economic conditions. Chartists saw political power as a factor of fundamental importance. They believed that if the working classes had a share in political power, then measures such as the Poor Law Amendment Act would never have seen the light of day, and factory owners would never have been able to enforce wage reductions.

Chartism: a failure?

On three occasions, despite massive popular support, the Chartists had failed to achieve their fundamental aim – parliament's acceptance of the People's Charter. It would therefore seem sensible simply to dismiss Chartism as an abject failure and the Charter as a senseless dream. However, this would be to underestimate the immediate and long-term importance of the Chartist movement.

Chartism breathed new life into working-class radicalism, which had declined rapidly after Peterloo and been deeply disappointed by the outcome of the reform agitation of 1830–32. It allowed a new and often impressive leadership to emerge, and it strengthened the development of an entirely separate working-class culture. Many people, men and women, were involved in political activities for the first time. They took part in activities as diverse as local gatherings, mass meetings and demonstrations, and became more politically aware through the speeches of men such as Stephens and O'Connor. The pages of the *Northern Star* furthered their political education, and made them aware of the dynamic and national importance of the Chartist movement. This new political involvement did not simply disappear in 1850. The 1850s and 1860s saw the growth of many distinctly working-class organisations, such as trade unions, co-operative societies and Sunday schools, while many prominent Chartists were involved in the formation of the Liberal Party in the late 1850s.

Most of the Six Points of the People's Charter, although very radical proposals in the 1830s, have been gradually adopted by parliament, though Chartism cannot be credited for their introduction. The property qualification for MPs was abolished in 1858; the secret ballot arrived in 1872; payment of MPs was introduced in 1912; and universal adult suffrage was granted in 1928. Constituency boundaries are regularly redrawn, though strict equality of size has never been attained. Annual parliaments have never been seriously considered, though some radical groups still promote the idea today.

Carlyle described Chartism as 'bitter discontent grown fierce and mad'. While this is an apt description of the movement in the short term, Chartism might be better understood as part of a long-term continuum of working-class actions that stretched from the 1790s, through the 1830s and 1840s, and into the unionism and socialism of the 1880s and beyond.

EXTRACT

3

Ramsden Balmforth was a noted pacifist, reformer and humanist. Here, in *Some Social and Political Pioneers of the Nineteenth Century* (1900), he suggests that, although the People's Charter was never accomplished, Chartism as a movement had significant achievements to its credit.

The Chartist movement was one to which all social and political reformers look back with a certain amount of pride, mingled with a greater amount of sadness. Pride, because it was a movement inspired by great ideals. Sadness, because its ideals were either shattered, or passed on, into other movements and other parties; and because its adherents were deluded and misled by one or two inordinately vain and self-seeking agitators.

... A cause of disunion was found in the character and temper of some of the leaders themselves. O'Connor was the most effective outdoor orator of his time, and the idol of the immense assemblages which were often brought together in those days. Unfortunately, both for the movement and for himself, he was a man of unbounded conceit and egotism, and regarded himself as a sort of uncrowned king of the working classes.

... It would be a great mistake to suppose that the Chartist movement was really fruitless. No movement of its magnitude and intensity can be fruitless. It may have looked too much to outward means; but it was an excellent means of political education for the working classes. It paved the way for later political reforms, and we owe it to the men who now lie in forgotten graves that our present political freedom closely approximates to the ideal of the Charter.

ACTIVITY
KNOWLEDGE CHECK

O'Connor's contribution to the Chartist movement

Write two paragraphs on O'Connor's contribution to Chartism: one highlighting his positive influence; the second underlining the harm he did to the movement.

TO WHAT EXTENT DID CHARTIST SUPPORT CHANGE IN THE YEARS c1838–50?

There were wide variations in the levels of support that Chartism received in the years c1838–50. Support was at its height during the agitation for the Charter in 1838–39, when mass meetings and torchlight processions in the north and Midlands attracted large and enthusiastic crowds of supporters. National support, however, declined during the 1840s, despite the growing number of signatures claimed by the 1842 and 1848 petitions.

The circulation of O'Connor's *Northern Star* is an important indication of Chartism's fluctuating support. In 1838, it had a circulation of 10,000, but during the mass agitation of 1839, its editions sold an average of 36,000 copies. Its popularity fell during the 1840s, selling fewer than 6,000 copies in 1845. In 1851, the year before it collapsed, the *Star* struggled to reach 1,500 in sales.

National support

Chartism enjoyed strong support in the expanding industrial areas of the Midlands and the north. There were well-organised local associations in the textile districts of Manchester and the surrounding towns: Ashton-under-Lyne and Stockport in particular had a vigorous Chartist presence. These were areas where agitation against the Poor Law had been strong, and the organisational skills developed by the anti-Poor Law associations were put to good use in sustaining the Chartists. The movement was especially strong among those textile trades, such as the handloom weavers, whose livelihoods were threatened by technological change.

Industrial areas in Scotland were also strong supporters of Chartism, especially after the government's suppression of the Glasgow weavers' strike in 1837–38. In Ireland, however, Chartism was never able to gain widespread support. Irish nationalist groups such as Young Ireland were more interested in campaigning against the Union, and regarded Chartism as a side issue and an essentially English concern. Little headway could be made because of the Catholic Church's unyielding opposition to Chartism.

Chartism was never able to make much headway in many areas of England. A. Brown's study of Chartism in Essex and Suffolk suggests that these two counties provided less than one percent of its strength because it was never able to gain the adherence of the region's large number of agricultural labourers. Opposition to Chartism was strong among landowners, the middle class and important church leaders. The Bishop of Norwich was notorious for his trenchant sermons that denounced Chartist leaders as irreligious, and the whole movement as contrary to Christian teachings.

While Chartism was strong in the northern towns, it had difficulty gaining much support in London. The capital had some small-scale industrial development, but it was not on the scale that was developing elsewhere in the country. London's sheer size, in terms of geography and population, meant that it was difficult to sustain allegiance to Chartism. During the 1840s, there was some increase in Chartist activity in London, partly because of fluctuations in the economy, but also because of the well-organised activities of the National Charter Association. These changing circumstances help to explain the large demonstrations that were held after the rejection of the 1848 petition.

Women and Chartism

During its early years, women provided substantial support for the Chartist movement. The historian Brown suggests that women provided one-third of the signatures on the 1839 petition. Women had important, though secondary, roles in the movement. They were involved in fundraising activities and running **Chartist Sunday schools**, as well as carrying out traditionally female activities, such as sewing banners or organising tea parties. More significant was their attitude towards local shopkeepers. Many women promoted 'exclusive dealing', patronising shopkeepers who were known to support Chartism, while boycotting those hostile to the movement.

Although there were some 100 female Chartist associations, including 23 in Scotland, women were never considered for roles in the national movement. A few leaders were prepared to support women's political rights, notably R.J. Richardson, who made a powerful argument for women's suffrage in *The Rights of Women* (1842). However, the attitude of most Chartists was that women should limit themselves to supporting their husbands and families, and should not engage in political activities.

KEY TERM

Chartist Sunday school
A school providing lessons in literacy and numeracy for adults and children, along with instruction in democratic ideas and the aims of the People's Charter. They were especially popular in the textile areas around Manchester, and were responsible for a significant improvement in working-class education.

Women's involvement in Chartist activities declined during the 1840s. The mass meetings of 1838–39 were supplanted from 1840 by the National Charter Association, and women were not offered a role in its committees and other organisations. They were reluctant to attend NCA meetings, which were often held in the traditionally male stronghold of the public house. Women were attracted to other organisations, such as religious and teetotal groups.

By 1848, women's adherence to Chartism had become insignificant. The only surviving photograph of the Kennington Common meeting of 10 April 1848 suggests that it was an overwhelmingly masculine event.

SOURCE 10

This address was published in the *Northern Star* on 9 February 1839. A meeting held in Newcastle led to the formation of the Female Political Union, an organisation of women dedicated to supporting the Chartist movement. The union issued the following address, aimed at 'Their Fellow Countrywomen'.

We have been told that the province of woman is her home, and that the field of politics should be left to men; this we deny. Is it not true that the interests of our fathers, husbands, and brothers, ought to be ours? If they are oppressed and impoverished, do we not share those evils with them?

We have seen that because the husband's earnings could not support his family, the wife has been compelled to leave her home, neglected, and with her infant children, work at degrading toil. We have seen a law enacted to treat poverty as a crime, to take from the unfortunate their freedom, to separate those whom God has joined together, and tear the children from their parents' care.

We have struggled to maintain our homes in comfort, such as our hearts told us should greet our husbands after their fatiguing labours. Year after year has passed away, and even now, our wishes have no prospect of being realised: our houses are half furnished, our families ill-fed, and our children are educated. The fear of want hangs over our heads, and we feel the degradation.

We have searched and found that the cause of these evils is the Government of the country being in the hands of a few of the upper and middle classes, while the working men who form the millions, the strength and wealth of the country, are left without the pale of the Constitution. For these evils there is no remedy, but to pass the People's Charter into law and emancipate the white slaves of England.

We tell the wealthy, the high and mighty ones of the land, our kindred shall be free. We tell their lordly dames we love our husbands as well as they love theirs. We harbour no evil wishes against anyone and ask only for justice; therefore, we call on all persons to assist us in this good work, but especially those shopkeepers which the Reform Bill enfranchised. We call on them to remember it was the unrepresented workingmen that procure them their rights, and that they now ought to fulfil the pledge they gave to assist them to get theirs – they ought to remember that our pennies make their pounds, and that we cannot in justice spend the hard earnings of our husbands with those that are opposed to their rights and interests.

A Level Exam-Style Question Section A

Study Source 10 before you answer this question.
Assess the value of the source for revealing the reasons why women were prepared to support the Chartist movement, and their attitude towards different social groups.

Explain your answer using the source, the information given about it and your own knowledge of the historical context. (20 marks)

Tip
Your answer should consider the language and the tone of the extract as well as its content, and whether a persuasive case is made overall.

Chartism and the middle class

In its early years, Chartism was not an exclusively working-class organisation, but enjoyed some support from the middle class, especially in London. However, by the end of 1838, most middle-class members had left the movement as they became concerned by the increasingly violent and aggressive tone adopted by several leading Chartists. There were attempts to expand Chartist support in the early 1840s, when alliances were suggested with both the Anti-Corn Law League (ACLL) and the Complete Suffrage Union, but a programme of joint action was never agreed.

The ACLL was formed in Manchester in 1838, with strong financial support provided by a number of rich industrialists. It claimed that the repeal of the Corn Laws would benefit the agricultural interest and, indeed, the industrialists, because repeal would form part of a growing trend towards free trade that would help to boost the economy. The ACLL claimed that the working classes would also benefit because repeal would inevitably lower the price of bread and other foodstuffs. Many Chartists, however, took a different view. After their disappointment over reform in 1832, they were reluctant to work with middle-class groups again. Some suggested that the reduced price of bread would give employers an excuse to continue to reduce wages. Members from both groups were initially keen to work together, but the differences between both the two leaderships and their members meant that they could never reach a clear arrangement for action. The philosophical gulf between the economic ideas of middle-class free traders and the political ambitions of the working class was too wide to be bridged effectively.

The Complete Suffrage Union (CSU) was formed in 1841 by Joseph Sturge to promote a single issue – universal male suffrage. His attempts to win Chartist support were initially successful, but faced the implacable opposition of O'Connor and the *Northern Star*. A meeting in December 1842 was convened, attended by CSU and Chartist representatives. O'Connor persuaded the meeting that the People's Charter was, and would remain, the sole objective of the Chartist movement. Faced with the unyielding opposition of Chartist leaders, and with little support among the middle classes, the CSU collapsed.

Chartism and trade societies

Attempts by the government to control the organisation of labour through unionisation and the options open to trade societies to help their members had been in place since the Combination Acts of 1799 and 1800. When legal punishment for striking or using collective bargaining to better working conditions was reintroduced in 1825, after just one year of a more lenient government position, trade societies and unions were struggling to meet the demands of their members. By the late 1830s, the rise of Chartism provided an outlet for those workers who saw an organisation that could affect political change in areas where their own trade societies were struggling.

However, the goals of many workers, trade societies and nascent unions in the Chartist movement were, for the most part, still aimed at improving the economic position of the working class. When the Chartist Convention of 1839 sent out a questionnaire to local associations supporting Chartism, 21 of the 23 that responded did not have a general grievance over the lack of the vote. Instead, they were more concerned with hardship caused by a combination of a lack of work, low pay and expensive food. Clearly, though, there were large numbers of workers who supported the Chartist cause, as evidenced by the many hundreds of thousands of genuine signatures on the petitions sent to parliament.

Chartists also played a key role in the foundation of new trade unions, using the knowledge and experience of organisation. Throughout the 1840s, Chartists were involved with the establishment of new unions or the extension of friendly societies into much more overt unions. The General United Tailors' Trade Protection Society and the Mechanics Protective Society of Great Britain were both formed in 1844, with Chartist influence very much to the fore. These had either grown from smaller, more localised societies to national bodies, or represented an umbrella organisation for these local societies. Despite the failure of the first and second Charter petitions, the experience of the Chartists in working on a national scale towards a political end had shown them that larger, more centralised organisations were more able to make their voices heard.

SOURCE

11 An extract in the Chartist newspaper the *Northern Star*, from a report sent from a London tailors' branch.

Unless the trades generally adopt the principles of a General Union, there is no hope of making a successful stand against the encroachments of the principal capitalists.

Another organisation that was established with a strong Chartist influence was the Miners' Association of Great Britain and Ireland (MAGBI). Again, despite being set up primarily to deal with working conditions for the miners, several of its senior officials had been active Chartists, and O'Connor was asked to offer his legal opinion on its founding constitution. However, despite the personal support for Chartism amongst the higher echelons of the MAGBI, this support did not seemingly extend to the membership, and attempts to distribute Chartist literature at meetings were met with opposition.

So, despite widespread support for the Chartist cause across both leadership and membership of trade associations, when industrial unrest did break out, the implementation of the Charter was rarely put forward as a condition for ending the strikes. This can be seen during the 1842 Plug Plot riots and accompanying strikes across the country. For the most part, the concerns of the miners were those that exercised the majority of workers – primarily low wages, long working hours and high rents.

ACTIVITY
KNOWLEDGE CHECK

Chartist supporters

1 a) Create a table listing all of the various groups that supported Chartism.

   b) Add a column to explain what each group hoped to gain through its support of Chartism.

   c) Add a further column to explain why support for Chartism from this group waned.

2 How far was the leadership of the Chartist movement responsible for the change in support for Chartism?

A Level Exam-Style Question Section B

To what extent did support for Chartism change in the years c1838–50? (20 marks)

Tip
First, outline the support that Chartism enjoyed in 1838. Then look at the different support it enjoyed in 1850. Explain what had changed, and why.

HOW EFFECTIVE WAS THE GOVERNMENT'S RESPONSE TO THE CHARTIST CHALLENGE?

Whig and Tory governments of the 1830s and 1840s realised that Chartism posed a greater threat to national stability than the post-war agitation of 1815–20. However, as the threat was greater, so too were the forces opposed to the Chartists of a different order. The year 1832 had seen the revitalisation of state power, with the bringing together of the propertied classes in a union that was determined to resist challenges to national order and to their own authority. While it continued to rely on local magistrates to maintain order, and a network of spies to keep it informed, the government was able to deploy new and effective weapons in its confrontations with the Chartists.

Government responses

Police forces

Peel was Home Secretary in 1829 when he introduced the Metropolitan Police Act. The haphazard and medieval system of parish officers and watchmen was replaced by a single, professional and uniformed force of around 1,000 men charged with maintaining order in London and surrounding counties. Troops could restore order by threatening to use armed force; Peel believed that a trained police force could suppress disorder without having to resort to guns and swords.

The Act proved so successful that it was extended by the Rural Police Act 1839, which empowered authorities in counties and boroughs to raise their own police forces, which were paid for by a local rate. Although the introduction of local forces developed slowly in many counties, the rural police did provide a further weapon to be deployed to deal with outbreaks of disorder.

The electric telegraph

While information provided by government spies was often invaluable in enabling central government to arrange precautionary measures against Chartist agitation, communication between the spies and London was inevitably very slow. This problem was overcome during the 1840s with the development of the electric telegraph. It proved invaluable in 1848, when the government received information almost immediately about the Chartists' intentions and their likely strength following the rejection of the third petition.

The Whig response to the Chartists

The government's response to the Chartists was measured at times, and was intended not to provoke a violent reaction. In 1838, the Whigs were attacked in the Press for failing to take strong action against Chartist speakers who called for the use of physical force. O'Connor was notorious for his slogan, 'Peaceably if we may, forcibly if we must', but the language of other Chartists was even more extreme. J.R. Stephens, although an ordained minister, was famous for the inflammatory speeches he delivered in Ashton-under-Lyne and surrounding mill towns, often rousing his audience with slogans such as, 'For children and wife, we'll fight to the knife.'

In the years 1838–39, ministers took no action against Chartist speakers or writers who were openly advocating the use of violent force. The *Northern Star* gained a large circulation because of its comprehensive coverage of Chartist activities and speeches, and many Whigs called for action against the paper. The *Northern Star's* attention to Chartist activities was unsurprising given that O'Connor was its proprietor. The government refused to curtail the paper, preferring to allow the free and open discussion of ideas. Equally, it was reluctant to respond to calls from local magistrates to supply military forces, fearing that the deployment of troops in troubled areas would only inflame difficult situations. However, strong action was taken after the 1839 petition and the Newport Rising. In 1839–40, some 500 Chartists were arrested throughout the country. Many, including prominent leaders such as Lovett, received prison terms, though these were often for short periods of a year or two.

The government's response, 1842–48

Conditions in 1842 were rather different. Chartism had grown in strength since 1839, thanks in part to the movement's stronger organisation through the NCA. The economic downturn of 1842 was especially severe, leading to widespread strikes and the Plug Plot riots after the rejection of the second petition. Troops and units of the Metropolitan Police were sent to trouble spots, especially in Lancashire and Yorkshire; and large numbers of spies were employed to discover the plans being laid by local organisations. As in 1839, hundreds were arrested, with several of those found guilty being transported to the colonies for up to seven years.

The events of 1848 in Britain need to be placed into a wider national and European context. The third petition was presented at a time of widespread rebellions in Europe, notably in France and the German and Italian states; but the government viewed the situation in Ireland as its most pressing concern.

The failure of the Irish potato crop in 1845 led to a devastating famine: by 1848, one million people had died, and a further one million had emigrated to north-west England and the USA. Early in 1848, the followers of Young Ireland were prepared to revolt against English rule. They hoped that Chartist disturbances in England would divert troops from Ireland and allow the planned revolt to succeed.

The government's response to the 1848 petition suggested that they were very concerned about the Kennington Common meeting of 10 April and its possible outcome; and it is possible that they feared the revolutionary outbreaks that had broken out in 1848 in France, the German states, Italy and the Austrian Empire might be repeated in Britain. Queen Victoria and Prince Albert were sent to the Isle of Wight for their own safety, while the aged Duke of Wellington organised London's defences. At 2pm that day, Lord John Russell wrote triumphantly to the queen that the meeting had proved a complete failure.

The power of the state
The year 1832 had established a new political settlement that separated the propertied classes from the rest of society. Russell's 'finality' speech of 1837 showed that the government and its supporters would not contemplate even a modest extension of the franchise, let alone the Six Points of the People's Charter.

Moreover, state power was extended in the 1830s through technological change and the creation of police forces outside London. Britain was not involved in European conflicts at this time, so could use its armed forces to maintain domestic peace. In these circumstances, it was meaningless for Chartists to debate matters of moral and physical force. Napier put the issue succinctly with his accurate declaration that 'we have the physical force, not they.'

Changing government attitudes
During the 1830s, the Whigs had shown little interest in working-class grievances. On the contrary, many of their measures, notably the new Poor Law, were important factors in giving birth to the Chartist movement. In the 1840s, however, Peel's government showed more interest in tackling what the writer Carlyle referred to as 'the Condition of England Question', the growing separation between rich and poor. Measures such as the Mines and Factories Acts showed that social change and improvement could be achieved without Chartist intervention.

The significance of Major General Napier
In April 1839, Major General Sir Charles Napier was appointed to command 4,000 troops in the 11 counties that comprised the Northern District. His biography, written by his brother, gives historians an invaluable insight into Chartist activities in the north, and into Napier's response to a large number of disturbances.

EXTEND YOUR KNOWLEDGE

Major General Sir Charles Napier (1782–1853)
A descendant of Charles II, Napier saw distinguished service in Spain during the Napoleonic Wars. He and his brother William were strong supporters of radical politics, and were members of the Bath Working Men's Association, which promoted the causes of universal suffrage and the ballot. After commanding the Northern District, Napier was sent to India, where he was responsible for the conquest of the province of Sindh.

Napier was an unusual choice for command in the north because he had displayed an active sympathy for the poor for many years. On 24 April, he wrote to his brother: 'These poor people are inclined to rise, and if they do, what horrid bloodshed! At this moment the best handloom weaver can only earn 5 shillings a week, the price of food being such that this will not give him bread, without firing [heating], clothes or lodgings; hence a good workman in full wages must starve! And with this fact our rulers are called statesmen!'

Despite his concerns, Napier was able to set them aside and act to maintain order or put down Chartist agitation. His strategy was a simple one. He often rejected requests from magistrates for small detachments of troops to be sent to their towns, fearing that they would be easy targets for local Chartists. Instead, he divided his forces into three large detachments, positioned around the north and close to major industrial centres. The largest division, of 2,800 men, was placed under his direct command in South Lancashire to respond to disturbances in the textile towns.

Napier's fears about possible violence were eased somewhat when he attended the mass meeting held on Kersal Moor later in May. O'Connor claimed an attendance of a million people, but Napier estimated just 20,000 men and 10,000 women and children. He believed that there were only 500, mostly young men, who would take up arms, and claimed that '50 dragoons would have routed all that came to fight.'

Napier's gloomy view of possibly rebellious activities in the north appeared justified in July, when the Chartists called for the 'sacred month'. Napier believed that the expected month of strikes would not take place because workers simply could not afford to lose their wages for a prolonged period. Although magistrates pleaded with him for troops as a precautionary measure, Napier refused their requests, advising them to take no provocative actions if the sacred month took place. His refusal to confront the Chartists during strike action meant that peace was maintained during the few days of strike action.

**A Level Exam-Style Question
Section A**

Study Source 12 before you answer this question.

Assess the value of the source for revealing Napier's attitude towards the Chartists, and the strength of the Chartist organisation in 1839.

Explain your answer using the source, the information given about it and your own knowledge of the historical context. (20 marks)

Tip

Remember to comment briefly on the language and tone of the extract, and what they reveal about Napier's attitude.

SOURCE

The following source is taken from the diaries of Sir Charles Napier for August 1839. The entries were cited in Sir William Napier's biography of his brother, published in 1857.

Journal, August 2nd. Sacred month! Do they imagine they can make the people of England stop work for a month? How are they to feed? Rob. What! All England turn thieves in a day. Why the thieves, were they two million, would be floored instantly by the ten million who were not thieves! It is a farce, but the attempt may produce a tragedy and to prevent that is in some degree my affair. I can however only do my own work and with such magistrates God knows what may happen.

August 5th. Meetings every night in the market-place, and good sense talked by the speakers: some a little outrageous, but nothing to demand notice. My advice to the magistrates is not to interfere unless the peace be broken: why should they? If the mob break the peace I will break their heads; we will have no burnings, no disgraceful proceedings, which the honest part of the Chartists deprecate: but when men assemble to express their political opinions it is unjust as well as foolish to disperse them.

August 6th. The plot thickens. Meetings increase and are so violent, and arms so abound, I know not what to think. The Duke of Portland tells me there is no doubt of an intended general rising. Poor people! They will suffer. They have set all England against them and their physical force: – fools! We have the physical force, not they. They talk of their hundred thousands of men. Who is to move them when I am dancing round them with cavalry, and pelting them with cannon-shot? What would their 100,000 men do with my 100 rockets wriggling their fiery talks among them, roaring, scorching, tearing, smashing all they came near? And when in desperation and despair they broke to fly, how would they bear five regiments of cavalry careering through them? Poor men! Poor men! How little they know of physical force!

Napier held the command of the Northern District until 1841, when he took command of a body of troops in India. For two years, he had worked hard to maintain order in the northern counties. He was aware that plans for a co-ordinated rising were being discussed in many towns, and that drilling and the stockpiling of arms were taking place, but he would take no actions that might provoke a violent Chartist reaction. It was largely thanks to his sensible command of his troops that, although there was much unrest in the northern towns in 1839–40, the region did not experience a second Peterloo.

The impact of the growth of the rail network

Both the Chartist movement itself, and the government's ability to respond to it, were influenced by the development of a national network of railways. The first passenger railway in England, between Liverpool and Manchester, was opened in 1830. It was an immediate success, and encouraged substantial investment in railways. Two waves of **railway mania**, 1836–38 and 1844–46, led to the creation of a substantial network of lines, covering over 5,000 miles by 1850.

The railways helped in the establishment of a national organisation for Chartism. Before the railways, lecturers and campaigners had taken several days to move from one part of the country to another, and had often been forced to travel by sea between England and Scotland. Railways meant that they could move easily from town to town and visit more organisations. Railways carried news as well as people, and journals such as the *Northern Star* were able to bring the latest news of Chartist activities to their readers. Many Chartists travelled by rail to attend different Chartist meetings, most notably the Kennington Common meeting in London in April 1848.

Railway construction also influenced the spread of Chartism. While Chartism was flourishing in urban areas, problems of communication and distance had limited its spread into the countryside. The historian Briggs noted the significance of the Great Western Railway between London and Cornwall in encouraging the development of rural Chartism in the West Country. The building of a large complex of engine repair shops at Swindon in the early 1840s attracted a large number of workers from other areas. One of these, David Morrison, established a Chartist organisation in the town and went on to open a branch of the Chartist Land Company. The influence of Swindon Chartists led to similar organisations being established throughout the West Country, and such patterns were established elsewhere in Britain.

The railways influenced the ability of the authorities to respond speedily to Chartist disturbances. The government's response to the Newport Rising of November 1839 was hampered by the absence of a nearby railway. Troops from Winchester had to be marched 100 miles to Bristol and crossed the River Severn by steamer, only arriving in Newport six days after the rising. The Home Secretary

KEY TERM

Railway mania
The success of the Liverpool and Manchester railway encouraged many people to invest heavily in railway company shares. There was a frenzy of investment in the decade from 1836, but when this collapsed in the mid-1840s many people lost their investments and were completely ruined.

ordered guns to be sent from Woolwich to Newport. Trains took them to Twyford in Berkshire, but they too faced a long march overland to Bristol.

Where railways lines existed, the authorities could respond far more effectively to Chartist disturbances. In 1838, the London and Birmingham Railway was opened. At Birmingham, it connected with the Grand Junction line, allowing direct links to be established between London, Birmingham, Liverpool and Manchester. The Bull Ring riots of 1839 took place in the same year as the Newport Rising, but the authorities' response was much more effective. A force of 60 Metropolitan Police travelled from London to Birmingham in a few hours, and played an important role in dispersing the rioters.

ACTIVITY
KNOWLEDGE CHECK

The government and the Chartists

1 On a sheet of A3 paper, draw a spider diagram of the various ways in which the government was able to counter Chartist activity throughout the country.

2 Which methods do you consider to have been the most effective? Explain your answer.

ACTIVITY
SUMMARY

Drawing conclusions on Chartism

1 By 1850, Chartism had failed to secure the Six Points, and there were many factors that contributed to its failure.

   a) Examine the following factors and consider the extent to which they contributed to the failure of Chartism:

   - Leadership divisions, especially between Lovett and O'Connor

   - Divided aims

   - Moral v physical force

   - Prevailing economic conditions

   - The government's response to Chartism.

   b) In your opinion, which of these factors was the most important in explaining the failure of Chartism? Justify your choice.

2 Although Chartism failed to secure the Six Points, what, in your opinion, did it achieve?

 WIDER READING

Behagg, C. *Labour and Reform: Working-Class Movements, 1815–1914*, Hodder (1991)

Briggs, A. *Chartism*, Sutton Publishing (1998)

Briggs, A. (ed.) *Chartist Studies*, Macmillan (1959)

Evans, E.J. *Chartism*, Pearson Education (2000)

Evans, E.J. 'Chartism revisited', *History Review* (March 1999)

Mather, F.C. *Chartism and Society*, Bell and Hyman (1980)

Nash, D. 'The Chartists: Charting a future democracy', *History Today* (May 2010)

Royle, E. *Chartism* (third edition), Addison Wesley Longman (1996)

Royle, E. 'Chartism', *History Today* (December 1985)

Thompson, D. *The Chartists*, Maurice Temple Smith (1984)

Ward, J.T. *Chartism*, Batsford (1973)

3.5 Contagious Diseases Acts and the campaign for their repeal, 1862–86

KEY QUESTIONS

- Why were the Contagious Diseases Acts introduced between 1862 and 1869?
- What was the impact of these Acts on prostitutes and ordinary women?
- Why were the Contagious Diseases Acts repealed?

INTRODUCTION

Between 1862 and 1886, Britain's political system witnessed two reform Acts that fundamentally changed the size and composition of the electorate. In 1867, Benjamin Disraeli's Conservative government passed the Second Reform Act. This legislation enfranchised urban working-class men for the first time. Before 1867, only one out of seven males in England and Wales could vote, which made for an electorate of about 1.43 million out of a population of 30 million. The Reform Act increased this to all male heads of households, enlarging the electorate to just under 2.5 million. Then, in 1884, William Gladstone's Liberal administration forced through the Third Reform Act. This increased the electorate to 5.5 million, including men owning land worth £10 or more, or paying an annual rent of at least £10. There was, however, a noticeable admission from both reforms. Women were completely excluded. Property was the essential qualification of a voter, but propertied women had no say over the government in power or the laws it passed. Before 1867, this was unexceptional as few men could vote either, but the extension of the suffrage to some working-class men while upper- and middle-class women were excluded from politics was troublesome for a society defined by class. Yet it was not the Reform Acts that transformed the place of women in British politics, but a series of laws passed with the consent of the nation's scientific and medical professions: the Contagious Diseases Acts of 1864, 1866 and 1869. These Acts, passed to regulate prostitution and prevent the spread of venereal disease, were to change fundamentally the question of female suffrage. Before 1869, the matter of women's votes was a niche for radical female intellectuals and idealistic philosophers like John Stuart Mill. A woman's place was in the home and her function was to produce children. The Contagious Diseases Acts, however, made it clear that without political representation, women could expect little justice from a government exclusively comprised of men. The outcry these Acts caused and the campaign for their repeal popularised the women's rights movement.

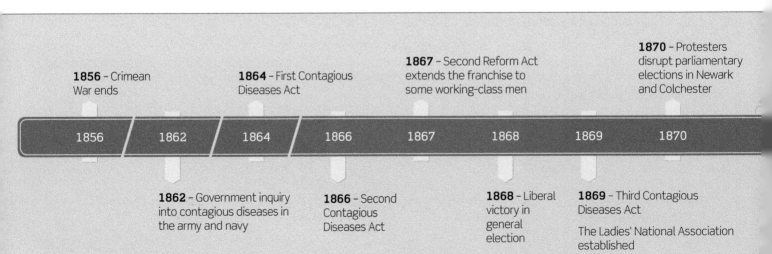

1856 – Crimean War ends

1862 – Government inquiry into contagious diseases in the army and navy

1864 – First Contagious Diseases Act

1866 – Second Contagious Diseases Act

1867 – Second Reform Act extends the franchise to some working-class men

1868 – Liberal victory in general election

1869 – Third Contagious Diseases Act

The Ladies' National Association established

1870 – Protesters disrupt parliamentary elections in Newark and Colchester

Women spoke out, challenging the government that represented a defining moment in British politics. Before 1869, women did not, as a rule, publicly question political matters. They were not expected to have a public presence over questions of government. During the 1870s and 1880s, in their attempts to repeal the Acts, women did just this. They shattered social conventions and provided a form of protest, largely based on questions of morality, that was phenomenally hard for the government to deal with.

WHY WERE THE CONTAGIOUS DISEASES ACTS INTRODUCED BETWEEN 1862 AND 1869?

Prostitution in Victorian Britain caused much moral indignation. Yet within society there was a growing acknowledgement that such practices were widespread, could not be prevented, and could even be viewed as something that was useful. It was widely believed that male sexual desire was natural and could not be repressed, whereas women's sexual desire was completely related to procreation. Prostitution was a valuable commodity for meeting the male demand for sex. With prostitution came the risk of venereal diseases, spread by sexual intercourse. With the advent of new statistical data collecting came a rising awareness of the extent of venereal infection. This caused alarm that the health of the nation was endangered and stimulated calls for the government to intervene.

The health of the army and the navy

During the Crimean War (1853–56) the health of the British army became a national concern. In a conflict marked by military incompetence, the army suffered more casualties from disease than on the battlefield. Hospitals and barracks lacked basic sanitation and were breeding grounds for infection. The most celebrated heroes of the conflict were not soldiers but nurses, notably Florence Nightingale and Mary Seacole. In the war's aftermath, the government looked to reform Britain's armed forces. At the centre of these efforts were enquiries into the health of the army and navy. A big problem was venereal diseases, like **gonorrhoea**, **syphilis** and scabies, spread through sexual activity.

High levels of disease occurred because of the army's dependence on prostitution. For the British army in peacetime, sexually spread diseases were the most common cause of infection. Common thought held that married men were usually reluctant to risk their lives in combat and made unreliable soldiers. Prostitution was therefore accepted as a necessity for allowing soldiers and sailors to fulfil their urge to have sex without the need for a wife. It was believed to be essential to sustaining a bachelor army and preventing homosexuality among soldiers.

KEY TERMS

Gonorrhoea
A sexually transmitted disease that causes an inflammatory discharge from the urethra or vagina.

Syphilis
A bacterial disease, usually spread by sexual intercourse, but also passed from a mother to her developing foetus. The earliest symptoms include sores. These later develop into a rash that usually affects the hands and feet. Usually 3-15 years after initial infection, if left untreated, syphilis causes large growths to develop on the skin, bone and liver.

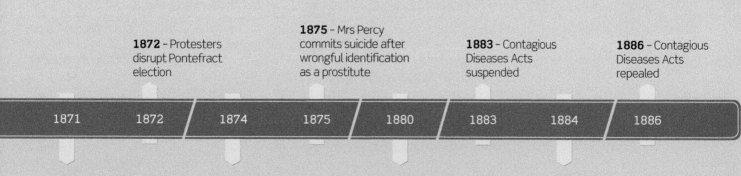

1872 – Protesters disrupt Pontefract election

1875 – Mrs Percy commits suicide after wrongful identification as a prostitute

1883 – Contagious Diseases Acts suspended

1886 – Contagious Diseases Acts repealed

| 1871 | 1872 | 1874 | 1875 | 1880 | 1883 | 1884 | 1886 |

1871 – Royal Commission investigates the effects of the Contagious Diseases Acts

1874 – Conservative victory in general election

1880 – Liberal victory in general election

1884 – Third Reform Act passed

SOURCE

1 Florence Nightingale attending to British soldiers in Scutari during the Crimean War. Despite her efforts to improve sanitation for injured troops, infection and disease actually increased during her time at the hospital.

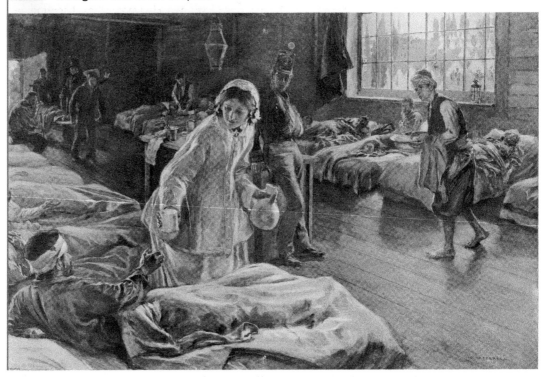

EXTEND YOUR KNOWLEDGE

Florence Nightingale (1820-1910)
The English social reformer Florence Nightingale earned fame during the Crimean War of 1854-56. For her work training and instructing nurses during the conflict, she became renowned as 'The Lady with the Lamp'. In 1860, she established the nursing school at St Thomas' Hospital in London, widely seen as the foundation of modern nursing. A promoter of sanitary reform and improvements to living conditions within British army barracks, Nightingale also encouraged what she regarded as appropriate forms of female employment.

The 1862 committee

The 1857 Royal Commission on the Health of the Army, established in response to the Crimean War, warned that levels of venereal infection were higher for soldiers and sailors than for other men of the same age outside the armed forces. This commission made no recommendations to solve this, but specified that medical checks on soldiers for venereal infections should be ended as they created a loss of respect among troops. Until 1859, soldiers had to undergo frequent medical checks; however, this practice was abandoned, as men were hostile to such invasive examinations.

The 1857 Royal Commission recommended the appointment of a statistical department to report annually on the health of the army. This department uncovered alarming statistics of the extent of sexually transmitted diseases within the army. In 1860, 37 percent of army hospital admissions were for venereal infections, with common fevers the next largest cause, with 25 percent. On average, 105 out of every 1,000 soldiers were in hospital because of sexually related illnesses. This meant that out of the home army's full strength of 60,000 troops, 586 men per day were inactive as a result of venereal infections.

In response, the government appointed a committee in 1862 to investigate how venereal disease within the army could be prevented. The central advocate of this committee was Nightingale; she was instrumental in selecting the members and questions of this investigation. She hoped to publicise the problem of venereal diseases in the armed forces. What she wanted was for the committee to recommend that the army should purify itself morally and end its reliance on prostitution.

Nightingale did not want the committee to suggest that the government should start regulating prostitutes.

Sir John Liddell, a member of the 1862 committee, instead looked to France, where, since 1802, the state had regulated prostitution with medical examinations of women. He went against Nightingale and argued that the state should regulate prostitutes by frequent medical checks. Nightingale believed that this practice, common on the Continent, was a disgusting infringement of prostitutes' rights. She suggested that soldiers might be persuaded to regulate their own health if the army issued penalties for concealing, but not contracting, venereal diseases. This was the official recommendation of the 1862 committee, along with establishing **lock hospitals** for prostitutes to visit voluntarily for treatment. However, this proposal found little support, with William Gladstone raising objections to such a scheme. The government ignored Nightingale and the 1862 committee.

EXTEND YOUR KNOWLEDGE

William Gladstone (1809-98)
Originally a Tory, Gladstone was the dominating Liberal politician of his age. Having entered parliament in 1832, he served as prime minister four times, during the periods 1868-74, 1880-85, 1886 and 1892-94. Gladstone was intensely religious, and his evangelical beliefs shaped much of his thinking. This Christian faith drove Gladstone's mission to rescue prostitutes. Even as prime minister, Gladstone was renowned for going out into London at night and bringing home young women. He and his wife would offer them food and shelter. While some raised doubts that his intentions were completely innocent, Gladstone did believe it a moral duty to save these women.

Prostitution and sexuality in Victorian society

In Victorian Britain, prostitution was not just a concern for the army and navy, but a much broader social dilemma. Fears abounded that it threatened marriages, the home, families and the nation. While police statistics estimated that there were about 30,000 prostitutes in England, some estimated the real figure to be as high as 500,000. Many of these were struggling to keep down additional work like waitressing and bartending, while up to 40 percent were domestic servants. For these women, venereal diseases presented a range of challenges. Gonorrhoea was believed to be relatively harmless, but the inflammation of the mucous membranes (the urethra for a man and the vagina for a woman) was painful. Worse was syphilis. If left long enough, syphilis caused blindness, deafness and insanity. The London Royal Free Hospital found that syphilis was responsible for 12.5 to 20 percent of all admissions to the ear and eye wards. Hereditary syphilis, passed from women to their children, was particularly debilitating. Within the civilian population, hereditary syphilis was a big killer for children aged less than 12 months. Up to 20 percent of child admissions to the Royal Free Hospital had the disease, with similar statistics found in Newcastle, Manchester and Birmingham. Conservative estimates reckoned that seven percent of the sick poor in London had venereal infections. These data convinced Britain's medical and military authorities that a wave of degenerative sickness was sweeping the nation. This was a threat to the health of the nation's population.

Prostitution engendered 19th-century notions of sexuality that involved perceived differences between men and women. Prostitution was quietly regarded by many as a social necessity. Female sexuality was understood to be wholly connected with reproduction. A woman's place was in the home and her first priority was to be a mother. Women were seen as lacking a sexual appetite; they were characterised as spiritual beings. In contrast, male sexuality was seen as animalistic and savage. This division between men and women was seen as a natural state. Indeed, these notions of sexuality were embodied in law. The Matrimonial Causes Act 1857 specified that a man could divorce a woman on the grounds of adultery. However, for a woman to divorce a man, she had to show additional reasons such as cruelty or desertion. Adultery on its own was not enough because such an act by a man was seen as natural. Sexual immorality was pardonable for a man, but not for a woman. Although unjust, at a practical level this emphasis on female fidelity was important in order to ensure the paternity of any children, which was essential to questions of inheritance. This double standard was further enshrined in law in that a man could use restraint to force his wife into sex, while a wife had to get a court order if her husband refused. Marriage was an important mechanism for moderating a man's sexual activity. The problem was how could unmarried men satisfy what were held to be biological needs? Men usually married later in life than women, while a woman's

KEY TERM

Lock hospital
In the 19th century, most British army and navy bases had a lock hospital. This was a hospital that had a ward specialising in the treatment of venereal diseases. The first of these opened in London in 1747. While sometimes for the treatment of the civilian population, they were usually within the administration of the military authorities. For example, the Royal Navy opened a lock hospital in Portsmouth in 1858, and another in Plymouth in 1863.

SOURCE

An image from 1871, depicting a man meeting a prostitute in Regent Street, London. The caption has the man's wife exclaiming, 'That girl seems to know you, George!' The cartoon was featured in *The Days' Doings*, a Victorian publication that portrayed society in a comedic light.

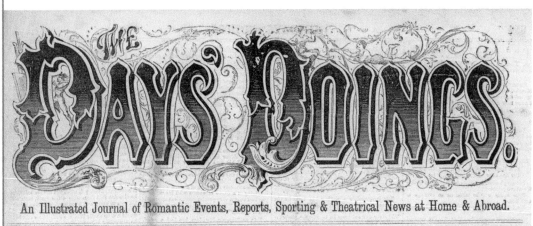

AWKWARD CONTRE-TEMPS IN REGENT STREET DURING THE HEIGHT OF THE SEASON.
"That Girl seems to know you, George!"

virginity was an important asset as a prospective wife. The solution was prostitution. While morally regrettable, the medical consensus that male and female sexuality were fundamentally different made prostitution a necessary social evil. Prostitution, however, for both the armed forces and for society, presented an immense medical challenge.

EXTEND YOUR KNOWLEDGE

Matrimonial Causes Act 1857

The Act reformed the laws on divorce and specified that adultery was no longer a criminal offence. Before this Act, divorces were decided by the Church of England and regarded as a religious matter. However, with the 1857 Act, divorces were to be granted by civil courts. Gladstone objected to this legislation, believing it harmed the Church, and he attempted to stop it passing through parliament. Along with the inequalities it brought over how a husband and a wife could apply for a divorce, it was also unfair in that it specified that a husband had to name his wife's adulterer in the legal proceedings. The same was not required by a wife who sought divorce on the grounds of adultery.

John William Acton (1813–75)

William Acton was a London surgeon of high reputation, specialising in the urinary and genital organs. He not only had medical knowledge of venereal diseases, but was concerned with the social issues created by prostitution. In 1857, Acton published a book that had a huge impact on government thinking on sexual health. In this book, entitled *Prostitution, considered in its moral, social, and sanitary aspects, in London and other large cities: with proposals for the mitigation and prevention of its attendant evils*, Acton outlined the problems prostitution created. However, Acton believed that because women in marriage only consented to sexual intercourse out of a desire for maternity, prostitution was a social necessity. Along with prostitution's role in the armed forces, the trade's importance for society more broadly encouraged Acton that it could never be eradicated. While Acton did not consider prostitution to be a moral evil, he was concerned that the diseases it spread presented a considerable social problem. Acton explained how venereal diseases were a danger to the health of the population and the condition of the armed forces.

Acton's book opened up discussions over how to deal with venereal infection and convinced many within Britain's medical profession that government intervention was essential. This was, after all, a time during which there was immense enthusiasm for intervening in the lives of the poor to bring about improvements in health and sanitation. During the 1850s, there were many organisations for the reform and salvation of prostitutes; such Christian work was popular with middle-class ladies. However, in 1860, Acton declared that charity and religion had failed to prevent prostitution and that scientific government regulation was called for. He was sure that movements for reforming prostitutes were ineffective. Acton was confident that the medical profession had the technology to solve the problem of venereal disease. Through regular medical checks of prostitutes, venereal disease could be identified and then treated.

At the same time, running through Acton's work was a belief that state regulation was necessary to save the health of women who, after working as prostitutes, would go on to live respectable lives. Acton wanted to change the widespread belief that once a woman became a prostitute she was on a road to inevitable ruin. He believed that prostitution was usually only a temporary position; a means for a woman to get through economically difficult times. The barrier to her resuming a normal life after such work was venereal infection. If the state protected women's health when they were prostitutes, they were given a chance to reform after their lives of sin.

ACTIVITY
KNOWLEDGE CHECK

Victorian prostitution

1 What threats did prostitution present to British society and the state?

2 Why was prostitution deemed necessary?

3 How significant was William Acton in the formation of political thought over prostitutes and how the state should deal with the problem of venereal disease?

KEY TERMS

Garrison town
A town or city where soldiers are permanently stationed.

Protected district
The series of naval ports and garrison towns where the regulations of the Contagious Diseases Acts were to be imposed on prostitutes. These became known as protected ports and protected towns. They were urban regions where soldiers and sailors could use prostitutes in the knowledge that they were being subjected to regular medical checks.

The Contagious Diseases Acts of 1864, 1866 and 1869

In 1864, the government passed the first Contagious Diseases Act, before an almost empty House of Commons and without debate. This legislation gave the police within ports and **garrison towns** the power to arrest prostitutes for medical examination. If a woman was found to be diseased, she could be detained in a lock hospital until cured. Failure to submit to examination would result in imprisonment. A second Act followed in 1866, once again without debate in the House of Commons. This time, the government introduced compulsory examinations for prostitutes once every three months. Prostitutes could be identified on the evidence of a single policeman before a magistrate. Examinations were to be performed on all suspected prostitutes within ten miles of a protected port or garrison town. The third Contagious Diseases Act was passed in 1869, extending this regulation to all garrison towns and allowing prostitutes to be held for five days before examination without trial. This Act established 18 **protected districts** across the UK. The 1869 legislation also made it legal for prostitutes to be detained in a lock hospital for up to a year and subjected to fortnightly inspections. It was hoped that these measures would ensure the safe regulation of prostitution.

SOURCE

3 In 1870, John William Acton provided his opinion over the value of the Contagious Diseases Acts. As he saw it, the legislation was in part a direct response to concerns that he had previously raised.

This Act, however, is something more than a means of imparting health both physical and moral, it forms the commencement of a new legislative era, being a departure from that neutral position previously held by English law with respect to venereal diseases, and admits that there is nothing in the nature of prostitution to exclude it from legislative action; but that, on the contrary, it may be necessary to recognise its existence, and to provide for its regulation, and for the repression, so far as possible, of its attendant evils; it is, in fact, the adoption—so far as it goes—of the principle for which I have always contended, that prostitution ought to be an object of legislation... Strange as it may appear, the same arguments that were urged against interference by the legislature with venereal maladies previously to the passing of the Contagious Diseases Bill — of whose futility that measure is the strongest possible acknowledgment—are still put forward with as much confidence as though they had never received such authoritative refutation, and must still be met and answered, so far as the civil population is concerned. Opposition to legislative interference is still based mainly on religious and moral grounds, the risk of encouraging sin, and the injustice of curtailing individual freedom. I yield to no man in my love of liberty and regard for religion. I am therefore especially careful in the following pages to show that the interference which I propose with personal liberty is unhappily necessary both for the sake of the community at large, and of the women themselves. Such interference is, in fact, not special – it is the extension to venereal disorders of the principle on which the Government endeavours to act in dealing with other forms of preventable disease, nor have the objections on religious grounds to the course which I propose any real foundation; on the contrary, religion is on my side.

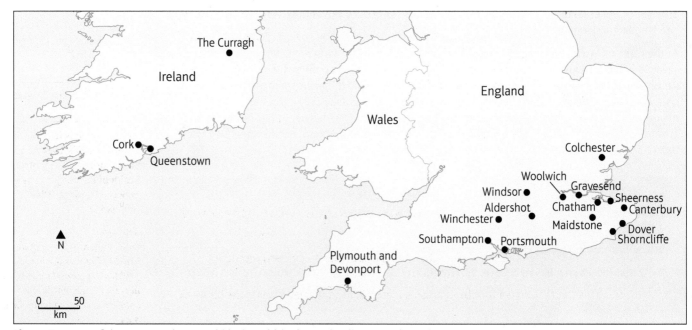

Figure 5.1 Map of the protected areas within the British Isles under the Contagious Diseases Act 1869.

Medical authorities like Acton and Elizabeth Garrett Anderson defended the Acts, believing the reduction of venereal disease to be benevolent and part of the moral duty of the state. While Acton hoped the legislation would improve public health, Anderson believed voluntary checks could not prevent infections. She was sure that the Contagious Diseases Acts would relieve the physical suffering of prostitutes, who otherwise would not visit hospitals early enough or remain long enough to be successfully treated.

EXTEND YOUR KNOWLEDGE

Elizabeth Garrett Anderson (1836–1917)

London physician Elizabeth Anderson cut a radical figure in Victorian society. After meeting the American-trained Dr Elizabeth Blackwell in 1859, Anderson keenly pursued a career in medicine in an age when women were excluded from the profession. After struggling to secure a medical education, she received the licence of the Society of Apothecaries in 1865, becoming the first woman qualified in Britain to enter the medical register. In 1870, she became the first woman to be awarded an MD from the University of Paris, and joined the British Medical Association in 1873. Following her admission, the association took efforts to prevent any more women joining, so Anderson was the only female member for 19 years.

SOURCE

'Lady Physicians', from the popular satirical journal *Punch*, December 1865. Response to Elizabeth Garrett Anderson's licence to practise, granted by the Society of Apothecaries in 1865.

LADY-PHYSICIANS.

Who is th s Interesting Invalid? It is young Reginald de Braces, who has succeeded in Catching a Bad Cold, in order that he might Send for that rising Practitioner, Dr. Arabella Bolus!

ACTIVITY
KNOWLEDGE CHECK

The Contagious Diseases Act

1 'The extent of the Contagious Diseases Acts was limited to regions of military and naval significance.'

   a) List the regions the legislation affected.

   b) What do you think the geographical limits of the Contagious Diseases Acts tell us about the government's priorities with regard to prostitution?

2 Why do you think the government took the measures that it did to protect its armed forces between 1864 and 1869?

A Level Exam-Style Question Section A

Study Source 3 before you answer this question.

Assess the value of the source for revealing William Acton's attitudes towards the Contagious Diseases Acts and to the dilemma prostitution posed to the legislature.

Explain your answer, using the source, the information given about its origin and your own knowledge about the historical context. (20 marks)

Tip

Think about how Acton wanted the Contagious Diseases Acts to be interpreted. He not only cites practical reasons for the Acts' introduction, but believes there to be a religious argument in favour of the regulation.

A Level Exam-Style Question Section B

How accurate is it to say the Contagious Diseases Acts were passed primarily to protect the health of the army and navy between 1864 and 1869? (20 marks)

Tip

Don't forget to mention that prostitution was a wide social problem, regarded by many as a necessary evil, not just for soldiers and sailors, but for all men.

WHAT WAS THE IMPACT OF THESE ACTS ON PROSTITUTES AND ORDINARY WOMEN?

The Contagious Diseases Acts fundamentally restructured the business of prostitution. State regulation consisted of medical examinations, hospital treatment and the registration of known prostitutes. Yet the ramifications of these Acts were much more extensive. Many upper- and middle-class women feared that the Acts endangered the dignity of women mistakenly identified as prostitutes. In appearing to lay the blame for venereal disease at the door of women, the government also provided a stark lesson to women of all social ranks: a parliament of men was more than capable of passing laws degrading to women and beneficial only to men.

Regulated prostitution

In 1990, historian F.B. Smith argued that the Contagious Diseases Acts had a noticeable impact on prostitution in Britain through the 1860s and 1870s. An 1871 Royal Commission, appointed to investigate the effects of the Acts, found considerable evidence that the legislation had improved conditions for prostitutes in protected areas. One lock hospital surgeon alleged that the provision of medical treatment encouraged infected women to travel voluntarily to protected regions, like Plymouth, and receive free medical treatment. He also claimed that the certificates given to disease-free prostitutes on release became valued assets. Prostitutes could use these clearance documents as a guarantee with clients, with some using them to secure increased payments. Church of England clergy working in lock wards in Aldershot, Chatham and Devonport reported that, while incarcerated and under treatment, both the health and self-esteem of prostitutes appeared to improve.

SOURCE

Captain Gore Jones, Royal Navy officer on HMS *Impregnable* and inspector of training ships at Plymouth and Devonport, reviewed the impact of the Contagious Diseases Acts before the 1871 Royal Commission.

The most remarkable feature connected with it is the improved state of the streets at the ports. One rarely or never now sees those brazen strumpets that one used to see in former days in the company of drunken sailors who molested everybody that passed along, and the number of brothels is also unquestionably very much reduced. The streets where brothels are known to exist are as quiet and as orderly as any other streets. Disease among the men is very much reduced and amongst the 3,000 boys that I have peculiarly charge of, it is almost unknown, although many of them are at that thoughtless age, about 17, when they would most probably, be more inclined to run after women than at any other age.

While health certificates became prized possessions for prostitutes, frequent checks and timely treatment increased the working life of women beyond the customary three to four years. While venereal diseases usually brought about a woman's premature death, the legislation appeared to be preserving their health and allowing them to remain in their business considerably longer than without regular investigations. The 1871 Royal Commission found that the most popular aspect of the Acts had been the reduced occurrence of scabies, commonly known as 'the itch'. This disease kept women awake at night, corrupted their fingers, and caused a constant scratching around their anal and genital regions. Of all venereal diseases, it was scabies that caused the most immediate discomfort. Treatment of this infection provided great relief to prostitutes. Furthermore, the status of prostitutes under the Acts was quite flexible. If women married or entered full-time employment, their names were removed from police registers. The Acts also reduced hospital admission rates for syphilis within the army. In protected areas, 37 out of every 1,000 soldiers were hospitalised with the disease, compared to 194 out of every 1,000 soldiers in unprotected areas.

Despite these findings, it must be remembered that the 1871 Royal Commission only interviewed certain types of witness. The bulk of the evidence collected came from Anglican ministers, doctors and military officers. Prostitutes were not sufficiently respectable for the government to consult, so the true extent of the Acts is much harder to determine. It was noticed by some that the laws made access to reform institutions harder for prostitutes who wanted help to leave their profession. For example, the Society for the Rescue of Women and Children refused to care for women from government hospitals as it was opposed to the Acts. The police were also unenthusiastic about the task of implementing the laws. Some within the police regarded the regulation of prostitution as an unnecessary distraction from preventing and detecting more serious crimes. There were worries that the official intervention had damaged social relations between prostitutes and their local communities; prostitutes effectively became outcasts.

SOURCE

The Lancet, one of Britain's leading medical journals, considers the regulation of prostitution in July 1868.

The Report of the Lords Committee appointed to consider the working of the Contagious Diseases Act is a very satisfactory one. It refers to three main points – the effects already produced by the operation of the Act, the propriety and practicability of extending its operation, and the measures whose adoption seems to be indicated for the successful prevention of 'contagious diseases'. Plenty of evidence has been obtained by the Committee to show that, where the Act has been in operation, not only has disease diminished in amount and severity, but women have been deterred from prostitution, and in a large number of instances reclaimed. There is no difficulty in the way of applying the Act generally to the country. Newcastle, Cheltenham, Gloucester, Exeter, Liverpool, Reading, and Bath are anxious to see the Act enforced. The military authorities desire its extension to Dover, Isle of Wight, Canterbury, York, Maidstone, Manchester, Dublin, Enniskillen, Cahir, and Gravesend. The Committee recommend that a Bill should be introduced into Parliament giving her Majesty power in Council to apply the Act of 1866 to all naval and military stations, and all towns and places – the inhabitants of which shall wish it, provided they can show adequate hospital accommodation, and that proper moral and religious supervision will be exercised over the unfortunate women treated. Lock hospitals, it is believed, would be best: and most economically established in connexion with existing hospitals; and it is thought that a certain kind of separation for the married, the not irreclaimable, and the hardened prostitutes should be carried out.

ACTIVITY
KNOWLEDGE CHECK

The navy and the Contagious Diseases Acts

Consider Sources 5 and 6 carefully and think about the sort of witness the government was interested in consulting over the Contagious Diseases Acts.

1 Which authorities did the government think were trustworthy over questions of prostitution?

2 Who were the Acts primarily intended to satisfy?

3 Who was the government not consulting?

It would seem that the Contagious Diseases Acts did improve health, both in the armed forces and for prostitutes. However, historian Judith Walkowitz argued in 1980 that this improvement was somewhat limited as there were no checks on men within the armed forces. While disease might have been contained, the limiting of checks to prostitutes meant that venereal infections could not be eradicated. Walkowitz also shows how the prevention of disease was undermined by the lack of medical knowledge around the subject. Although the medical authorities were confident they could cure gonorrhoea and syphilis, treatment was limited. For syphilis, a course of mercury was customary. This would be either through pills, vapour baths or ointment. While this could reduce the symptoms, syphilis was essentially untreatable. Scabies, caused by a skin infestation of mites, could be successfully treated by bathing an infected patient in a diluted solution of potassium sulphate, which killed the infestation.

Historian Paula Bartley has explained how it was hard to define what a prostitute was during this time. Most only worked in the profession part-time, to survive economically challenging circumstances, and many balanced this work with other jobs. The threat of mistaken identity appeared very real, thanks to the Acts' rather ambiguous definition of a 'common prostitute'. The police needed no proof that a woman had performed sexual acts for money to make an arrest. Reports from brothel keepers and secret informants, or even just ill repute, were enough to have a woman investigated as a prostitute.

Despite this, from a medical perspective, the Acts fulfilled their purpose to such an extent that in 1869 the medical profession moved to extend the regulation beyond protected areas to the civilian population throughout Britain. However, outside of these medical circles were concerns that the impact of the Acts on prostitution, and women more generally, were far from beneficial. While there had been little immediate opposition to the three Contagious Diseases Acts, the suggestion that they might be enforced nationally raised public concerns about the legislation that would escalate into a movement for its repeal.

Believing that the regulation introduced before 1869 had been beneficial, medical men and the civil authorities became increasingly active in promoting the extension of the Contagious Diseases Acts. In 1867, the Harveian Society of London (a medical association) reported that further state intervention was needed to reduce the high levels of venereal infection in the military and civilian population. Following this report, the Association for Promoting the Extension of the Contagious Diseases Act of 1866 to the Civilian Population was formed, and campaigned for the Act's extension, largely through the medical press, especially through the journal *The Lancet*. The membership of this movement included many Church of England clergymen and politically liberal doctors. While this movement campaigned for the extension of the Acts, between 1868 and 1869 opposition to the Acts increased. Activists like Harriet Martineau and Elizabeth Wolstenholme were becoming angry with the growing efforts of the authorities to interfere in the personal liberties of women.

Medical examinations and the speculum

The actual medical examinations performed on prostitutes for venereal infection were controversial. Doctors would use a metal instrument, known as a **speculum**, to allow internal observation. This exposing device was, in the opinion of medical authorities like Acton, absolutely vital for a complete medical examination of female genitalia. However, the speculum quickly became notorious. Medical examinations were unpopular with prostitutes, being brutally quick and degrading. In Devonport, such checks were performed, embarrassingly, in a room with clear windows and could be observed by dock workers. Above all else, it was the speculum that caused outrage. Fears abounded in society that doctors secretly enjoyed employing the device in investigations. The level of internal exposure it produced offended female propriety. The penetration of the speculum was conceived as a form of instrumental rape. Many worried that an inspection by speculum could destroy a virgin's modesty and degrade a pure mind. The medical checks, if performed on a virgin, could corrupt their sexual innocence. Some even believed the examinations were enough to rob a woman of her virginity altogether. Even in sexually experienced women, it was feared that the use of the speculum encouraged the development of sexual fetishes. There were also medical concerns over the instrument, which could cause cross-contamination between women. On one occasion, a doctor used the speculum on a young woman with an unbroken hymen who died during the inspection from what was recorded as an inflammation of the brain. Such accounts were deeply worrying. The speculum appeared both degrading and potentially dangerous.

Double standards

The Contagious Diseases Acts had an impact on women who were not prostitutes. Along with medical examinations, the legislation encouraged new forms of thought over government and sexuality. The Acts appeared to legalise prostitution by accepting that the business could not be extinguished. The state could not regulate prostitution without also appearing to condone it, and this was a massive problem for Victorian society. Contemporary notions of sexuality maintained that men had sexual desires while women were pure, interested in sexual intercourse only for procreation. Yet, the Contagious Diseases Acts, in forcing medical examinations on prostitutes instead of soldiers and sailors, appeared to place the blame for venereal disease on women. The state appeared to be accepting prostitution as a necessity for male sexuality, but, conversely, blamed women for the problems this created. In Britain, there was a growing feeling that prostitutes were victims, rather than conveyers, of male vice, yet now they were to suffer degradation to protect public health. This injustice was to become central to the popular unrest the legislation aroused. That the government, consisting entirely of men, had passed laws blaming women for the diseases spread by man's licentiousness was construed to be so immoral and unfair that the Acts radicalised women and triggered a campaign that would fundamentally change British politics.

KEY TERM

Speculum
A metal instrument that, when inserted into an orifice, causes it to dilate. The vaginal speculum made the direct observation of the cervix possible. This became popular in the 1830s with French specialists, but was harder to introduce into Britain in the 1840s and 1850s. The most successful speculum was the curved, blade-like Sims Speculum, developed for use on American slaves in the mid-19th century.

A Level Exam-Style Question Section B

What was the impact of the Contagious Diseases Acts for women between 1864 and 1870? (20 marks)

Tip
Make sure that you distinguish between the impact of the Acts on prostitutes who were regulated, and on women who were not prostitutes but were still affected by the implications of the Acts.

ACTIVITY
KNOWLEDGE CHECK

Medical inspections
1 How could it be argued that the medical inspections brought in by the Contagious Diseases Acts were excessive and demeaning to prostitutes?

2 How might it be shown that the examinations were effective and the laws warranted?

3 In your opinion, did the state have an obligation to regulate prostitution?

WHY WERE THE CONTAGIOUS DISEASES ACTS REPEALED?

The national movement against the Acts developed a variety of different tactics to put pressure on parliament to repeal the legislation. On the face of it, these efforts were successful in bringing about the abolition of the Acts in 1886. However, the extent to which this can be attributed to campaigners has been a subject of much historical attention.

The formation of the Ladies' National Association for the Repeal of the Contagious Diseases Act

The proposal to extend the Contagious Diseases Acts beyond ports and barrack towns sparked a hostile public response. In October 1869, Elizabeth Wolstenholme invited her friend Josephine Butler to lead a campaign against the Acts. On 31 December 1869, over 120 women, including Butler, Wolstenholme, Nightingale, Lydia Becker and Harriet Martineau, signed a protest against the Acts and announced the formation of the Ladies' National Association for the Repeal of the Contagious Diseases Acts (LNA). The number of signatures quickly increased to over 2,000. This group of women, which included many **Quakers** and **Unitarians**, made eight allegations against the Contagious Diseases Acts:

1 The Acts had passed through parliament in secrecy.

2 The legislation undermined the legal protection formally accorded to men and women.

3 The offence of prostitution was unclearly defined within the Acts.

4 The laws unfairly punished one sex for the vice of prostitution, which was largely the fault of men.

5 The Acts made the path to evil easier for men.

6 The implementation of the Acts was cruel and degrading, with the medical examinations brutalising women.

7 The Acts would increase disease, rather than prevent it.

8 The solution to the problem of venereal diseases was not 'physical', but had to be 'moral'.

These eight declarations represented the principle arguments that would be used against the Contagious Diseases Acts for the next 16 years. Before long, this popular movement had captured the public's imagination, and branches of the LNA were established in major cities across the country.

The role of Elizabeth Wolstenholme (1833–1918)

During the 1860s, Wolstenholme was a member of the National Association for the Promotion of Social Science. This organisation, more commonly referred to as the Social Science Association, was founded in 1857 to promote public health, penal reform, industrial relations and female education. In 1869, at a meeting of the Social Science Association in Bristol, a group of members, angered at recent proposals to extend the Contagious Diseases Act to civilian regions, founded the National Anti-Contagious Diseases Act Extension Association. Under the leadership of Charles Taylor, this became the National Association for the Repeal of the Contagious Diseases Acts. Wolstenholme was part of these early movements against the legislation, and from these experiences conceived of the LNA. Wolstenholme could not lead this movement, being something of a radical. She refused to comply with mid-Victorian expectations of respectability. She was openly hostile to marriage, believing it was legally disadvantageous for a woman. In 1875, she partnered Ben Elmy without a legal ceremony. When she became pregnant she agreed to marry, but only to avoid damaging the campaign against the Contagious Diseases Act. While Wolstenholme recognised she was unsuited to lead the LNA, she also refused to invite Florence Nightingale or the feminist social theorist Harriet Martineau. Both were unmarried and childless. Instead, Wolstenholme invited Butler to lead the movement.

KEY TERMS

Quaker
A member of a Christian movement founded by George Fox c1650. Quakers live by peaceful principles and believe that Christ works directly on the soul. As a result, they reject formal forms of worship.

Unitarian
A protestant Christian who rejects the Trinity. The Trinity maintains that God consists of Christ, the Father and the Holy Ghost. Unitarians believe that God is not composed of three parts, but is one unified deity.

Elizabeth Clarke Wolstenholme (1833–1918)

A keen promoter of women's rights, Wolstenholme campaigned for girls to be made economically independent. In the early 1860s, she established the Manchester Board of School Mistresses. In 1865, she supported John Stuart Mill's election to parliament and praised his efforts to have women included in the Reform Act 1867. She was also prominent in campaigns to secure women the right to keep their own property in marriage, partially fulfilled by the Married Women's Property Act 1870.

Harriet Martineau (1802–76)

Often referred to as the first female sociologist, Martineau wrote extensively on society, and on religious and domestic life from a feminine perspective. With Queen Victoria one of her readers, Martineau drew attention to marriage and children in domestic life. Politically quite radical, she was a close friend of the naturalist Charles Darwin.

The role of Josephine Butler (1828–1906)

Elizabeth Wolstenholme's choice of Butler to lead the LNA was an inspired appointment. The campaign against the Contagious Diseases Acts was difficult. For a group of women in Victorian society to speak out publicly against government policy was radical, but for the subject of the protest to be prostitution would open female protesters up to charges of impropriety. To promote the interests of prostitutes was, in terms of reputation, a risky course for members of the LNA, so it was vital that its leadership maintained impeccable morality. Of the LNA's 33 national leaders, 12 were single, six widowed and over 20 were childless. These women had to avoid any scandalous behaviour to avoid attempts to discredit them.

To lead this campaign a woman of undoubted morality was required. To hold most credibility in society and avoid questions of impropriety, she would also preferably be both a wife and a mother. Butler fitted this description completely. Married to an Anglican Church minister, George Butler, she was charismatic, strong-willed, fashionable and generally regarded to be beautiful. She was a devout Christian, with strong **evangelical** convictions. Importantly, her leadership was driven out of maternal love. Aged just six, Butler's daughter had tragically died after falling down the stairs. This loss left Butler devastated. She became passionate about finding women in a worse state than her own and bringing them salvation. Usually this meant prostitutes. Butler founded a refuge for fallen women and regularly visited destitute prostitutes in workhouses. Taking pity on these women, she vehemently

KEY TERM

Evangelical

A form of Christianity that maintains salvation can be achieved by the belief that Christ died to redeem man of his sins, an act also known as the Atonement. There were several parts to Victorian evangelicalism. A belief in the Atonement was central. This was combined with a belief that it was a Christian's duty to spread the word of God and convert non-believers, and finally, a belief that the New Testament of the Bible was true and the basis for Christian faith.

opposed anyone who blamed them for their plight. She was adamant that prostitutes were more sinned against than sinning. For Butler, the Contagious Diseases Acts appeared to be legalising prostitution and were therefore morally abhorrent.

SOURCE

Josephine Butler recalls the moment she decided to take on the leadership of the LNA. Butler made these reflections some years after the repeal of the Contagious Diseases Act and they were published in 1909, after her death.

I spoke to my husband then of all that had passed in my mind, and said, 'I feel as if I must go out into the streets and cry aloud, or my heart will break.' And that good and noble man, foreseeing what it meant for me and for himself, spoke not one word to suggest difficulty or danger or impropriety in any action which I might be called to take. He did not pause to ask, 'What will the world say?' or 'Is this suitable work for a woman?' He had pondered the matter, and looking straight, as was his wont, he saw only a great wrong, and a deep desire to redress that wrong – a duty to be fulfilled in fidelity to that impulse, and in the cause of the victims of the wrong; and above all he saw God, who is of 'purer eyes than to behold iniquity,' and whose call (whatever it be) it is man's highest honour to obey; and his whole attitude in response to my words cited above expressed, 'Go! and God be with you.'

I went forth, but not exactly into the streets, to cry aloud. I took the train to the nearest large station – Crewe – where there is a great manufactory of locomotives and a mass of workmen. I scarcely knew what I should say, and knew not at all what I should meet with. A friend acquainted with the workmen led me after work hours to their popular hall, and when I had delivered my message, a small group of leaders among the men bade me thrice welcome in the name of all there. They surprised me by saying, 'We understand you perfectly. We in this group served an apprenticeship in Paris, and we have seen and know for ourselves the truth of what you say. We have said to each other that it would be the death-knell of the moral life of England were she to copy France in this matter.' From Crewe I went to Leeds, York, Sunderland and Newcastle-on-Tyne, and then returned home. The response to our appeal from the working-classes, and from the humbler middle class in the northern and midland counties and in Scotland, exceeded our utmost expectations. In less than three weeks after this first little propagandist effort, the workingmen of Yorkshire, recognised leaders in political and social movements, had organised mass meetings, and agreed on a programme of action, to express the adhesion of the working-classes of the north to the cause advocated.

Yet Butler was reluctant to lead the campaign, requiring persuasion from Wolstenholme and desiring the consent of her husband before agreeing. As the honorary secretary of the LNA, Butler was an immense asset, and very charismatic. Following the Royal Commission that had been set up in 1871 to investigate the impact of the Contagious Diseases Acts (see page 114), one of the commission's members, Peter Rylands, recalled the effect of Butler's testimony. While he did not agree with all of her opinions, he remarked that there was something holy about Butler; it was clear to him that 'the spirit of God was there'. This was an image Butler cultivated, personally identifying with St Catherine of Siena. In 1878, Butler wrote a biography of St Catherine, believing her to be a pioneering female activist.

EXTRACT

1 The portrait of Josephine Butler used to commemorate her on a Royal Mail set of stamps that honour British humanitarians. The stamps were issued on 15 March 2016.

However, although Butler was an inspirational leader, her impact on the anti-Contagious Diseases Acts campaign was not always positive. At the 1871 Royal Commission, Butler's condemnation of the degrading effects of the Acts in Portsmouth and Devonport appeared underwhelming when she confessed to having no first-hand knowledge of prostitution in these protected areas. Her testimony was based on hearsay, including her allegations of police misconduct. At a later select committee inquiry in 1881, she revealed that she had not been to a protected district since Canterbury in 1873. So there was a certain disconnection between Butler's leadership and the women most affected by the Contagious Diseases Acts. At the same time, while presenting herself as God's agent won her allegiance from fellow campaigners, some of her work with prostitutes appeared indulgent. Along with her sister, who had also lost a daughter, Butler would take pictures of her dead daughter to women in lock hospitals to weep over them.

Historian F.B. Smith has argued that Butler's uncompromising demands to repeal the Acts prevented important reforms to the welfare of prostitutes. At the 1871 Royal Commission, John Stuart Mill proposed that the existing regulation might be replaced by a system of voluntary examinations in private clinics. Butler completely blocked this compromise, as it would still place the blame for prostitution on women and appear to legitimise immoral behaviour. Such a system of regulation was therefore delayed until 1883. Butler's unrelenting campaign to completely abolish the Acts possibly delayed improvements to prostitutes' experience of medical examinations. Despite this, Butler was a strong character who added direction to the LNA. She wanted seduction made illegal, when performed by both women and men. She also proposed changes to laws covering illegitimacy. Butler believed that part of the problem was that men were driven from the company of women at an early age and so developed a belief that prostitution was an excusable sin. She was particularly outspoken on the use of the speculum. It was not just a degrading instrument, but because it was performed by men on women, the procedure effectively became a sexual attack. Butler's claims that doctors were performing instrumental rape were sensational.

EXTEND YOUR KNOWLEDGE

John Stuart Mill (1806–73)

The influential Utilitarian philosopher, and between 1865 and 1868 Liberal MP for Westminster, was an outspoken promoter of women's rights. Mill's 1869 essay, *The Subjection of Women*, argued that women needed to be made equal to men and that marriage was a mechanism that reduced them to something resembling slaves. This text became a seminal work for women's rights campaigners. On the passing of the Reform Act 1867, Mill proposed that the word 'man' should be changed to 'person', so as to include women within this extension of the franchise. Despite observing that female property owners hardly presented a threat to the state, his motion was defeated in the House of Commons by 194 votes to 73.

The role of James Stansfeld (1820–98)

Although Butler was a formidable figure within the LNA, the question of leadership was often troublesome. James Stansfeld and Henry J. Wilson (1833–1914) were both responsible for organising the movement. Stansfeld worked in Gladstone's cabinet until the Liberal election defeat in 1874. A Unitarian brewer, he was a leading radical MP within the government. Before 1874, Stansfeld was constrained from campaigning due to his responsibilities in the cabinet, but from 1874, he took a dominant role in leading the national movement for the repeal of the Contagious Diseases Acts. Prior to 1874, while Butler guided LNA policy, Stansfeld reshaped the movement into a more effective political pressure group. He continued to cultivate popular support, but adopted new strategies. He looked to develop scientific arguments against the Acts based on facts. This transformed the campaign from a moral venture to a pragmatic one. Stansfeld encouraged the formation of the National Medical Association in 1875, which enlisted medical professionals to campaign against the Acts. This pressure paid off in 1879, when the Conservative government agreed to establish a committee of inquiry into the Acts. This continued to gather information until 1882. When the Liberals returned to power in 1880, Stansfeld was appointed to this inquiry.

Stansfeld's role created some tension with many middle-class women within the LNA. They felt that men were too influential within the movement. Women such as Butler, feeling threatened by the men in the LNA, preferred to make alliances with working-class men, who were generally easier to manage. Butler relied on Stansfeld's organisational skills, but felt his prominence in the movement to be a threat. Likewise, she resented Henry Wilson's belief that the repeal was not especially a problem for women, but for all society. Both Wilson and Stansfeld were central to the LNA's success, however. Wilson was instrumental in getting the Liberal Party to support the repeal, while Stansfeld would eventually push through the final repeal in 1886. Unlike Butler, Wilson and Stansfeld were eligible to become Members of Parliament. Both radicals, they were Liberal MPs and so had political influence in parliament.

SOURCE

A letter from Mr George Brunswick to the *Leeds Mercury*, 4 January 1870, just a few days after the formation of the LNA.

The writer of your London letter, in noticing the opposition to the Contagious Diseases Act, says 'it would be well if the Ladies' Committee could enlist the support of some medical men of high repute.' Professor Newman, in a recent letter, says, 'certain doctors have the ear of the Privy Council and indoctrinate it. The Privy Council moves the Ministry, if it be not quite the same body; and the whispers of the Ministry carry the Doctors' Bill through Parliament. Thus we are under an insidious despotism.' The fact that the Ladies' Committee has originated and is maintained without assistance from doctors of a certain class is significant of their attitude to this question. Yet there have been numerous medical men who enjoy the confidence of their fellow citizens who have both written and spoken against the Contagious Diseases Act, but their influence has not had the weight it deserves, because they are cut off from all legal life by laws which give monopoly to a certain class of doctors only. It cannot be denied that there are men who stand outside the ranks of the legally orthodox practice of medicine, not only because they cannot practice as **allopaths** do, or believe in the contradictions of the so-called pharmacopeia, but because their minds can comprehend more than is allowed by the dominant medical sect. The country is now beginning to reap the fruits of this unjust state of things by the enforcement of the obnoxious Act under consideration, as well as by another absurd and tyrannical medical enactment which has lately excited great inquiry... Those who have been instrumental in promoting the Contagious Diseases Act are now seeking to extend its operations to other towns than those to which it is now confined. If the people wish to resist it they must take the question of health promoting into their own hands.

KEY TERM

Allopath
An individual who treats diseases with conventional means, such as drugs to counter symptoms.

A Level Exam-Style Question Section A

Study Source 8 before you answer this question.

Assess the value of the source for revealing anti-Contagious Diseases Act protesters' attitudes towards professional doctors and the attitudes of the government towards these same doctors.

Explain your answer, using the source, the information given about its origin and your own knowledge about the historical context. (20 marks)

Tip
Think about how the government used professional medical authorities and what this says of the extent to which it would let doctors shape its legislation. Consider how undermining the authority of medical professionals was important for arguments in favour of repealing the Contagious Diseases Acts.

Forms of protest and political influence

In its campaign against the Contagious Diseases Acts, the LNA employed a series of different tactics. Petitions against the Acts, attracting hundreds of thousands of signatures, were an early form of protest, but the LNA developed more influential ways of exerting pressure on parliament. The LNA found that even without parliamentary representation, it was possible to have political impact. A way of achieving this was to single out parliamentary candidates, usually Liberals, and undermine them throughout their election campaign unless they supported the repeal of the Acts.

Interfering in elections

One notable success for the LNA was the 1870 candidacy of Henry Storks for Newark. Storks had been the governor of Malta and had enforced the Contagious Diseases Acts rigorously across the Mediterranean island. Repeal campaigners ruthlessly targeted Storks for his behaviour on Malta, placing so much pressure that he withdrew his candidacy on the day of the election. A new Liberal candidate was elected who opposed the Acts. This was a huge coup for the LNA and showed the extent of its support. However, the triumph was short-lived. Storks stood again in 1870 for Colchester. When protesters entered their own pro-repeal candidate, it split the Liberal vote and handed the Conservatives victory.

EXTRACT

Josephine Butler's recollections from the Colchester election in 1870. She recalls contrasting reactions from different elements of the population of the town, which was directly regulated by the Contagious Diseases Acts. These comments were made after the repeal of the Contagious Diseases Act and were published in Butler's 1909 autobiography.

The National Association, which was daily increasing in vitality and in boldness of operation, effectually prevented the further extension of the system we opposed, and by means of successful contests at by-elections – pre-eminently that of Colchester in October–November, 1870, where the Government candidate, Sir Henry Storks, was defeated on this one question by over 400 votes – forced the Government to look seriously into the matter. I give some prominence to this hotly contested election at Colchester, as it proved to be somewhat of a turning-point in the history of our crusade. A public meeting had been arranged for in the theatre. I was with our friends previous to this meeting in a room in a hotel. Already we heard signs of the mob gathering to oppose us. The dangerous portion of this mob was headed and led on by a band of keepers of houses of prostitution in Colchester, who had sworn that we should be defeated and driven from the town. On this occasion the gentlemen who were preparing to go to the meeting left with me all their valuables, watches, &c. I remained alone during the evening. The mob were by this time collected in force in the streets. Their deep-throated yells and oaths, and the horrible words spoken by them, sounded sadly in my ears. I felt more than anything pity for these misguided people. It must be observed that these were not of the class of honest working people, but chiefly a number of hired roughs and persons directly interested in the maintenance of the vilest of human institutions... I may be excused, perhaps, for mentioning an amusing incident of the election. I was walking down a by-street one evening after we had held several meetings with wives of electors, when I met an immense workman, a stalwart man, trudging along to his home after work hours. By his side trotted his wife, a fragile woman, but with a fierce determination on her small thin face; and I heard her say, 'Now you know all about it; if you vote for that man Storks, Tom, I'll kill ye!' Tom seemed to think that there was some danger of her threat being put in execution. This incident did not represent exactly the kind of influence which we had entreated the working women to use with their husbands who had votes, but I confess it cheered me not a little.

ACTIVITY
KNOWLEDGE CHECK

Public responses to the protest

1 Read Extract 2. How do you think different elements of society reacted to the LNA's campaign?

2 How could protesters place pressure on voters to support their cause?

In 1872, H.C.E. Childers sought re-election in Pontefract. Childers was First Lord of the Admiralty, and because the Admiralty had zealously supported the Contagious Diseases Acts, protesters targeted Childers' election campaign. Childers was a popular figure in Pontefract, so when the LNA organised demonstrations against his re-election, these were met with local hostility and violence. Childers was returned to parliament, but with a greatly reduced majority. Anti-Contagious Diseases Acts protesters received the credit for this drop in support. This practice of manipulating public sympathy and influencing the electing of MPs was a powerful way for the LNA to campaign. However, its influence was fragile. The problem was that protesters were almost entirely dependent on Liberal candidates and were unable to exert influence over Conservative MPs. This position was made clear when Benjamin Disraeli's Conservative Party won the 1874 general election. The LNA lost the Liberal MPs who were sympathetic to its cause. While popular protest through the influencing of Liberal MPs could be sensational, it risked weakening the Liberal Party and allowing the Conservatives to increase their power.

SOURCE
9

A poster encouraging voters to support the repeal of the Contagious Diseases Acts at the January 1881 by-election in Wigan. The Conservatives won this election, with Francis Powell being returned to parliament. However, he was unable to take his seat on account of corrupt practices. He was later returned to parliament in 1885. This poster shows how campaigners appealed to both Liberal and Conservative voters.

WIGAN ELECTION.

A PUBLIC

MEETING

WILL BE HELD ON

THURSDAY, JAN. 6th, 1881,

IN THE

PUBLIC HALL, KING STREET,

TO PROMOTE THE UNCONDITIONAL REPEAL

OF THE

CONTAGIOUS DISEASES ACTS

RELATING TO WOMEN.

CHAIR TO BE TAKEN AT 8 O'CLOCK.

THE MEETING WILL BE ADDRESSED BY

J. BIRBECK NEVINS, Esq, M.D.

OF LIVERPOOL;

T. CARSON, Esq., M·R·C·S·I.

OF LIVERPOOL;

WILLIAM T. SWAN, Esq.

OF LONDON, REPRESENTATIVE OF THE NORTHERN COUNTIES LEAGUE FOR THE ABOLITION OF STATE REGULATION OF VICE.

EDMUND JONES,

PRESIDENT OF THE NATIONAL WORKMEN'S LEAGUE FOR REPEAL OF THE CONTAGIOUS DISEASES ACTS.

ELECTORS! No question upon which either Mr. LANCASTER or Mr. POWELL will have to record his Vote, if returned to Parliament, is of greater importance than whether the one-sided, unjust, and unconstitutional CONTAGIOUS DISEASES ACTS, 1866-9, should continne to disgrace our Statute Book, or be unconditionally repealed.

Every Voter, Liberal or Conservative, is earnestly invited.

WALL, PRINTER, WALLGATE, WIGAN.

Drawing attention to women mistaken for prostitutes

Another tactic to gain support against the Contagious Diseases Acts was to draw attention to women who had been incorrectly identified as prostitutes. The most dramatic of these was the case of Mrs Percy, who was mistaken for a prostitute in Aldershot in 1875. Mrs Percy drowned herself while the police were investigating her behaviour. Butler appreciated the publicity value of such a story, noting privately how 'Every good cause requires martyrs... and this woman's death will... be a means in the hands of Providence, of shaking the system'. Other accounts of incorrect identification caused equal sensation, such as Elizabeth Holt in 1870, who claimed to have been wrongly held in Maidstone jail, and Cardine Whybrow of Chatham, who, despite being identified as a prostitute, claimed to be living with her mother and home early every night. There were several other claims of mistaken identity, but these had little weight. Elizabeth Holt was found to have received treatment in a lock hospital on five occasions prior to May 1870, while Cardine Whybrow had actually been living in the attic of a brothel. Nevertheless, such cases fuelled public fear that the Contagious Diseases Acts risked the dignity of innocent women.

Co-operation with prostitutes

One noticeable failure of the LNA was its inability to mobilise working-class women against the Acts. By 1882, it was apparent that the campaign had failed to sway public opinion in the subjected ports and towns. While this proved not to be a barrier to repeal, as the local authorities in these areas eventually objected to the Acts, there were anomalies. In Plymouth and Southampton in the early 1870s, campaigners succeeded in persuading prostitutes to resist the legal requirements of the Acts. In Plymouth throughout 1870, public meetings and pamphleteering agitated prostitutes and brothel-keepers to such an extent that they refused to co-operate with the police and doctors. In what became known as the 'Siege of Devonport', campaigners worked with prostitutes in resisting medical examinations. When women who refused examination were sent to court, campaigners provided legal and financial support throughout trials. Several women were able to argue that they were no longer prostitutes and so should avoid examination. Nevertheless, by 1871, this expensive campaign had run out of steam, and prostitutes in the area were compliant with the laws by 1872.

ACTIVITY
KNOWLEDGE CHECK

LNA campaigning

1 Make a list of all the different ways the LNA exerted pressure on the government to repeal the Contagious Diseases Acts.

2 How effective was each of these actions?

EXTRACT

3 From F.B. Smith's 1971 article, 'Ethics and disease in the later nineteenth century: The Contagious Diseases Acts', which appeared in the journal *Historical Studies*. Smith portrayed the majority of prostitutes as passively agreeing with the Acts, providing them with very little agency of their own.

Many of the army prostitutes were hopelessly wretched. Almost certainly of low intelligence and general capacity... Modern studies of prostitutes reveal that they still bitterly resent compulsory medical examinations. Yet there were some who did not mind.

EXTRACT

From Judith Walkowitz's seminal *Prostitution and Victorian Society*, published in 1980. Walkowitz's work was important in moving attention around the Contagious Diseases Acts away from traditional military histories that focused on the practical value of the legislation for the armed forces. Instead, Walkowitz stressed the cultural and political role of the Acts in galvanising female protest. Much of Walkowitz's important work focused on just two case studies: Plymouth and Southampton.

Repealers were most active in subjected districts in 1870, during the early popular phase of the campaign, and later in 1876, when under Stansfeld's leadership they tried to revive public interest in repeal. In the early 1870s, repeal agitation was most successful in two southern ports, Plymouth and Southampton that were placed under the supervision of the Admiralty. In both districts numerous public meetings in support of repeal were held, local branches of the LNA and National Association were formed, and hundreds of registered prostitutes were incited to resist the legal requirements of the acts. These cities provide a comparative local study of the repeal campaign and the operation of the acts in two subjected districts. The local campaigns in Plymouth and Southampton were in many ways a microcosm of the national movement. Because of their smaller dimensions, it is possible to scrutinize the motives and interests of supporters and opponents of the acts that were also played out on the national level.

EXTRACT

From Catherine Lee's 'Prostitution and Victorian society revisited: The Contagious Diseases Acts in Kent', published in 2012 in *Women's History Review*. While building on Walkowitz's study, Lee emphasised that the impact of the Contagious Diseases Acts varied from location to location. Lee looked beyond Plymouth and Southampton to examine prostitutes' responses. Lee's gender analysis portrays prostitutes as agents who both rejected and complied with the regulation. This revised many of Walkowitz's conclusions about how prostitutes responded to the Contagious Diseases Acts.

The ten Kentish naval dockyards, garrison towns and sea and river ports made subject to the CD Acts were widely heterogeneous and experienced the operations of the legislation differently, both from one another and from the south coast ports investigated by Judith Walkowitz... The Kentish evidence suggests a widely heterogeneous response to the CD Acts amongst the women directly affected. This ranged from well-publicised outright disobedience, to the partial compliance demonstrated by those who, for example, said that they had no objection to being examined but refused to sign the submission form, or those who objected to remaining longer in the lock hospital than was necessary to achieve the superficial appearance of a cure. As has been seen, the statistics relating to medical inspection also suggest that a large number of women cooperated fully... The hitherto little-examined evidence relating to control of the Kentish prostitutes under the CD Acts poses a challenge to the notion that events in Southampton and Plymouth were typical or represent the wider history of the Acts. Moreover, a narrative of prostitutes' cooperation with the CD Acts as part of a strategy of survival is entirely consistent with 'the presentation of women not only as victims and resisters of patriarchal social formations, but also as colluders, survivors, and beneficiaries'.

THINKING HISTORICALLY   Evidence (6b)

The strength of argument

This exercise is designed to help you consider the value of secondary extracts and how to analyse the evidence and arguments you are presented with by different historians.

Answer the following:

1 Read Extract 3.

   a) What is weak about this historian's claim?

   b) What could be added to make it stronger?

2 Read Extract 4.

   a) Is this an argument? If yes, what makes it one?

   b) How might this argument be strengthened?

3 Read Extract 5.

   a) How has Lee expanded her explanation to make the claim stronger?

   b) Can you explain why this is the strongest claim of the three extracts?

4 What elements make a strong historical claim?

The Acts repealed

The campaign against the Contagious Diseases Acts had immediate impact. As one concerned MP observed, 'We know how to manage any other opposition in the House or in the country, but this is very awkward for us – this revolt of the women. It is quite a new thing; what are we to do with such opposition as this?' The 1871 Royal Commission into the effects of the legislation was an early sign that parliament took seriously the demands of protesters. Occurring just over a year after the LNA's formation, the report emanating from this inquiry made clear that it had been a response to popular pressure.

SOURCE
10

The report from the 1871 Royal Commission into the impacts of the Contagious Diseases Acts. The commission concluded that the legislation was working effectively and rejected the allegations of the LNA. Yet such an inquiry represented a significant triumph for the LNA's campaign.

These proceedings had a considerable effect on the public mind. In July 1868 the Lords had reported that in no case had any objection been made to the Act in places to which it had been applied, while meetings had been held in many important towns not subject to its operation favourable to its introduction. But before the end of the following year a formidable opposition had arisen. An active and influential organization was arrayed against the Act. Public meetings were held in most of the subjected districts, and in several large towns, at many of which meetings inflammatory statements were made as to the character and operation of the new law. Most of those statements, so far as they had any foundation whatever, were perversions of the truth; but they had their effect. Nevertheless the movement against the Acts was supported by many persons of station and intelligence, and among others by several ladies who resented this legislation as insulting to their sex, and tending to the depravation of public morals. In the midst of this agitation the House of Commons was moved to repeal the Acts, and after a long discussion, with closed doors, Your Majesty's ministers undertook to advise Your Majesty to refer the whole question to a Royal Commission to inquire into and report upon the administration of the Contagious Diseases Acts... Among the means adopted by some of the opponents of the Acts to bring them into public odium, have been charges of misconduct or gross negligence on the part of the police in putting the law in force against common prostitutes. Cases have been brought forward in publications and speeches at public meeting, not only of cruel insults offered to innocent women through the agency of the Acts, but of repeated wrongs to the unhappy women through the agency of the Acts, but of repeated wrongs to the unhappy women who have been or are subjected to them. We have made inquiry into every case in which names and details were given. We have requested the persons who have made these statements to substantiate them. In some instances the persons thus challenged have refused to come forward; in others, the explanations have been hearsay, or more or less frivolous. The result of our inquiries has been to satisfy us that the police are not chargeable with any abuse of their authority, and they have hitherto discharged a novel and difficult duty with moderation and caution... The charges thus rashly made and repeated, have contributed much to excite public indignation against these enactments.

The LNA's campaign was ultimately successful. In 1883, the Contagious Diseases Acts were suspended, and in 1886, they were repealed. While the House of Commons discussed the suspending of the Acts, Butler and her followers held continuous prayers next to parliament throughout the night. The efforts of the protesters had succeeded in exerting influence on parliament, and the forms of protest utilised were very difficult for politicians to deal with. Influencing election results and raising fears over wrongful identification were useful tactics, but what made the protest so forceful was its success in convincing large elements of society that the Contagious Diseases Acts were immoral.

Despite this, the direct relationship between the LNA and the repeal of the Acts is hard to specify. While the campaign encouraged a political climate in which the Contagious Diseases Acts appeared as shocking evidence of society's sexual double standard, Butler could not claim complete credit for their repeal. While Gladstone's family supported a repeal, from 1883 to 1886 the Acts remained law, with the Liberal Party distracted by the question of Irish Home Rule. Repealing the Acts was not a priority. Indeed, the laws were only eventually repealed when anti-Contagious Diseases Act campaigner and MP James Stansfeld demanded Gladstone repeal the Acts in exchange for support for Irish Home Rule. Facing a divided government over the Irish question, Gladstone agreed to repeal the Acts.

In addition to these political negotiations, there is evidence that the medical profession was less enthusiastic about the continuation of the Acts. New understandings of the long-term consequences of gonorrhoea and syphilis persuaded many that regulation was no longer a viable option. As both diseases were found to cause long-term health problems, such as infertility and pelvic ailments, the belief that science could cure venereal disease was undermined. There was a loss of confidence that infected patients could be treated. Instead of regulation, the medical profession was moving to promote chastity and precaution. Rather than curing infections, trying to stop individuals from contracting them altogether was the priority. For this, the Contagious Diseases Acts were clearly not sufficient.

THINKING HISTORICALLY Cause and consequence (7c)

The value of historical explanations

Historical explanations derive from the historian who is investigating the past. Differences in explanations are usually about what the historians think is significant. Historians bring their own attitudes and perspectives to historical questions and see history in the light of these. It is therefore perfectly acceptable to have very different explanations of the same historical phenomenon. The way we judge historical accounts is by looking at how well argued they are and how well evidence has been deployed to support the argument.

Approach A	Approach B	Approach C
Political change is caused by decisions taken by politicians. It is imposed from the top by great men. Ordinary people then fall into line and do whatever they are told.	Political change is the result of popular clamour. The pressure of public opinion and desire for reform causes political change.	Political change is inevitable. The great movements of history point us to this fact. Political progress and the growth of democracy have been unstoppable forces in history.

Work in groups of between three and five. (You will need an even number of groups in the class.)

In your groups, devise a brief explanation of the repeal of the Contagious Diseases Acts, of between 200 and 300 words, that matches one of the approaches above. Present your explanation to another group, who will decide on two things:

1 Which of the approaches is the explanation trying to demonstrate?

2 Considering the structure and the quality of the argument and use of evidence, which is the best of the three explanations?

3 If you choose a 'best' explanation, should you discount the other two? Explain your answer.

ACTIVITY
KNOWLEDGE CHECK

The LNA and the government

1 What were the causes of the repeal of the Contagious Diseases Acts?

2 What does this say about the government's attitudes towards the LNA?

Conclusion

Protests against the Contagious Diseases Acts radicalised women and provided a basis for future movements. This changed British politics. For the first time, women on a large scale were speaking out in public on a political question. The techniques adopted during the protests would provide important lessons to future female rights campaigners, especially the targeting of individual parliamentary candidates and the publicity violence could attract. The LNA provided a model of how women could organise themselves to exert political influence over parliament.

The LNA's campaign not only popularised the cause of female rights, but changed thinking over the place of women in politics. As the state had appeared to make prostitution safe for men, without care for women, it became apparent that a government without female virtue could be an immoral political system. With women excluded from government, men had passed legislation to legalise sinful behaviour. Protesters asserted that to redeem this situation required the moral superiority of women. Women ensured that the family was run as a model of moral government, so it was believed that feminine morality had to be introduced into politics to improve national government. The Social Purity Alliance, founded in 1873 and led by Butler, promoted this view that female morality would redeem a political system corrupted by male vice. In 1885, this social purity movement successfully campaigned to have the age of consent raised to 16 and the police granted powers to close brothels. This was after the discovery of a 'white slave trade', in which under age girls were abducted and transported to Belgium to be sold into prostitution. Such a scandal seemed to confirm fears over the threat male sexuality represented to society.

From attempts to repeal the Contagious Diseases Acts came a belief that women were to be agents of national moral regeneration. Male vice caused female misery, but if women entered politics they would raise the moral standards of all society. The Contagious Diseases Acts became the ultimate embodiment of the sexual injustice allowed by a political system that excluded women. Butler realised the implications of such thought. The Acts demonstrated that women needed a voice; they needed representation and this could only be achieved through suffrage. Butler believed that women needed the vote and a share in the nation's law making if legislation like the Contagious Diseases Acts was to be avoided. The impact of the LNA was far more extensive than achieving the repeal of the Acts. It fermented new and increasingly radical thoughts over the role women had to play in politics.

Despite this, there were limits to the impact the LNA's campaign could have on wider questions of women's rights and the vote. That extended women's rights were so closely connected with Butler's campaigns did provide some ammunition for anti-suffragists. In associating themselves with prostitutes, members of the LNA were often criticised as immoral. Those opposed to women having the vote looked at the LNA's efforts to defend the rights of prostitutes as evidence of women's unsuitability to be granted political representation.

Whether Butler's campaign against the Contagious Diseases Acts had been directly responsible for their repeal was not a pressing consideration in the 1880s. What mattered was that it seemed as though the popular protests against the legislation had undermined the government's position on prostitution. Against the government's dependence on scientific authority and medical opinion, the LNA had deployed a moral argument that parliament found hard to counter. By organising themselves and developing effective means of exerting pressure on parliament, despite their exclusion from the electorate, women had found a voice. The movement for women's rights had been popularised like never before. While historians might debate the true extent of the Acts, the women's movement had unarguably been permanently changed. Over the three decades following the repeal, the voice of women in British politics would continue to get louder and become ever more focused on the question of female suffrage.

ACTIVITY
KNOWLEDGE CHECK

The impact of the LNA's campaign

1 How successful was the LNA in getting the Contagious Diseases Acts repealed?

2 Was the repeal of the Contagious Diseases Acts primarily because of James Stansfeld's political position in William Gladstone's government?

3 What were the long-term impacts of the LNA's campaigning and the part played by women in this movement?

ACTIVITY
SUMMARY

Moral protests

1 Make a series of notes outlining the key thoughts surrounding the Contagious Diseases Acts. Use these headings:

- The necessity of the Acts for society and the state

- The arguments for repealing the legislation.

2 Under your first heading, you should be able to explain why it was thought necessary for the Acts to be introduced, including questions of the armed forces, male sexuality and health.

3 Under the second heading, try to use the arguments employed by the LNA after 1869.

WIDER READING

Bartley, P. *Prostitution: Prevention and Reform in England, 1860–1914*, Routledge (2000)

Mathers, H. *Patron Saint of Prostitutes: Josephine Butler and the Victorian Scandal*, History Press (2014)

McHugh, P. *Prostitution and Victorian Social Reform*, Routledge (2013)

Petrie, G. *A Singular Iniquity: The Campaigns of Josephine Butler*, Macmillan (1971)

Smith, F.B. *The Contagious Diseases Acts Reconsidered*, Society for the Social History of Medicine (1990)

Walkowitz, J. *Prostitution and Victorian Society*, Cambridge (1980)

3.6 The Women's Social and Political Union, 1903-14

KEY QUESTIONS

- How effective was the WSPU as a political organisation between 1903 and 1914?
- How far were individual women responsible for the WSPU's success before 1914?
- How far was the Liberal government to blame for the continued failure of legislation for female suffrage between 1909 and 1913?

INTRODUCTION

The late 19th century was a disappointing time for women's rights activists. The 1884 Reform Act had given the vote to many working-class men, and although 40 percent of men remained unenfranchised, it was feared that women had missed the chance to secure the vote. An amendment to the Reform Act 1884 to enfranchise 100,000 propertied women had been wrecked by Prime Minister William Gladstone, who had persuaded 104 Liberal MPs to reject the measure. This was a severe blow to women's hopes. Fears abounded that the age of reform was over and the opportunity gone. Through the 1890s, little progress was made. Between 1886 and 1892, women's suffrage was not debated once within the House of Commons. Millicent Fawcett's National Union of Women's Suffrage Societies (NUWSS), established in 1897, spearheaded the campaign for women's suffrage, but their tame tactics and limited ideas produced little success. The NUWSS avoided outdoor meetings, public appeals and by-election interfering – the very tactics that had secured anti-Contagious Diseases Acts protesters influence with parliament. Despite this, there was a growing consensus that female suffrage would eventually be achieved. Britain in the early 1900s witnessed increasingly radical and often violent forms of political protest. The rise of the Independent Labour Party (ILP), which secured electoral significance in the 1906 general election, provided a socialist voice to the nation's industrial workers. Along with industrial unrest, the Irish Home Rule movement completely divided parliament, with the Liberal Party seeing many of its members co-operate with the Conservatives in opposing Irish self-governance. Seeing that increased militancy within both the Labour movement and the Irish Home Rule campaign was putting pressure on parliament to introduce fundamental reforms, many women grew impatient.

1903 – Women's Social and Political Union established

1906 – Liberal Party wins general election

Christabel Pankhurst ends WSPU's alliance with the Labour Party

1909 – Failure of the women's suffrage bill

| 1897 | 1903 | 1904 | 1905 | 1906 | 1907 | 1908 | 1909 |

1897 – Formation of the National Union of Women's Suffrage Societies

1905 – WSPU begins militant action

1908 – Herbert Asquith becomes Liberal prime minister

250,000–500,000 assemble in Hyde Park demanding female suffrage

WSPU escalates militancy. Window smashing begins

From 1903, with the formation of the Women's Social and Political Union (WSPU), the women's suffrage campaign took on a more militant character. Although this revitalised the movement and brought it to the verge of parliamentary reform, escalating violence and increasingly terrifying forms of protest threatened to derail efforts to secure women the vote. While between 1903 and 1908 the WSPU reinvigorated the cause of women's suffrage, historians are divided over the impact of violence between 1909 and 1914. Winning the vote was a long, hard process. A fragile political context, personal objections to women's franchise and the complexities of parliamentary procedure all undermined attempts to enfranchise women. However, as the vote became a realisable proposition, almost within the grasp of women, the effect of militant tactics became harder to measure. So much so that by 1914, on the eve of the First World War, it was hard to know if women's suffrage had become an inevitability, or had been fatally damaged by the violence that the WSPU had inspired.

HOW EFFECTIVE WAS THE WSPU AS A POLITICAL ORGANISATION BETWEEN 1903 AND 1914?

The performance of the WSPU can be crudely divided into three periods. The first, from 1903 to 1905, was relatively quiet, with the organisation securing little attention. It did not expand significantly during this period. The year 1905 marked the start of the WSPU's sustained militancy campaign. This transformed the organisation, bringing it to the public's attention and winning much support. Its membership expanded considerably. From 1908, we see a third period begin: a time of escalating violence and increasingly shocking forms of militant protest. This would continue to increase until 1914.

Early tactics of the WSPU, 1905–8

In 1903, Emmeline Pankhurst established the Women's Social and Political Union (WSPU). Initially, membership consisted of a small group of working-class women, mostly wives of ILP supporters. By the summer of 1905, the organisation included some 30 members. Emmeline Pankhurst and her daughters Christabel and Sylvia had been supporters of the ILP, believing that, if elected, Labour MPs would promote female suffrage. However, even when a majority of MPs in the House of Commons agreed with the principle of votes for women, as was the case in 1884 and again by 1906, there was still no change. The Pankhursts calculated that if even a parliament of pro-women MPs would not enfranchise women, then a political movement was called for that would challenge the government, forcing it to reform the electorate. Unlike the NUWSS's efforts to reform through peaceful protest, the WSPU announced its motto as 'Deeds, not words'.

1911 – May: Second Conciliation bill passed

1912 – Third conciliation bill defeated

Arson campaign begins

1914 – Outbreak of First World War

1918 – Representation of the People Act secures women the vote

| 1910 | 1911 | 1912 | 1913 | 1914 | 1915 | 1916 | 1917 | 1918 |

1910 – January: Liberals lose majority in general election

Conciliation committee

First conciliation bill passed

November: 'Black Friday'

December: General election returns hung parliament

1913 – January: Failure of government franchise bill

June: Emily Davison killed at Epsom Derby

Government passes 'Cat-and-Mouse Act'

In 1905, Christabel Pankhurst made the decision to adopt the moderate militant tactics of meeting disruptions, demonstrations and heckling. Christabel initiated the militancy campaign by disrupting a speech by Sir Edward Grey at a public meeting. Accompanied by fellow WSPU member Annie Kenney, she was imprisoned for this act. Christabel had grown impatient with suffrage campaigns for reform through parliamentary measures. This move to militancy drew inspiration from the **Irish Home Rule** movement, whose leader Charles Parnell had decided to oppose all Liberal candidates, even those in favour of Home Rule. Christabel and Emmeline Pankhurst believed such tactics, which had won the Home Rule movement political influence, could also further the cause of women's suffrage. Parnell's approach was not to target individual MPs on the question of Home Rule, but to put pressure on the government. Such an approach required an autocratic control over the WSPU, just as Parnell had dominated the Home Rule movement. Like Parnell, the WSPU wanted to enrage and shock the government; it wanted to be hated, even feared, and force the state into retributive acts that would encourage public support for women's suffrage.

SOURCE

In her autobiography, appearing after her death in 1958, Christabel Pankhurst's reflections were published on how the disrupting of meetings and heckling secured the WSPU much needed press attention.

We had certainly broken the Press silence on votes for women, that silence which, by keeping women uninformed, had so largely smothered and strangled the movement. This newspaper silence had, at the same time, protected politicians from criticism of their offences, omissive and commissive, against the suffrage cause. Mother and I – in the pre-militant days – called on the editor of one of the most important newspapers in the country, asking for the publication of a leading article drawing attention to a Woman Suffrage Bill. The editor, we found, was away; an associate received us. Mother put her request. 'I cannot do this without the editor's authority,' he told us, and went on to explain that in all his twenty years' association with this newspaper its practice had been, as far as possible, to ignore the woman suffrage question. But where peaceful means had failed, one act of militancy succeeded and never again was the cause ignored by that or any other newspaper. Weird rumours were heard now and again of newspaper potentates meeting in conclave and agreeing to be blind and dumb concerning the doings of the militants, but the rumours were false or else the agreements broke down.

From 1905, the WSPU pursued tactics of disrupting meetings and heckling politicians. Throughout 1906 and 1907, militant action increased, including **suffragettes** chaining themselves to railings in Downing Street and to statues in the House of Commons' lobby. Interruptions to meetings also grew more frequent. On 25 October 1906, a WSPU group broke into the lobby of the House of Commons, waving flags and making speeches. Ten were arrested for breaching the peace and went to prison. Of these, nine were middle- and upper-class women. The arrest of respectable ladies caused public outrage. The notion of socially elite women in jail presented the WSPU with a powerful tool for creating sympathy with middle- and upper-class audiences. For example, one of the imprisoned women was Mrs Cobden Sanderson, daughter of renowned reform politician Richard Cobden. Her arrest shocked polite society and won the WSPU support, even from peaceful members of the NUWSS. However, it also exposed class divides. The impact of working-class women going to prison never produced the same public response. Indeed, this creation of martyrs through imprisonment made women protesters appear as unjustly punished victims of a male-controlled state. This tactic was a valuable propaganda weapon, building public sympathy and showing the government to be brutal and reactionary. Breakfast meetings to celebrate the release of women from prison became a fruitful way of raising both support and funds.

In February 1907, the WSPU held the first 'Women's Parliament' at Caxton Hall, Westminster. Participants then marched on parliament, only to be attacked by the police. Thirty-eight women went to court, most being sentenced to a few weeks in Holloway prison, including Sylvia and Christabel Pankhurst. Such militant acts attracted immense support, much of it crucial to the success of the peaceful campaign of the NUWSS. WSPU militancy won publicity for the women's suffrage campaign, which helped the NUWSS to build up its membership. In 1907, the NUWSS organised its own mass meeting, assembling 3,000 supporters for what became known as the 'Mud March'.

Increased militancy after 1908

The turning point came in 1908. Until 1908, the WSPU had pursued peaceful forms of protest aimed at arousing public sympathy and drawing political attention to the question of women's suffrage. However, the failure of these tactics, which became apparent after the huge 1908 Hyde Park meeting failed to influence the government at all, encouraged the WSPU to move towards more violent forms of militancy.

SOURCE 2

In July 1910, the journal *Punch* commented on the work of Edith Garrud, the first female professional martial arts instructor. A suffragette, Garrud trained the WSPU's bodyguard unit in jiu-jitsu self-defence.

THE SUFFRAGETTE THAT KNEW JIU-JITSU.
THE ARREST.

The question of female suffrage was not, in 1908, an urgent one for the Liberal government. Having won a landslide victory in the 1906 general election, the Liberals were far more concerned with their programme of radical social welfare reforms, resistance from the Conservative-controlled House of Lords, the question of Irish Home Rule and a worsening national trade balance. In April 1908, Herbert Henry Asquith replaced Henry Campbell-Bannerman as prime minister. Asquith was sceptical of whether the majority of women wanted the vote. He reasoned that representation within parliament was not a universal right, noting that children were not included. He refused to consider the question of female suffrage unless there was a clear demonstration that there was sufficient demand in the country. In response, a huge meeting of somewhere between 250,000 and 500,000 women met in Hyde Park in June 1908, demanding the vote. Despite this impressive gathering, Asquith was unmoved. The prime minister's refusal to acknowledge popular calls for suffrage convinced the WSPU's leaders that moderate peaceful protest was no longer of use. Christabel Pankhurst directed a mass campaign of window-breaking in the belief that only violence could influence the government. The autumn of 1908 marked the start of the WSPU's violent militancy. Christabel was sent to prison for two months for window breaking, but this was just the start of the violence that would escalate over the following six years. The purpose was to target private property to convince the government and the public that orderly daily life could not continue while women were excluded from politics. Asquith himself became a popular target for violence. As well as being assaulted on a golf course, slates were thrown at his car, and within parliament there were fears that he might be assassinated.

SOURCE 3

Christabel Pankhurst explaining the importance of the Hyde Park meeting in the WSPU newspaper *Votes For Women* on 18 June 1908. Appealing for support from readers for the peaceful demonstration, Christabel explained how the protest had been requested by the government to show support for female suffrage.

The Prime Minister lately challenged women to show that they want the vote, and his challenge was at once taken up. A space of eight days is to see two great and imposing demonstrations in support of Woman Suffrage. The first of these has already taken place. In last Saturday's procession were represented women of all political parties, and of every class. It is very doubtful whether there has ever been so representative a procession of men for any political object. A little while ago even women themselves would have hesitated to adopt the plan so foreign to their traditions and training, of marching through the streets to demand the vote. But when some women are ready to suffer violence, and to undergo imprisonment, no earnest Suffragist can refuse to give public expression to her convictions by walking in procession... On Sunday next, June 21, the seven processions organised by the Women's Social and Political Union will march to Hyde Park to demand the immediate extension of the Parliamentary franchise to women. Not only members of the Union and their friends, but also members of other associations and of the general public, will walk in the processions, men as well as women being welcome.

Although the Prime Minister refuses to throw light on the matter, Mr Herbert Gladstone, in the course of the Woman Suffrage debate, pointed to the holding of great meetings as the legitimate and effective method of inducing the Government to grant votes to women. He held up to us, as an example, the mass meetings organised by men in the days which preceded the various extensions of the franchise, and referred in particular to the gathering in Hyde Park, in 1867. It was, he argued, not the destruction of the railings, but the number and earnestness of the demonstrations that gave that meeting its importance. It remains to be seen whether next Sunday's demonstration, which seems likely to be the largest ever held in Hyde Park, will have the same effect on the political situation as had the smaller gathering in 1867. This is the moment for applying all possible pressure upon the Government... Further, this great gathering will show whether agitation by way of great public meetings is an adequate means of bringing pressure to bear on the Government. If the Government refuse to obey the will of the people, as expressed in public meetings, then it will be evident that by militant methods alone can the vote be won.

ACTIVITY
KNOWLEDGE CHECK

Hyde Park, 1908

Study Source 3.

1 How useful do you think this source is for examining how Christabel Pankhurst considered increased militancy to be the only way to influence the Liberal government after the 1908 Hyde Park meeting?

2 How useful is this source for examining the attitudes of the government towards the women's suffrage movement?

In June 1909, the WSPU organised a march on parliament. During this protest, the windows of the Home Office, Treasury and Privy Council were smashed. Later in the month, jailed protesters began hunger strikes, refusing all food. The government introduced **force-feedings**, but this only created scenes of heroic sacrifice on the part of the protesters. Force-feedings became a great propaganda coup. It would be four years before the government came up with a solution to the hunger strikes. The passing of the Temporary Discharge for Ill-Health Act 1913 somewhat undermined the propaganda effect of force-feedings that had won so much public support for the WSPU since 1909. The government recognised that force-feedings were politically damaging, but hoped that the legislation would resolve the problem of hunger strikes. This Act, also known as the **Cat-and-Mouse Act**, ordered that when women on hunger strike became ill, they were to be released until healthy enough to be rearrested. They would be kept under surveillance until re-arrest. This was demoralising to WSPU members and personally damaging to Emmeline Pankhurst's own health. However, it also aroused much public hostility and was hard to enforce on a practical level. It seemed to surrender any claims the government had to moral authority. It was not an effective government solution to the problem of hunger strikes.

KEY TERMS

Force-feeding
When imprisoned women went on hunger strike and became dangerously ill, liquid food was forced into them through tubes, inserted either through the mouth or nose. They would be forcibly held down on a chair while this was done. This was not only mentally, but physically painful. Often, women were sick, and many were injured through this process.

Cat-and-Mouse Act
The name applied to the Temporary Discharge for Ill-Health Act 1913 as a comparison to a cat's practice of playing with its prey before finally killing it. The analogy between this and the Liberal government that introduced it was an unflattering one.

The most notorious act of militancy was on 18 November 1910, when the government refused time to debate legislation for women's suffrage. The WSPU responded by sending 300 women into the House of Commons. In what became known as 'Black Friday', this group clashed with the police around parliament. The police were deliberately rough, assaulting many women, sometimes sexually, leaving several with serious injuries. This was the police's attempt to teach the women a lesson. Christabel declared an all-out sex war against men, while Emmeline felt the enemy was not men, but specifically the Liberal Party. Either way, after this event, the WSPU tried to avoid street protests, favouring acts of property destruction. In 1911, militancy grew more intense, and in 1912, the WSPU targeted artworks and set fire to pillar boxes, while continuing its relentless programme of window smashing. The same year saw the start of widespread acts of arson. Throughout 1913, a campaign of even greater intimidation was directed by the WSPU. Thirteen paintings in Manchester Art Gallery were hacked apart, while streetlights, golf greens and train carriages were all damaged.

SOURCE 4

The force-feeding of an imprisoned suffragette in 1909.

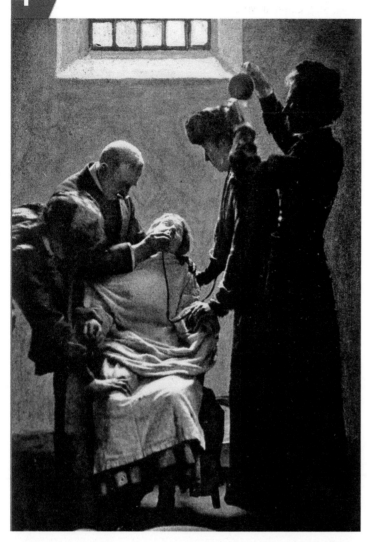

completely. Women were supposed to build sympathy among society for their cause, not intimidate the state with terrorism. Beyond the NUWSS, the violence produced increasingly hostile responses. In 1908, Mrs Humphry Ward established the Women's National Anti-Suffrage League for women who did not want the vote. In 1909, Lords Curzon and Cromer formed the Men's League for Opposing Women's Suffrage. These two organisations united in 1910 to form the National League for Opposing Women's Suffrage, a movement that included 97 branches nationwide. Even within the WSPU there were concerns that the militancy was excessive. Ex-WSPU member Teresa Billington-Greig believed the violence was dishonest, as it had been engineered by the Pankhursts to win publicity.

Pre-1908 violence appears to have been useful in promoting women's suffrage, yet the violence between 1908 and 1914 was counterproductive. However, considering that the government clearly refused to act in response to peaceful forms of protest between 1905 and 1908, the WSPU believed that violence was the only way forward for the campaign.

The WSPU's organisation and support

The WSPU's militant tactics won the organisation immense support and popularised the women's suffrage movement. While the WSPU and NUWSS are often seen as rivals, between 1903 and 1909 they were essentially two wings of the same movement. Tensions only arose with the WSPU's post-1908 increase of violence. The early militant campaign created public sympathy, although it aroused some male opposition to female suffrage. While growth was slow between 1903 and 1905, the advent of militancy sparked a boom in membership. In 1906, the WSPU had three branches, but by 1911 it had 122. Between 1906 and 1910, membership expanded rapidly, and by 1910, the circulation of its journal, *Votes for Women*, was over 40,000. It is hard to know how many women participated within the WSPU as the organisation did not maintain formal membership.

Although Christabel and Emmeline provided forceful direction and inspiration to members, the WSPU's leadership included several key supporters who helped to organise the movement. Before 1905, the five main WSPU speakers were Emmeline, Christabel, Adela and Sylvia Pankhurst and Teresa Billington-Greig. In 1905, they were joined by Annie Kenney, the poverty-stricken daughter of a textile worker. Kenney added a much needed working-class element to the WSPU's leadership and provided a strong accomplice to Christabel. In 1906, Emmeline Pethick-Lawrence and her husband, Frederick, joined the WSPU, adding much financial and organisational skill. Emmeline Pethick-Lawrence became treasurer, working diligently to ensure the WSPU was well-funded. Frederick organised the WSPU's staff and established its newspaper, *Votes for Women*. The couple also encouraged the use of pageantry, music and drama to popularise the cause. Emmeline Pethick-Lawrence designed suffragette clothing in white, green and purple, respectively symbolising purity, hope and dignity. The Pethick-Lawrences administered the WSPU on a daily basis. Such support was essential to the Pankhursts' grip over the movement.

EXTEND YOUR KNOWLEDGE

Millicent Fawcett (1847–1929)

Leader of the NUWSS from 1897 to 1919, Fawcett had campaigned for female suffrage since the late 1860s. Through the 1870s and 1880s, she had fought for the repeal of the Contagious Diseases Acts. In 1907, she was elected the NUWSS's first president. Although keeping the Liberal Party separate from her suffrage campaigning, she was from 1886 a Liberal Unionist, believing that Irish Home Rule would be a national disaster for Britain. By 1912, she was disillusioned with the Liberals' attempts to give women the vote, so she formed an alliance between Labour and the NUWSS. Although recognising the value of WSPU militancy early on, she grew increasingly concerned that the violence had gone too far and was damaging the arguments in favour of female suffrage.

While the post-1908 violence secured the WSPU increased publicity, it alienated many non-violent campaigners. Millicent Fawcett was particularly disappointed. The NUWSS had campaigned patiently since 1897 for female suffrage. For Fawcett, part of the case for women's votes was that women were morally superior to men, but the WSPU's violence undermined this idea

SOURCE 5

The WSPU fife and drum band formed in 1909. Here, it appears in the fashionable West End of London.

Peaceful demonstrations

Examine Source 5.

1 Consider what such a source might tell us about the appeal of the WSPU.

2 Who do you think such displays were aimed at?

3 To what extent would such spectacles encourage support for the movement?

4 How important do you think such displays were in comparison with militant violence?

Central Committee (unelected)

Role: decide policies, control publications, make appointments to paid positions, control finances

Membership: Sylvia Pankhurst (secretary)
Emmeline Pethick-Lawrence (treasurer)
Christbabel Pankhurst (chief organiser)
Annie Kenney (salaried organiser)

Subcommittee (unelected)

Role: assist Central Committee

Membership: friends and relatives of the Pankhursts

'A Home' sessions

Role: receive instructions about new policies and strategies

Membership: WSPU members

Meets every Monday afternoon in the WSPU's Headquarters, Lincoln's Inn Fields London

Eleven regional offices

(Bristol: Torquay; Manchester; Preston; Rochdale; Birmingham; Leeds; Newcastle; Glasgow; Edinburgh and Aberdeen)

Role: implement the aims and objectives of the WSPU but with considerable local autonomy

Emmeline Pankhurst

Role: Roving ambassador for the WSPU, speaking at meetings, organising by-election campaigns, arranging demonstrations and urging militancy

Figure 6.1 Central committee, subcommittees and regional offices of the WSPU.

By 1906, the WSPU's leadership was organised into an unelected central committee, consisting of Sylvia Pankhurst as secretary, Annie Kenney as paid organiser, and Emmeline Pethick-Lawrence as treasurer. Overall leadership remained with Christabel and Emmeline Pankhurst. This committee was assisted by a sub committee made up mainly of friends and family of the Pankhursts. This central leadership was based in Lincoln's Inn Field, London. The central committee controlled all WSPU publications, finances and paid appointments. In 1910, there were 98 office-working women in London, along with 26 individuals responsible for regional districts. While the Pankhursts operated in London and the home counties, local branches of the WSPU in the provinces held considerable autonomy. In 1911, while there were 64 London and home county branches, there were 58 WSPU branches throughout the rest of England, Wales and Scotland. Sylvia Pankhurst observed that the national leaders in London usually ignored the regional branches, but occasionally tensions arose between the London WSPU and its provincial organisations. For example, the Liverpool branch of the WSPU, founded in 1906, was a very working-class organisation. Instead of the more fashionable drawing-room meetings typical of the middle- and upper-class WSPU in London, the Liverpool branch preferred open-air meetings, which were more popular with working-class women. When the central WSPU leadership demanded the Liverpool branch hold drawing-room meetings to encourage middle-class membership, the Liverpool branch refused.

The social base of the WSPU changed noticeably between its 1903 formation and 1914. While at first it was largely composed of northern working-class women, with connections to the ILP, in 1906 Christabel severed the organisation's alliance with Labour and moved the WSPU's base from Manchester to London. This move was because of an increasing disillusionment with the ILP in terms of its seriousness in securing women the vote, and also to secure the movement's popular support outside of Manchester. This geographical and political adjustment transformed the WSPU's social composition. Without its socialist connotations, wealthy women were encouraged to join. The WSPU's ability to recruit from Britain's social elite, facilitated by the shift away from Labour, was very good for its finances. Wealthy women had more money to donate and more free time to devote to demonstrations. Between 1906 and 1907, the WSPU spent £2,494 on campaigning, but by 1907 it was able to raise £20,000. It soon employed more fully paid members of staff than the Labour Party. Christabel and Emmeline encouraged socialist members to tone down their politics to aid this gentrification of the WSPU. For example, Adela Pankhurst failed to conceal her socialist views from Conservative supporters within the WSPU, causing much offence. Fearing this would damage the organisation, Emmeline persuaded Adela to emigrate to Australia so as to avoid any future embarrassment. The WSPU quickly became a fashionable, elitist, London-centric movement, dominated by wealthy socialites. This made it particularly uncomfortable for many working-class members. Despite creating a class divide, the Pankhursts emphasised that gender was the uniting factor for the WSPU.

EXTEND YOUR KNOWLEDGE

Historians and the WSPU
Historical evaluations of the WSPU's support have been divided between socialist feminist and radical feminist interpretations. Socialist feminists have seen the WSPU as an extension of wider movements to reduce class distances and increase democracy, while radical feminist historians have emphasised that the WSPU pursued not class conflict, but a sex war against men.

KEY TERM

Property-based suffrage
During the 19th and early 20th centuries, property was the essential qualification for voting. It was widely maintained that only those who had a stake in the nation should have a say in its law making. Usually the definition of property was land, real estate or wealth derived from property. In Liberal political thinking, there was a constant fear that separating property from political representation would damage the welfare of the nation by creating an essentially disinterested electorate.

It is hard to see how class divisions after 1906 did not dominate the WSPU's membership, but Emmeline and Christabel were always eager to stress that their movement was not socially elite. They appealed to all women as sisters in their campaign for suffrage. This was a persuasive rallying cry. Yet questions still remained as to whether it was preferable to work for universal suffrage, which would be hard to achieve, or aim for limited **property-based suffrage**, which, though hardly aiding working-class women, would establish the principle of votes for women.

Even before the WSPU split from Labour, securing the support of working-class men was difficult. Many in Labour feared women would vote Conservative or Liberal, while their admission to the workplace would drive wages down. The relations between the WSPU and Labour were always strained, with working-class men disliking middle- and upper-class women interfering in their movement. To many, the Pankhursts appeared overly dramatic and privileged. One notable exception was the Labour leader Keir Hardie, who was a personal friend of the Pankhursts before 1906. By 1907, however, the Labour Party conference rejected women's suffrage, preferring instead to link female suffrage with the campaign for extended male suffrage.

EXTEND YOUR KNOWLEDGE

Keir Hardie (1856–1915)
A Scottish socialist and the first Labour MP, Hardie formed the ILP in 1893 and organised the LRC in 1900, which was to become the Labour Party in 1906. At the 1906 general election, Labour won 29 MPs, securing electoral significance. Hardie resigned in 1908 and spent the later years of his life campaigning for votes for women. He remained a close friend of Sylvia Pankhurst.

Nevertheless, it is possible to ascribe too much credit for the increased support for the women's suffrage movement to the WSPU. The NUWSS noticed an increase in popularity before the WSPU's formation. The NUWSS grew rapidly between 1902 and 1906, increasing from 17 to 31 branches. Its practice of pressing the question of women's suffrage to all parliamentary candidates in 1903, before the general election of 1906, and working to ensure local political associations only selected candidates pledged to women's votes was crucial. The NUWSS was successful in this work, ensuring that in 1906, regardless of WSPU militancy, the House of Commons included 415 MPs committed to female suffrage. It was the NUWSS and not the WSPU that made sure the 1906 Liberal government included a majority of members who would react sympathetically to women's suffrage campaigning. While the WSPU won the cause much-needed publicity, the NUWSS put in the political leg work to make female suffrage a realistic proposition.

At the same time, it is important to note that the WSPU was not alone in committing militant acts. Militancy probably began in the 1890s, with the North of England Society for Women's Suffrage and the Women's Franchise League. Throughout the 1900s, militant acts were also orchestrated by the **Women's Freedom League (WFL)**, the Men's Political Union, the Women's Tax Resistance League, and the East London Federation of Suffragettes. However, it was the scale and organisation of the WSPU that made it so important in the campaign for female suffrage. Between 1905 and 1908, the WSPU galvanised the women's franchise movement.

KEY TERM

Women's Freedom League (WFL)
Formed in 1907, this group campaigned for female suffrage, but avoided violence. It pursued militant forms of protests like tax avoidance. Originally established by members unhappy with the WSPU's leadership, it included upwards of 4,000 members.

SOURCE

Christabel Pankhurst explains her mother's belief that militancy was the correct response to the failure of the third conciliation bill in 1912. This extract appeared in Christabel's posthumous autobiography, *Unshackled: The Story of How We Won The Vote* (1959).

The resolution of the evening pledged those present to 'continue the militant agitation and to oppose the Government and their Parliamentary allies until the introduction of a measure for women's enfranchisement'. Property meant much to the Government, said Mother, and it was through property that the Suffragettes would reach the Government. She wanted citizens who owned property to go to the Government and say: 'Examine the cause that leads to the destruction of property. Remove the discontent; then women will return to what they formally were, the most law-abiding half of the community.'

'I incite this meeting to rebellion!' went on Mother. 'And my last word is for the Government. You have not dared to take the leaders of the Ulster rebellion for their incitement. Take me, if you will. But I tell you this: that so long as those who incite to armed rebellion and the destruction of human life are at liberty, you shall not keep me in prison. Women in this meeting, although the vote is not yet won, we who are militant are free. Remember only the freedom of the spirit and join this magnificent rebellion of the women of the twentieth century'... Mother had again chosen the harder part in 1912, as she had chosen it in 1905, when militancy began. In 1905 she chose, for the sake of womanhood, the ruin and ostracism and all the suffering implicit for her in her eldest daughter's act, which was also her own act and but the first link in a chain of future acts. In 1912, dedicating herself anew, Mother chose, if it should so happen, a convict's grave... Mother and I could have ended militancy as easily as we began it! When we declared the Conciliation Bill Truce, there was a truce. When we declared the end of the truce and the renewal of militancy, militancy was renewed.

A Level Exam-Style Question Section B

'The WSPU's popularity was a response to government inactivity in advancing the cause of women's suffrage.'

To what extent is this a fair judgement of the rise of the WSPU between 1903 and 1914? (20 marks)

Tip
Consider and compare with how far the WSPU's popularity was secured through its radically militant forms of protest.

ACTIVITY
KNOWLEDGE CHECK

The case for militancy

1 How did WSPU militancy escalate between 1905 and 1913?

2 Do you think that the increased use of violent forms of militancy was a just response from the WSPU to government responses?

3 How important was militancy for the WSPU's popularity between 1905 and 1909?

4 How important was militancy for the WSPU's popularity after 1909?

HOW FAR WERE INDIVIDUAL WOMEN RESPONSIBLE FOR THE WSPU'S SUCCESS BEFORE 1914?

Christabel and Emmeline Pankhurst dominated the WSPU. They were inspirational, driven, determined and often ruthless leaders. Yet their management has been the subject of much historical attention. The extent to which they organised and directed the WSPU has been revised; it is hard to know how much control they had over individual members. At the same time, their militant strategy is still a controversial subject. Historians agree on its value before 1908, but Emmeline and Christabel's leadership between 1908 and 1914 has been sharply criticised.

Emmeline and Christabel Pankhurst

Emmeline Pankhurst and her eldest daughter, Christabel, were at the helm of the WSPU throughout its existence. They were the undoubted powerhouse of the organisation. Christabel enforced a clear strategy of militancy from 1905, while Emmeline provided a magnetism that attracted many dedicated women to the movement. The initial move to establish the WSPU came from Emmeline, who, after 20 years of experience campaigning for female suffrage and a growing disillusionment with the ILP's commitment to women's rights, believed a new militant movement composed of women was required. Emmeline had experienced limited militant tactics with the **Women's Franchise League** during the 1890s. She was an influential speaker, whose argument that women had a unique point of view that required political representation found sympathy among female audiences. She did not claim that women and men were equal, but that women required specific consideration in law making that could only be ensured through female suffrage. This resonated with mothers and wives.

KEY TERM

Women's Franchise League
A political organisation that Richard and Emmeline Pankhurst founded in 1889. Through its campaigning, this organisation won women the right to vote in local council elections.

EXTEND YOUR KNOWLEDGE

Emmeline Pankhurst (1858–1928)
Founder of the WSPU, Emmeline was born in Manchester. Her early political experiences were with her husband Richard, who, in 1885, attempted to become Liberal MP for Rotherhithe. Despite Richard Pankhurst's radical views, including abolishing the House of Lords, he was defeated due to anti-Liberal Irish voters. Although allowing the Conservatives victory, Irish Home Rule campaigners decided that voting against the government was more important than voting against the Conservatives who were unsympathetic to the Irish cause. Emmeline was left distraught, but never forgot the lesson. She had five children, Christabel (1880), Sylvia (1882), Frank (1884), Adela (1885) and Henry (1889), though Christabel remained her favourite, which caused immense jealously, particularly from Sylvia. Together with Richard, Emmeline founded the Women's Franchise League in 1889, which successfully campaigned for women to vote in local elections. Although a supporter of the ILP during the 1890s, Emmeline eventually joined the Conservative Party in 1926, and in 1928, stood as the Conservative candidate as MP for Whitechapel and St George's, before ill health ended this ambition.

Both Emmeline and Christabel were adored by many WSPU supporters, with the notable exception of Theresa Billington-Greig. Christabel conceived of the militant campaign in 1905, having noticed the impact on the government of disturbances over unemployment. After a meeting of unemployed men had to be dispersed by the police and was branded a riot in March 1905, an unemployment bill previously abandoned by the government was reintroduced and passed. Militant disturbances, it seemed, could shake the government into action. In November 1905, Christabel disrupted a public meeting, before spitting on a policeman to ensure she was arrested. Both Emmeline and Liberal politician Winston Churchill tried to pay a fine for Christabel to avoid imprisonment, but she refused. Christabel therefore recognised that imprisonment could be a valuable tool to secure public sympathy. She provided inspiration to other young women to do the same. Dazzlingly clever, strong-willed and attractive, she cut a heroic figure. Emmeline and Christabel were at the forefront of new tactics like window breaking and heckling. Christabel inspired several acts of arson from 1912, including the burning of anti-suffrage cabinet minister Lewis Harcourt's house. Christabel also directed acts of arson on churches, believing the Church of England upheld existing political prejudices against women. Between 1913 and 1914, around 50 churches were attacked.

Emmeline Pankhurst being arrested outside Buckingham Palace in May 1914 while trying to present a petition to King George V.

The 1906 move away from the ILP was also very much an initiative of Christabel and Emmeline Pankhurst. Historians have traditionally seen this as a shift to the right on the part of the WSPU. Christabel was sure that Labour and the Liberals were both unwilling to support women's votes, but thought that the Conservative Party would introduce suffrage for propertied women to gain an electoral advantage over the Liberals, as it had done in 1867 with the Second Reform Act. In 1907, Christabel was in contact with the Conservative leader Arthur Balfour, who doubted women wanted the vote.

Emmeline and Christabel were eager to run the WSPU like an army. Indeed, they felt that as they engaged in militant behaviour and illegal forms of protest, an almost militaristic system of authority was required. Sometimes, however, their autocratic style alienated members, causing several splits. Arguably, their inability to compromise or concede to any opinions other than their own weakened the movement. In 1907, disillusioned with the undemocratic nature of the WSPU, Charlotte Despard and Teresa Billington-Greig left to form the WFL. They took with them a fifth of the WSPU's members in their bid to forge a more working-class, pro-Labour movement. This was after Billington-Greig had drafted

a constitution at the WSPU's annual conference, attempting to make the WSPU more democratic. Christabel and Emmeline were horrified at the proposal and removed Billington-Greig from the WSPU's leadership. This was the first of seven splits. In October 1912, the Pethick-Lawrences found themselves on the wrong side of Emmeline and Christabel's wrath. After quarrelling over the recent escalation of violence, Emmeline persuaded the couple to take a break in Canada. On returning to England, they found that they had been banned from the WSPU altogether.

EXTEND YOUR KNOWLEDGE

Historians and the WSPU leadership
Emmeline and Christabel's leadership has been subject to much historical scrutiny. Traditionally, they have been seen as despotic autocrats, with historian David Mitchell in 1977 comparing the WSPU to a terrorist gang. Feminist historians have tended to agree, with Jill Liddington and Jill Norris believing the WSPU's leadership had been excessively dictatorial. More recently, however, this has been revised. Paula Bartley and June Purvis both produced biographies of Emmeline Pankhurst in 2002. They argued that Emmeline's experience of the divided suffrage movement before 1903 made her keen to prevent disagreements within the WSPU. At the same time, there was no formal membership of the WSPU and no one was forced to remain in the organisation against their wishes.

Sylvia Pankhurst

Christabel's younger sister, Sylvia Pankhurst, was an early supporter of the WSPU. Born in 1882, she abandoned her studies at the Royal College of Arts in 1906 to devote herself completely to working for the WSPU as its secretary. She designed banners, gifts and flags for the movement, which were sold in the WSPU shop that she ran. Sylvia was arrested later in 1906 for disrupting a court case. Although she did not approve of the escalating militancy after 1908, and failed to persuade Emmeline and Christabel to moderate the WSPU's tactics, Sylvia was regularly in and out of prison for acts of militancy. In spring 1913, she was arrested three times, going on hunger strike on the third occasion. She was arrested again in July, but after the introduction of the Cat-and-Mouse Act was released and then rearrested several times. Sylvia recognised the political value of imprisonment and force-feedings. In 1911, she published *The Suffragette: The History of the Women's Militant Suffrage Movement, 1905–1910*, which outlined the actions of the WSPU. This was a work of propaganda intended to win support for the movement, and it emphasised the sacrifice suffragettes made through militancy.

When Christabel severed connections between the movement and the ILP, Sylvia remained close to Labour and worked to promote women's suffrage among working-class audiences. Unlike her older sister Christabel, Sylvia was a socialist. She quickly grew tired of the WSPU's increasingly fashionable, socially elite composition. Sylvia believed that the move away from Labour was typical of Christabel's 'incipient Toryism'.

The move to the Conservatives and the emphasis on extending the franchise to propertied women can be seen as a pragmatic move by Emmeline and Christabel, making the principle of women's votes easier to achieve. A broad appeal for votes for all women would have been difficult to sell to parliament.

However, Sylvia provides a good example of how Emmeline and Christabel's leadership was limited. Sylvia kept close links with Labour and remained a very close friend of Keir Hardie, the ILP's leader. While Emmeline and Christabel focused their attention on winning support from wealthy middle- and upper-class women, Sylvia devoted her efforts to campaigning in London's East End, appealing to working-class families.

SOURCE

8

Sylvia Pankhurst describes the conditions inside prison. Recalling her imprisonment in October 1906, Sylvia's account, appearing in her book *The Suffragette: The History of the Women's Militant Suffrage Movement, 1905–1910*, published in 1911, was intended to attract sympathy for the WSPU's campaign. However, Sylvia also drew attention to the difference in treatment for women of different classes.

We were ushered into a row of rather dark cells adjoining each other in an old part of the prison, which is chiefly occupied by prisoners on remand who have not yet been tried. These women, we were horrified to find, are treated exactly like second class prisoners, except that their dress is blue instead of green, and that some to whom permission has been given are allowed to wear their own clothes, and to have food sent in to them at their own expense. We were now offered the same privileges, but these we declined. On consulting the prison rules, however, I found that first class misdemeanants are entitled to exercise their profession whilst in prison, if their doing so does not interfere with the ordinary prison regulations... The food served out to us was exactly like that of the second class except that instead of oatmeal gruel, a pint of tea was substituted for breakfast and a pint of cocoa for supper... The soups or meat for each prisoner was served in a cylindrical quart tin into the top of which, like a lid, was fitted another shallow tin holding the potatoes. One did not clean these tins oneself as one did the other utensils, and probably because the kitchen attendants were overburdened with work, they were always exceedingly dingy and dirty-looking. Everything was as badly cooked and as uninviting as it could be. The cocoa, which was quite unlike any cocoa that I have ever tasted, had little pieces of meat and fat floating about in it. It was evidently made in the same vessel in which the meat was cooked. To cut up our meat, in addition to the wooden spoon, which is common to the second and third classes, we were now provided with 'a knife.' This knife was made of tin. It was about four inches in length and Mrs. Drummond later on aptly described it as being 'hemmed' at the edge. There was no fork. On November 6th my sentence came to an end, and the newspaper representatives were all eager to hear from me what the inside of Holloway was like. I was thus able to make known exactly what the conditions of imprisonment had been both before and after our transfer to the first division.

A Level Exam-Style Question Section A

Study Source 8 before you answer this question.

Assess the value of the source for evaluating the attitudes of WSPU leaders such as Sylvia Pankhurst towards the imprisonment of women and the variation in treatment of women of different classes.

Explain your answer, using the source, the information given about its origin and your own knowledge about the historical context. (20 marks)

Tip
What do you think made the experience of prison, as recorded here by Sylvia Pankhurst, such a valuable resource for promoting the suffrage campaign? How important is class in Sylvia's observations on prison?

While the WSPU leant increasingly towards the Conservative Party under the leadership of Christabel and Emmeline after 1906, many WSPU members, including Sylvia, remained politically close to Labour. Sylvia wanted the WSPU to be a socialist organisation, working with and representing working-class women and families. In 1913, the political differences between Sylvia and her mother and older sister became too great. Sylvia left the WSPU after quarrelling with her mother, and founded the East London Federation of Suffragettes (ELFS). This consisted of working-class women, rather than the upper-class socialites of the WSPU. The ELFS included male members and was a democratically organised society.

Emily Davison

Along with divisions within the WSPU, recent historical research has emphasised the role of individual, autonomous militant protesters. It has been suggested that much window breaking and violent behaviour was not directed by the WSPU, but performed on individual members' private initiative. It is doubtful the Pankhursts had much control over such action. One notable example of this was Emily Wilding Davison (1872–1913) who joined the WSPU in 1906. After working as a teacher and studying at the University of Oxford, Davison quit her job in 1908 to campaign full-time for the vote. Davison was a particularly violent campaigner, who frequently acted without the WSPU's instruction, often resorting to stone throwing or arson. She also underwent force-feedings in prison and was arrested several times. During the 1911 census, she hid in the chapel beneath the Houses of Parliament the night before registration, so that she could appear as residing in the 'House of Commons'. In 1912, she spent six months in Holloway Prison for arson before falling down a staircase to win relief from the force-feedings. She was left with head and spinal injuries that never fully healed.

In June 1913, Davison was killed after colliding with the king's horse at the Epsom Derby. It is unclear whether this was suicide or if she was attempting to attach a WSPU flag to the horse. Her motives remain a mystery. The WSPU was eager to show she had martyred herself, but historians suggest she intended to return home after, having kept her return rail ticket. This lack of knowledge over her intentions shows how independently she worked. The WSPU had little control over the actions of such members. Nevertheless, the WSPU's leaders seized on the propaganda opportunity Davison's death presented. Her funeral was used by the WSPU as a unique publicity stunt, with thousands of suffragettes attending. This won the WSPU much public sympathy. The actions of Davison provide a microcosm of wider questions about the role of Emmeline and Christabel Pankhurst. While they undoubtedly inspired women to heroic deeds and created an organisation that cultivated militancy, they were logistically unable to control all their members. Not all militant activities were directed by the Pankhursts. Very often, the WSPU's success relied on individual members outside of the Pankhurst family, such as Davison.

The WSPU's position by 1914

By 1914, the WSPU had enjoyed immense success and popularity, but was in a precarious position. In both cases, the leadership of Emmeline and Christabel, and the heroism of individuals such as Sylvia Pankhurst and Davison, were central. There can be little doubt that, while autocratic, Christabel and Emmeline provided many women with inspirational characters. They often ruled by charm; winning genuine devotion from their followers. Emmeline and Christabel believed that a more democratic style of government was unsuitable to a militant organisation like the WSPU, which practised illegal activities.

So while the Pankhursts' leadership aroused several splits and alienated many WSPU members, as well as outsiders to the organisation, Emmeline and Christabel did mould the WSPU into an effective political force. Christabel, in particular, was central to the adoption of militant tactics that brought the question of female suffrage to the forefront of British politics. Yet she also bears much of the responsibility for the increasingly violent tactics that shocked observers after 1908. After 1912, however, Christabel's role in the WSPU diminished when she fled to France to avoid imprisonment. From Paris, she orchestrated the WSPU through regular meetings with Annie Kenney. In particular, it was from Paris that Christabel directed the WSPU's arson campaign. While Christabel's authority diminished after 1912, Emmeline's grip loosened too. In 1913, Emmeline was sentenced to three years' penal servitude for threatening to blow up Lloyd George's house. Emmeline's constant imprisonments, with the cycle of starvations, force-feedings, releases and re-arrests ruined her health, leaving her much weakened. With the Liberal government's repressive response to violence and Christabel's absence, the WSPU's leadership was somewhat undermined by 1914.

The problem was that the WSPU's autocratic nature was limited and inflexible. When votes for women was not on the government's agenda, militant tactics won the support the movement so badly needed. However, Emmeline and Christabel lacked ideas over how to influence government when it was seriously considering extending the franchise to women between 1909 and 1914.

EXTRACT

Martin Pugh's comments made during an interview for the *Guardian* newspaper in 2000. The historian Pugh attempted to undermine the reputations of Christabel and Emmeline Pankhurst and Annie Kenney.

In the diary Kenney appears frequently and with different women. Almost day by day Mary says she is sleeping with someone else... Biographers, while acknowledging a small lesbian element in the movement, have all skirted around the issue.

EXTRACT

Historian June Purvis, writing in 2003, recalls challenging Pugh over his claims to discredit the WSPU's leadership.

In an exchange of views with Martin Pugh in *The Times Higher Education Supplement* in January 2002, I questioned his representation of Emmeline Pankhurst, including a claim made in an 'Observer' article that his forthcoming book would reveal how Emmeline, Christabel and Annie Kenney, a working-class woman who became a key figure in the WSPU, led 'a promiscuous lesbian lifestyle'.

EXTRACT

A review of the Pugh–Purvis historical debate over the reputations of the WSPU's leadership by the historian Jill Liddington. This appeared in 2003 on the *Times Higher Education* website.

Pugh's biography is also controversial because of his critical take on the Pankhursts, pronouncing them 'a rather dysfunctional family'. He may have a point. Yet they were all highly political, and politically active families are not routinely cosy. As the youngest daughter, Adela, put it: 'It was the family attitude – Cause First and human relations - nowhere... if (Emmeline) had been tolerant and broadminded, she would not have been the leader of the suffragettes.'

EXTRACT

Jacqueline Devries provides another review of the Pugh–Purvis debate, this time in 2002 in the historical journal *Victorian Studies*.

At times Pugh's revisionism shades into a reaction to feminist methodologies and analysis of gender politics and identities... Although he is not the first to argue that the suffragists' spectacular demonstrations might actually have delayed victory, he pushes the argument further, claiming they brought little innovation to the movement and decisively failed in their political strategy. He constructs this argument mainly from an analysis of neglected Public Record Office sources on by-elections, which reveal the inefficacy of the Pankhurst strategy to oppose the election of Liberal MPs. On a strictly parliamentary level, Pugh may be right.

THINKING HISTORICALLY   Evidence (6c)

Comparing and evaluating historians' arguments

Between 2000 and 2002, historians Martin Pugh and June Purvis engaged in a debate over the reputation of Christabel and Emmeline Pankhurst. Each historian produced their own biography, with Pugh provocatively demeaning the Pankhursts' credentials. His allegation that Annie Kenney and Christabel Pankhurst were lesbian lovers was particularly controversial. Purvis worked to undermine Pugh's work, and defend the reputation of the Pankhursts. She believed that they were good leaders who had made tough decisions that were necessary to lead a militant movement successfully.

1 Extract 4 supports Pugh and Extract 3 supports Purvis.

   a) Which extract has the better-supported claim?

   b) How could you add something to Extract 4 to make the claim stronger?

2 What is particularly strong about the claim in Extract 3 compared to the others?

3 According to Extract 2, what is unorthodox about Pugh's argument?

4 How does Extract 3 challenge the argument in Extract 1?

5 Consider all the sources. Which do you think is the best argument? Explain your answer.

A Level Exam-Style Question Section B

How far were Emmeline and Christabel Pankhurst responsible for the rise of militancy within the women's suffrage movement between 1903 and 1914? (20 marks)

Tip

Consider the roles of Emmeline and Christabel within the WSPU, the level of autocratic rule they exerted and the roles of others, like the Pethick-Lawrences and Emily Davison.

ACTIVITY
KNOWLEDGE CHECK

Leading the WSPU

1 What evidence is there that Christabel and Emmeline Pankhurst held great control over the WSPU?

2 What does the 1906 split from the Labour Party show about the Pankhursts' leadership?

3 What evidence is there that Christabel and Emmeline Pankhurst's authority over the WSPU was limited?

4 Do you think the Pankhursts' autocratic leadership was justified between 1903 and 1914?

HOW FAR WAS THE LIBERAL GOVERNMENT TO BLAME FOR THE CONTINUED FAILURE OF LEGISLATION FOR FEMALE SUFFRAGE BETWEEN 1909 AND 1913?

While the WSPU gathered increasing support, the Liberal government under Asquith was not inactive. It had to respond to the campaign for women's suffrage. Between 1909 and 1913, a series of measures to give women the vote, initially proposed by individual members, but eventually introduced by the government, were debated. However, several political obstacles prevented success, such as the prime minister's personal opposition, the 1910 constitutional crisis and debates over the form of female suffrage. By 1912, the WSPU's violent hostility to the government left many pro-women's suffrage MPs disillusioned and unwilling to support legislation that would grant them the vote.

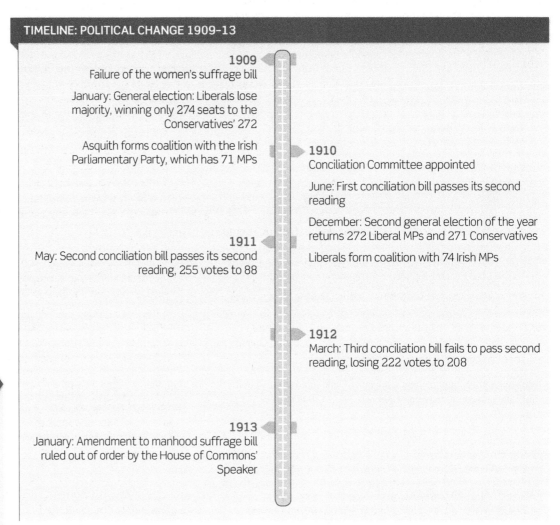

TIMELINE: POLITICAL CHANGE 1909–13

1909
Failure of the women's suffrage bill

January: General election: Liberals lose majority, winning only 274 seats to the Conservatives' 272

Asquith forms coalition with the Irish Parliamentary Party, which has 71 MPs

1910
Conciliation Committee appointed

June: First conciliation bill passes its second reading

December: Second general election of the year returns 272 Liberal MPs and 271 Conservatives

Liberals form coalition with 74 Irish MPs

1911
May: Second conciliation bill passes its second reading, 255 votes to 88

1912
March: Third conciliation bill fails to pass second reading, losing 222 votes to 208

1913
January: Amendment to manhood suffrage bill ruled out of order by the House of Commons' Speaker

KEY TERMS

Private member's bill
A proposed bill that is introduced for debate into the House of Commons by an individual MP and is therefore not part of the government's planned legislation.

Second reading
To become law, a bill must pass through several readings in parliament, after which a vote is taken. The bill expires if it does not become an Act before a parliamentary session ends and an election is held. While both the first and second conciliation bills passed their second readings, they failed to secure further time to pass into law. For the first conciliation bill, this was because the early election of December 1910 ended the parliamentary session.

Reasons for the failure of the women's suffrage bill, 1909

Thanks to the efforts of the NUWSS, the Liberal government that took power in 1906 included a majority of MPs pledged to grant women the vote. Although the government made no mention of women in its manifesto, the NUWSS was hopeful that the government would pass legislation to extend the franchise. In 1909, Liberal MP Geoffrey Howard introduced a **private member's bill** for both male and female suffrage, based on a three-month residential qualification. This was not a government move. This carried by 35 votes on its **second reading**, but failed to proceed after extensive debate wasted the time allocated to its passing. Both Christabel and Fawcett disliked the bill, believing full adult suffrage was unpractical and represented the government's attempt to introduce a measure so radical that it could never pass. In part, this revealed a pragmatic approach to the question of the vote among the NUWSS and WSPU leadership; they conceived of only a limited extension to the franchise.

There were two key obstacles to franchise reform in 1909. These were not only responsible for the failure of the 1909 women's suffrage bill, but continued to prove troublesome between 1909 and 1913. Most serious was the party deadlock between Conservatives and Liberals over the question of women's votes. While most MPs supported such a reform, they differed over the form it should take. Many Conservatives wanted women to have equal suffrage rights with men, with the vote based on the existing property-based franchise – women could have the vote if they had property or income. The Liberals rejected this, fearing it would add Conservative votes to the electorate. Instead, many Liberals favoured extending the suffrage criteria so that women and more working-class men would have the vote. Of course, the Conservatives refused to agree to this, as they suspected it would add votes for Labour and the Liberals. This impasse was to prove virtually impossible to resolve fully.

The other big obstacle to female suffrage throughout 1909–13 was the personal opinion of the prime minister, Herbert Asquith. Wherever possible, he undermined legislative attempts that would enfranchise women. Asquith could not comprehend why women would want the vote and regarded militant protesters as unnatural. In many ways, Asquith held a Gladstonian view of political change, believing that too much too quickly would fundamentally damage political stability. He was loath to allow militancy to dictate government policy, fearing that agitation was not the same as public opinion. He was, after all, a lawyer, and in any question of change considered whether it would improve government and whether it was really wanted. To confirm his views, he needed only to look at his wife Margot and daughter Violet, who were both adamantly opposed to female suffrage and detested the actions of the WSPU. This reinforced Asquith's view that only very extreme women could possibly want the vote. Female suffrage was a question that he hoped would just go away. He was far more concerned with the problems of Ireland, social reform, industrial unrest and the House of Lords' crisis.

EXTEND YOUR KNOWLEDGE

Herbert Henry Asquith (1852–1928)
Liberal prime minister between 1908 and 1916, Asquith's first position as Home Secretary had come in 1892 in William Gladstone's government. A keen supporter of free trade, Asquith was at the helm of a Liberal government that, from 1906, introduced a series of radical welfare reforms, most notably the 'People's Budget'. These reforms included improvements to schools, old-age pensions, workers' rights and health care for low earners. On becoming prime minister, Asquith reorganised the cabinet, assigning key positions to able men like David Lloyd George and Winston Churchill. While critical of his approach to the question of women's suffrage, historians have generally judged Asquith's government as one of the most successful of the 20th century, despite his failure to provide leadership during the first two years of the First World War. Under Asquith, the Liberals delivered the beginnings of the welfare state.

Asquith was a frequent target of militant violence, having been attacked on a golf course in Scotland by suffragettes desperate to rip his clothes off. He was only saved by the timely intervention of his daughter, Violet. Then, in 1913, he was assaulted by women brandishing dog whips. In public and at social events, respectable women heckled him. Such disrespect left Asquith offended, but also somewhat confused. Rather than change his mind, however, these displays of militancy strengthened his resolve. He came to see women protesters as analogous to the rebellious Irish protesters and dangerous trade unionists. Biographers of Asquith, such as Roy Jenkins, have considered the prime minister's attitudes to female suffrage to be bizarre.

The conciliation bills, 1910 and 1911

In January 1910, with mounting pressure over the House of Lords' refusal to pass the 1909 Budget and facing a constitutional crisis, Asquith called a general election. The Liberals returned to government, but lost their majority. Despite this, a majority of MPs still wanted female suffrage, so an all-party committee was appointed to address the question. Supported by the NUWSS and the WSPU, the committee consisted of 54 MPs and was chaired by the Conservative Earl of Lytton, brother of the WSPU's celebrated member, Lady Constance Lytton. These MPs found a path to conciliation between Conservatives and Liberals over how to give women the vote without handing one party a big electoral advantage. This conciliation committee drew up a bill, approved by Conservatives and Liberals, for limited women's franchise. The WSPU suspended militant hostilities while the House of Commons debated the measure. This legislation proposed that women householders and business occupants, with an income of £10 a year or more, would be allowed to vote. Marriage would not be a disqualification, but a husband and wife could not both vote on the basis of the same property. This would have given the vote to women who could already vote in local government elections. The first conciliation bill was criticised in the House of Commons for granting the vote to only a million women, mostly widows and spinsters. Christabel denounced the bill, preferring extended female suffrage, but it passed its second reading in July 1910 by a staggering 110 votes. Asquith opposed the bill, while Liberals Lloyd George and Winston Churchill believed it did not go far enough, providing votes only to the Conservative Party. The vote was a great step forward, but because of the **1910 constitutional crisis**, Asquith prioritised government business in the cabinet, taking women's suffrage off the agenda.

In November 1909, the House of Lords vetoed David Lloyd George's 'People's Budget'. In 1910, the House of Lords begrudgingly approved the Budget, but to ensure such an event did not happen again, the government introduced legislation prohibiting the House of Lords from vetoing bills relating to finance. However, the House of Lords tried to stop this bill too.

KEY TERM

1910 constitutional crisis
In 1910, the House of Lords had the power to veto bills passed in the House of Commons. This meant that it could stop them becoming law, despite popular support. The House of Lords' decision to veto Lloyd George's 1909 Budget triggered the constitutional crisis, in which the elected Liberal government had been blocked by an unelected, largely Conservative, House of Lords. The Parliament Act 1911, which prohibited the House of Lords from vetoing bills relating to finance, ensured this did not happen again.

Asquith had to get the support of King George V, who threatened to flood the Lords with Liberal supporters if the Lords did not co-operate. With this threat, the Lords passed the legislation. While this crisis was resolved by the Parliament Act 1911, in 1910 it damaged efforts to pass legislation granting women the vote. This political crisis meant that further parliamentary time for the first conciliation bill was refused.

EXTEND YOUR KNOWLEDGE

The People's Budget

The 1909 Budget, popularised as the 'People's Budget', was the flagship policy of Asquith's Liberal government. Supported by Winston Churchill, the Chancellor of the Exchequer, Lloyd George introduced the measure believing it would reduce poverty. Increased income tax, (five percent) for incomes over £2,000 and 7.5 percent for incomes over £5,000, along with a 20 percent tax on the value of land when it was inherited or sold, would fund a dramatic increase in public spending on national insurance, providing health care to low earners, and old-age pensions. The 20 percent land tax made this very unpopular with land-owning members of the House of Lords.

SOURCE

9 The Home Secretary, Winston Churchill, expressed his opposition to the first conciliation bill in a debate in the House of Commons on 12 July 1910. Shortly after this, the bill passed, despite Churchill's opposition.

This Bill is neither one thing nor the other. It is not a genuine democratic reform nor a fairly balanced restricted mitigation of the grievance which exists. It is an enormous addition to the franchise of 1,000,000 persons, and altogether a capricious and one-sided addition to that franchise. It is the Bill we now have to divide upon. We have to decide and vote not for a principle, not for a Bill, but for this Bill now before the House of Commons. I have been making as good an examination as is in my power of the actual proposals, and shape, and character of the Bill. The more I study the Bill the more astonished I am that such a large number of respected Members of Parliament should have found it possible to put their names to it. And, most of all, I was astonished that Liberal and Labour Members should have associated themselves with it. It is not merely an undemocratic Bill; it is worse. It is an anti-democratic Bill. It gives an entirely unfair representation to property, as against persons... I can easily understand the Noble Lord the Member for Oxford hurrying from his academic groves to welcome this windfall, but I am bound to say when I see a Liberal Member or a Labour Member voting for provisions like this I feel he must either be very innocent or must have been intimidated. But quite apart from this one-sided aspect, apart from the question of the property or the non-property, let the House look at the absurdity of the Bill. I can understand a man who says, 'I am in favour of votes for women,' and a man who says, 'I am against votes for women,' but what is to be said for a man who says he is in favour of votes for women, but not for mothers and wives, unless they are faggot votes? The basic principle of this Bill is to deny votes to mothers and wives – that is to say, to deny votes to those who are upon the whole the best of their sex. Fancy this proposition that we Members of Parliament are asked to commit ourselves to, and to defend on the platforms of the country, that a young, inexperienced girl of twenty-one should have a vote, and the mother of seven or eight children, who for twenty-five years has kept and directed the policy and economy of a family, should be refused the vote; that a woman who has nobody to keep but herself out of her wages or income is to have a vote, and the woman who keeps by her labour an invalid husband and her family is to have no vote unless the unfortunate husband is rich enough to put her in for a property qualification!

Arguments against the first conciliation bill
Study Source 9.

1 Summarise Winston Churchill's arguments against the passing of the first conciliation bill.

2 Given that the bill passed, how significant was such opposition from a cabinet minister?

In November, parliament dissolved for another election, due to the total breakdown in relations between the House of Lords and the House of Commons. The WSPU resumed its hostilities. A riot broke out in Parliament Square, with 300 women being assaulted by the police, three of whom died as a result. Asquith promised the next parliament would include a bill for female suffrage. True to his word, a second conciliation bill was passed in May 1911, this time by 255 votes to 88. However, Lloyd George then announced his opposition to the measure, fearing it would create thousands of Conservative voters. The cabinet refused the bill more parliamentary time, but agreed that a week would be given to a similar measure in 1912, if it could again pass its second reading. Asquith personally pledged his support for this, guaranteeing the measure would have time for debate.

SOURCE

10 A letter to *The Times* from Emmeline Pankhurst justifying the use of militant protest before the second conciliation bill, 20 March 1911.

I have read with interest your leading article in to-day's issue of *The Times* entitled 'Woman Suffrage and its Advocates,' and desire with your permission to reply to that part of it which refers to what may be described as an organized boycott of the Census. The National Committee of the Women's Social and Political Union, of which I am a member, has decided after very long and full consideration to adopt this form of protest against the determined refusal of the Government to give to women the *status* of citizenship. The Census is a numbering of the people. Until women count as people for the purpose of representation in the councils of the nation as well as for purposes of taxation and of obedience to the laws, we advise women to refuse to be numbered. You point out how important is the Census for statistical purposes. We fully recognize this vital importance. It is an added reason for our protest. The statistics obtained through the Census will form the basis of legislation affecting women which a Parliament of men responsible only to men will pass into law. It is because we know from actual experience how always inadequate and often unjust is such legislation that we deliberately and after much thought refuse to provide the information until facilities are given by the Government for the passing into law of a Woman's Suffrage Bill, the second reading of which is fixed for May 5 next. There is a very simple and obvious way out of the difficulty, which, let me point out, has only arisen because of the unreasonable behaviour of a small minority of the Cabinet. That is to give to women a pledge such as the Prime Minister has already given to the Irish... Let him assure us that he will not veto our Bill, but will allow such time after second reading as is necessary to carry it to third reading... Once we have won the vote the methods you condemn will no longer be necessary. Until we have won it we are determined to do all in our power to make clear to our rulers the truth of the axiom that government to be effective must rest upon the consent of the governed.

In March 1912, a third conciliation bill, essentially the same measure as that which secured a majority of 167 votes in 1911, was defeated by 14 votes. This was a terrible blow to women's suffrage campaigners. In response, the NUWSS moved to make an alliance with the Labour Party, and the WSPU resumed militant activities, this time more aggressively than ever before.

Part of the reason for the failure of the third conciliation bill was the damaging effect of the WSPU's militant violence. Had it passed, Asquith was publicly pledged to allow further time to pass legislation for women's suffrage. Its defeat represented the loss of the WSPU's best peacetime chance to secure the vote. This was effectively the same measure parliament had passed by a majority of 167 in 1911. Yet in 1912 it was defeated. In part, this was because Asquith persuaded the Irish Nationalist MPs to drop their support for the bill in order to secure legislation for Irish Home Rule. All but three Irish MPs voted against the 1912 bill. This does not account for the dramatic loss of support, however, and the loss of 167 votes (the Irish Parliamentary Party had only 74 votes). Much more serious was the 42 previous supporters who voted against the measure, and the 91 MPs who approved of female suffrage in 1911, but abstained in 1912. This collapse in support was because of the doubt created by the WSPU's militant violence. The WSPU had alienated a majority of MPs. Teresa Billington-Greig certainly held this view, believing the Pankhurst-inspired violence, so close to the conciliation bill, had been suicidal.

Violence turned opinion against women's cause, creating great hostility and feeding prejudices. For many, the vote was a responsibility, not a right, and the WSPU's tactics called into question the character of women. Violence made women appear irresponsible, and too reckless to be trusted with political representation. While many Conservatives feared change would create disorder, Liberals worried that giving in to militancy would encourage violence from Irish protesters.

The government franchise bill, 1913

In 1913, a new franchise bill, supported by Labour, Liberal, and Conservative MPs, was debated. This would extend the vote to working-class men. An amendment was proposed to strike the word 'male' from the bill so as to include women. This measure was suggested by Lloyd George, so that any extension of the franchise would include working-class women too. While this found support from the House of Commons, the Speaker of the House, the Conservative MP James Lowther, shocked everyone by declaring that such an amendment would change the character of the bill and invalidate it. Lowther was personally opposed to the extension of the franchise to women. Although probably as surprised as everyone else by Lowther's actions, Asquith was greatly pleased and refused to draft a replacement bill. More WSPU violence followed.

SOURCE 11

The pro-militant newspaper, *Votes for Women*, provided the following analysis of the failure of the 1913 franchise bill amendment to include female suffrage. Appearing on 7 February 1913, this publication placed the blame for the continued failings to enfranchise women firmly on the Liberal government, and defended acts of violence as necessary for placing pressure on parliament. While this had been the WSPU's newspaper, when the Pethick-Lawrences were expelled from the organisation in 1912, they took the publication with them. However, it remained supportive of WSPU militancy.

The Conciliation Bill was a measure contrived on a really non-party basis, having been drafted by a committee of genuine Suffragists drawn from all parties in the House of Commons. Experts computed that it would have enfranchised about a million women... Let us restate the position. A private member's Bill, drawing support from both sides of the House, could only be carried provided the Government were prepared to remain neutral not merely as to the actual voting, but as to the nature of the Bill itself. This proviso was not fulfilled in the case of the Conciliation Bill, and it is already evident that it will not be fulfilled for the new Bill. More than that, it is a proviso inherently incapable of fulfilment under modern political conditions. We therefore say definitely that this method of attempting to deal with Woman Suffrage is foredoomed to failure, and only those can advocate it who are either deliberately putting women off or who have themselves not sufficiently considered the situation. We are thrown back on the only other method, the one which is in strict accordance with the practice of the Constitution, the introduction by the Government of a Government measure for the enfranchisement of women... The guerrilla war conducted by the militants continues with unabated vigour. Pillar-boxes in different parts of the country have been tampered with, and the campaign has been extended to the Tower of London, the Archbishop's Palace, and to the golf courses. However much the public may dislike and resent these actions, they are a sign that large numbers of women feel keenly their exclusion from citizenship, and do not intend to let Society rest until their grievances are redressed. We are glad to see that the strong protest made last week in our columns by Mr. Nevinson against the treatment meted out by the police to Mrs. Drummond has drawn the attention of the *Manchester Guardian* to the facts, and that that paper is demanding an inquiry.

Asquith's opposition, parliamentary procedure and the political deadlock over the form female suffrage should take were all important for the failure of the government to give women the vote between 1909 and 1913. Yet the escalating WSPU militancy has also been seen as an immensely damaging feature, contributing to the failure of women to win the vote before 1914. The WSPU's violent forms of protest increased opposition within parliament to female suffrage. When, in 1910, Millicent Fawcett discussed legislation with Lloyd George, she was informed that recent militancy made reform impossible. Although a supporter of women's franchise, Lloyd George claimed that the recent demonstrations had left his wife alienated from the suffrage campaign. He grew increasingly displeased with the WSPU, believing in November 1911 that Christabel had lost all sense of proportion. The intense wave of violence triggered by Asquith's failure to grant time to the recently passed second conciliation bill persuaded Lloyd George that the militancy was out of control. Likewise, the leader of the Labour Party, Ramsay MacDonald, regarded the window smashing and hunger strikes as a hysterical response to the bill's failure.

SOURCE 12 A WSPU poster reacting to Asquith's failure to grant further time to pass the Second Conciliation bill.

THE RIGHT DISHONOURABLE DOUBLE-FACE ASQUITH.

A. PATRIOT.

Citizen Asq—th: "Down with privilege of birth up with democratic rule!"

Monseigneur Asq—th: "The rights of Government belong to the aristocrats by birth—men. No liberty or equality for women!"

VOTES FOR WOMEN.

Women! The Government refuse to give you the vote. Therefore, work against the Liberal Candidate, the nominee of the Government.

Electors! The Government pose as champions of the Constitution, but deny constitutional liberty to women. We call upon you to support the Women.

Vote against the Government and keep the Liberal out.

On behalf of The Women's Social and Political Union,

EMMELINE PANKHURST.
EMMELINE PETHICK LAWRENCE.

When, in late 1910, the WSPU feared Asquith was delaying the vote and launched an attack on Downing Street, accosting Asquith and smashing his car's windows, many pro-suffrage MPs lost enthusiasm for the cause. From late 1910, there was reduced support within parliament for women's suffrage. While post-1910 violence dampened the enthusiasm of pro-suffrage MPs, the particularly aggressive waves of violence between 1911 and 1913 really damaged parliament's efforts to extend the franchise. The WSPU's attempts to target private property and destroy social order, including the destruction of churches and politicians' homes with bombs and arson, played into the hands of anti-suffrage groups, who used such actions as evidence of women's unsuitability for politics. From 1912, parliamentary debates moved away from how to enfranchise women to discussions about how to prevent the violence. Public support was badly shaken.

While it would be fair to say that by 1912 pro-suffrage advocates had won the debate over women's franchise, violence undermined this. Before 1911, Conservative Party conferences had on six occasions passed votes in favour of female suffrage. In 1912 and 1913, conferences voted to oppose the measure. A similar example of reduced support appeared in 1912, when the MP George Lansbury sought re-election with a mandate for female franchise. Despite a huge majority in 1910, his stance on women's votes lost him his seat to an anti-suffrage candidate.

SOURCE

13 A letter written by Emmeline Pankhurst and addressed to members of the WSPU, emphasising the need for militant action. This was published on 10 January 1913 and demanded that, should the amendment to the franchise bill fail, further violence would be justified.

The Prime Minister has announced that in the week beginning January 20th the Women's Amendments to the Manhood Suffrage Bill will be discussed and voted upon. This means that within a few short days the fate of these Amendments will be finally decided.

The W.S.P.U. has from the first declined to call any truce on the strength of the Prime Minister's so-called pledge, and has refused to depend upon the Amendments in question, because the Government have not accepted the responsibility of getting them carried. There are, however, some Suffragists – and there may be some even in the ranks of the W.S.P.U. – who hope against hope that in spite of the Government's intrigues an unofficial Amendment may be carried. Feeling as they do, these Suffragists are tempted to hold their hand as far as militancy is concerned, until after the fate of the Amendments is known.

But every member of the W.S.P.U. recognises that the defeat of the Amendments will make militancy more a moral duty and more a political necessity than it has ever been before. We must prepare beforehand to deal with that situation!

There are degrees of militancy. Some women are able to go further than others in militant action and each woman is the judge of her own duty so far is that is concerned. To be militant in some way or other is, however, a moral obligation. It is a duty which every woman will owe to her own conscience and self-respect, to other women who are less fortunate than she herself is, and to all those who are to come after her.

If any woman refrains from militant protest against the injury done by the Government and the House of Commons to women and to the race, she will share the responsibility for the crime. Submission under such circumstances will be itself a crime.

I know that the defeat of the Amendments will prove to thousands of women that to rely only on peaceful, patient methods, is to court failure, and that militancy is inevitable. We must, as I have said, prepare to meet the crisis before it arises. Will you therefore tell me (by letter, if it is not possible to do so by word of mouth), that you are ready to take your share in manifesting in a practical manner your indignation at the betrayal of our cause.

> **A Level Exam-Style Question Section A**
>
> *Study Source 13 before you answer this question.*
>
> Assess the value of the source for revealing WSPU attitudes towards the failure of parliament to pass legislation granting women the vote, and Emmeline Pankhurst's opinion regarding militancy.
>
> Explain your answer, using the source, the information given about its origin and your own knowledge about the historical context. (20 marks)
>
> **Tip**
> *Think about how the WSPU justified the use of militancy as a response to government failures to extend the vote to women. How does the WSPU newspaper conceptualise suffragette violence?*

Conclusion

By 1914, the WSPU had clearly run out of steam. It lacked ideas and its leadership was increasingly disjointed. While it could claim a great deal of credit for successfully bringing female suffrage to the public's attention between 1903 and 1908, its handling of protests between 1909 and 1913, while the government sought a legislative solution to women's votes, is difficult to assess. It would seem that the WSPU very probably impeded attempts at reform and provided valuable ammunition to those who opposed female suffrage. It was the NUWSS that, from 1912, worked with Labour to ensure the vote remained a priority in mainstream politics. The NUWSS's Election Fighting Funding Committee (EFF), which campaigned for pro-suffrage Labour candidates, was valued by the Labour Party during by-elections between 1913 and 1914. Despite this, the WSPU's earlier militancy had contributed to the NUWSS's growth. The attention it won for the cause between 1903 and 1908 was crucial to later efforts to secure the vote. The First World War provided the chance for the WSPU to seize the initiative, as it eagerly supported the government. It was fiercely anti-German and campaigned hard for recruits for the armed services. In 1917, the government passed the representation of the people bill by 385 to 55 votes. In each party, there was a majority in favour, with even Asquith changing his mind and supporting women's suffrage. The coalition government set up during the war to replace Asquith's ailing administration removed the party deadlock over which party female voters would benefit the most. For all their campaigning, this was the impasse that neither the WSPU nor the NUWSS had really been able to resolve. The 1918 Representation of the People Act enfranchised 13 million men and 8.4 million women. Ultimately, while the WSPU lacked flexibility during the government's attempts to pass laws granting women the vote between 1910 and 1913, it adapted quickly to the challenge war presented.

THINKING HISTORICALLY   Change (7a)

Convergence and divergence

WSPU militancy, 1905–13				
1905	**1908**	**1909**	**1910**	**1912**
Christabel Pankhurst initiates militancy by disrupting a political meeting	Hyde Park meeting, including 250,000 to 500,000 suffrage campaigners	Window smashing campaign under way	Black Friday, where women clash with police around parliament	Christabel Pankhurst initiates arson campaign

Political events, 1905–13				
1908	**1909**	**1911**	**1912**	**1913**
Asquith becomes prime minister and asserts that women do not want the vote	Failure of private member's bill to extend the franchise to women and men	Failure of the second conciliation bill	Failure of the third conciliation bill	Failure to amend the franchise bill

1 Draw a timeline across the middle of a landscape piece of A3 paper. Cut out ten small rectangular cards and write the above events on them. Then place them on the timeline, with WSPU militancy above the line and political events below. Make sure there is a lot of space between the events and the line.

2 Draw a line and write a link between each event within each strand, so that you have five links that join up the events in the WSPU part of the timeline and five that join the political events. You will then have two strands of event: WSPU militancy and political.

3 Now make as many links as possible across the timeline between WSPU militancy and political change. Think about how they are affected by one another and think about how things can link across long periods of time.

You should end up with something like this:

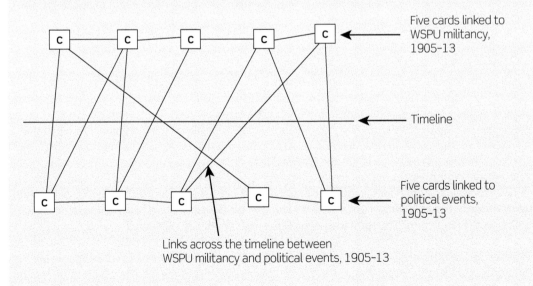

Five cards linked to WSPU militancy, 1905–13

Timeline

Five cards linked to political events, 1905–13

Links across the timeline between WSPU militancy and political events, 1905–13

Answer the following:

4 How far do different strands of history interact with one another? Illustrate your answer with two well-explained examples.

5 At what point do the two strands of development converge (i.e. when do the events have the biggest impact on one another)?

6 How useful are the strands in understanding the role of militancy on political action?

ACTIVITY
KNOWLEDGE CHECK

Militancy

1 Did militancy help or hinder parliamentary efforts to enfranchise women?

2 In your opinion, was the WSPU's use of violence after 1908 justified?

ACTIVITY
SUMMARY

Parliament and militancy

1 Produce your own double-sided timeline of government attempts to provide women with the vote and militant activity.

   a) Down one side, list all the government measures for enfranchising women.

   b) Down the other side, list, chronologically, the WSPU's responses.

   c) Consider specific responses such as Black Friday and Davison's death at the Epsom Derby, but also include dates notable for escalations in violence and changes in the WSPU's political affiliation.

   d) Consider how parliament reacted to different displays of protest from the WSPU, but also think about how WSPU militancy influenced parliament, both positively and negatively.

2 On balance, do you think the WSPU was more influencing of, rather than influenced by, the actions of the Liberal government of 1906–14?

WIDER READING

Bartley, P. *Emmeline Pankhurst*, Routledge (2002)

Bentley, M. and Stevenson, J. (eds) *High and Low Politics in Modern Britain*, Oxford University Press (1983)

Joannou, M. and Purvis, J. (eds) *The Women's Suffrage Movement: New Feminist Perspectives*, Manchester University Press (1998)

Liddington, J. and Norris, J. *One Hand Tied Behind Us: The Rise of the Women's Suffrage Movement*, Virago (1978)

Marcos, J. (ed.) *Suffrage and the Pankhursts*, Routledge (1987)

Pugh, M. *The Pankhursts*, Penguin (2001)

Purvis, J. *Emmeline Pankhurst: A Biography*, Routledge (2002)

Rosen, A. *Rise Up, Women! The Militant Campaign of the Women's Social and Political Union, 1903-14*, Routledge (1974)

Smith, H. *The British Women's Suffrage Campaign, 1866-1928*, Pearson (2007)

3.7 Trades union militancy, 1915–27

KEY QUESTIONS

- To what extent did the trade union movement secure increased influence between 1915 and 1919?
- To what extent was there a trade union revival between 1919 and 1921 in the aftermath of the First World War?
- Why did the General Strike fail to influence the Conservative government in 1926?

INTRODUCTION

The First World War (1914–18) fundamentally changed Britain, politically, economically and socially. In 1914, Britain had confidently entered the war as the world's leading imperial power, controlling one-third of the globe's land, one-quarter of its people, and dominating its trade thanks to its immense industrial and financial power. Its wealth was largely derived from heavy industry, built on iron production and coal mining. These were industries in which labourers were poorly paid and worked in terrible conditions. However, the tremendous loss of life during the war, upwards of 820,000, encouraged many to believe that the working classes had suffered; they had paid a sacrifice that entitled them to increased wages and improved working conditions. The wartime demand for industrial produce, particularly munitions, presented a challenge for industrial workers. Rising costs of living, increasingly expensive rent, long hours, restricted movement between jobs and an influx of unskilled labour all contributed to worsen the condition of many industrial labourers. Because of the increased demands for labour during the war, workers were able to campaign for improvements. Industrial unrest challenged traditional British society, and this continued after the war. Working-class labourers made up 70 percent of the nation's workforce. Through the war and 1920s, trade unions tapped into this rich potential support.

The potential of militant industrial protest and the memory of sacrifice during the war convinced some trade unionists that the traditional capitalist system, in which business owners exploited their workers for profit, would change. That the lot of the worker would improve and that profits would be more evenly shared was a radical hope. Yet the 1920s were hard times, with Britain's industrial output collapsing after the short-lived post-war economic boom, and employers determined to reduce wages.

1915 – Glasgow rent strikes and industrial militancy

1919 – Glasgow 40-hour week strike

General Council of the TUC established

1921
15 April: Black Friday

| 1914 | 1915 | 1918 | 1919 | 1920 | 1921 | 1922 |

1914 – Triple Alliance of trade unions formed

August: Commencement of the First World War

1918 – End of the First World War

1922 – Fall of the coalition government; Conservative government forms

In 1926, tensions in the coal industry reached breaking point and the central TUC General Council, which represented the federation of trade unions, called a general strike across the nation. For all the post-war change, this move completely failed, and the government reasserted its control over the union-organised working classes. While the rise of the trade union movement between 1915 and 1926 appeared to herald a new era of industrial relations between employees and the employed, Stanley Baldwin's Conservative government was able to completely neutralise the threat of industrial action during the General Strike. It was the government elected to parliament that controlled the country, not the trade unions.

TO WHAT EXTENT DID THE TRADE UNION MOVEMENT SECURE INCREASED INFLUENCE BETWEEN 1915 AND 1919?

The First World War saw the rise in influence of Britain's trade unions. These organisations, which sought to unite workers and lobby for their improved conditions, saw their support increase between 1914 and 1919. In 1913, 4,189,000 workers were members of trade unions, but by 1919 this figure had risen to 8,081,000. The economic challenges of war led the government to nationalise much industry, including Britain's railways and coal mines. This brought the unions into direct contact with the government, removing the business owners and allowing for direct negotiations. The government had to co-operate with unions to ensure industrial production remained constant.

The roles of Ernest Bevin and James Henry Thomas

For Britain's working classes, the First World War presented challenges and opportunities. The war saw a huge strain placed on the British labour market. Out of a total male working population of 15 million, 4,970,000 were recruited into the army, 407,000 into the navy and 293,000 for the air force. Combined with a shortage of imported raw materials, British industrial production, including munitions, declined rapidly. By July 1915, mining produce had fallen 21.8 percent, including coal output; iron and steel production was down 18.8 percent; engineering was down 29.5 percent; and shipbuilding fell 16.5 percent from pre-war levels. This did two things. Initially, it worsened living conditions for industrial workers. The cost of living, including housing rent, food, coal and industrial products, all went up. The cost of living increased to such an extent that by March 1915, coal miners were demanding a 20 percent rise in wages to meet the growing expenses of rent and food. However, the higher demand for industrial workers also put labourers and trade unions into a strong position to negotiate for improved working conditions and increased wages between 1915 and 1918.

1925 – April: Britain returns to the gold standard

31 July: 'Red Friday'

1927 – Trades Disputes Act

| 1923 | 1924 | 1925 | 1926 | 1927 | 1928 | 1929 | 1930 |

1924 – January: Minority Labour government forms after general election

October: Conservatives win general election; Stanley Baldwin becomes prime minister

1926 – 3 May: General Strike begins

12 May: General Strike ends

SOURCE
1 Coal miners working a narrow coal seam in Pontypool, South Wales, c1910. Such work was immensely dangerous.

Even before the war, trade unionists had realised that to improve working conditions and pay, it was essential for the unions of different industries to collaborate and co-ordinate industrial unrest. At the forefront of these efforts to unite union militancy were Ernest Bevin and James Thomson. Bevin (1881–1951) was originally a van driver. In 1911, he became a trade union official for the Dockers' Union. In 1916, he was elected to the executive committee of the National Transport Workers' Federation (NTWF), formed in 1910. A Labour loyalist, Bevin was later defeated as the parliamentary candidate for Central Bristol in 1918, but during the war he was pivotal in forming NTWF policy. He realised that the transport union had to collaborate with the coal and railway unions to win workers improved pay and working conditions.

James Henry Thomas (1874–1949) was responsible for the National Union of Railwaymen (NUR). After growing up in poverty, Thomas had worked for the Great Western Railway (GWR), eventually becoming an engine driver. In 1910, he became Labour MP for Derby and oversaw the 1911 national rail strike, the first of its kind. He was instrumental in the 1913 creation of the NUR, serving as its assistant secretary. Thomas rose to prominence throughout the First World War, supporting the war and becoming general secretary of the NUR in 1916. In parliament, Thomas was able to support Lloyd George's coalition government, which formed in late 1916, by cracking down on unofficial strikes and ensuring reasonable industrial harmony. Thomas worked with Lloyd George from within parliament to secure improvements to workers' pay and conditions. After the war, Thomas worked on the TUC General Council during the years 1921–24 and 1925–29. He got on well with the upper classes. His 1920 book, *When Labour Rules*, calmed middle-class readers by assuring them that they had nothing to fear from limited nationalisation and equal opportunities for workers. Thomas became a favourite of King George V and a friend of aristocrats and plutocrats.

The Triple Alliance and the war

Both Thomas and Bevin eagerly promoted the formation of the Triple Alliance at the beginning of the war. The Miners' Federation of Great Britain (MFGB) united with the NTWF and the NUR. These three unions, representing miners, railwaymen and transport workers, together formed the Triple Alliance in 1914. Bevin had been elected to the NTWF's executive committee and represented transport workers, while 'Jimmy' Thomas had been instrumental in forming the NUR in 1913, bringing together the leading railway unions. Recognising that the union movement had to work together to exert influence on the government, Thomas and Bevin believed that the Triple Alliance would allow for the effective co-ordination of strike action. As Labour MP for Derby, Thomas worked on the newly formed parliamentary committee of the TUC, which represented the combined interests of the trade unions, from 1917 to 1921. He then served on the TUC General Council that replaced the parliamentary committee after 1921.

Although the strained labour market placed the Triple Alliance in an improved position, the war also placed new pressures on workers. The Munitions of War Act 1915 was a government response to fears over insufficient shell and ammunition production. Under the Act, private companies supplying essential wartime supplies were brought under the authority of the ministry of munitions. The Act gave it powers to regulate wages, hours and employment conditions. The ministry of munitions was empowered to resolve industrial conflicts. Government committees would arbitrate on disagreements between workers and employers to ensure production was not undermined by industrial disputes. For example, in 1915, the ministry's committee on production reviewed wages in the shipbuilding industry. This committee determined national wage rates in engineering and industry, and revised national wages every four months throughout the war. The committee granted a 12.5 percent bonus in October 1917 to skilled workers in engineering and foundries, but this caused strikes by semi-skilled and unskilled labourers, forcing the government to extend the wartime bonus to all workers.

However, the Munitions of War Act also placed constraints on skilled workers in essential industries. To prevent skilled workers moving into unskilled but better-paid engineering work, the government stipulated that workmen could not leave employment without a leaving certificate from their previous employer. This was intended to ensure production from skilled labour did not decline, but in reality it handed employers immense power over their workers. It meant that there was no competition for labour and that, if dismissed, a labourer would struggle to find new work. Employers could treat workers badly and know they had control over their future employment prospects. Leaving certificates became, in effect, 'character notes'. This hindrance to finding new employment caused much anger with workers.

Another grievance for workers was **dilution**. This use of semi-skilled or unskilled labour, including women, for skilled work caused much anger, as it undermined the privileged position of skilled workers. On the Clyde, there was much unrest over dilution, where some 14,000 female workers were employed, which caused strikes in May 1917. While coal miners did not suffer from dilution, with coal mining a highly skilled job not easily acquired by new employees, there was much anger that when miners were recruited for the army, they were not always the newest miners, but often older workers who had worked in the coal industry since before the war. When, in April 1916, the government required miners for tunnelling operations under the trenches of the Somme battlefield, it agreed to take miners who had entered work since 1914 and were single.

The shortage of labour meant that many new men were employed in coal mines who were not members of unions. This caused concern with union members, and in March 1915, strikes broke out in South Wales over the issue. By March 1916, the employment of non-union members had become so serious that the government had to intervene. It made employers make trade union membership a condition of employment for all miners for the duration of the war. So while Thomas and Bevin made sure that in the Triple Alliance the trade unions had influence as a coherent militant group, there were many new challenges presented by the war.

KEY TERM

Dilution
The practice of employing unskilled or semi-skilled workers for skilled work.

ACTIVITY
KNOWLEDGE CHECK

Trade unions in the war
1 a) List the different ways in which the war created hardships and grievances for industrial workers.

 b) List the different ways in which the war created opportunities for workers to secure improvements.

2 Overall, do you think conditions for workers improved or deteriorated during the war?

The roles of Manny Shinwell and James Maxton

During the war, the centre of industrial unrest was Glasgow. More specifically, it was in the shipyards and workshops along the banks of the river Clyde. Nowhere did the industrial militancy of the trade union movement have more influence than on Clydeside. Glasgow regarded itself as the 'Second City' of the empire and was the heart of British heavy industry. It was home to 370,000 shipbuilders, coal miners, iron makers and engineers, composing 35 percent of the city's workforce. Contemporaries feared that if a revolution happened in Britain, like the one that had swept the tsar from power in Russia in 1917, it would happen on the Clyde. The industrialisation and socialist agitation along the river Clyde earned the region the reputation of 'Red Clydeside'. At the forefront of this industrial unrest were radical trade unionists, such as Manny Shinwell and James Maxton.

Emanuel 'Manny' Shinwell (1884–1986) was born in London and grew up in Glasgow, becoming an early member of the ILP. Shinwell worked in a clothing workshop, and in 1906, joined Glasgow Trades Council as a delegate of the union. A committed socialist, he was prominent in Clydeside during the national dock strikes of 1911. During the war, Shinwell worked as local secretary of the Glasgow branch of the British Seafarers' Union, which represented the interests of seamen and dock workers in the city. Shinwell earned fame for his militancy against the police, and in 1918, he stood unsuccessfully as the Labour candidate for West Lothian. In the 40-hours movement in 1919, Shinwell was a key figure in securing the support of seafarers for the strike. He was tried afterwards and found guilty of incitement to riot, serving five months in prison. He became a Labour MP at the 1922 election. In Ramsay MacDonald's 1924 Labour government, Shinwell was appointed parliamentary secretary to the mines department.

James Maxton (1885–1946) was born in Glasgow into a Conservative family. Maxton became a schoolteacher, but was shocked by the poverty of his Glaswegian students and turned to **socialism**. In 1904, he joined the ILP. Between 1913 and 1919, he was chairman of the Scottish Labour Party, opposing the war and making regular speeches condemning the conflict. Maxton was a good public speaker. When he refused to be conscripted into the army, he was sent to work on barges and became involved in union militancy through this employment. He organised strikes in the shipyards on Clydeside, becoming part of the Clyde Workers' Committee. This committee was formed to campaign against the Munitions Act 1915 and was critical of the war.

The Clyde Workers' Committee initially came together in October 1915. Maxton was key in advocating and organising this. In 1916, Maxton was arrested for sedition and served a year in prison. In 1918, he was elected to the National Council of the Labour Party. The discontent over leaving certificates introduced through the Munitions Act eventually provoked strikes at the Fairfield Yard on the Clyde in August 1915. Two Fairfield shipwrights were dismissed and then had adverse remarks made on their leaving certificates. The strike that this caused encouraged the government to introduce the Munitions of War Amendment Act of January 1916, which was then extended by legislation in 1917 that abolished leaving certificates.

The events and significance of the Glasgow Rent Strike, 1915

In 1915, strikes by Clydeside engineers for a pay rise marked the start of unrest that would escalate until May 1916. However, this militancy was neither political nor revolutionary; it was industrial. Discontent grew out of the desire for all society to share the sacrifices war entailed. Many workers disliked that food distribution businesses were making big profits, while landlords made money from the increased demands of industry. The influx of workers to the city to sustain increased wartime production created a shortage of housing. Property owners took this opportunity to dramatically increase rents. In the city district of Govan, a centre of shipbuilding, housewives protested against this by refusing to pay rent. Under the direction of Mary Barbour (1875–1958), Helen Crawford (1877–1954) and Agnes Dollan (1887–1966), the Glasgow Women's Housing Association led this rent strike that continued through 1915, spreading across the city. Working men soon joined the women's protest, with shipbuilders demanding better pay and conditions. Crawford and Dollan were both suffragettes, being members of the WSPU before the war. Dollan worked as the treasurer of the Glasgow Women's Housing Association that had been formed in 1914, while Barbour was central in organising tenant committees and eviction resistance. Indeed, with locals in Glasgow, the rent

KEY TERM

Socialism
The economic and political theory of social organisation that argues that the means of production, distribution and exchange should be owned or regulated by the community, usually in the form of the state.

Trades union militancy, 1915–27   3.7

protesters become popularly known as 'Mrs Barbour's Army'. Crawford and Barbour would both go on to campaign for an end to the war altogether in 1916.

In November 1915, the government passed the Rents and Mortgage Interest Restriction Act in response to the Glasgow rent strikes. This Act limited rent and mortgage rates to the levels at which they had been before the war in August 1914. The government introduced this measure on 25 November, following increasing support for the rent strike on the Clyde from industrial workers. Under Maxton, the Clydeside Workers' Committee threatened to call a general strike in support of the rent strikes. On 17 November, shipbuilders came out in sympathy with the protesting women. Then, when a landlord attempted to prosecute 18 protesters for refusing to pay rent, Lloyd George telephoned the landlord's solicitor, urging the prosecution to be delayed for the sake of protecting the production of munitions and war supplies. Within a month, the government had passed the legislation restricting rents and mortgage rates. This represented a huge triumph. Through industrial militant protest in an area essential for wartime industrial production, the rent strikers and trade unions had won a considerable improvement in living conditions. Combined with the success in removing employment leaving certificates, the rent strike was significant as it showed the extent of influence the labouring classes had attained under wartime conditions.

What makes Clydeside political activism so important within the context of Britain's growing trade union movement is that, during the war, the militant protest there was both dramatic and successful. The government and press feared the region and the trade union militancy there. Revolutionaries and radical left-wing agitators such as Maxton and Shinwell earned Glasgow a reputation as a centre of socialism. Between 1915 and 1919, the government became increasingly worried that a socialist revolution might develop in the city. While such fears were largely exaggerated, the Clydeside industrial unrest won improved conditions for workers between 1915 and 1919. Red Clydeside became emblematic of the trade unions' growing influence.

The 40-hour strike, 1919

In January 1919, a local general strike throughout Glasgow was organised by the Joint Strike Committee, in protest for a 40-hour week. With the war over and the millions of men conscripted into the army and navy quickly being demobilised, there was a dramatic increase in the number of workers looking for jobs. While in the war there had been a shortage of labour, now there was a huge surplus. The Joint Strike Committee of Glasgow calculated that the solution to this problem was to reduce the number of hours employees worked. By limiting all workers' hours to 40 per week, it hoped that jobs would be created, tackling the problem of unemployment. Of course, such measures were unpopular with employers and the government. In early 1919, shipbuilders and engineers on the Clyde and in Belfast had already appealed for and secured a reduction in working hours, from 53 per week to 47. This was agreed by employers and encouraged trade unions to move for even shorter working weeks. Several Glasgow trade unionists wanted to try to get 30-hour weeks, but in the end, Clydeside and Belfast workers came out on strike for a 40-hour week.

In fact, the most intense strike action was in Belfast, but it was on the Clyde that the most dramatic impacts of the 40-hour strike were felt. In Glasgow, the authorities overreacted and the government became convinced a revolution was unfolding. In panic, it despatched tanks and troops to the city to check any socialist uprising. A riot broke out in George Square when police tried to disperse protesters; this became known infamously as the 'Battle of George Square'. While the wartime strikes were not political, the 1919 general strike marked a change in attitude, with trade union-organised industrial workers realising the potential for militant protest to influence government policy. Worryingly for the government, during the strike, the **red flag** was raised on the municipal flagpole, sparking fears of a socialist revolution. The unrest spread to London, with the London Underground going out on strike. Between February and March 1919, it did seem that Britain might be on the verge of a revolution.

'Red Clydeside'

The rise of this perception of 'Red Clydeside' and the fears of social revolution in 1919 had an important impact on trade union influence. Through fears of socialist agitation, the trade unions' influence actually increased. For example, Winston Churchill, in the turmoil of the spring of 1919, remarked that the trade unions were an effective device for preventing the discontent of post-war

Red flag
Since the French Revolution, red flags have been symbolic of revolutionary left-wing politics. As the 19th century progressed, the red flag became emblematic of socialism. The red flag assumed its full symbolic significance with the 1917 Russian Revolution. In Britain, the appearance of this symbol usually provoked fear of revolutionary agitation.

155

SOURCE

The 'Battle of George Square', in Glasgow, 1919. This riot convinced many that Glasgow was in the grip of a revolutionary movement, and led to the deployment of military forces.

unemployment and reduced wages from spiralling out of control and into all-out revolution. Unions benefited from fears of a revolution, as the government hoped that trade unionists would control industrial unrest. While revolutionaries required military force to be suppressed, trade unionists could be appeased with negotiations. In Glasgow in 1919, the authorities overreacted, believing a revolution was underway, and prematurely resorted to military intervention rather than negotiation.

The experience of war probably did not radicalise Glasgow's industrial society. It was never really an area of socialist revolution, but between 1919 and 1922 it did become a centre of Labour support. Indeed, while the Labour Party failed in the election of December 1918, winning only one out of 15 Glasgow seats, in 1922 the party won ten. This group of Glaswegian Labour MPs, including Shinwell and Maxton, formed a united political group at parliament, determined to improve working-class conditions. This core of Scottish Labour MPs had first-hand experience of how organised industrial militancy could secure political reform. Between 1915 and 1919, Clydeside had been at the forefront of the labour movement's increasing influence.

EXTRACT

1

Historian Alastair Reid reviews Iain McLean's 1983 *The Legend of Red Clydeside*. McLean argues that the Red Clydeside movement was not an influential socialist movement, but a myth created by the government's overreaction and long-term economic factors affecting Clydeside industry.

McLean carries out an equally thorough empirical revision of each of the other dramatic incidents in the standard story of 'Red Clydeside', most of which seem to have been produced as much by government over-reaction as by extraordinary local militancy. This is all thoroughly argued and full of suggestive insights: it will be important for a long time to come as the first major revision of the revolutionary mythology of 'Red Clydeside'... His analysis of the economic and legal background to housing grievances could have been more clearly and economically expressed, but it does show that housing was already a problem before the outbreak of the First World War, as profits were squeezed between rising building costs and the low wages of manual workers, while other lucrative opportunities were drawing more and more capital abroad.

EXTRACT 2

In 1990, historian John Foster rejected Reid and McLean's evaluation of the Red Clydeside industrial unrest, arguing that as the war progressed it became an increasingly threatening and potent influential socialist movement. Foster instead provides a statistical analysis to emphasise the considerable extent of the Clydeside industrial unrest.

Reid claims that it was this 'practical socialism' which emerged as the victor. Looking at strikes in Clydeside shipbuilding between 1915 and 1917 (but curiously not 1918 and 1919) he finds no evidence of a rank-and-file revolt... In fact this revisionist reconstruction bears surprisingly little relationship to any historical reality. Quite remarkably, neither author sees fit to examine the central phenomenon of the Red Clyde, that is, the overall scale, sequence and character of its strike activity... The data on strike activity shows just how dangerous this concentration is. Figure 1 [below] makes it clear that the climax of industrial unrest on the Clyde occurred not in 1915 but at the end of the war and was principally located in shipbuilding and heavy industry. Figure 1 also supplies some measure of the exceptionality of the Clyde. No other place in Britain witnessed industrial action of anything like the general strike proportions seen in the west of Scotland in January 1919. The strikes of 1915, which certainly caused the government some concern, are dwarfed by the 1 ¼ million days lost in January 1919 – or even by the 300,000 days lost at the beginning of 1918. Naturally enough, McLean and Reid have little reason to consider why the west of Scotland might be so exceptional, and this leads to the second major flaw in their accounts. Although they are ostensibly analysing regional politics, both remain geographically non-specific. No attempt is made to place the west of Scotland within the very uneven political economy of Britain's regional development.

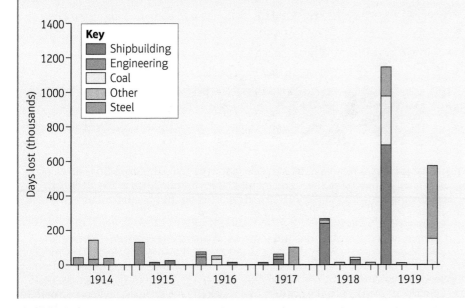

EXTRACT 3

In his 2015 article on the labour movement in Glasgow between 1915 and 1919, Paul Griffin argued that the development of the Red Clydeside movement should be understood as a rather ambiguous movement. Rather than a single socialist labour organisation, Red Clydeside, Griffin argues, should be understood as a diverse movement with varied aims.

The geographical approach towards labour history uncovers tensions and contradictions within labour histories such as Red Clydeside. Anna Chen (2013) recently commented that 'people of colour have been part of the fabric of British society for centuries, but you won't find many in official histories' either from the right or the left. Her intervention highlights the continued importance of pursuing histories, such as Red Clydeside, with greater recognition of the experiences and agency of people of colour. The hostilities considered represent an example of the complex and sometimes hostile interconnections between the politics of race and class. Within Red Clydeside, these intersections were reflective of longer trajectories of communication, and this reveals the ambivalent nature of labour identities and their subsequent demands... This paper has principally considered intersections between class and race, and that focus is justified through tensions emerging in 1919, but gender and masculinity also offer a further important lens to scrutinise labour demand making.

THINKING HISTORICALLY Change (8a, b & c) (II)

Judgements about change

If two professionals were asked to track a patient's health over time, one might approach this task by measuring heart rate, weight and cholesterol, while the other professional might assess the patient's mental well-being, relationships and ability to achieve their goals. Both are valid approaches, but result in different reports. What is true in this medical case is true in historical cases. Measuring change in something requires: (a) a concept of what that something is (e.g. 'What is "health"?', 'What is an "economy"?'); (b) judgements about how this should be measured; and (c) judgements about what relevant 'markers of change' are (how we distinguish a change from a temporary and insignificant fluctuation).

Historians have differed in their accounts of industrial change and development in Glasgow between 1915 and 1919 and debated the appropriateness of the term 'Red Clydeside' to characterise the story of the industrial unrest in this period.

Look at Extracts 1, 2 and 3 about 'Red Clydeside' and then answer the questions below.

1 Do all three accounts agree that there was serious industrial unrest on the Clyde, caused by the war?

2 Do all three accounts agree on the chronology of change? In other words, do they see change happening at the same time and at the same pace?

3 Do all three accounts agree in characterising change as rapid, dramatic and impacting on the industrial unrest as a whole?

4 Do the historians all think of the industrial unrest in the same way? For example, do they all focus on radicalism and the extent of the strikes?

5 Generalising from these examples, to what extent do historians' judgements about change depend on what historians decide to look at and how they decide to measure change?

SOURCE 3

From a pamphlet printed in February 1919 and circulated by the Joint Strike Committee of Glasgow, which had orchestrated the 40-hour strike. This was published in the aftermath of the 'Battle of George Square' in January 1919 and reported on the government attack on the labour movement, calling on the workers of Britain to unite.

Ever since the Armistice was signed it has been evident that a big unemployment crisis was imminent unless steps were taken to absorb into industry the demobilised men of the Army and Navy. Thousands are being demobilised every day. Over a hundred thousand workers in Scotland have been dismissed from civil employment. They are out of a job. There are no jobs for them. There is only one remedy: reduce the hours of labour. The Joint Committee representing the Scottish Trades Union Congress Parliamentary Committee, the Glasgow Trades and Labour Council, and a number of other important Unions initiated the movement for a Forty Hours Week with a view to absorbing the unemployed. A strike for this object began on 27th January... The demonstrators were, however, met by a vicious bludgeoning attack by the police. The authorities had evidently determined to break the strike by force, and had made their plans accordingly... Remember that this was a peaceful and orderly demonstration of workers from all districts of the Clyde area. It was met by police batons, which were used indiscriminately upon men, women, and children. Since then the authorities have imported thousands of troops into the city with machine guns and tanks for the purpose of breaking the spirit of the strikers and forcing them back to work. On the following day the offices of the Glasgow Trades and Labour Council, the centre of Scottish Trade Unionism, were forcibly raided by the police. Three years ago we were told by spokesmen of the Employers that, after the war, the workers would have to be content with longer hours. Here then is the secret of the determination to crush by any and every means attempts to secure shorter hours. The organized workers of Scotland put forward an orderly and legitimate demand for the Forty Hours. The Government's reply is bludgeons, machine-guns, bayonets and tanks. In one word, the institution of a Reign of Terror.

ACTIVITY
KNOWLEDGE CHECK

Red Clydeside

1 What was the significance of Clydeside for the influence of the trade union movement between 1915 and 1919?

2 To what extent did the industrial unrest in Glasgow improve conditions for the labouring classes in the city?

A Level Exam-Style Question Section A

Study Source 3 before you answer this question.

Assess the value of the source for revealing the Strike Committee of Glasgow's attitudes towards the government's response to the 1919 40-hour strike and how the government wanted the strikes to be interpreted.

Explain your answer, using the source, the information given about its origin and your own knowledge about the historical context. (20 marks)

Tip

Consider who this source was aimed at. Workers within Glasgow were the main target audience, but was this also intended to be seen by government officials and members of trade unions beyond Clydeside?

TO WHAT EXTENT WAS THERE A TRADE UNION REVIVAL BETWEEN 1919 AND 1921 IN THE AFTERMATH OF THE FIRST WORLD WAR?

During the First World War, Britain's trade unions increasingly exerted influence over government policy. With peace came a determination among the trade union movement to hold onto and to consolidate the wartime gains. With the rail and coal industries nationalised came a belief held by many trade union leaders that state control of industry could continue in peacetime and that there would be no return to the pre-war position whereby industry was run for the profits of business owners. There was a widespread belief that Britain's social order had changed permanently. Yet while trade unions hoped to consolidate wartime gains, the government was eager to return industry to private ownership, with business owners wanting to restore profits. During the years 1919 to 1921, there was immense conflict between these groups. By 1921, the trade unions' position was very different to what it had been in 1919. For all the efforts of the unions, the government became increasingly sophisticated at dealing with industrial disputes between 1919 and 1921.

The Triple Alliance

With peace in 1918 came a determination among employers and the government to roll back the regulations of the wartime economy. Employers wanted to return to a competitive system, while the government was desperate to avoid industrial unrest and return nationalised industries to private ownership. However, returning industries to private ownership aroused hostility from trade unionists. Marxist historians such as John Foster have described this post-war period as a crisis for capitalism, with private competition undermined by state ownership and inflated workers' wages. While there was initially an economic boom in Britain after the war, by 1920 Britain was struggling to recapture trade markets it had dominated in 1914. In 1919, with much of Europe in economic ruins, especially the industrial regions of France and Germany, and peacetime demand for industrial products high, Britain's industries benefitted. However, the increased pay and reduced hours that British industrial labourers had won in the war meant that it was not long before British industry was found to be uncompetitive. High costs of production meant that the economic boom was short-lived. To improve competitiveness, business owners looked to increase the hours and reduce the wages of workers.

Nationalisation

The war broke the traditional history of trade unionism. High demand for labour meant that the government had to work alongside the working population like never before. In December 1916, the government had had to seize the South Wales coalfield in response to the declining coal production. The government did this to eliminate employers' profits and disputes and to increase efficiency. By March 1917, this measure to nationalise coal production was extended to the entire country under the Defence of the Realm Act. With state control came a national regulation of wages. The profits from coal were pooled and then divided to provide national wages for all coal miners. In September 1917, the government increased wages by one shilling and six pence a day, and then in July 1918 raised it again by the same amount.

By 1919, it was apparent to employers and the government that the industrial system of 1914 was gone. The relationship between employer and employee had changed. Traditionally, the government had acted as an arbitrator in industrial disputes, but now, because of nationalisation, it was the chief negotiator with employees. Until 1921, the government maintained ownership of the coal mines and railways. However, after the war there was a case for continued nationalisation. Before the war, Britain's railways had been inefficient, regularly running an excess of rolling stock and different companies maintaining duplicate track. With wartime nationalisation came a move for efficiency, with state planning rationalising rolling stock and track. Such efficiencies convinced trade unionists such as Thomas and the MFGB's president, Robert Smillie, that nationalisation could continue, and promised a radical new organisation of society where labour was not inseparable from capitalist profits. In his book *When Labour Rules*, published in 1922, Thomas wrote about his belief that with the nationalisation of the coal and rail industries by the government there was a chance of realising the 44-hour week if Labour were able to secure profits from industry going to all rather than into the pockets of a few.

At the start of 1919, the Triple Alliance represented a considerable force in British politics and a serious challenge to the government. In March 1919, Thomas negotiated with the government to ensure railway wages would not be severely reduced. Thomas managed to win railway workers the prolongation of wartime bonus wages into peacetime. When the government refused to make a permanent settlement on the continuation of wartime bonuses, Thomas called a strike in September 1919. The government panicked at the prospect of a united Triple Alliance strike, and deployed troops at Paddington and Woking railway stations in London. However, the 1919 railway strike was not supported by miners and transport workers. The miners were waiting for a government commission to report on the future of their industry. The miners had already won a two shilling pay rise (about 20 percent of total wages) in 1919, and had seen their hours cut from eight to seven.

SOURCE 4

Report in *The Times* of a speech by Robert Smillie, president of the MFGB, on 13 August 1919, calling on miners to strike should the government fail to keep the coal-mining industry nationalised, as recommended by the Sankey Commission.

Capitalism did not intend to allow the mines to be nationalized. At the present time the mineowners were spending hundreds of thousands of pounds upon propaganda. The miner's leaders had in the past been called 'agitators,' but now dukes were engaged in propaganda work, and they were also agitators. They had become agitators where their own interests were concerned. The propaganda work would be good for the dukes; it would let them see what life really was. All classes of capitalists knew that when nationalization of the mines took place it would not end there. Landlords knew that if the minerals were nationalized, the surface would be nationalized next. The surface was as necessary for the nation as the mineral wealth underneath it. The capitalists knew that, if they allowed the mines to be nationalized, other industries would follow, and that people would continue to aim at a cooperative commonwealth for their own needs. It was asserted that the Bolshevists were spending thousands of pounds in this country, but the sums mentioned were not to be compared with those being spent in support of the propaganda against the nationalization of the mines... If the Prime Minister and the Cabinet allowed their capitalist friends to frighten them and prevent the finding of the Coal Commission from being carried out, he felt it would be the duty of organized labour, and certainly of the miners, to use their industrial power to force the hands of the Government. (Cheers.) This would be one of the things which probably in the coming year they might have to deal with.

Prime Minister Lloyd George realised that wages would have to be reduced to make British coal competitive in foreign markets, but wanted to avoid industrial strikes against the government. He had set up a Royal Commission to determine if coal should remain nationalised. Formed in 1919, the Sankey Commission, named after its chairman, the Labour lawyer and judge John Sankey (1866–1948), investigated the coal industry. This removed the immediate threat of coal strikes between 1919 and 1921, but in March 1921, Lloyd George's coalition government returned the coal industry to private owners. This was despite the Sankey Report recommending that the mines remain nationalised. The government did not want the expense or trouble of running the coal industry, but rather wished to act as an arbitrator between employers and workers. Within one day of resuming their ownership of the coal mines, the employers announced cuts to wages to increase competitiveness. During 1921, pay for coal miners fell 30 percent, yet the cost of living actually increased. The coal miners came out on strike. They hoped for support from the railway and transport unions to make their protest effective.

ACTIVITY
KNOWLEDGE CHECK

The nationalised coal industry
Using Source 4, and your own knowledge, consider the question of nationalisation.

1 What is Robert Smillie's opinion of the nationalised coal industry?

2 How far was the nationalisation of Britain's coal mines during the war a temporary measure?

3 Was the question of state control over the mines specific to the mining industry, or did it engender wider concerns over all private property?

The impact of Black Friday, 1921

On what became known as 'Black Friday', on 15 April 1921, the leaders of the transport and railway unions ordered workers not to strike in sympathy with the miners. Ernest Bevin of the NTWF was personally in favour of supporting the coal miners, but was also aware of how brittle his union was because the trade depression threatened the jobs of his members. He begrudgingly followed the other Triple Alliance leaders, refusing to support the miners. This was widely seen as a betrayal of the miners, with Robert Williams of the NTWF and Thomas of the NUR being singled out by the MFGB as responsible. The NUR and NTWF accused the MFGB of wanting support but refusing the rail and transport factions of the Triple Alliance a part in government negotiations. By the end of 1921, hunger had forced the miners to return to work.

The failure of the miners' strike and the refusal of the NUR and NTWF to support them led to the collapse of the alliance. Trust between the coal, railway and transport unions had been lost. This preceded a decline in industrial unrest. While in 1921, 85,870,000 days of work were lost to industrial disputes, this sank to 19,850,000 in 1922 and 10,670,000 days in 1923. Nevertheless, the unrest between 1919 and 1921 revealed the full extent of change due to the war and the increased influence of the trade unions. Economist John Maynard Keynes explained that, while before 1914 inequalities had been accepted, with workers accepting the distribution of wealth and established order of society, in post-war Britain such thought had been weakened. Keynes argued that the war had encouraged workers to want a change to the way produce was shared between employers and the employed. Since Keynes, Marxist and left-wing historians have maintained that the post-war unrest was the result of the reduced legitimacy of the capitalist system in the eyes of workers.

SOURCE 5

On 29 September 1919, the *Daily Express* publicly condemned the autumn railway strike. To its readers, the newspaper framed the strike not as a conflict between employers and workers, but as a direct challenge to the rights and liberties of the British people. Such rhetoric was intended to compare the railway union's actions with those of the revolutionaries in Russia and raise fears of a move towards socialism.

The little band of conspirators who forced their duped followers into a strike against the whole nation did not reckon with a power that will crush them. The people will not submit to tyranny... No King, no peer, no commoner can succeed in trampling on British Liberty... The conspiracy hatched against the People by a handful of hare-brained agitators, has the word FAILURE written across it. It is unthinkable that at the very moment when the nation, struggling to free itself from the entanglement of five years of terror and disruption, with the first gleam of daylight... should, at the behest of a group of conspirators, be plunged into Anarchy from which there can be no recovery. This is not a struggle between trade unionism and employers. It is not a fight between masters and men. It is a challenge by a few conspirators to the liberties, the rights, and the honour of Great Britain.

Government action and union responses to Black Friday

Black Friday reveals several things about the post-war labour movement. Among workers, there was a determination to keep hold of the hard-won wage increases that war had brought. There was also a great awareness of the potentially revolutionary and politically influential weapon that unified strikes presented. Yet the unions had failed to co-operate with each other. Without support from the transport and railway unions, the coal miners were doomed to fail, as the government could import cheap foreign coal to keep the economy going. Black Friday also revealed that, with the war over, the government was determined to counter industrial efforts to secure influence.

State apparatus for strikes

During the war, government had passed the Defence of the Realm Act, which regulated industrial relations, but in October 1920 this was replaced by the Emergency Powers Act (EPA). This allowed the government to declare a national state of emergency in times of severe industrial unrest, make provisions for maintaining supplies, give full power to the cabinet and civil service, and allow for the quick passing of emergency legislation to regulate militancy. The EPA was invoked before Black Friday, with troops being deployed into areas likely to be the sites of strikes. However, despite this state of emergency being called, in the end the Act was not required in 1921.

Throughout 1919, the government had built up an effective anti-strike apparatus and quietly gained much experience and knowledge of how to deal with strikes. In February 1919, it appointed the Industrial Unrest Committee, which became the Strike Committee, led by ex-railway manager Eric Geddes, to counter strike activity. This committee was not needed in the strikes of 1919 because of the Triple Alliance's failure to work together, but the government kept it in place; effectively, this was a

strikebreaking machine. In October 1919, realising that the name 'Strike Committee' might be antagonistic, the cabinet changed the name to the more neutral sounding Supply and Transport Committee (STC). This had policy-making power. From October 1919 to November 1921, the STC met 46 times, reviewing and resolving most industrial crises. Geddes was unhappy with his role on the STC, convinced that it was not the position of the government to orchestrate strikebreaking. Believing the government should be neutral, he resigned, only to be reappointed in 1920 because of the government's failure to find a permanent replacement. He remained sceptical, disliking the STC's secrecy, emphasis on using the military and avoidance of conciliatory measures for disputes. Nevertheless, the STC worked out the government's response to strike action.

It found ways of reducing the impact of strikes, making plans to recruit volunteers to replace striking labourers in essential services. Churchill suggested the use of volunteers as special constables to avoid using the army, which, if dispersed, might leave the government open to an organised revolution. The STC established the Volunteer Service Committee (VSC), providing a structure of volunteer response to strikes. The STC also oversaw co-operation between the government and businesses to stockpile resources, especially coal and oil. For example, in 1919, the government worked with the British Petroleum Company to maintain fuel reserves, and agreed to cut import duties on oil so that it could build up oil holdings.

In 1921, before Black Friday, the STC reacted quickly to prevent the coal miners' strike from causing disruption. It halted coal exports, put troops on alert and called a state of emergency. In the end, military intervention was avoided, but it was clear the government was well prepared. On 16 April 1921, the cabinet reviewed the coal strike and concluded the STC had prevented a general strike spreading to the railways and transport. In August 1921, the STC was disbanded as a cost-saving measure, but the Home Office kept the nucleus of the committee together for future use. In 1923, the STC was revived under the control of Britain's top civil servant, John Anderson, and would play a crucial role in the disturbances of 1926.

What all this government activity amounted to was an attempt to revert to a pre-1914 state of industrial relations, where labour (workers) and capital (owners) debated pay and conditions, with the government serving as an arbitrator of last resort. While trade unions had gained influence between 1915 and 1921, the state had taken steps to limit the impact of strike action, and with these measures undermined some of the TUC's strength.

The formation of the AEU and TGWU and the importance of the Council of Action

While the government prepared for future conflict, so did the trade unions. Bevin wanted to ensure Black Friday could never happen again and worked to replace the old loose alliance with a centralised structure for industrial militancy co-ordination. In 1921, a new General Council of the TUC was formed to counter the government's and employers' relentless attacks on wages and hours. The council tried to win the trust of the major unions and, by 1924, had secured the support of the NUR and MFGB. Nevertheless, only Bevin and the newly formed Transport and General Workers' Union (TGWU) conceived of this council as a permanent alliance. From 1922, the TGWU replaced the NTWF as the leading transport union. Bevin worked to make the TGWU the nation's largest trade union by the early 1930s, providing immense support for the Labour Party. Bevin served as the TGWU's general secretary and oversaw the amalgamation of workers in transport, docks, passenger services and road haulage.

The AEU

The TGWU was not the only powerful union to emerge from the tensions of 1919–21. In 1920, the Amalgamated Society of Engineers (ASE), formed in 1851, became the Amalgamated Engineering Union (AEU). The ASE had represented iron-founders, builders, carpenters and skilled engineering workers. These were respectable skilled workers who, being paid higher wages, were able to pay one shilling a week to their union. This created a valuable fund for providing workers with money when a strike was called. The financial strength of the ASE deterred employers from pushing their workers into strikes. While the ASE was a powerful union in the late 19th century, in 1920 it expanded into the AEU by absorbing local and regional unions for skilled engineering workers.

The Council of Action

KEY TERM

Council of Action
Established on a local level to organise and direct strikers throughout the General Strike. Across the country, over 500 of these were formed. These were trade union councils that, during the General Strike, styled themselves as 'councils of action' or 'strike committees'. In practice, it was these local councils that orchestrated the strike.

In response to the risk of Britain entering into a war with Soviet Russia in August 1920, the trade unions and Labour Party had formed the **Council of Action**, along with about 350 local Councils of Action. With Soviet Russia at war with Poland, many feared that Britain would go to war against the revolutionary state. The Council of Action was to co-ordinate opposition to any attempt by the British government to aid Poland's war effort. The council would orchestrate strikes to prevent the manufacture and export of munitions and military supplies to Poland, should Britain get involved in the conflict. The council succeeded in raising extensive public opposition to intervention in the Polish conflict. In October 1920, 6,000 protesters gathered in London, opposing the war. The local Councils of Action were formed either through regional Labour branches or trade councils. For example, the Leeds Council of Action was formed by the local Labour Party, while the Manchester Council of Action was formed by the city's trade council. Initially, the Home Office feared this left-wing movement might present a revolutionary threat to the state. Such fears were exasperated by the actions of more radical Councils of Action such as Birmingham council, which moved for an extension of remit beyond simply opposing war with Russia. Birmingham council recommended the nation's councils address questions of unemployment and oppose business profits. It wanted the movement to become anti-capitalistic on a more general basis. However, few trade unionists or Labour supporters conceived of these councils as a revolutionary movement. Between 1920 and 1921, they were largely confined to opposing military aid for Poland.

By 1921, the Council of Action and the local Councils of Action were losing popular support, with the diminished chance of war with Russia. In the spring of 1921, the Polish secured victory over the Soviets and ensured their independence at the Peace of Riga. British government reports into the potential of the councils concluded that they were unable to mount a serious general strike. Their lack of support convinced the government, by 1921, that a general strike would be a fiasco. Nevertheless, the Councils of Action remained in place after 1921, performing a propagandist role in the labour movement. These councils provided an infrastructure for co-ordinating future industrial conflict. By 1921, while the government was well equipped for any potential trade union militancy, the unions reorganised after Black Friday.

A Level Exam-Style Question Section B

'The trade union movement represented a revolutionary threat to the British state between 1919 and 1921'.

Is this a fair statement regarding the industrial unrest in Britain after the First World War? (20 marks)

Tip
Make a point of defining what the statement means by 'revolutionary'. Revolution would entail some kind of change to Britain's political system. The alternative would be that industrial disputes between 1919 and 1921 involved specific rights and conditions for workers, such as wages and working hours.

ACTIVITY
KNOWLEDGE CHECK

Trade unions after the war

1 What was the cause of Black Friday?

2 What was the significance of the Triple Alliance's collapse?

3 Would it be fair to say that the biggest problem facing the trade union movement between 1919 and 1921 was government opposition?

WHY DID THE GENERAL STRIKE FAIL TO INFLUENCE THE CONSERVATIVE GOVERNMENT IN 1926?

Between 1921 and 1926, trade union militancy declined following the collapse of the Triple Alliance. However, throughout 1925, tensions in the coal-mining industry meant that the industry was once again in confrontation with the government. This time, however, the railway and transport unions were determined to avoid a repeat of Black Friday. By the spring of 1926, an all-out strike was called by the central TUC. Yet this militancy completely failed to influence the government. There were several causes for this failure. A lack of organised workers' support, the efficient organisation of counter-strike measures by the government and the lack of determination from the TUC General Council have all been cited as causes of the General Strike's failure.

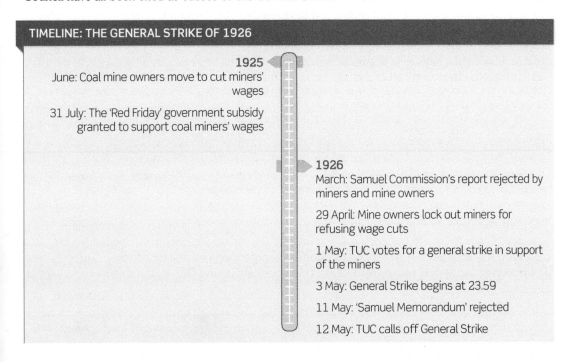

TIMELINE: THE GENERAL STRIKE OF 1926

1925

June: Coal mine owners move to cut miners' wages

31 July: The 'Red Friday' government subsidy granted to support coal miners' wages

1926

March: Samuel Commission's report rejected by miners and mine owners

29 April: Mine owners lock out miners for refusing wage cuts

1 May: TUC votes for a general strike in support of the miners

3 May: General Strike begins at 23.59

11 May: 'Samuel Memorandum' rejected

12 May: TUC calls off General Strike

Reasons for the General Strike

Long-term causes, 1921–26

The long-term causes of the 1926 General Strike can broadly be broken down into several categories:

- The change in industrial relations brought about by the First World War

- The fall in the production and price of coal

- Rising trade union discontent after the embarrassment of Black Friday

- The determination of mine owners to maintain profits, even in an unstable economic period, by cutting wages and raising hours

- The 1925 return to the gold standard and overvalued strength of the pound.

In their bid to recapture international markets, between 1921 and 1926, business owners who were making a loss, particularly coal mine owners, made efforts to cut wages. Between 1921 and 1925, it is likely that British workers saw a total average fall in wages of £12 million per week. Yet wage reductions did not increase British competiveness, and only reduced home demand for products and domestic spending, which further increased unemployment. Increased competition from German and American mines kept international coal prices low. This temporarily abated between 1923 and 1925, when the French seized control of German mines in the Ruhr and American miners went on strike, but by 1925, British coal mine wages were again targeted for cuts.

Between 1921 and 1925, British trade stagnated, the demand for coal declined and unemployment hit one million. This situation was exacerbated by Britain's return to the gold standard. Despite his own reservations, the Chancellor of the Exchequer, Winston Churchill, decided on this policy that attempted to peg the pound to gold reserves in the Bank of England to stabilise the value of the currency, avoid inflation and restore the City of London to the dominant centre of global finance. In 1918, the **Cunliffe Committee** on Currency and Foreign Exchange recommended that Britain had to strengthen the pound to pre-war parity with the dollar and return to the gold standard within seven years. The committee advised that, in order to do this, the government had to maintain a **balanced budget**, limit the issue of bank notes and reduce the **national debt**. In 1925, the pound was set to the value of $4.86, the level it had been in 1914, a decision that was initially supported by economist John Maynard Keynes. Keynes later argued that this choice had strangled the British economy and triggered a global recession.

KEY TERMS

Cunliffe Committee
Established to plan out how Britain could return to financial stability after the economic chaos of the First World War. This was chaired by Walter Cunliffe, who was governor of the Bank of England between 1913 and 1918.

Balanced budget
When a government is not spending more than it is receiving in revenue. If a government is spending less than it receives, this is known as a budget surplus. When more is being spent than received, this is called a budget deficit. Revenue usually consists of taxes.

National debt
The amount of money that a government has borrowed. By spending more than it receives in revenue, a government runs a deficit. To be able to spend more than it receives in revenue, it is essential for a government to borrow money.

Gold standard
The commitment to fix domestic currencies to a nation's gold reserves. In theory, all money in circulation was backed by gold and could be exchanged for bullion if presented to the Bank of England.

Deflation
The economic process whereby the price of commodities decreases, usually accompanied by an increase in the value of money. This is usually considered a damaging process as it means the costs of debt increase and wages decrease.

EXTEND YOUR KNOWLEDGE

Winston Churchill (1874-1965)
Churchill first entered parliament in 1900 as a Conservative MP. He joined the Liberals in 1904 in opposition to the Conservatives' hostility to free trade. He held government positions between 1906 and 1914, and oversaw the disastrous Gallipoli campaign in 1915. In 1924, he rejoined the Conservative party upon which the prime minister, Stanley Baldwin, appointed him Chancellor of the Exchequer, a position in which Churchill served until 1929. Churchill was responsible for the return to the gold standard in 1925, a decision he later regretted as the worst mistake of his career. Throughout the General Strike, Churchill was an advocate for using the military to maintain order, including the use of tanks and machine guns to protect food convoys. Churchill had become increasingly hard-line right-wing after the war, having a profound dislike of socialism and fear of revolution. In 1940, he became prime minister and led Britain to victory in the Second World War. He was to be prime minister a second time from 1951-55, until illness forced his resignation. He was to remain an MP until 1964, a year before his death.

The **gold standard** created **deflation**, causing a shortage of currency and constraining the economy. The reduction in currency caused wages to fall and created increased unemployment. As the pound was stronger, British exports became more expensive, necessitating further wage cuts. The British economy was too weak to support such a strong pound. The gold standard was an act of economic vanity.

EXTEND YOUR KNOWLEDGE

Britain and the gold standard
Britain was on the gold standard between 1819 and 1914, with the period 1880 to 1914 witnessing a global economic system committed to backing currency with gold. Britain was forced to abandon the gold standard in 1914 due to the financial pressures of the First World War, and had to print more money than could be backed by national gold reserves. Britain returned to the gold standard in 1925, but was forced to abandon it in 1931 due to an economic recession that drained the nation's gold reserves. While the gold standard supported the value of the pound, it restrained economic expansion by limiting the money that could be in circulation.

The coal industry, already struggling, was particularly badly hit by this policy. Business owners continued to try to make profits, despite the troubled economic conditions. With the new gold standard, wages would have to be cut by ten percent to keep British products competitive. Nonetheless, coal miners were encouraged that their wages might be protected by the government after a dispute in the textile industry was resolved by a government commission recommending that textile wages remain constant. This victory for the textile workers boosted the TUC's confidence that the reversal of wartime wage increases was not inevitable.

SOURCE

6 *The Times* considers Winston Churchill's decision to return Britain to the gold standard and the effect it might have on the coal industry, 7 August 1925.

On the previous day, by a brilliant speech in the House of Commons, Mr. Churchill had rendered a notable service, not only to the cause of sound finance, but also to that of morality in dealing with currency. Currency questions are admittedly difficult for laymen to understand. The public is largely at the mercy, therefore, of every fluent expert. There has been a great campaign in criticism of the gold standard. Much of the coal crisis has been attributed to it. It has been blamed, indeed, for the plight of the export industries in general, in spite of the fact that the depression has lasted for years, whereas the gold standard is only a few months old, and that the coal crisis is by no means confined to this country. The Chancellor of the Exchequer revealed the real implications of Mr. Keynes's proposal to make the currency, instead of prices, the 'shock absorber' in our economic system. If prices of our exportable goods are too high, Mr. Keynes would effect the adjustment by debasing the currency. By this means wages would be reduced without the consent, and even without the knowledge, of those who earned them. But the possibilities of manipulating currency do not end at that point. A depreciating exchange gives a bounty on exports, with the result that prices are raised, and that, in turn, leads to a further fall in exchange, and ultimately to a demand for higher wages. Mr. Churchill likened the process, as others have done before him, to snipping an inch off the yard measure or an ounce off the pound as a means of maintaining the incomes of drapers and grocers and of robbing the consumer unawares.

ACTIVITY
KNOWLEDGE CHECK

The gold standard

1 **a)** Produce a table with two columns. Label the first column 'Advantages' and the second 'Disadvantages'.

   b) Examine Source 6 and use your own knowledge to complete the table by adding the perceived advantages and disadvantages of the return to the gold standard.

2 Was Churchill's decision to return to the gold standard a bad decision? Explain your answer.

3 What implications did the return to the gold standard have for Britain's coal industry?

'Red Friday'

The immediate causes of the General Strike were the coal conflict of July 1925 and the subsequent breakdown of industrial relations between the trade unions, employees and the government. Under financial pressure, in June 1925, coal mine owners attempted to abolish the 1924 minimum wage agreement. This had specified that the profits on 87 percent of all coal sold would constitute miners' wages. Owners were to take profits from the remaining 13 percent of receipts from coal sales. However, when the French pulled out of the Ruhr and German coal competition returned, Britain's coal pits faced financial strain, with owners looking to cut wages by 13 percent and increase daily working hours from seven to eight hours. Miners rejected this and the government was unable to find a compromise. A court of inquiry was proposed in July. It reported that the coal industry had to be more efficient, that wages should be agreed before profits were taken by owners, but that owners had to reorganise the industry. Both miners and owners rejected this judgement. The General Council of the TUC ordered an embargo to halt coal imports in support of a coal strike. While the Chancellor of the Exchequer, Churchill, and many hard-line Conservatives were prepared for confrontation, Prime Minister Baldwin hoped to avoid conflict. Baldwin hoped to resolve the coal dispute through negotiation, while Churchill believed a show of government strength, demonstrated by defeating a strike, would show the trade unions that the government was in control of events.

Baldwin backed down to prevent the strike, offering a nine-month government subsidy of £23 million to support coal miners' wages. This avoided the immediate need for wage reductions. The subsidy was agreed on 31 July 1925, which became known as '**Red Friday**'. This subsidy for wages was supported by owners and miners, and bought the government crucial time to organise for future industrial militancy. At the same time, Baldwin appointed the Samuel Commission to investigate the coal industry and provide a long-term solution to the crisis. The government thus hoped to avoid coal strikes or, should they happen, be prepared for the threat of the NUR, MFGB and TGWU uniting and forcing an all-out strike.

KEY TERM

Red Friday
When the government granted a subsidy for coal miners' wages on 31 July 1925. The day was seen as a triumph for trade unions and provided what was, at the time, believed to be a reversal of the Triple Alliance's capitulation on Black Friday in 1921.

Stanley Baldwin (1867–1947)
Conservative prime minister serving three terms, from 1923 to January 1924, November 1925–1929 and 1935–1937. Baldwin had moved against Lloyd George's coalition government in 1922 and served as Chancellor of the Exchequer in Andrew Bonar Law's Conservative government. He replaced Bonar Law, who retired as prime minister on health grounds in 1923, immediately calling an election that Baldwin then lost to Ramsay MacDonald's Labour Party, which formed a minority government. Baldwin returned to victory in the 1924 general election.

The subsidy of Red Friday was a short-term solution, but it polarised opinion and intensified the slide towards a general strike. For trade unions and left-wing thinkers, the government subsidy of miners' wages encouraged hope that capitalism might quickly be replaced by socialism. The principle that the state would intervene to support industry and undermine the competition of capitalist markets had been established and this was widely seen as a huge victory for the working classes. The government had backed down. Clearly, to right-wing politicians and anti-socialist Conservatives, Red Friday was a catastrophe, reflecting poorly on Baldwin. Even Ramsay MacDonald, leader of the Labour Party, was critical, believing the subsidy would encourage revolutionaries. He worried that socialist agitation would discredit the Labour Party's growing credentials as a legitimate and responsible political organisation.

The breakdown of negotiations, 1926

Red Friday was only a short-term solution; one that intensified support for and opposition to industrial militancy. While Walter Citrine, the acting secretary of the TUC, observed that the General Council remained pessimistic about its long-term chance of securing miners' wages, it was staggeringly oblivious of the need to prepare for industrial action. In contrast, the government used the nine-month respite to effectively organise counter-strike measures, expertly administered by the STC. Resources were stockpiled, local networks of volunteers established, while independent organisations for anti-strike action were put in place. The Economic League and the Organisation for the Maintenance of Supplies (OMS) both recruited middle- and upper-class volunteers who might work public services and keep the country moving in the event of a strike. The OMS included several aristocrats, including Lord Jellicoe, who had commanded the British fleet at the Battle of Jutland in 1916, and Lord Hardinge as president, who had previously been Viceroy of India. By February 1926, the government believed it was ready for any industrial militancy, having established a system of administration to keep open the nation's roads and coal and food supplies. Military forces were deployed in sensitive areas.

The TUC was, by comparison, completely inactive. The unions refused to grant powers to the General Council to call an all-out strike and conduct government negotiations. The problem was that there was a lack of trust between the unions, especially after Black Friday, with Thomas seen as a master of intrigue. So while the government grew ever more confident at the prospect of a showdown with the unions, the TUC's position rapidly deteriorated.

The Royal Commission on the coal industry, the Samuel Commission, recommended that the coal industry be rationalised, the government continue manipulating coal revenues, and that wage levels be reduced temporarily while the industry was reorganised. It also stated that the coal industry should not be nationalised. In March 1926, this was completely rejected by both mine owners and workers. The Samuel Commission proposed the amalgamation of mines and increased research into coal production. It advocated that profits should be shared between owners and miners. This clearly angered owners, while its proposed reduction in wages offended the MFGB. No one accepted the report. The MFGB refused to consider any wage reductions at all.

Baldwin and the Conservative government worked to try to get owners and the unions to compromise, but an impasse had been reached. On 29 April, things escalated when owners locked out miners who refused to accept wage reductions. The TUC responded by calling on the unions to unite, and powers were finally granted to the General Council for conducting the dispute and co-ordinating strike action. With this delicate position, the spark to hostilities came from a poster. During government–TUC negotiations, Jimmy Thomas produced an OMS poster calling for recruits. This was seen as a provocation, as the government was moving to counter strike action. The OMS, without the government's instruction, had acted rashly in distributing posters. In response, on 1 May, the TUC voted for a general strike in sympathy to the miners. The strike was to commence at one minute to midnight on 3 May. The government appealed to the General Council to concede on working hours, but the MFGB was resolute in its opposition to cuts and longer hours. Under pressure from hardline anti-trade union Conservatives in the cabinet, Baldwin was unable to back down and repeat the embarrassment of Red Friday. Likewise, the TUC could not climb down and risk a repeat of Black Friday. The General Strike became unavoidable.

ACTIVITY
KNOWLEDGE CHECK

The roots of the general strike
1 By 1926, was a general strike inevitable?
2 How might Red Friday have been interpreted by trade unionists and Conservative politicians?
3 Do you think that the government's efforts to put anti-strike measures in place increased the likelihood of industrial conflict in 1926?

The roles of the media, government and TUC

Government responses to the General Strike

The problem with the General Strike was not so much a lack of support among trade unions and workers, as the effective government response to the crisis. The question, then, is just how well did the government deal with the strike, and to what degree did it consider the industrial unrest to be a constitutional threat? While Baldwin was committed to peacefully resolving the dispute, hard-line Conservatives in his government and the hostile Conservative press, led by Winston Churchill's *British Gazette*, eager to avenge Red Friday, pushed Baldwin towards tough action. The two priorities for the government were maintaining food supplies and essential services, and preserving law and order. On both counts, the government was well organised. Orders went out on 3 May to begin mobilising volunteers, and on 5 May, instructions were sent to the Boards of Guardians to refuse relief to strikers. The government had recruited some 300,000 to 500,000 middle- and upper-class volunteers, but few of these were ever needed. In London, for example, of 114,000 volunteers recruited by 11 May, only 9,500 were given work. The government always had a massive reserve of labour to draw on. These were used to man power stations and docks, and to act as special constables and transport workers. The London Underground was operated by 2,000 Cambridge University undergraduates. This support ensured good food distribution and transport maintenance. The docks were particularly essential to keeping supplies moving. At Dover, 460 Cambridge students worked the docks, providing a particularly ostentatious display of upper-class solidarity. Ninety-seven students worked the South East Railway. Such acts heightened class tensions; the work of the middle and upper classes in undermining the effect of the working-class strike was tantamount to a class war.

A Level Exam-Style Question Section A

Study Source 7 before you answer this question.

Assess the value of the source for revealing Stanley Baldwin's attitudes towards the General Strike and how far this is useful in showing how the government wanted the public to interpret the industrial militancy.

Explain your answer, using the source, the information given about its origin and your own knowledge about the historical context. (20 marks)

Tip
Would it seem, from this evidence, that Baldwin was presenting the strike as a challenge to the British political system, or a specific industrial dispute? If so, think about how this might have provoked reactionary measures against the strike action.

SOURCE 7

Stanley Baldwin broadcast the following message on the BBC on 8 May 1926, in the midst of the General Strike.

What is the issue for which the Government is fighting? It is fighting because while negotiations were still in progress the TUC ordered a general strike, presumably to force Parliament and the community to heed its will. With that object the TUC has declared that the railways shall not run, that transport shall not move and that the unloading of ships shall stop, and that no news shall reach the public. The supply of electricity, the transportation of food supplies of the people have been interrupted. The TUC declare that this is merely an industrial dispute, but their method of helping the miners is to affect the community. Can there be a more direct attack upon the community than that a body not elected by the voters of the country, without consulting even trade unionists, and in order to impose conditions never yet defined should disrupt the life of the nation and try to starve it into submission? I wish to make it as clear as I can that the Government is not fighting to lower the standard of living of the miners or of any other class of workers. My whole desire is to maintain the standard of living of every worker, and I am ready to press the employers to make every sacrifice to this end, consistent with keeping industry in its proper working order... I am a man of peace. I am longing and working and praying for peace. But I will not surrender the safety and security of the British Constitution. You placed me in power eighteen months ago by the largest majority afforded to any party for many years. Have I done anything to forfeit that confidence? Cannot you trust me to ensure a square deal for the parties and secure even justice between man and man?

The government formed a civil constabulary reserve from former soldiers and members of the Territorial Army, preventing the widespread use of armed forces. These efforts were effective and meant that, as the strike continued, the government grew increasingly confident that it could break the union's resolve. In towns, local authorities kept food and coal supplies flowing, particularly in Liverpool, which was responsible for a fifth of the nation's imports. In Plymouth, two battleships brought in food that was unloaded by 20,000 volunteers. There was no breakdown in order, as the government had feared.

One area the government organisation did fail to resolve was the railways. It was difficult to move freight throughout the strike. On 5 May, only one percent of freight could be moved, rising to six percent by 12 May. Passenger services were easier to maintain, with 22.4 percent of services running by 12 May. While law and order was maintained, there were several disturbances in Plymouth and London, and some violence around a few coalfields. In Glasgow, miners clashed with the police. In total, 1,760 arrests were made during the strike. Perhaps the most iconic act of violence was the derailing of the famous steam locomotive, the *Flying Scotsman*, by protesters at Newcastle on 10 May.

SOURCE

8
The aristocratic grandson of the 2nd Earl of Lichfield working as a volunteer train driver during the General Strike of 1926.

The media

With Churchill as editor, the *British Gazette* was published throughout the strike as the government's newspaper. While it sought to inform the public that the government was in a strong position and that the disruption of the strike was minimal, it also raised fears that the strike represented a revolutionary threat to the state. While the BBC claimed to be impartial, it refused to publish content that would be damaging to the government. Formed in 1922, the BBC depended on the government for its licence, on which its income depended. To oppose the government, therefore, was not an option for the fledgling organisation. The BBC did, however, take on a conciliatory tone during the strike, broadcasting a speech by the Archbishop of Canterbury in which he called for an end to the strike and a return to negotiations. However, the BBC avoided controversy and in any way supporting the strikers, in part because of Churchill's demands that the government seize control of the news organ. He wanted the BBC used for the government's advantage, but by avoiding sympathy for the strikers, the BBC avoided being taken over by the government. In comparison, the TUC's propaganda was severely restrained, with the government not only preventing the BBC from broadcasting in sympathy to the unions, but curtailing the print of the TUC's pro-strike paper, the *British Worker*. Churchill ordered the requisitioning of the *British Worker's* newsprint, forcing it to reduce its publications to four pages, from its usual eight. Churchill justified this hard line towards the TUC's newspaper on the grounds that it was harder to feed a country than to wreck it. He believed the government had a right to propaganda, unlike the TUC.

SOURCE

9
From the government's publication, the *British Gazette*, edited by Winston Churchill. This was published on 8 May 1926. The publication sought to inform readers of the nation's stability throughout the strike, but also aroused fears that a social revolution was likely.

No serious disorder has occurred in any part of the country. The work of feeding the people and of maintaining light and power and essential communications is being successfully accomplished. Over 2,000 trains were run on May 6, or nearly double the day before. A further substantial improvement both on the main lines and in the metropolitan and suburban services is arranged for to-day. The protection of 'buses in London proved yesterday most satisfactory, and they are constantly increasing in numbers. Nevertheless, as was to be expected, the situation is becoming more intense and the climax is not yet reached. Orders have been sent by the leaders of the Railway and Transport Trade Unions to do their utmost to paralyse and break down the supply of food and the necessaries of life... Intimidation both by disorderly crowds and picketing has occurred in many places, and may soon occur in many more. His Majesty's Government have directed all authorities to repress and overcome these criminal obstructions. The recruitment of Special Constables in all parts of the country is being vigorously and rapidly pressed forward. It is proposed to raise the numbers of Special Constables in London as quickly as possible to 50,000. Other important measures to increase the forces at the disposal of the Government and to enable widespread protection to be afforded are also being taken. An organised attempt is being made to starve the people and to wreck the State, and the legal and constitutional aspects are entering upon a new phase. The newspaper services are steadily improving.

SOURCE 10

A tank leaving Wellington Barracks in London in May 1926. Such movements demonstrated the military strength the government had at its disposal.

The limited use of armed force demonstrates that the Baldwin government never really took seriously the threat of revolution or civil war. The strike was most probably not a threat to the constitutional position of the government. Although since the 1920 formation of the Communist Party of Great Britain the government had feared strike action might lead to a political move against the state, the Communist Party had little influence over strikers. The Conservative press tried to encourage fears that a revolution was likely and emphasised the socialist sentiments of the movement, but the limited violence and use of the army show that Baldwin did not believe a revolution was brewing. When the army was used, it was to demonstrate strength or to protect food supplies.

The reasons for the failure of the General Strike

The extent of the strike

The failure of the General Strike has been attributed to the chaotic and sporadic support that the TUC secured. However, a close inspection shows that during the nine days of industrial militancy from 3 May until 12 May 1926, there was a good response from trade unions and workers. Between 1.5 and 1.75 million workers came out in support of the one million coal miners already locked out. This was an immense response. While the TUC had prepared poorly for the industrial action, making no arrangements until 27 April, the TGWU's general secretary, Bevin, believed the strike was a success in terms of support. Traditional histories have cited local responses to the TUC's General Council call for an all-out strike as somewhat limited, but recent research has revised this. The failure of the General Strike cannot be attributed to a lack of worker solidarity. To call out up to 1.75 million within a day was a triumph given the preparations made. Most of these were workers in transport, power stations, printing, building, iron and steel production and the chemical industries. On the final day of the strike, these were joined by shipbuilders and engineers. Much of the credit for this belongs to Bevin and the Powers and Orders Committee, which directed this unrest. They secured ten agreements from power stations to cut electricity to London. Local responses to this central call for action were often quite competent. For example, in the textile centre of Bradford, strike organisation was effective. The Bradford Council of Action was well organised and called out nearly 10,000 workers on strike. The strike found almost 100 percent support in the town. Elsewhere, there was a solid response, with 40,000 workers in Leeds, 7,000 in York and 100,000 in Merseyside, all uniting on strike. Ninety-eight percent of all locomotive drivers and firemen went on strike at the TUC's insistence. Even in rural areas like Devon there was an impressive response. In quiet towns like Torquay and Newton Abbott, railwaymen came out. Eighty percent of the GWR workers went on strike supporting the miners.

Yet despite this support, the organisation and extent of the strike was far from perfect. Many London power stations remained in operation, while the Strike Organising Committee only ever had symbolic control over the movement. Many workers, known as 'Blacklegs' to those who went on strike, continued working. On Merseyside, out of 92 1,000-tonne ships in port on 4 May, 25 had left by 15 May, with 50 new arrivals. In Barnsley, the power station remained working. The strike was clearly not as effective as its leaders would have liked, but the support was considerable and cannot be blamed singularly for the strike's failure.

SOURCE

11 An undergraduate student provides technical skills for lubricating the moving parts of a steam locomotive during the General Strike, 1926. Such voluntary work offered an alternative form of labour to employers for keeping essential services running.

The TUC's capitulation

On 12 May, the TUC called off the strike. The cause of this has been a big question ever since. Arthur James Cook, the general secretary of the MFGB between 1924 and 1931, blamed James Thomas and the leaders of the TUC. Cook believed, most probably correctly, that they had never fully supported militancy. By calling off the strike, the General Council appeared to have betrayed the workers it represented. The historical consensus supports this, with Renshaw and Phillips both agreeing. Thomas himself admitted in the House of Commons that he had wanted to end the strike before it got out of hand. Thomas and the General Council were eager for the protest not to escalate beyond an industrial dispute, so when hardliners like Churchill alleged that a revolution was unfolding, the General Council grew increasingly keen to cut a deal. At the same time, the memory of Black Friday sustained a constant pessimism among the TUC leaders that victory was impossible. The government's claims that it had to protect the nation from the trade unions were persuasive. How could 42 million citizens be held to ransom by some four million labourers? While parliament had been democratically elected, the trade union leadership appeared autocratic.

The chance to withdraw came from Herbert Samuel, chair of the Coal Commission, who offered to settle the dispute. The TUC believed Samuel would allow for a face-saving solution. Samuel proposed that the coal industry be reorganised and miners' wages cut for one year. A National Wages Board would be established to ensure wages remained fair. The mines rejected this. The TUC suggested a wage reduction after the reorganisation of the industry, but the MFGB refused to consider any cuts. On 11 May, this proposal, known as the 'Samuel Memorandum', was rejected. On 12 May, the General Council met Baldwin to announce the end of the strike. Bevin tried to get the prime minister to promise no strikers would be victimised for their part in the protest, but no agreement was made. Arthur Pugh and Walter Citrine sent out orders to end the strike, completing a remarkable capitulation.

While workers had supported the strike, and the government had organised an effective response, it seems the TUC General Council never believed wages could be protected. It desperately hoped the Samuel Memorandum could be enforced, but the MFGB constantly refused to compromise.

While miners would not accept the deal, there is also doubt that Baldwin would have been able to support Samuel's suggestions. His proposals would have involved the government committing to help sustain wages, and after Red Friday, Baldwin could not afford any such compromise, especially after such recent success against the strike. It would have been politically damaging.

SOURCE 12

The circular issued by the TUC General Council to call off the General Strike on 12 May 1926.

The General Council, through the magnificent support and solidarity of the Trade Union Movement has obtained assurances that a settlement of the Mining problem can be secured which justifies them in bringing the general stoppage to an end. Conversations have been proceeding between the General Council representative and Sir Herbert Samuel, Chairman of the Coal Commission, who returned from Italy for the express purpose of offering his services to try to effect a settlement of the difference in the Coal Mining Industry. The Government has declared that under no circumstances could negotiations take place until the general strike had been terminated, but the General Council feel as a result of the conversations with Sir Herbert Samuel and the proposals which are embodied in the correspondence and documents which are enclosed that sufficient assurances had been obtained as to the lines upon which a settlement could be reached to justify them in terminating the General Strike... The General Council accept the consequences of their decision with a full sense of their responsibility not only to their own membership but to the Nation at large. They have endeavoured throughout the crisis to conduct their case as industrial disputes have always been conducted by British Trade Unions, without violence or aggression. The General Council feel in taking the last steps to bring the crisis to an end that the Trade Union Movement has given a demonstration to the World of discipline, unity and loyalty without parallel in the history of industrial disputes.

SOURCE 13

The popular journal *Punch's* interpretation of the strike, 19 May 1926. The TUC is depicted using the General Strike as a lever to move the constitutionally elected government. However, the weight of parliamentary democracy is too much for the trade union militancy to overcome.

THE LEVER BREAKS.

The threat of the TUC
Examine Source 13 closely.

1 Is *Punch* sympathetic to the TUC?

2 How seriously do you think the journal takes the challenge of the TUC to the British constitution?

3 Consider the strikers in this cartoon. In being used as a lever, which is broken by the TUC, is *Punch* distinguishing between the TUC's leadership and its members?

Trades Disputes Act 1927

When strikers returned to work, it was clear their leaders had achieved nothing and had presided over a catastrophe. Employers tried to ensure strikers could never repeat the response of 1926, many even attempting to make union membership a barrier to employment. Tramway workers in Cheltenham were made to work longer hours for the same wage. In Glasgow, 368 out of 5,000 tramway workers were suspended. Many workers struggled to get their old jobs back, while wages were often cut. The coal miners remained locked out until November 1926. They were forced back into work through hunger. In Yorkshire, owners forced miners to accept seven-and-a-half-hour days (up from seven), while in South Wales, Scotland and the north-east wages were cut. It was clear the General Strike had failed.

After the strike, the trade union movement was divided by allegations of betrayal and accusations that the General Council had failed to protect its members from post-strike victimisation. There was a decline in membership, from 5,219,000 to 4,392,000 by 1932. The unions also acknowledged that capitalism was not at an end and worked to improve relations with employers. The historian Chris Wrigley has shown that there was collaboration before 1926 too. Rather than see 1926 as a turning point, industrial relations between unions and employers were evolutionary, not revolutionary. Likewise, while the government promoted wage reduction, it wanted to sustain good industrial relations.

Historians and the General Strike's legacy
Marxist historian Martin Jacques argued that 1926 was a turning point for trade unions, with the defeat so decisive that the movement did not recover until the Second World War. Alan Bullock's right-wing analysis claimed that after 1926, workers were disillusioned with the trade unions and membership declined. Renshaw suggests that after 1926, the movement accepted unemployment as unavoidable. Gordon Phillips and Hugh Clegg have revised this by suggesting that, although the trade unions failed to save the wages of miners, 1926 did not mark such a clear defeat of the movement. Rather than see the General Strike as a turning point, they have emphasised that post-General Strike industrial relations improved. Employers had been warned of the dangers of industrial conflict, while the trade unions recognised the limits of strike action. Phillips and Clegg argued that the unions were on a trajectory that did not change in 1926. Chris Wrigley supported this by asserting that unions only ever desired industrial peace after the First World War and that the TUC's behaviour during and after 1926 was no different.

The government took action to avoid future general strikes by passing the Trades Disputes and Trade Unions Act in 1927. The government considered curbing the trade unions' influence over Labour by limiting the funding they could provide. In March 1927, a bill was drawn up for regulating strike action, passing into the Trade Disputes and Trade Unions Act later in the year. This restrained trade unions and their association to the central TUC. This Act made it illegal for a general strike to be called. It specified that if a strike was called to exert influence on the government, it was illegal.

While the General Strike was a failure, the impact of this was limited. The government's victory did not undermine the trade union movement. In any analysis of why the General Strike failed, the extent and ramifications of the defeat have to be qualified.

The failure of the strike
1 To what extent was the General Strike a class conflict?

2 Was the General Strike betrayed by its leaders, or beaten by Baldwin's Conservative government?

3 How far would you agree that the General Strike was inevitably doomed to failure, even before it had commenced?

A Level Exam-Style Question Section B

How far does the government's anti-strike organisation following Red Friday explain the failure of the 1926 General Strike? (20 marks)

Tip
Consider the position of the General Council. Was its pessimism justified or was it sustained by an impressive government response to the strike? Or did the General Council concede on 12 May because it had never believed it could prevent miners' wages from being cut? Was this a question of the council betraying union members, or of an effective government operation against the strike action?

Conclusion

Arguably, the General Strike of 1926 was no more than an industrial dispute over the wages of coal miners. Certainly most trade unionists, like Bevin, Thomas and Citrine, were keen that the protest did not get out of hand and worked to show that the militancy was about a specific grievance. They wanted audiences to know that the government's stability was never at risk and that this was not a political revolution. It was not a move towards socialism or communism, like the revolutions that Europe and Russia witnessed after 1917. There is much evidence to support this interpretation. The government did not need to rely on the army and navy to maintain order, and parliament was never targeted by an organised revolution. Furthermore, the response of volunteer labour from the middle and upper classes ensured the constitutional political system was not in danger. Efforts to reform British politics did not come from industrial agitation, but from the Labour Party. After the war, Labour completely obliterated the Liberal Party to become the premier left-wing force in British politics. By 1929, Ramsay MacDonald was back in power, having won the general election, and Labour would govern until the economic crisis of 1931 led to calls for a National Government of Conservatives and Labour to navigate Britain through the turbulent times.

While Marxist historians have shown the prominence of class tensions throughout the General Strike, and, indeed, throughout the agitation from 1917 until 1926, the General Strike was not a move to overthrow any particular class or governing element of society. The years between 1917 and 1926 were dogged not by left-wing ideology, but by the struggle to return to the competitive economic system of 1914. Moments like Black Friday and the General Strike were born out of the difficulties of returning to the traditional relationship between owners and labourers. To a degree, this traditional relationship could never be fully restored after the mutual sacrifice of the First World War. However, socialists were gravely mistaken if they believed capitalism was on the verge of collapse, despite the hope provided by Red Friday. There was to be no new way of sharing profits between employers and the employed. For all this, the General Strike had settled a big question that had hung like a spectre over Britain since 1917: who really ruled the nation – parliament or the trade unions? The government's ease in defeating the trade unions in 1926 answered this resoundingly. Baldwin's Conservative government had conclusively shown that Britain's future was to be determined through democratic elections and constitutional parliamentary government, not through the militancy of the trade unions or socialist revolutions.

ACTIVITY
SUMMARY

Government and the trade union movement

1 a) Draw a table using the following headings:

	Strike action	Government measures	Effect of government measures	Response of the trade union leadership
Black Friday, 1921				
The General Strike, 1926				

b) Complete the table. Under the heading 'Government measures', compare the preparations of Baldwin's government with that of the STC in 1921. Under the heading 'Response of the trade union leadership', compare the actions of the Triple Alliance in 1921 with those of the General Council of the TUC in 1926.

2 Using your table above, answer the following questions:

a) Was the failure of the General Strike of 1926 a repeat of Black Friday?

b) In 1921 and 1926, was the government well prepared for industrial unrest?

c) To what degree do you think the failings of 1921 and 1926 were both the result of weak trade union leadership?

WIDER READING

Clegg, H.A. *A History of British Trade Unions since 1889, Vol. II 1911–33*, Clarendon Press (1985)

Laybourn, K. *The General Strike of 1926*, Manchester University Press (1993)

Morris, M. *The General Strike*, Pluto Press (1976)

Phillips, G.A. *The General Strike: The Politics of Industrial Conflict*, Weidenfeld and Nicolson (1976)

Renshaw, P. *The General Strike*, Eyre Methuen (1975)

Wrigley, C. (ed.) *A History of British Industrial Relations, 1914–1939*, Harvester Press (1982)

Wrigley, C. and Shepherd, J. (eds) *On the Move: Essays in Labour and Transport History presented to Philip Bagwell*, A & C Black (1991)

Preparing for your A Level Paper 3 exam

Advance planning

Draw up a timetable for your revision and try to keep to it. Spend longer on topics that you have found difficult, and revise them several times. Aim to be confident about all aspects of your Paper 3 work, because this will ensure that you have a choice of questions in Sections B and C.

Paper 3 overview

Paper 3	Time: 2 hours 15 minutes	
Section A	Answer 1 compulsory question for the option studied, assessing source analysis and evaluation skills.	20 marks
Section B	Answer 1 question from a choice of 2 on an aspect in depth for the option studied.	20 marks
Section C	Answer 1 question from a choice of 2 on an aspect in breadth for the option studied.	20 marks
	Total marks =	60 marks

Section A questions

There is no choice of question in Section A. You will be referred to a source of about 350 words long, printed in a Sources Booklet. The source will be a primary source or one that is contemporary to the period you have studied, and will relate to one of the key topics in the Aspect of Depth. You will be expected to analyse and evaluate the source in its historical context. The question will ask you to assess the value of the source for revealing something specific about the period, and will expect you to explain your answer, using the source, the information given about its origin and your own knowledge about the historical context.

Section B questions

You will have a choice of one from two questions in Section B. They will aim to assess your understanding of one or more of the key topics in the Aspect of Depth you have studied. Questions may relate to a single, momentous year, but will normally cover longer periods. You will be required to write an essay evaluating an aspect of the period. You may be asked about change and continuity, similarity and difference, consequences, significance or causation, or you may be given a quotation and asked to explain how far you agree with it. All questions will require you to reach a substantiated judgement.

Section C questions

You will have a choice of one from two questions in Section C. Questions will relate to the themes of the Aspects of Breadth you have studied, and will aim to assess your understanding of change over time. They will cover a period of no less than 100 years and will relate either to the factors that brought about change, or the extent of change over the period, or patterns of change as demonstrated by turning points.

Use of time

1. Do not write solidly for 45 minutes on each question. For Section B and C answers, you should spend a few minutes working out what the question is asking you to do, and drawing up a plan of your answer. This is especially important for Section C answers, which cover an extended period of time.
2. For Section A, it is essential that you have a clear understanding of the content of the source and its historical context. Pay particular attention to the provenance: was the author in a position to know what he or she was writing about? Read it carefully and underline important points. You might decide to spend up to ten minutes reading the source and drawing up your plan, and 35 minutes writing your answer.

Preparing for your A Level exams

Paper 3: A Level sample answer with comments

Section A

These questions require you to analyse and evaluate source material with respect to its historical context.

For these questions remember to:

- look at the evidence given in the source and consider how the source could be used in differing ways to provide historical understanding
- use your knowledge of the historical context to discuss any limitations the source may have
- use your historical understanding to evaluate the source, considering how much weight you would give to its argument
- come to a judgement on the overall value of the source in respect to the question.

Study Source 4 in Chapter 3 (page 69) before you answer this question.

Assess the value of the source for revealing the extent of feeling among the population for franchise reform and the attitude of the government to such reform.

Explain your answer, using the source, the information given about its origin and your own knowledge about the historical context. (20 marks)

Average student answer

Source 4 is very useful for revealing the extent of feeling among both the population and the government for franchise reform because it is a newspaper record about a political meeting arranged by those in favour of reform, and the manner in which the event was broken up by government soldiers. By presenting the events as they unfolded, the article offers the chance to see the extent of feeling from both sides.

The source is a newspaper article produced just after the 'Peterloo Massacre', which was an unfortunate turn of events that saw the death of 11 people when soldiers were sent to break up a political meeting about franchise reform. The article itself seems to present the facts of the tragedy in such detail as to suggest the author was either present at the meeting or received first-hand accounts of it from others. In this regard, it is invaluable for shedding light upon the extent of feeling that existed about reform from both government and the population since it offers a prism through which to observe the actions of both sides. In terms of the population, the fact that they are holding a meeting about the issue is suggestive that it was desirable for them, while the fact that the government sent troops to break the meeting up demonstrates a strong sense of ill-feeling on its part for franchise reform. Since the attitudes of both parties are present, the source is therefore very useful.

> A reasonable introduction that conveys a clear argument and some awareness of the source's provenance. It does not integrate these as effectively as a higher-level response might have done.

> This paragraph offers some useful own knowledge and analytical comment, but does not fully develop the point effectively.

In addition, the source is from a reputable newspaper that was generally well regarded, and so it has a good claim for reliability. Given this standing, the representation of events can largely be accepted as a fair account of the day and, therefore, of great utility for making an assessment of both the government and the general population's feelings. Furthermore, as a newspaper, it also presents facts about the event that can be effectively used to draw more valid conclusions about each side's position. In particular, it mentions that '80,000' people were in attendance, which would suggest that the extent of feeling from the population was substantial since such numbers were not common at a time when travel was more difficult. It also mentions some prominent figures who spoke at the event, such as Henry Hunt, which offers a sense of the quality of those who attended rather than simply figures. In doing this, the article arguably humanises the issue for the people.

> This is quite a short paragraph, but it has some appropriate focus on the question demand and considers the quality of the material. This provenance is used in a general fashion and could have developed a greater sense of judgement if it was explored a little further. There is some useful analysis that could also be further developed.

Despite the evident strengths of the source, it is nonetheless a newspaper article that is arguably intended to sell papers in addition to presenting news. In this sense, there remains the possibility that some of the material is over-dramatised for commercial purposes and, therefore, any consideration of the evidence should be done cautiously. In this regard there could be some reservations about the commentary, although, given the seeming lack of over-exaggeration or deliberately one-sided reporting, the source nevertheless retains some usefulness. Even if it was a little dramatised, the events are still recorded based upon what took place and the part of both groups is given fair representation. Furthermore, given the context of the massacre – four years after the end of the Napoleonic Wars, and during a period of depression in Britain – there is perhaps a lingering sense of revolutionary fears that arguably tainted any such reporting of political meetings. In this sense, perhaps any over-exaggeration that might exist is in fact the product of recent events that only goes further to offer insight into the extent of personal feeling on both sides.

> This paragraph offers some developed commentary about the provenance of the material and starts to develop an interesting point towards the end that could be explored further.

In conclusion, therefore, the source is ultimately quite useful since it presents the opportunity to explore the feelings of both government and the people by neutrally presenting the facts of an event in which both parties took part. In doing so, it arguably gives the reader the chance to consider for themselves the extent of feeling by interpreting the description as they see fit.

> This conclusion is reasonably clear and presents a consistent, albeit quite general, argument.

Verdict

This is an average answer because:

- it lacks substantive judgement based on the question asked
- although the source's provenance is considered, it lacks detailed explanation or development
- it does not come to a strong, reasoned judgement.

Use the feedback on this essay to rewrite it, making as many improvements as you can.

Paper 3: A Level sample answer with comments

Section A

These questions require you to analyse and evaluate source material with respect to its historical context.

For these questions remember to:

- look at the evidence given in the source and consider how the source could be used in differing ways to provide historical understanding
- use your knowledge of the historical context to discuss any limitations the source may have
- use your historical understanding to evaluate the source, considering how much weight you would give to its argument
- come to a judgement on the overall value of the source in respect to the question.

Study Source 4 in Chapter 3 (page 69) before you answer this question.

Assess the value of the source for revealing the extent of feeling among the population for franchise reform and the attitude of the government to such reform.

Explain your answer, using the source, the information given about its origin and your own knowledge about the historical context. (20 marks)

Strong student answer

The source is very useful in assessing the extent of feeling among both the general population and the government towards the issue of reform because it is about that theme specifically. Furthermore, being a document that presents the actions of both sides, it is of considerable value in that it offers the chance to interpret each side's feelings, while the potential limitations it has on the grounds of potential exaggeration are perhaps outweighed by the insight it offers overall.

An introduction that considers debate and provenance, while presenting a clear argument.

Certainly it can be suggested that the source is a little limited in that it is a newspaper article about the 'Peterloo Massacre', which was the result of significant tensions between reformers and government in 1819. Given the general nature of newspapers – and especially the 'Annual Register' that was established by Edmund Burke, a politician with distinct views about the issue of reform – it would be fair to say that it might offer a partisan opinion and, therefore, be of little value. However, even if this were the case, it still has value since it would at least offer some indication of the level of feeling about the issue from the chosen perspective. Indeed, if it were felt to be heavily exaggerated, then that would imply that the issue was of great importance and was therefore particularly emotive given the efforts undertaken to convince the audience it was intended for; in this case, an educated class primarily. With regard to the perspective, it would seem that the paper broadly suggests that the massacre was the result of an anxious government that was fearful of reform given that it places the origin of the action at the feet of the yeomanry who 'lost all command of their temper'. Although this could be interpreted as perhaps human fallibility rather than a deliberate intention, the fact that these troops were sent into a peaceful meeting by officials of the government would suggest that even without the loss of temper, the hope was to break up the crowd and avoid promoting their demand for reform. In this sense the source, by detailing the cause of the massacre, offers some useful insight into the feelings that existed towards reform.

There is a clear consideration of provenance that is integrated into the overall discussion of the question focus. The material is analytical and well-considered, developing a clear line of argument.

Developing this idea, the fact that the source depicts a meeting designed to promote the cause of reform also offers useful insight into the extent of feeling that existed among the general population. In one sense, this might easily be interpreted as very well disposed towards the issue since 80,000 turned up to hear the speakers. Given the challenges of travel at the time, and also the general awareness of government ill-feeling towards reform, that so many people chose to attend is testament to their commitment to the demand. Furthermore, it also mentions 'clubs of reformers', which would go even further to suggest that people were very keen on the issue to the extent that they formed their own organisations to campaign for it. While one could say that political clubs were quite popular during this period – there were many such organisations littering the country, and that the existence of them does not necessarily mean reform was their main focus since there were other political concerns that were occupying attention as the source identifies; there were in fact more franchise reform clubs (such as the London Corresponding Society) than any other because that issue offered the chance to make gains in all the others – a political voice was the starting point. In this sense, the source is valuable because it not only shows the strength of feeling of the general population, but also highlights how politically well versed they were.

Here, the context of the source is used nicely to develop the argument. Own knowledge is supportive of the overall analytical discussion and argumentation.

The source is also valuable because it offers the chance to interpret the extent of feeling from either side since it does not focus on one or the other, but rather just presents the events of the day. In this sense, while it is appropriate to interpret the presence of such large numbers as evidence of support and the presence of troops as evidence of fear on the government's part, it also invites deeper consideration; the fact that the meeting was taking place could equally imply that those who had staged the event were keen to spread their message and perhaps maintain any momentum for their cause that had developed. In addition, the presence of troops, if the context is considered more thoughtfully, could simply have been the result of government fears of revolution rather than reform. In this regard, 1819 was only two years after the Pentridge Rising, which intended to overthrow the government. Therefore, it would be equally plausible to suggest the troops were a reactionary action to the possibility of a repeated attempt – an interpretation that merits some attention given that the source also mentions that many of the attendees had 'caps of liberty', which were popularised during the French Revolution of 1789.

Own knowledge is integrated well with the source material to develop an effective and analytical paragraph.

Overall therefore, the source has a great deal of value for assessing the extent of feeling on both sides because it allows for a variety of interpretations to be drawn rather than pushing the reader towards one opinion or the other. By simply presenting the events of 16 August 1819, it not only gives tangible evidence of the strength of feeling but also presents the complexities of the political scene in the early 19th century; this itself is invaluable for drawing objective conclusions.

A clear and well-reasoned conclusion that reaches a judgement based on the analytical argument presented in the body.

Verdict

This is a strong answer because:

- it focuses explicitly on the source when developing an answer

- the provenance of the source is consistently used to develop well-considered points
- it reaches a clearly substantiated judgement that has been justified in the body.

Paper 3: A Level sample answer with comments

Section B

These questions require you to show your understanding of a period in depth. They will ask you about a quite specific period of time and require you to make a substantiated judgement about a specific aspect you have studied.

For these questions remember to:

- organise your essay and communicate it in a manner that is clear and comprehensible
- use historical knowledge to analyse and evaluate the key aspect of the question
- make a balanced argument that weighs up differing opinions
- make a substantiated overall judgement on the question.

How far was the growth of Chartism in the years 1838 and 1848 politically motivated? (20 marks)

Average student answer

The growth of Chartism was completely politically motivated because those who were involved in the development of the movement believed that by gaining political reform the lives of workers would be greatly improved. While there were also some specific economic difficulties that inspired some members, the address of these concerns was only possible by changing the political system.

Chartism was a broad movement of workers who came together to try to force political change in the country in order to improve their lives. This was because they had no political voice and were very much at the mercy of those who employed them. Given this impotent position, the only way to make any headway was to gain the vote so as to be able to influence those in power to address their wider concerns over employment and living conditions. Prominent leaders of the Chartist movement, such as William Lovett from the London Working Men's Association, believed the only way to achieve the franchise was to create a large body of reformers who would be powerful enough to force political change. Therefore, Lovett, along with others such as the Birmingham Political Union and the Great Northern Union, created Chartism – perhaps the biggest working-class organisation of the 19th century.

In addition to seeking the vote, the Chartists also sought wider reforms, such as a secret ballot, the payment of MPs, annual parliaments, equal-sized constituencies and the removal of property qualifications for being able to stand for parliament. These demands were encapsulated in the 'People's Charter', which was drawn up in Birmingham in August 1838 and became the manifesto of the organisation. By looking at the nature of these demands, it is clear that the Chartists were definitely politically motivated since what they were asking for was rooted in that field. Adopting any of the demands would have had a profound effect upon the existing political system – especially annual parliaments that we don't even have today. Since these demands – referred to as 'points of the charter' – were the focus of the entire movement, it is therefore clear that the movement was politically motivated.

> A clear introduction that acknowledges a brief debate and presents an argument that has some reasoning applied.

> This paragraph has some argument, but it is a little general and not effectively developed. The evidence in support is appropriate, if a little unspecific.

> This paragraph has some relevant knowledge, but the material is quite descriptive and lacks a real focus on the question demand.

Despite the 'People's Charter' being so evidently political in its orientation, the document was only created after the decision was made to form a movement and, therefore, there must have been some other motivation that encouraged the initial gathering. In one sense this was the desire of politically motivated individuals like Lovett and Julian Harney, but the fact that the majority of supporters were workers – from the Great Northern Union and London Working Men's Association – suggests that perhaps the underlying motivation was economic. In this sense, politics was not necessarily the motivation, but perhaps the only way for the real motivation of economy to be achieved. Given this idea, it is still reasonable to suggest political motivation was the main reason.

> A debate is acknowledged and an argument is developed using some useful, if general, evidence in support. There is some clear reasoning here, but it could be more sharply developed in terms of the question demand.

In conclusion, therefore, the rise of Chartism was the result of political motivations because, even if the economy was what brought the movement together, it was political change that would bring about any improvements to economic and social concerns that the Chartists actually had.

> This conclusion neatly sums up a consistent argument in a straightforward manner.

Verdict

This is an average answer because:

- it is quite descriptive and general throughout
- although own knowledge is used in support of the answer, this material could be more precise
- it does not really cover the timeframe.

Use the feedback on this essay to rewrite it, making as many improvements as you can.

Paper 3: A Level sample answer with comments

Section B

These questions require you to show your understanding of a period in depth. They will ask you about a quite specific period of time and require you to make a substantiated judgement about a specific aspect you have studied.

For these questions remember to:

- organise your essay and communicate it in a manner that is clear and comprehensible
- use historical knowledge to analyse and evaluate the key aspect of the question
- make a balanced argument that weighs up differing opinions
- make a substantiated overall judgement on the question.

How far was the growth of Chartism in the years 1838 and 1848 politically motivated? (20 marks)

Strong student answer

To a great extent, it is reasonable to suggest that the Chartist movement was borne from a desire to change the political system because it was an organisation that was predominantly made up of those who were towards the bottom of the social order and, therefore, had the most to gain from achieving political reforms. In this sense, the equally compelling suggestion that the movement was inspired by economic motives is actually bound up within the broader benefits that political reform offered, and, therefore, because political change covers many more specific motivations it was perhaps the general aim of the Chartist movement.

> This introduction acknowledges some debate, but integrates it into the overall argument that has some reasoning and clear direction.

It is reasonable to suggest that Chartism was motivated by political desires since it was guided by its 'People's Charter', which was created in August 1838 and became the manifesto of the whole movement not only until 1848, but throughout its entire existence. Given the overt political nature of this document – it issued six points that were very radical for the early 19th century, including things such as a secret ballot and annual parliaments – it is fair to say that the movement was entirely political. This is because had any one of the demands been achieved, then the existing system would have been significantly different. Britain in the mid-19th century was still very much run by those with substantial property – even despite reform in 1832, and therefore with a growing industrial class there was still substantial under-representation; Manchester, for example, despite having a population of 182,000 in 1831, had no MP. By focusing their attention on what they felt were important oversights in British politics, the Chartists were arguably seeking to inject greater equality into the system by creating an environment wherein even the poorest individual's voice might be heard. This was perhaps most evident in their demand for the payment of MPs and the removal of property qualifications in order to stand as an MP, each of which would have made it easier for working people to participate fully in the governance of their country. In pressing for this reform, it is certainly evident that political motivations were central to the growth of Chartism.

> There is a clear discussion here that relates well to the question demand and offers awareness of the context in which the question is set. It successfully integrates this context into the overall argument set out in the introduction and uses some evidence to support the argument being developed.

Furthermore, the nature of the movement also suggests that it was politically motivated. It was perhaps the first large-scale working-class movement to challenge the existing, privilege-based system and, on this basis, was undoubtedly perceived by those in power as a political organisation. Supporting this was also the manner in which the movement behaved; both the 'moral force' and 'physical force' aspects of Chartism were politically active. In the case of the former, pamphleteering and speech making on the issue of reform was seeking to induce such change, while 'physical force' was more directly political; the Newport Rising in 1839, which saw a pitched battle between Chartists and government forces, and the Chartist petitions of 1838,

> This paragraph starts to develop a reasoned, analytical argument about the question's stated factor and it uses some good evidence in support of the points advanced.

1842 and 1848 especially. Given the activity of the Chartist movement, it is difficult to suggest how they were not politically motivated; their very existence made them so and their actions only amplified this.

Despite the compelling evidence to suggest that Chartism was a political movement, the initial impetus for its creation was undoubtedly economic deprivation; the conditions of the working class and their exploitation for economic gain by their employers. Considering the long hours they were forced to work and the low wages they received, it is fair to suggest that the movement certainly sought to improve these wrongs. However, these problems had always been present during Britain's Industrial Revolution, yet Chartism did not formally emerge until 1838. In this sense it is perhaps more reasonable to suggest that, while economic concerns added to the growth of the movement, it was not the main cause of its birth. Given the changes to the political system in 1832 that saw the new middle class gain the vote, and also other reforms such as the abolition of slavery in 1833 and the amendment to the Poor Law in 1834, it is more likely that the working classes saw the opportunity to push for their own reforms under this seeming 'era of progression'. Within this context, coupled with the actual manifesto aims enumerated in the 'People's Charter', it would seem that bringing about political change was the overriding motivation for the emergent movement.

◄— Another analytical and well-directed paragraph that develops a clear line of argument using well-selected own knowledge. Some debate is considered and related effectively to the argument being made.

Reinforcing this idea is also the fact that any economic discontent could be mitigated through political change anyway. In this sense, by promoting greater political rights for workers, and a more equality-based system generally, then those who were being exploited would have had the necessary political tools with which to remedy their position, in particular if they themselves could stand and vote for MPs sympathetic to their needs. Considering the charter's aims, these featured prominently – along with things like the secret ballot that would protect those who wanted to vote against their landlords – and, therefore, it would be fair to say that empowering the more vulnerable in a political sense, would also empower them to address their economic difficulties. On this basis, seeking political change was clearly more beneficial than just seeking a narrow economic reform and, as such, was perhaps the reason for Chartism's growth throughout the 1840s.

◄— This paragraph considers counterargument and successfully links it to the argument presented in the introduction to provide a well-balanced and thoughtful response to the question demand.

In conclusion, therefore, although it might be suggested that Chartism was the product of economic discontent during the mid-19th century, the overriding reason for its growth was political change. It was the first major working-class challenge to Britain's government, and its aims were to transform the existing privilege-based system into a more equality-based platform on which all of those living in the country would be able to progress.

◄— A consistent conclusion that draws the themes in the essay together into an effective judgement.

Verdict

This is a strong answer because:

- it is clearly analytical and offers a well-defined argument
- throughout the response there is good use of precise and well-selected evidence to support the points made
- it considers a counterargument and includes this as part of the overall evaluation, reaching a reasoned conclusion.

Paper 3: A Level sample answer with comments

Section C

These questions require you to show your understanding of a subject over a considerable period of time. They will ask you to assess a long-term historical topic and its development over a period of at least 100 years, and they require you to make a substantiated judgement in relation to the question.

For these questions remember to:

- organise your essay and communicate it in a manner that is clear and comprehensible
- use historical knowledge to analyse and evaluate the key aspect of the question covering the entire period
- make a balanced argument that weighs up differing opinions
- make a substantiated overall judgement on the question.

To what extent was the extension of the franchise the result of political rivalry in the years 1828 to 1928? (20 marks)

Average student answer

The extension of the vote was the product of a variety of different factors, not least the rivalry between the two main parties in Britain: the Whigs and the Tories, which later became the Liberals and Conservatives. While the influence of extra-parliamentary pressures from groups such as the Chartists certainly kept the issue of reform alive, it was the continual desire for power that each of these parties held that drove reform.

It is very appropriate to suggest that the extension of the franchise was the result of political rivalry because over the course of the period in question there was very little substantive pressure from outside of the political arena. Although during the early 19th century there was a greater sense of revolutionary threat following the 1830 revolution in France and the 'Days of May', which threatened the financial stability of the British economy when hundreds of people were encouraged to withdraw their savings from banks in the hope that this pressure would force political change, as the century wore on similar such threats diminished. For example, the Representation of the People Act 1884 saw no real threat posed at all by outside interests, and yet reform was still passed. This was arguably because of other interests among the political establishment rather than any sense of threat, and, therefore, it is more appropriate to suggest that political rivalry was the main influence.

Reinforcing this idea of diminishing threat promoting the idea that rivalry was more important is the fact that such rivalry has always existed within the political arena. In this sense, while outside pressures such as revolutionary threat or popular demand might rise and fall throughout the period, rivalry is always present. For example, in the years leading up to the 1867 Act which gave skilled workers the chance to vote, the driving force behind this reform was the ongoing discord between the Liberal William Gladstone and the Conservative Benjamin Disraeli. These figures were prominent members of their respective parties and sought to advance their own careers at the expense of the other. In particular, Disraeli sought to use the popular demand for reform as a vehicle to drive him into power and, therefore, he was prepared to offer a far more extensive reform bill than even his liberal opponents were prepared to support. As a result of debate in parliament, Disraeli accepted any amendment proposals except those from Gladstone and was therefore able to get reform passed – albeit much more radical than was initially intended. The motivation for this reform was ambition and rivalry and, as such, it was clearly the main cause of franchise reform.

This introduction offers a general argument and acknowledges some debate. However, it could be more focused in terms of how the debate relates to the argument presented. This would sharpen the argument and allow for a better sense of direction in the essay.

This paragraph offers some good ideas and there is an argument presented that is generally analytical. It does not develop this analysis very far.

This paragraph has some focus, but it drifts into narrative quite quickly. Once again, the analysis is generally undeveloped beyond some tantalising phrases.

Although there is a reasonable claim to suggest that reform was encouraged on the grounds of progressive thought – attitudes naturally evolve over time as circumstances change and therefore governments can act to reflect this change – actually the motivation for power is far more influential. For example, there is the suggestion that the Representation of the People Act 1928, which extended the vote to women over the age of 21, was entirely motivated by enlightened thinking since there was almost no political challenge demanding such reform. However, looking more closely at the political motivations surrounding even this 'progressive' Act, it is evident to see that the underlying motivation was political rivalry. Following the previous reforms (1832, 1867, 1884 and 1918), the electorate was naturally expanding and broadly balanced in terms of political affiliation. Therefore, in order to secure the remaining votes available in Britain and thereby gain a political advantage, it could be said that the 1928 Act was passed. Far from being an altruistic motivation, it was entirely considered in terms of tactical political gain.

> This paragraph offers some clear debate that is related to the question demand. It also contains some good own knowledge that is used to support the points being made. Once again, however, these points are not really developed very far, which limits the opportunity for evaluation.

In conclusion, therefore, while there are some interesting claims that can partially be supported for why the vote was extended – threat of revolution and natural evolution, in particular – the most consistent motivation was undoubtedly the ever-present rivalry that existed among the British parliamentary parties.

> This conclusion has a judgement that is generally supported by the main body. It is related to the question demand, but the overall focus could be sharper, which in turn would enhance the evaluation that is being made.

Verdict

This is an average answer because:

- it is quite narrative throughout and does not cover the breadth of the timeframe asked for
- the points made are developed in a general way, albeit with some good own knowledge
- it does not evenly consider a counterargument.

Use the feedback on this essay to rewrite it, making as many improvements as you can.

Paper 3: A Level sample answer with comments

Section C

These questions require you to show your understanding of a subject over a considerable period of time. They will ask you to assess a long-term historical topic and its development over a period of at least 100 years, and they require you to make a substantiated judgement in relation to the question.

For these questions remember to:

- organise your essay and communicate it in a manner that is clear and comprehensible
- use historical knowledge to analyse and evaluate the key aspect of the question covering the entire period
- make a balanced argument that weighs up differing opinions
- make a substantiated overall judgement on the question.

To what extent was the extension of the franchise the result of political rivalry in the years 1828 to 1928? (20 marks)

Strong student answer

To a great extent, it is reasonable to suggest that the extension of the franchise was the result of political rivalry since this is a continual presence within the years 1828–1928. Even with the evolution of political attitudes and occasional extra-parliamentary threat, which some might argue really forced politicians into accepting a wider franchise, the underlying motivation for such reform remained closely tied to political rivalry, since this was the constant threat that drove those in power to even consider changing their political environment.

> In this introduction there is a clear argument being developed that integrates an awareness of debate and uses this to inform the overall idea being presented.

Foremost, it can be suggested that political rivalry is the driving force behind extending the franchise because it is within the political system itself that the change has to come. Given this principle, those individuals, such as Disraeli and Gladstone, who were so instrumental in bringing about reform (1867 and 1884 respectively), needed the incentive to modernise the system from which they benefited. While this might have come from popular pressure, such as the Hyde Park riots in 1866, the state had effective tools with which to combat such threat. In 1819, it used troops to disperse a reform meeting, and in the early 20th century, when challenged by the suffragettes, it passed the Cat-and-Mouse Act to allow the rearrest of those women who sought to evade prison by going on hunger strike. Since the state has the means to meet any physical challenge, it is therefore more reasonable to suggest that any motivation for reform came from themselves, and in the case of Disraeli and Gladstone in particular, it is evident to see the role played by rivalry.

> This paragraph is clearly analytical and starts to build the argument presented in the introduction. There is some supporting evidence and, to make this even better, a little more would be useful.

Reinforcing this idea is the nature of change over time itself. While it could be suggested that reform was a natural development that reflected the growth of modern views about representation – for example, allowing women to vote in 1918 – actually this can better be seen in the light of political incentive. Indeed, after the first reform in 1832 that gave the vote to the middle class, arguably the door to reform was open and therefore further change became expected from the growing population. Having tentatively extended the vote – ostensibly because of the threat posed by the 'Days of May' and 'Swing' riots, but more realistically because of the threat to Tory power in the House of Lords – the increase to the electorate raised the stakes for party rivalry. In this regard, the growth in numbers – now 18 percent of the adult male population – made it less certain as to who would support your party; it also made bribing the electorate more expensive. Given these changes, the relationship between the main parties arguably became more strained and therefore enhanced any previous rivalry that existed. This view is further supported by the introduction of a secret ballot in 1872, which made it even harder to be certain of support to the extent that only by introducing reform did parties feel they could be sure to swell their ranks – winning over a draft of newly enfranchised, grateful voters.

> Like the previous paragraph, this is nicely analytical and continues to build a clear argument that is consistent and focused. There is more supporting evidence here that enhances the points being made.

As compelling as this argument may seem, progress as a motivation for reform has certainly been a popular interpretation, especially when considering the Representation of the People Act 1928 that extended the vote to women over the age of 21. Here, there is a strong willingness to maintain that it was entirely motivated by enlightened thinking since there was almost no political challenge demanding such reform and both parties supported it. On the surface, this would appear convincing; however, underlying this progressive sentiment is a deeper vein of political incentive. This is because by 1928 there was little difference between the parties in terms of public support, and, therefore, it can reasonably be argued that to gain an edge each party sought to extend the female franchise from the 1918 restriction of 30 years to 21 years. Though this change had the appearance of altruism, underneath it was the desire to secure more voters that brought this reform about – especially since the young Labour Party was growing into a more viable political contender. Given this additional threat to the traditional parties, and on the basis of political motivations in the previous century, it is more probable that political rivalry continued to be the primary motivation for franchise extension.

> This paragraph introduces some debate, but relates it effectively to the overall argument using logical development and a good awareness of context.

In conclusion, therefore, the means by which Britain eventually became a representative democracy was located in the far more cynical desire among each political party to ensure their ability to retain power over the other. While throughout the period there were undoubted pressures from the public itself, this was only to serve as ammunition to use against political rivals, since that demand actually made reform an effective weapon in the constant and ever-pressing battle for political dominance. It is the consistency of this motivation, particularly when considering such a broad timeframe, which makes rivalry so instrumental because it is always present and therefore something that will always need to be thought about.

> A clear judgement is made here that is well supported in the body of the essay.

Verdict

This is a strong answer because:

- it is clearly analytical and offers a well-defined argument
- throughout the response there is good use of precise and well-selected evidence to support the points made
- it considers a counterargument and includes this as part of an overall developed evaluation.

Index

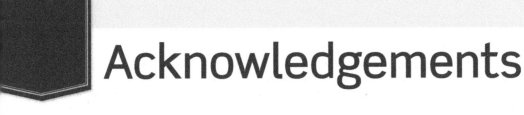

Acknowledgements

The authors and publisher would like to thank the following individuals and organisations for permission to reproduce photographs and text in this book.

(Key: b-bottom; c-centre; l-left; r-right; t-top)

Alamy Images: Interfoto 119, Mary Evans Picture Library 9, National Geographic Image Collection 6; **Bridgeman Art Library Ltd:** Private Collection/© Look and Learn 8, The Stapleton Collection 66; **Getty Images:** Corbis Historical/Michael Nicholson 52; **London School of Economics and Political Science:** 122; **Mary Evans Picture Library:** 13, 70, 90, 93t, 110, 146, 171, Illustrated London News Ltd 23, 26, 94, 108, 156, 168, 169, Marx Memorial Library 91, Roger Worsley Zrchive 152, Roger-Viollet 93b, Spaarnestad Photo 170, Sueddeutsche Zeitung Photo 133, The March of the Women Collection 134; **People's History Museum:** 54; © **The Trustees of The British Museum. All rights reserved.:** 75; **TopFoto:** 131, British Library Board 96, Oxford Science Archive / Heritage Images 113, The Granger Collection 42, 138, World History Archive 79

Cover image: Mary Evans Picture Library: The March of the Women Collection

All other images © Pearson Education

Maps
Figures 1.1 and 1.2 from *The Extension of the Franchise, 1832–1931*, Heinemann (Bob Whitfield 2001), pp.28, 74 © Bob Whitfield 2001, Reproduced with permission from Pearson Education Ltd.

Text
Extract p.86 from Chartism revisited, *History Review*, Issue 33, March (Evans, E. 1999), reproduced with permission; Extract p.92 from *Chartist Studies*, Macmillan: St Martin's Press (Briggs, A. 1959), reproduced with permission of Palgrave Macmillan; Extract p.123 from Ethics and disease in the later nineteenth century: the contagious diseases acts, *Historical Studies*, Vol. 15, Issue 57, p.126 (Smith, F. B. 1971), publisher Taylor & Francis Ltd, www.tandfonline.com reprinted by permission of the publisher; Extract 4 p.124 from *Prostitution and Victorian Society*, Cambridge University Press (Walkowitz, J. 1980) p.152, Copyright © 1980 Cambridge University Press; Extract 5 p.124 from Prostitution and Victorian Society revisited: the contagious diseases acts in Kent, *Women's History Review*, Vol. 21, Issue 2, pp.303, 313, and 314 (Lee, C. 2012), reprinted by permission of the publisher (Taylor & Francis Ltd, http://www.tandfonline.com); Extracts pp.130 and 136 from *Unshackled: The Story of How We Won the Vote*, Hutchinson (Pankhurst, C. 1959) p.55, reproduced with permission from The Random House Group UK and Dr Helen Pankhurst; Extract p.132 from *Votes For Women*, 18/06/1908, WSPU (Women Social and Political Union) newspaper, p.249 (Pankhurst, C.), Reproduced with permission; Extract on page 139 from *The Suffragette: the History of the Women's Militant Suffrage Movement, 1905–1910*, Gay & Hancock (Pankhurst, S. 1911) pp.125–8, Reproduced with permission; Extract 1 p.140 from Diary reveals lesbian love trysts of suffragette leaders, *The Observer*, 11/06/2000 (Thorpe, V. and Marsh, A.), http://www.theguardian.com/uk/2000/jun/11/vanessathorpe.theobserver, comments made by Martin Pugh. Courtesy of Guardian News & Media Ltd; Extract 2 p.140 from Emmeline Pankhurst: a biographical interpretation, *Women's History Review*, Vol. 12, Issue 1, p.76 (Purvis, J. 2003), reprinted by permission of the publisher (Taylor & Francis Ltd, http://www.tandfonline.com); Extract 3 p.140 from Pankhursts and provocations, *Times Higher Education*, 31/01/2003 (Liddington, J.), https://www.timeshighereducation.com/books/pankhursts-and-provocations/174443.article, reproduced with permission; Extract p.141 from The march of the women: A revisionist analysis of the campaign for women's suffrage, 1866–1914 (review), *Victorian Studies*, Vol. 44, No. 2, Winter pp.347–9 (DeVries, J. 2002), Copyright © 2002 Indiana University Press, reprinted with permission of Indiana University Press; Extract p.156 from Glasgow Socialism, *Social History*, Vol. 11, No. 1, January, pp.91–3 (Reid, A. 1986), reprintcd by permission of the publisher (Taylor & Francis Ltd, http://www.tandfonline.com); Extract 2 p.157 from Strike action and working-class politics on Clydeside 1914–1919, *International Review of Social History*, Vol. 35, Issue 01, April, pp.37–8 (Foster, John 1990), Copyright © Internationaal Instituut voor Sociale Geschiedenis 1990, reproduced with permission; Extract 3 p.157 from Labour struggles and the formation of demands: The spatial politics of Red Clydeside, *Geoforum*, 62, June, p.129 (Griffin, P. 2015), Copyright © 2015 with permission from Elsevier.